The MAILBOX®

IDEA MAGAZINE FOR TEACHERS®

2012–2013 YEARBOOK

The Education Center, LLC
Greensboro, North Carolina

The Mailbox® 2012–2013 Kindergarten Yearbook

ISBN 978-1-61276-415-3
ISSN 1088-5552

Printed in the United States of America.

The Mailbox® Yearbook
PO Box 6189
Harlan, IA 51593-1689

HPS249269

Contents

Departments

Features

www.themailbox.com

Common Core Skills Index

English Language Arts

Reading: Literature

Reading: Informational Text

Reading: Foundational Skills

Writing

Speaking and Listening

Language

Math

Counting and Cardinality

Operations and Algebraic Thinking

Number and Operations in Base Ten

Measurement and Data

Geometry

Arts & Crafts

Sensational Self-Portraits

Once students complete these personalized projects, choose one or more of the options below.

- **Open house:** Display the projects for each parent to find his child's portrait.
- **Attendance:** Laminate the portraits and store them in a basket. Upon arrival at school, invite each child to move her portrait to a designated area. To see who is absent, simply look at the portraits that remain in the basket.
- **Student of the week:** Feature each student's portrait during his special week.
- **Student progress:** Have each child make another portrait later in the year and compare the developmental progress between the two projects.

Materials for one self-portrait:

mirror
scissors
crayons
paper

Steps:

1. Look in the mirror. Get crayons to match your skin, eye, hair, and clothing colors.
2. Draw a picture so that it looks like you and what you are wearing today.
3. Draw a line around your drawing. Cut along the line.

Mindy Crowder
Southhampton Academy
Courtland, VA

Flashy Apple

These colorful projects look good enough to eat!

Materials for one apple:

apple template
white construction paper square
green and brown construction paper scraps
scissors
crayons
glue

Steps:

1. Color the whole square red, green, and yellow.
2. Trace the apple template on the white side of the square and cut it out.
3. Tear a leaf shape from the green paper scrap and a stem shape from the brown paper scrap.
4. Glue the stem and leaf to the apple.
5. Draw a face.

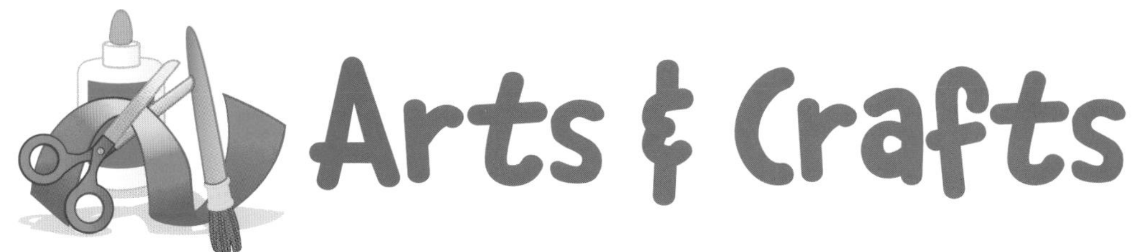

Arts & Crafts

Shapely Cats

These projects double as a "purr-fect" geometric shape review. (K.G.B.6)

Materials for one cat:

9" x 12" orange construction paper
black construction paper shapes—half of a 5" circle, 3" circle, 2 small triangles, four 1" x 2" rectangles, 1" x 4" rectangle
crayons
glue

Steps:

1. Draw a fence along the bottom of your paper.
2. Use a white crayon to draw a face and whiskers on the circle (head).
3. Arrange the shapes to form a cat standing on the fence. Glue the shapes in place.
4. Draw details as desired.

Katherine Pattison, St. Raphael School, Santa Barbara, CA

Fall Foliage

Students are sure to include color words when they write about these pretty painted trees! (W.K.2)

Materials for one tree:

shallow containers of paint in fall leaf colors
4½" x 6" brown construction paper
9" x 12" light blue construction paper
2" x 12" green construction paper strip
crumpled and clipped paper towels (one for each container of paint)
sentence strip
scissors
glue

Steps:

1. Trim the brown paper so it resembles a tree trunk. Glue it to the light blue paper.
2. Fringe-cut the green paper so it resembles grass. Glue it across the bottom of the light blue paper.
3. Dip a paper towel in a container of paint and dab it on the tree to make leaves. Continue to make leaves with different colors.
4. Write a sentence about your tree on a sentence strip. Glue it to the grass.

Nancy Myers-Alvarez, Watchung School, Montclair, NJ

I see red, yellow, and orange leaves on my tree.

Arts & Crafts Special

Gifts From Little Hands

Fingerprint Wreaths

When parents receive these ornaments as holiday gifts, they are sure to think the ornaments are "thumb-thing" special!

Materials for one ornament:

5" white card stock circle
student photo, trimmed into a 3" circle
green and red paint
ribbon
glue
tape

Steps:

1. Glue the photo to the center of the circle.
2. Make a green thumbprint wreath around the photo.
3. Add some red fingertip prints (berries).
4. Tape a ribbon loop to the back to make a hanger.

Jill Tittsworth, Chief Joseph Elementary, Meridian, ID

Holiday Banners

Invite students to make a banner of their choosing. If desired, secure a wood dowel and ribbon to each banner for easy hanging.

tip
Add a bit of liquid soap to the paint for easier cleanup.

Materials for one banner:

white piece of fabric
gold glitter glue
paintbrush
blue, yellow, and brown paint (menorah)
green, red, and brown paint (holiday tree)
permanent marker

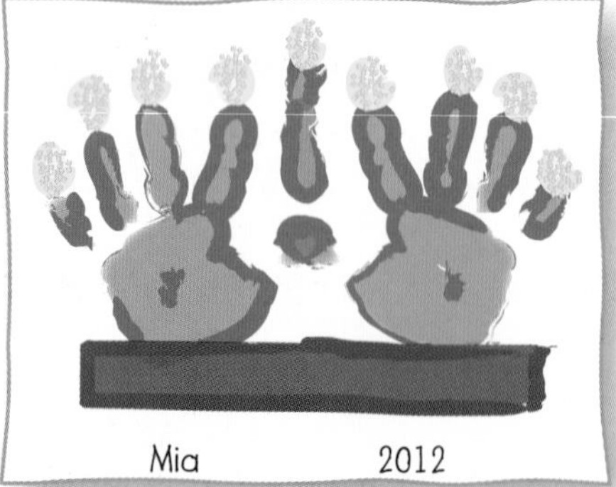

Menorah

Steps:

1. To make eight candles, use blue paint to make a left and a right handprint on the fabric so the thumbs overlap.
2. Paint a slightly taller blue candle *(shammash)* above the overlapped thumbprints.
3. Paint a brown base below the candles.
4. Make a yellow fingerprint flame at the top of each candle.
5. Spread a small amount of gold glitter glue on each flame.
6. Use the marker to write the artist's name and year on the fabric.

Holiday Tree

Steps:

1. Make six green handprints on the fabric to make a tree.
2. Make red fingerprints (ornaments) on the tree.
3. Paint a brown trunk below the tree.
4. Use gold glitter glue to make a star at the top of the tree.

Sarah Toybes, Dede Boudinet, and Francesca Bland, Old Bonhomme Elementary, Olivette, MD

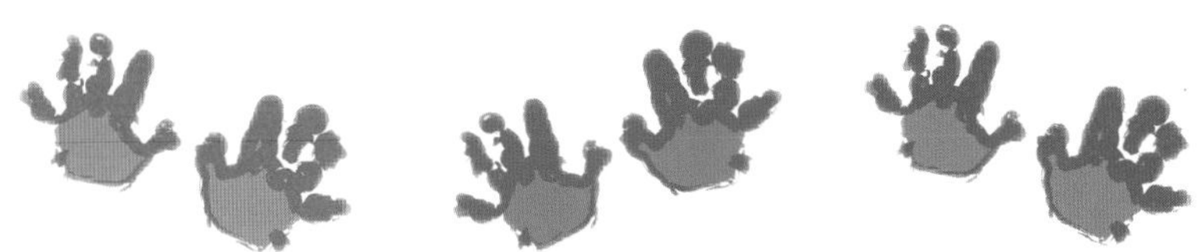

"Hand-y" Calendars

These unique calendars take several days to complete, but they make holiday gifts parents are sure to treasure! For each child, stack and staple thirteen 9" x 12" sheets of construction paper across the top. Help each child make a set of handprints on the cover and add a title. Next, have each child use a glue stick to attach monthly copies of 2013 calendar grids, in order, to the bottom half of each page. Then, for every month, help each child make a corresponding project using prints of his hand, palm, or arm like the ones shown below. Glue each project above the corresponding calendar grid.

Anastasia Rossio, Youngstown, OH

Projects to Get You Started

Labeling pictures: Have each child label the print(s) she made. (W.K.2)

Writing a response: Ask students a theme-related question about a project, such as "Where do you think the leprechaun hid his gold?" Have each child write to respond. (W.K.3)

Reading poetry: Give each child a copy of a poem that matches the monthly print or have her copy the poem on her paper. (RL.K.10)

"For the Rabbit"
For the rabbit, give three cheers.
One for its long, furry ears!
Two for its tail, fluffy and short!
Three for its nose, a button of sorts!

Writing a sentence: Have each student write a sentence that tells about the month or her monthly print. (W.K.2)

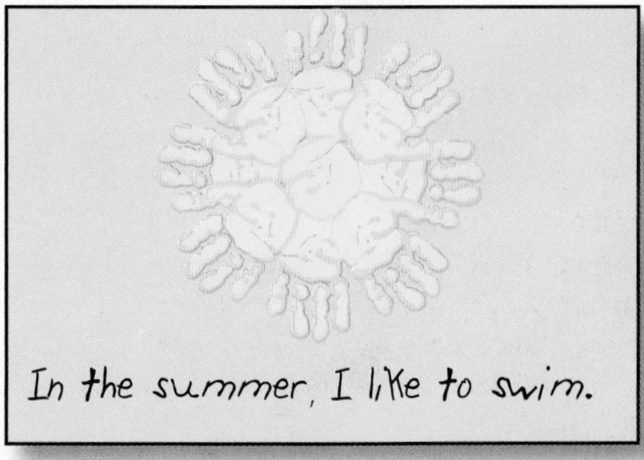

In the summer, I like to swim.

Crafts You Can Use!

These crafts are not only fun for students to make, they are the perfect props for several skill-based activities. Check it out!

"Heart-y" Flowers

Make It

To make a flower, glue five overlapping hearts together. Trim a photo and glue it to a cupcake liner. Glue the cupcake liner to the center of the flower. Then attach a green construction paper stem and leaf. *Ellen Moser, South Kortright Central School, South Kortright, NY*

Use It

- **Write a message (L.K.1f):** Help each child write a Valentine's Day message, attach it to the flower, and give it to a loved one.
- **Count by fives:** Have students step forward with their flowers, in turn, as you lead the group in counting the total number of petals by fives.
- **Respond to a prompt (W.K.2, 3):** Display the flowers under the title "Our 'Heart-y' Garden" and have youngsters write and draw to respond to a prompt, such as "What Cute Critters Are Hiding in Our Garden?"

Fabulous Fliers

Make It

Attach strips of masking tape to a large paper diamond (kite) to make cross lines. Paint the kite as desired. When the paint is dry, carefully peel off the tape. Then attach a crepe paper tail.

Use It

- **Write a story (W.K.3):** Have students write a story about a magic kite. Display each child's completed story alongside his kite.
- **Read color words(RF.K.3c):** Have students match color word cards to the color panels on the kites.
- **Long *i* review (RF.K.3b):** Have students write words and draw pictures featuring long *i* on the back of their kites.

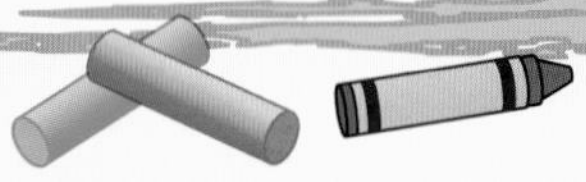

tip These shamrock crafts make a beautiful background for a bulletin board!

A Patch of Clovers

Make It

Arrange up to ten real clovers or clover cutouts on a work surface as desired. Lay a sheet of white paper atop the clovers and tape it in place. Rub the side of an unwrapped green crayon atop the paper until the clovers appear. *Jennifer Reidy, Halifax Elementary, Halifax, MA*

Use It

- **Compare sets (K.CC.C.6):** Guide youngsters to compare sets of clovers on two different crafts. Have them use the words *greater than* and *less than* with each comparison.
- **Respond to a prompt (W.K.3):** Have students write to respond to the prompt "If I got lost in a clover patch,…"

"Egg-cellent" Eggs

Make It

Put a large egg cutout in a box lid. Spoon about three dollops of tempera paint (same or different colors) onto the egg. Then drop in a plastic egg and tilt the lid to make the plastic egg roll through the paint and over the egg cutout several times. (For faster rolling, partially fill the egg with small stones to make it heavier.) When a desired effect is achieved, set the cutout aside to dry. *Rachel Dabbert, Transfiguration School, Wauconda, IL*

Use It

- **Science:** Have each child prepare a second egg cutout in the same manner. Cut one of his eggs so the cut resembles a jagged crack and help him curl the edges back so it looks like the egg hatched. On the unpainted side of the uncut egg, direct him to drizzle glue along the perimeter. Next, have him glue his eggs together, painted-sides out. To finish, have him draw and cut out a chick to glue on the opening. Then have him write sequenced steps from an egg, to an egg crack, to an opening, to a chick!
- **Make a graph or tally chart:** Use the egg colors as data to make a graph or tally chart. Use the information to determine the least and most popular egg color.
- **Solve word problems (K.OA.A.2):** Announce an egg-related word problem and invite students to use their eggs, act out the scenario, and solve the problem. Continue with different word problems.

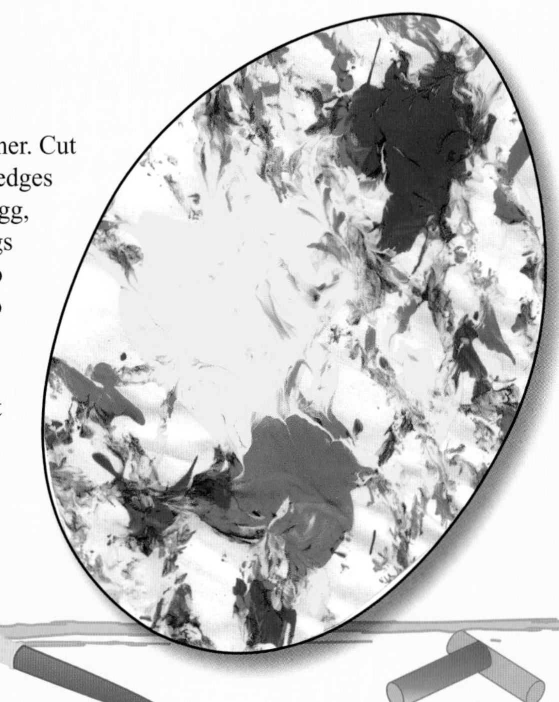

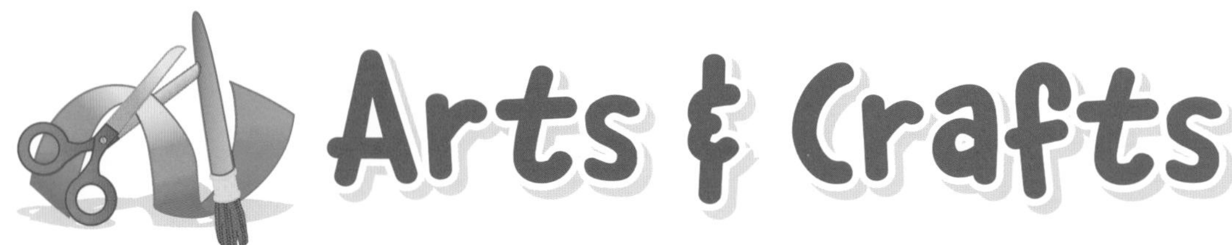

Fuzzy Chick

Have students use this spring chick as inspiration as they respond to the prompt "If I had a pet chick, I…"

Materials for one chick:

white chick shape
yellow paper scraps
2 small black circles
orange paper triangle
2 orange paper rectangles
yellow craft feathers
glue

Steps:

1. Tear the yellow paper scraps into small pieces.
2. Drizzle glue on the chick shape.
3. Cover the chick shape with the torn paper.
4. Glue the circles (eyes), triangle (beak), rectangles (legs), and feathers to the chick shape.

Sue Fleischmann, Sussex, WI

A Beautiful Bouquet

For this project, cut pictures of flowers from calendars, magazines, or catalogs. If desired, have students draw or paint their own bouquets for a personal touch.

Materials for one bouquet:

picture or drawing of flowers
9" x 12" construction paper
skin-tone paper
4 green paper strips
scissors
crayons
glue

Steps:

1. Trace your hand on skin-tone paper and cut out the tracing.
2. Glue the paper strips (stems) to the palm of the hand cutout and glue the fingers and thumb onto the stems so it looks like the hand is holding the stems.
3. Glue the hand (with the stems) to the bottom of the construction paper.
4. Glue the flower picture to the tops of the stems.
5. Write a message.

Stacy Wingen, Howard Elementary, Howard, SD

Math Crafts

Arts & Crafts with Terrific Triangles

Youngsters pair geometry and art when they make these summer-themed crafts.

Super Shark

Materials for one shark:
copy of the triangle patterns on page 14
9" x 12" sheet of blue construction paper
glue stick
scissors
crayons

Steps:
1. Cut out the triangle patterns.
2. Arrange the triangles on the blue paper (water) to form a shark.
3. Glue the triangles in place.
4. Draw an eye, teeth, and other details of your choice.

Cathy Lesinski, Thomas White Elementary, Saginaw, MI

tip

Watercolor-painted triangles make a cool color contrast on solid blue paper.

Sun designs will vary!

Let It Shine

Materials for one sun:
yellow construction paper triangles (sizes can vary)
9" x 12" blue construction paper
glue

Steps:
1. Arrange triangles to form several different sun pictures.
2. Choose your favorite sun and move those triangles onto the blue paper (sky).
3. Glue the triangles in place to show a sun in the sky.

For more exploration with triangles, encourage each student to use a variety of paper triangles to create a larger shape or object of her choice. ***Using shapes to create new shapes (K.G.B.6)***

Triangle Patterns

Use with "Super Shark" on page 13.

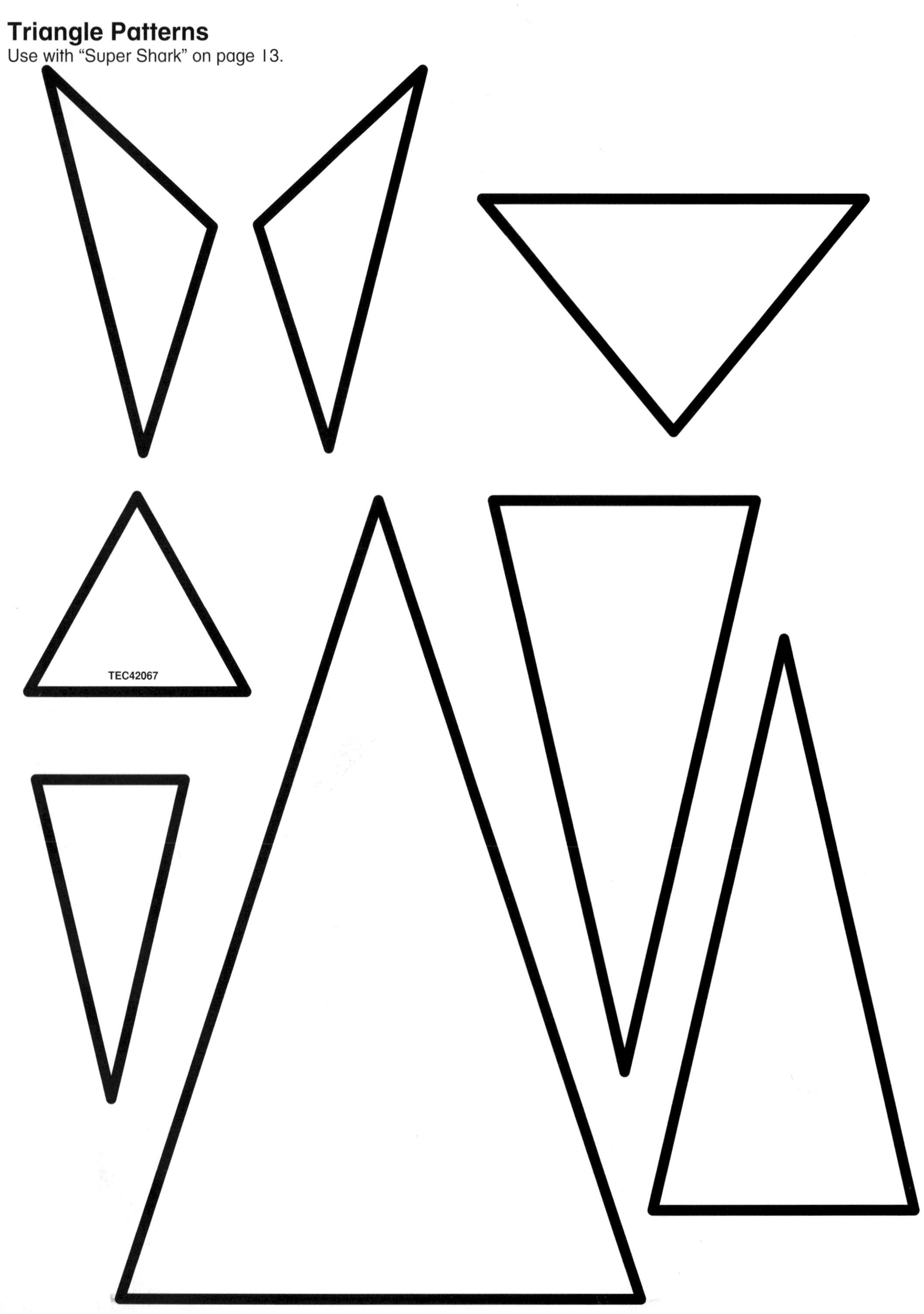

The Book Corner

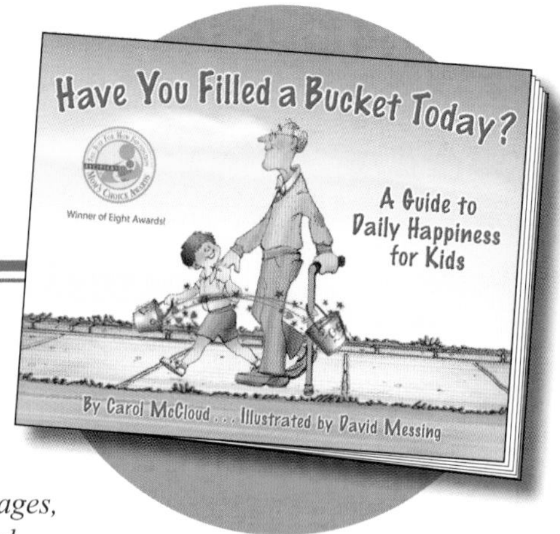

Have You Filled a Bucket Today?

Written by Carol McCloud
Illustrated by David Messing

Everyone carries an invisible bucket with them wherever they go. Bucket fillers are loving, caring people who make others feel special. Bucket filling is easy to do for all ages, doesn't cost any money, and doesn't take much time. In fact, sharing and receiving kind words and deeds can fill a bucket, and a full bucket means a happy person!

Promote positive behavior with this activity! Draw a bucket on a sheet of chart paper and gather self-adhesive craft foam shapes (or shape cutouts). After a read-aloud of the story, ask a student to share a way he could fill someone's bucket. Write his words on the bucket. Then encourage him to stick a shape above the bucket. Continue with each child, and soon the bucket will be full—just like the buckets in the story! If desired, add some colorful lines to the bucket as in the story's illustrations and then display it to use as a reference. ***Dictating information, reinforcing positive character traits (RL.K.1)***

Katrina Oldham, Goodview Elementary, Winona, MN

Share my toys.
Tell my friend she's pretty.
Tell my mom I love her.
Ask a friend to play.
Give my sister a cookie.
Say hi to my neighbor.
Smile at people.

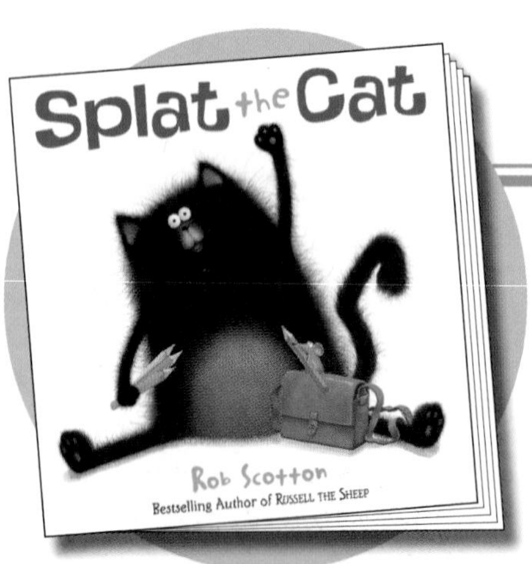

Splat the Cat

By Rob Scotton

It's Splat's first day of Cat School, and he is nervous! He tucks his mouse friend, Seymour, into his lunchbox for moral support and grudgingly sets off. But how will Seymour do at a school where all the students want to chase him? Fortunately, Seymour finds that he is one handy mouse to have around, and Splat learns that Cat School is indeed fun and exciting!

With this activity, youngsters think about animal characteristics, just as Splat's teacher does! Draw a Venn diagram on the board and label it as shown. Ask students to imagine they are cats in Cat School. Have them name characteristics of cats. As you write each one, prompt your young cats to meow enthusiastically. Next, repeat the process with mice, encouraging youngsters to squeak. Finally, tell students that they are at a school that has both cats and mice. Have students name characteristics these two critters have in common. As you write each one, have students run in place as if they're chasing mice or running away from a cat! ***Creating a Venn diagram, descriptive words (SL.K.2; L.K.6)***

Kathryn Davenport
Partin Elementary
Oviedo, FL

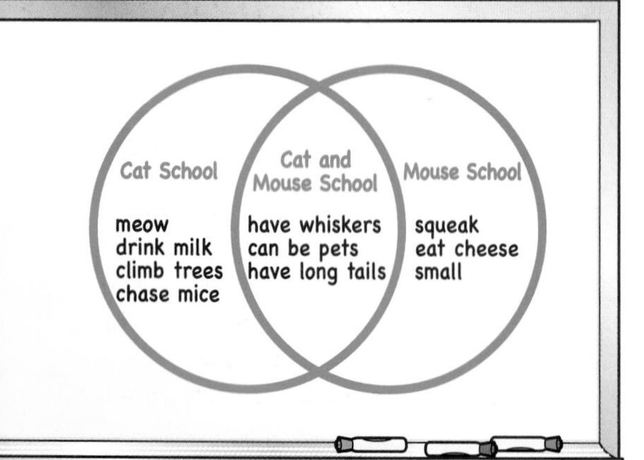

The Book Corner

Literacy Ideas for Teachers®

Stellaluna

By Janell Cannon

When Stellaluna, a baby fruit bat, is separated from her mother, she finds a home in a nest of baby birds. The birds' ways are not natural for Stellaluna, but she tries to adapt. She is eventually reunited with her mother; but in the meantime, she learns valuable lessons in cooperation, flexibility, and friendship.

Prompt students to recall story details with this bat diagram! Feature a bat cutout labeled as shown. Then, after a reading of *Stellaluna*, have youngsters tell what birds do, what bats do, and what both animals have in common. Write students' responses in the corresponding sections of the bat. **For added fun**, invite youngsters to take turns acting out different details. Have remaining students name the details and tell on which bat body part each phrase should be recorded. ***Comparing and contrasting (RL.K.9)***

Teresa Phillips, Belle Terre Elementary
Palm Coast, FL

Stone Soup

By Marcia Brown

When three tired and hungry soldiers approach a village on their long journey home from the wars, they are hopeful to be greeted with generous hospitality. Instead, the local people fear there is not enough food for all, so they hide all that they have. The wise soldiers, however, convince the villagers that a wonderful soup can be made from stones. The people are intrigued and, one by one, begin to offer vegetables, meat, barley and more so that the soup is fine enough for the richest of kings. Following the dinner, the soldiers are even offered comfortable resting places. By the time the soldiers depart, the villagers have learned a lesson on sharing, inadvertently, by simply making stone soup!

Your students' retelling of the story is packaged in this class-made shape book. After reading the story aloud, have students name important story parts and the steps in making stone soup. Write each response on a separate pot-shaped paper (booklet page). Then have small groups of students work together to draw a matching illustration on each page. Bind the completed pages in order between construction paper pot-shaped covers. If desired, record your students' summation of the main idea on the back cover. Set the book in your reading area for what is sure to be a popular pick for reading again and again! ***Retelling a story, identifying the main idea (RL.K.2)***

Cindy O'Brien, Greentown, PA

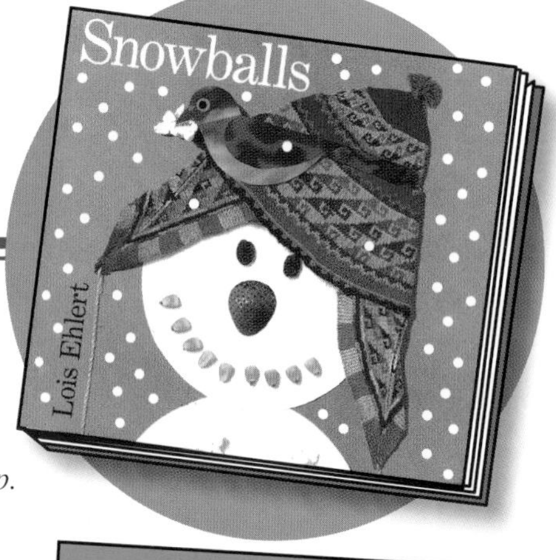

Snowballs

By Lois Ehlert

Combine a sack of "good stuff" with the perfect snowball day, and what do you get? An entire snowpal family: a snow dad, a snow mom, a snow boy, a snow girl, and snow pets—a cat and a dog! But all snow families come to an end when the weather warms up.

Youngsters create snowpeople reminiscent of the ones in the story! Have each child glue three small paper plates (snowballs) to a sheet of construction paper. Next, instruct him to decorate the snowballs with collage items so they resemble a snowpal. Then give him a copy of the poem card on page 21 and write his responses to name his snowperson and some of the collage items he used. Attach each project and card on a board to display a seasonal scene. ***Writing (W.K.2)***

Diane Bonica
Deer Creek Elementary
Tigard, OR

The displayed projects are ready-to-use data to create a snow family graph.

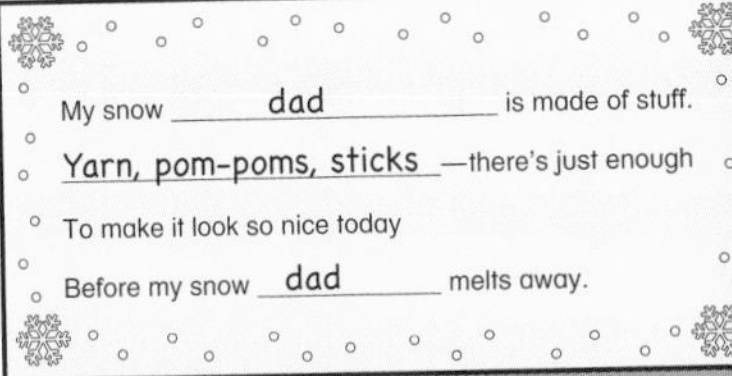

My snow dad is made of stuff.
Yarn, pom-poms, sticks —there's just enough
To make it look so nice today
Before my snow dad melts away.

Elmer

By David McKee

Elmer the patchwork elephant has an excellent sense of humor and makes all the elephants laugh. But Elmer feels as if he's being laughed at! So he rolls around in some elephant-colored berries to be the same color as the other elephants. That's when Elmer learns that the elephants love him for who he is.

Read the story aloud and then guide youngsters in completing these engaging post-story options.

- For this partner center, cut out an enlarged copy of the elephant pattern on page 21 for every two students. Set out the cutouts, colorful paper squares, dice, and glue. When two students visit the center, each child rolls a die and counts the appropriate number of squares. Then they put their sets together, count the total number of squares, and glue the squares on the elephant. Youngsters continue until the entire elephant is covered and looks just like Elmer! ***Adding sets, counting (K.CC.B.5)***
- Write "*E* is for *Elmer* and..." on a sheet of chart paper. Then have students brainstorm words that begin with short *e*. Write their words on the chart paper. Next, have each child glue tissue paper squares on an elephant cutout (pattern on page 21).When the glue is dry, trim any squares overlapping the edges and then display the elephants around the chart paper. ***Beginning sound short* e *(RF.K.3)***

E is for Elmer and...
elephant
egg
extra
elf
exit
elbow

Jill Tittsworth
Chief Joseph Elementary
Meridian, ID

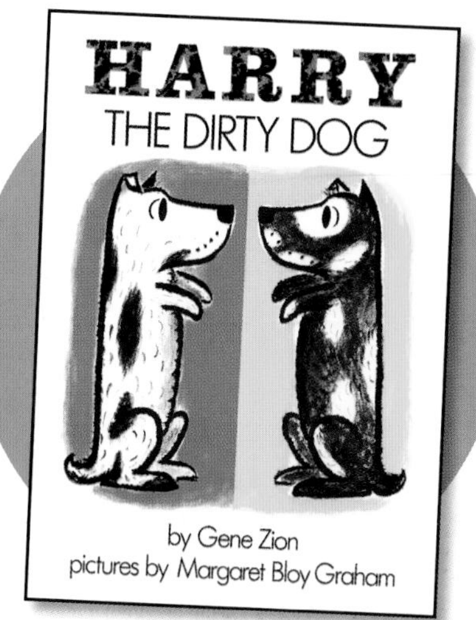

Harry the Dirty Dog

Written by Gene Zion
Illustrated by Margaret Bloy Graham

Harry the dog likes everything—except getting a bath. So he hides the scrub brush and then runs away and gets very dirty! When he comes back home, his family doesn't recognize him. Harry digs up the scrub brush and insists they give him a bath. Who knew Harry was under all that dirt!

Harry likes many things but dislikes getting a bath. No doubt there is something your students dislike as well! Encourage youngsters to share their likes and dislikes with this graphic organizer activity. Give each child a copy of the organizer on page 22. Have her draw and label a picture in each section, showing two things she likes and one thing she dislikes. Then encourage each student to share her organizer and have her classmates guess which item she doesn't like. ***Making text-to-self connections, using a graphic organizer (RL.K.10)***

Colleen Dabney, Williamsburg-James City County Public Schools, Williamsburg, VA

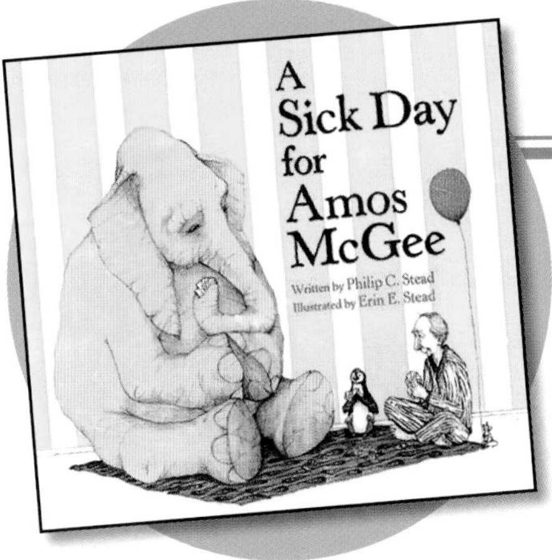

A Sick Day for Amos McGee

Written by Philip C. Stead
Illustrated by Erin E. Stead

Amos McGee works at the zoo. While there, he spends special time with his friends. He plays chess with the elephant, sits with the penguin, takes care of the rhino, and reads to the owl. One day, Amos is sick and stays home. So his friends come to his house to take care of him!

Make a sign labeled with the question "What happens next?" Gather youngsters in a circle and lead them in singing the song shown as they pass the sign. When the song is finished, say, "Amos McGee wakes up in the morning." Then ask the child with the sign, "What happens next?" After he replies, sing and pass the sign again, prompting the next child with the sign to continue describing story events. Repeat the activity until students reach the conclusion. ***Retelling a story in sequence (RL.K.2)***

(sung to the tune of "Are You Sleeping?")

Be a good friend.
Be a good friend.
It is not
Hard to do.
If you are a good friend,
If you are a good friend,
Friends will be
Good to you.

The Book Corner

Literacy Ideas for Teachers®

In the Tall, Tall Grass

By Denise Fleming

During a caterpillar's journey through the tall, tall grass, it encounters a variety of munching, humming, and flapping critters!

Youngsters show what other critters might be in tall, tall grass with this wall display! Cut slits in a long length of green bulletin board paper (grass) and attach it to a wall. Give each child a paper programmed with the sentence starter shown. Encourage her to draw a picture of a creature that might be found in the grass. Next, instruct her to complete the sentence and give more information, describing what she knows about the creature. Then help her tuck her paper in the grass, securing it in place with tape. Look at all those new creatures in the grass! ***Writing informative text (W.K.2)***

adapted by an idea from Angie Kutzer, Garrett Elementary, Mebane, NC

In the tall, tall grass there is a
mouse. A mouse is small and gray,
and it makes a squeaky noise.

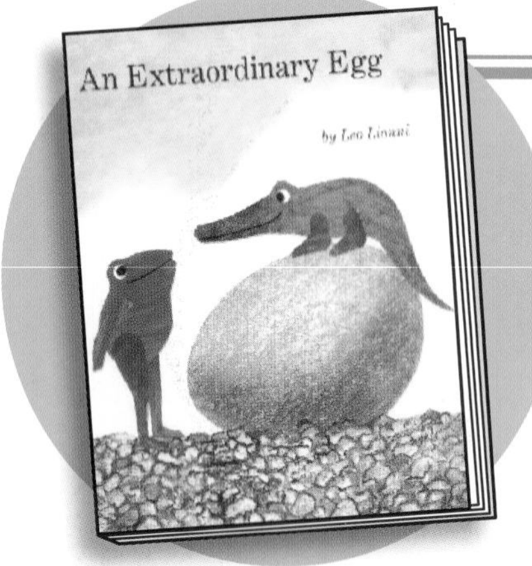

An Extraordinary Egg

By Leo Lionni

Three frog friends living on Pebble Island are thrilled to have what they think is an extraordinary egg—a chicken egg. When the egg hatches, they excitedly welcome the "chicken" and lead the green, scaly creature to the water. When the frogs' new friend meets its mother, the three frogs laugh when they learn the mother called her baby "my sweet little alligator"! What an extraordinary egg!

A classroom replica of Pebble Island is the result of this question-and-answer activity. Make a mound of play dough on a tray and place a container of pebbles nearby. Next, pose a question about the story (see suggestions) and invite a child to respond. After sharing, have him press several pebbles into the mound of play dough. Continue with other questions until each child has had a turn and the play dough is covered with pebbles. Then label a small sign "Pebble Island" and put it in the play dough. ***Answering questions about a story (RL.K.1; RL.K.3)***

Suggested questions:

Who are the main characters?
What does Jessica the frog find when she is exploring?
Where does the story take place? Is that place big or small? Explain.
Why do you think the frogs laugh when they hear the mother called her baby "my sweet little alligator"?
Why do Jessica and the hatched creature become close friends?
Who is your favorite character?
Why do you like or dislike the story?
What is the setting of the story?
Why do you think Marilyn the frog believes the egg is a chicken egg?

Poem Card

Use with "*Snowballs*" on page 18.

My snow ______________________ is made of stuff.

______________________—there's just enough

To make it look so nice today

Before my snow ____________ melts away.

TEC42064

Elephant Pattern

Use with "*Elmer*" on page 18.

Name ______________________________ Graphic organizer (RL.K.10)

Like It or Not!

Note to the teacher: Use with "*Harry the Dirty Dog*" on page 19.

Building Math Skills

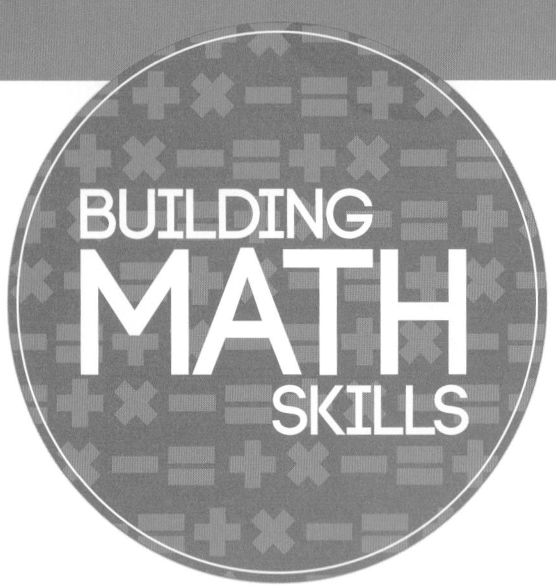

Squares Inside Squares

Characteristics of a square, visual-spatial reasoning (K.G.B.5)

Students build shapes during this discovery-style activity. Cut paper to make four of each of the following: 1" x 12" red strips, 1" x 10" orange strips, 1" x 8" yellow strips, and 1" x 6" green strips. To begin, draw a square on the board and discuss with students the shape's characteristics. Next, give each of four volunteers a red strip and have them use the strips to form a square. Use a glue stick to secure the corners and display the shape. Guide subsequent groups of four to form smaller squares with the remaining sets of color strips. Then lead youngsters to fit the smaller squares inside the largest red square. If desired, adjust the number and size of the paper strips to repeat the activity with different shapes.

Hiromi Yasukawa
Shanghai Community International School
Shanghai, WA

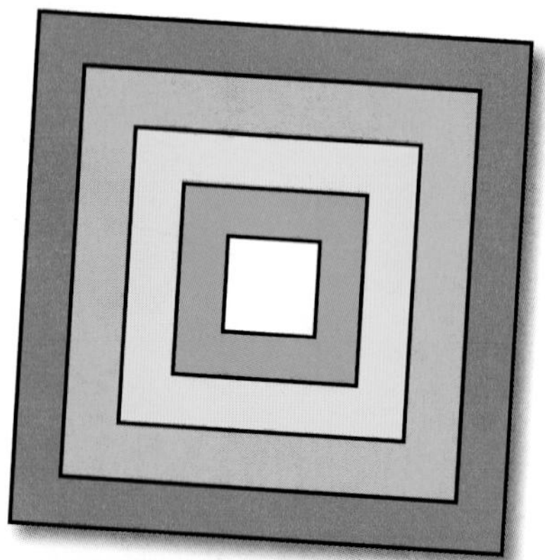

Just Hanging Around

Number order

Monkeys hang from a vine with the help of your students! For this center activity, cut apart a copy of the monkey cards on page 29 and hole-punch the cards where indicated. Display an artificial vine in a student-accessible location. Twist ten green pipe cleaners along the vine and bend the ends to make hooks. Place the monkey cards near the vine. A child puts the monkeys on the hooks in numerical order. **For an added challenge**, have students hang the monkeys in descending order from 10 to 1.

Judy Spradlin
Tate's School of Discovery
Knoxville, TN

Plenty of Practice!

Number sense

From recognizing numbers to addition and subtraction, number cards can be used with activities throughout the year. Give each child a set of number cards from 1 to 12 on a metal ring. Then choose one or more of the activities below for magnificent math practice.

Number recognition (K.CC.A.3): Have a student roll a pair of large dice, count the dots, and name the number. Instruct each child to flip her cards on the ring to show the matching number at the top of the stack.

Number order: Have each student in a small group show a number. Encourage classmates to guide the group to stand in ascending or descending number order.

Addition: Write a number on the board. Instruct each child to choose a number from her ring and add it to the featured number. Then have her write a number sentence to match.

Subtraction: Roll a pair of dice and have students write the number on a sheet of paper. Instruct each child to choose a number card (smaller than the number rolled) and write a corresponding subtraction number sentence. Then invite youngsters to compare their number sentences.

Suzanne Ward
Caledonia Centennial
Caledonia, Ontario, Canada

Later in the year, give each child different number cards to add to her ring and modify activities accordingly. For example, have a child roll three dice for number recognition to 18.

See page 30 for a **practice sheet** on patterning.

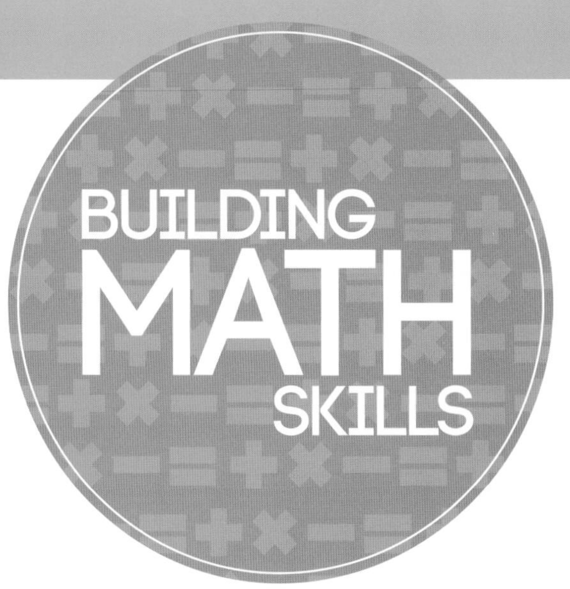

A frog sees nine flies. After it has a snack, there are two flies left. How many flies did the frog eat?

Snacktime for Froggy

Subtraction (K.OA.A.2)

This hands-on activity is sure to foster a student's ability to solve word problems. Have each child draw a frog on a sheet of paper and roll black paper scraps to make ten balls (flies). Then say a word problem for students to solve with their froggy and fly manipulatives. After checking for accuracy, invite a volunteer to explain how he solved the problem. Continue with different word problems.

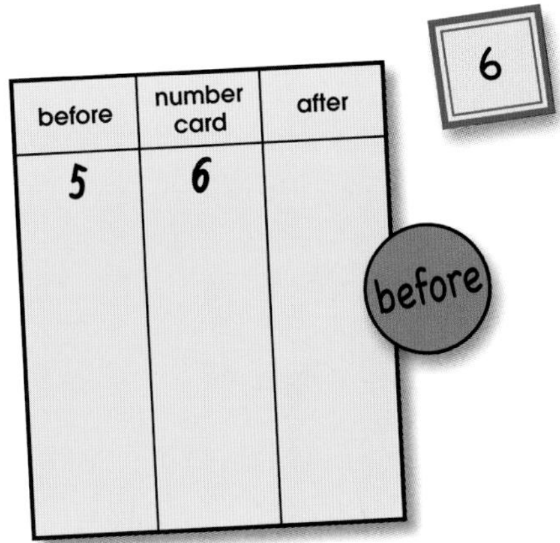

Drop and Write

Number order

Review numbers that come before and after a number with this easy-to-prepare center activity. Label opposite sides of a paper circle "before" and "after." Put the circle, number cards from 1 to 29, and paper at a center. A child labels her paper as shown. Next, she takes a card and writes the number in the middle column. Then she drops the paper circle, finds the matching column on her paper, and records the correct number.

Doria Owen, William Paca Old Post Road Elementary, Abingdon, MD

Shapely Comparisons

Analyzing and comparing three-dimensional shapes (K.G.B.4)

Ask each student to bring from home an object that is an example of a three-dimensional shape. (Have a few extras on hand in case a youngster forgets.) To use the shapes, direct each child to find a partner with an object that has a different shape than his. Have the partners name the shapes of their objects and discuss ways they are alike and different. Then guide youngsters to repeat the activity with a new partner. **For practice with two-dimensional shapes**, have partners compare attribute blocks.

See page 31 for a practice page on **one more and one less.**

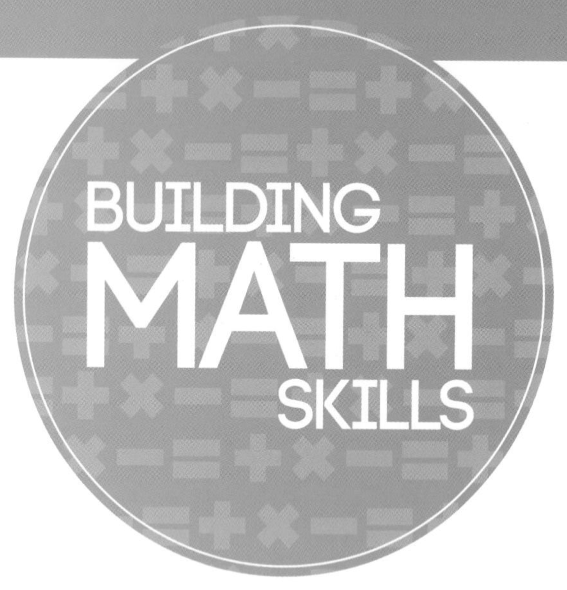

Time Mime

Time to the hour

Here's a kid-pleasing way to practice using an analog clock. Draw a giant clockface without hands on the board. Stand in front of the clock and use your arms to show a time. Ask a volunteer to name the time. For added fun, guide students to pose before a similar clock for classmates to read each time.

Kate Wonders, Carlisle Elementary, Carlisle, IA

Shopping for a Pet

Counting coins

Each day, display a few stuffed toy animals as if they were on sale at a pet shop. Attach a price tag to each one. Then give each of a few students a bag of manipulative coins and encourage him to shop for an animal. To "purchase" a pet, have him count the matching coin combination for his chosen animal. Then invite him to keep his new pet on his desk for the remainder of the day.

Kathy Dailey, Hillside Elementary, Ashburn, VA

Math on the Line!

Number sense

Gather youngsters to practice a variety of math concepts with a single number line! Number cutouts from 0 to 10 and glue them to a length of paper. Then choose one or more of the activities below.

Whole group: Post the number line on a magnetic surface and place two magnets above different numbers. Then have each child write the numbers on a sheet of paper and circle the larger one. Continue with different number pairs. *Comparing numbers (K.CC.C.7)*

Small group: Give each child an individual whiteboard and marker. Secretly cover one of the numbers between 1 and 9. Then invite each student to write the number before the missing number, the missing number, and the next number. *Missing numbers*

Center: Put addition and subtraction flash cards, counters, and paper by the number line. A child takes a card and uses the counters and number line to solve the problem. Then he writes the equation on his paper and shows how he knows. He continues with other cards. *Addition or subtraction (K.OA.A.1)*

Amber Dingman, Sterling, MI

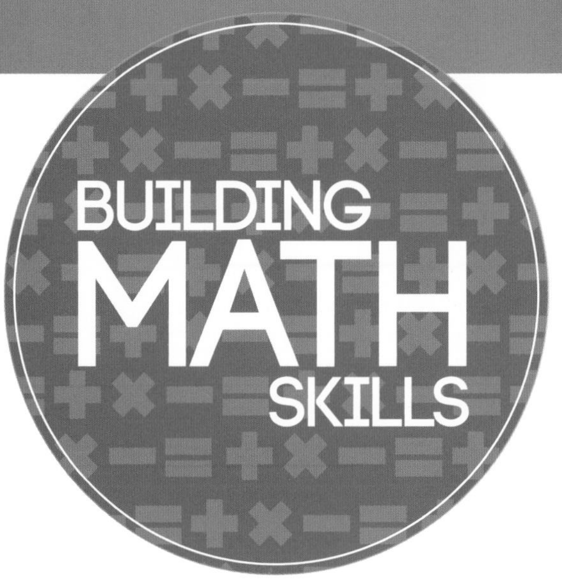

Hungry Birds

Sharing equally, number relationships

Youngsters play the role of a mother bird sharing an equal number of worms at this center. Label a resealable plastic bag with the numbers 2, 3, 4, and 6. Put 12 lengths of yarn (worms) in the bag. Set out the bag, six large pom-poms (birds), and a large brown paper nest. A child chooses a number on the bag and puts that many birds on the nest. Then she takes the worms and "feeds" the baby birds, making sure each baby gets the same amount of worms. If desired, have her draw a picture to show her work. Then she repeats the activity for a different number on the bag.

Suzanne Kobb
South Bend, IN

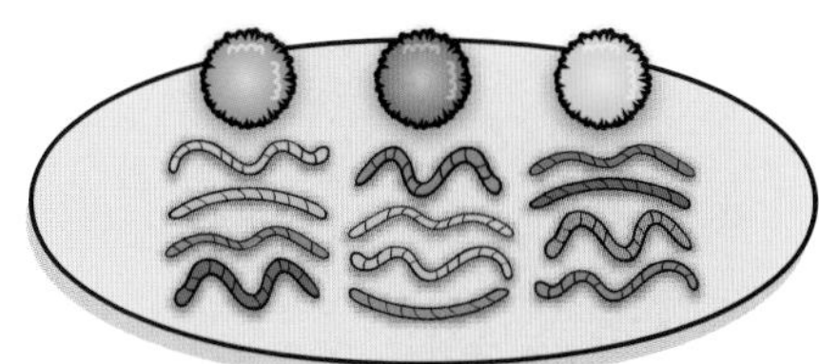

Ramp It Up!

Solid shapes (K.G.B.4)

Have students compare the attributes of solid shapes with this hands-on math exploration. To prepare, lean a personal whiteboard on a wooden block to make a ramp. Nearby, set out a collection of real-world solid shapes that will slide, roll, or slide and roll (on different releases) on the ramp. Then overlap two yarn lengths to make a Venn diagram and label it as shown. Invite a volunteer to choose an object. Ask youngsters to predict whether that object will roll, slide, or both. Have the volunteer use the ramp to test his classmates' predictions. Then have him place the object in the correct area of the diagram. Continue with the remaining objects.

Kimberly Richman, The Learning Zone, Des Moines, IA

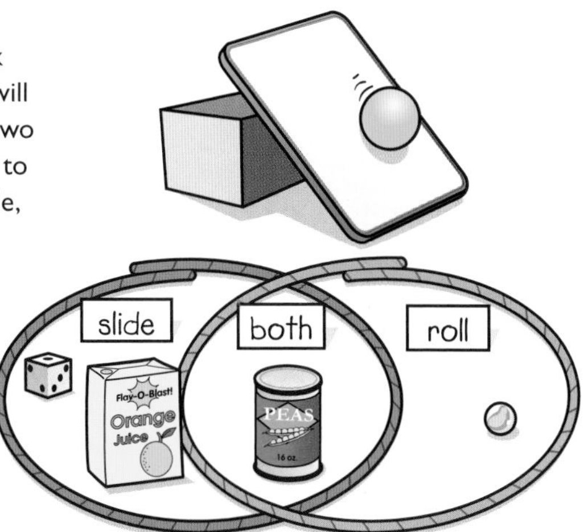

There are ten bunnies in the garden and six bunnies outside the garden, so...

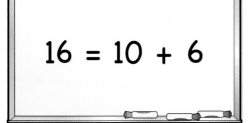

16 = 10 + 6

Into the Garden?

Decomposing numbers into tens and ones (K.NBT.A.1)

Kindergartners pretend a supersize ten frame is a garden in this whole-group activity! To make the garden, use tape to form a ten frame on the floor, making sure each section is large enough for a student to stand. Then invite from ten to 19 students to pretend to be bunnies and have them hop to the garden. Lead the class in counting the total number of bunnies and write that number on the board. Then point to ten bunnies, signaling each one to hop onto a garden section. Guide youngsters to conclude that the ten bunnies in the garden plus the remaining bunnies outside the garden equal the recorded number. If desired, complete the corresponding equation on the board. Continue with a different number of bunnies for additional number practice!

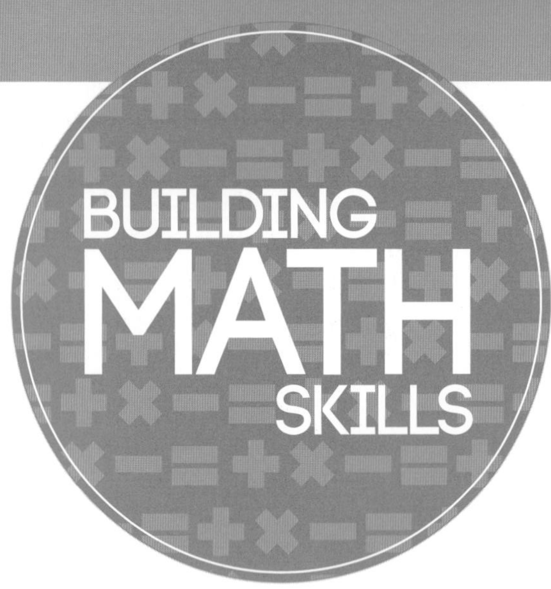

Fill the Chart

Writing numbers (K.CC.A.3)

Students will pick up the pace to complete this quick-to-prepare activity. Give each child two rows of a blank hundred chart. Set a timer for a desired amount of time and say "Start!" Each child races to write the numbers from 1 to 10 in the top row before the timer rings. If he beats the clock, he waves to show his success. When all classmates complete the task, restart the timer and signal youngsters to write the next ten numbers in the sequence. **For practice writing numbers to 100**, give each child a blank hundred chart and have him race to write numbers row by row.

Extension! To use the resulting number grid, give directions such as "Trace the number 13 with a blue crayon" or "Use a green crayon. Color the box with the number that is before 18."

Laurie Brewer, Davis Elementary, Greenwood, MS

Sizing Up Animals

Measurement (K.MD.A.2)

Students compare the average heights of animals with this fun activity. To prepare, use the bonus information shown to cut a length of bulletin board paper for each animal, matching the length of the paper to the height of the animal. Give one strip to each of a small group of students. Have group members color or paint their strip so it resembles the animal it represents. Then guide youngsters to compare the heights of the animals and make comparison statements using appropriate vocabulary, such as *taller*, *shorter*, and *tallest*. For added fun, invite youngsters to explore how many children tall the elephant and the giraffe are by laying head to toe along the cutout.

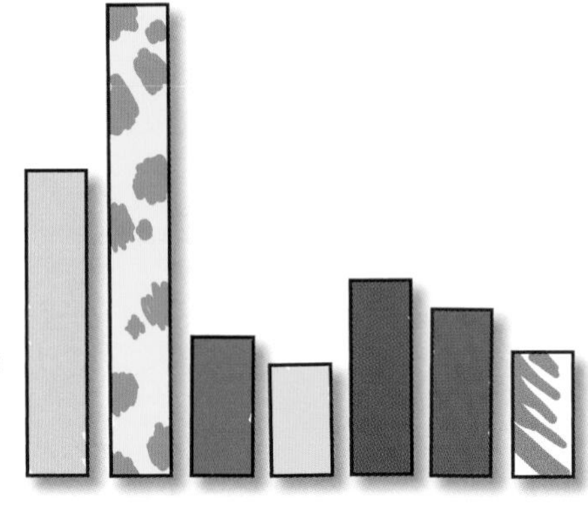

Susan Winter, Shekou International School, Shekou, China

Average Animal Heights
African elephant, 11 feet; giraffe, 17 feet; red kangaroo, 5 feet; lion, 4 feet; grizzly bear, 7 feet; gorilla, 6 feet; zebra, 4.5 feet

Taking Attendance

Counting sets (K.CC.B.5), concept of addition

Combine sorting and counting to find out if all students are present. Choose a sorting criterion, such as boys and girls or students wearing long sleeves and students wearing short sleeves. (Be sure all students fit into one of the categories.) Ask a child in each group to count the total number of students in her group, including herself, and write the number on the board. Next, help students determine how many students are present altogether and write that number on the board. Lead youngsters to then compare the written total to the total number of students in the class and figure out the number of students missing, if any.

Kim Sykes, Methacton Mennonite Preschool, Norristown, PA

Go to page 33 for a practice page on graphing and page 34 for one on addition.

Monkey Cards

Use with "Just Hanging Around" on page 24.

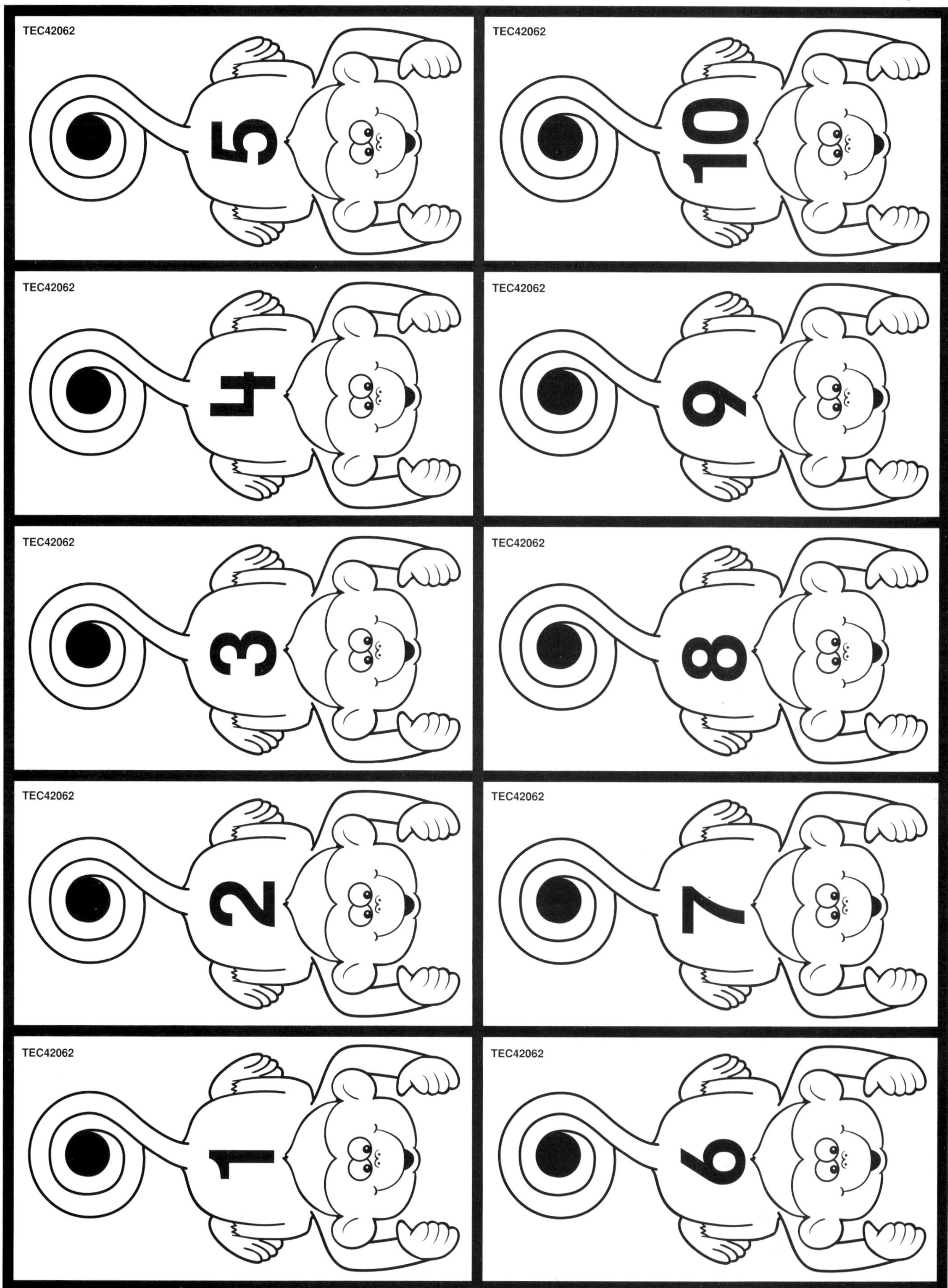

Name ____________________

A Playful Pup

Draw to match and extend each pattern.

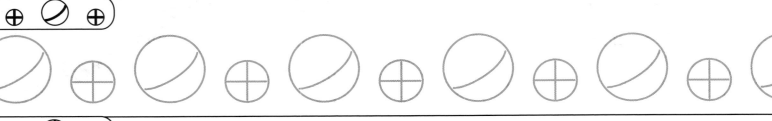

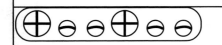

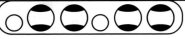

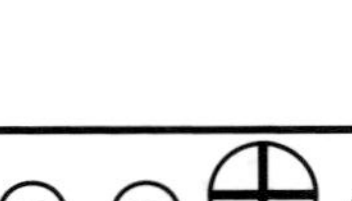
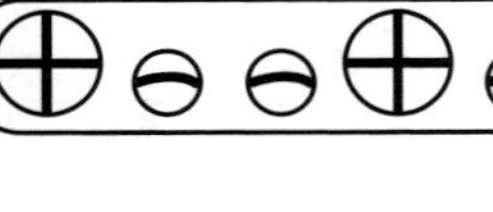

Bonus: Draw red and blue balls to show a pattern.

Name ____________________

Presents Aplenty

1 2 3 4 5 6 7 8 9 10 11 12

Write the number that is **one more**.

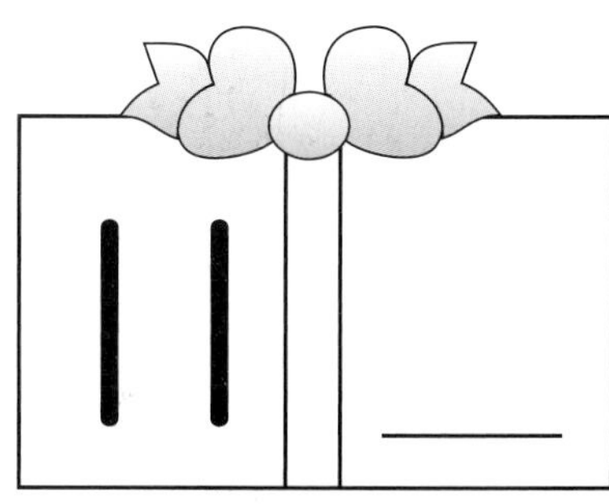

Write the number that is **one less**.

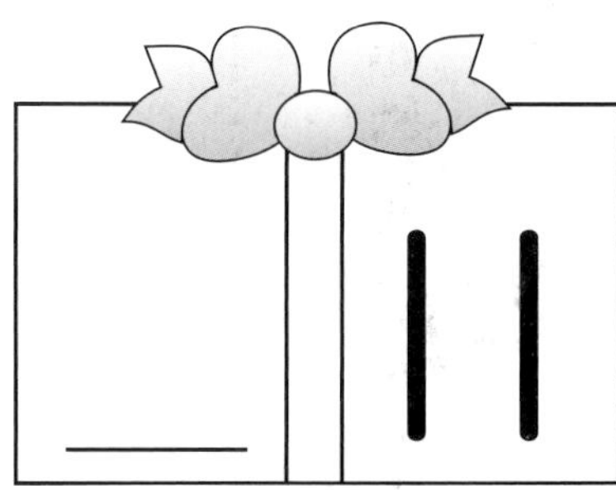

Bonus: Write each number that is **one more** and **one less** than 3.

Name ____________________

Goodies to Go

Circle **yes** or **no** to tell if there are equal parts.

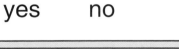

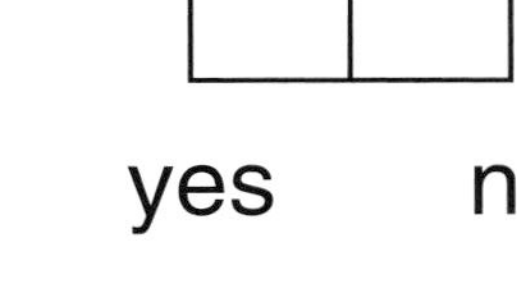
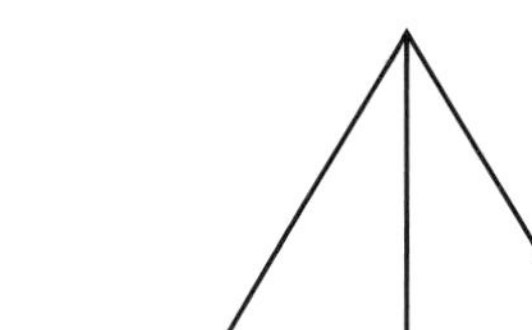
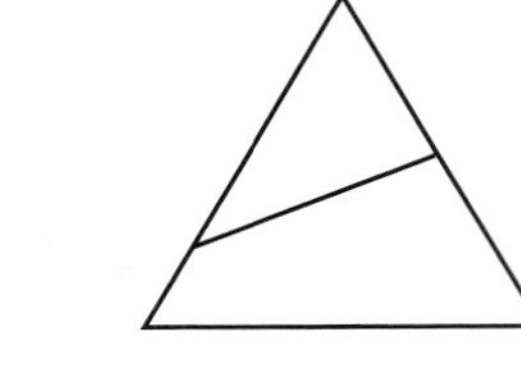
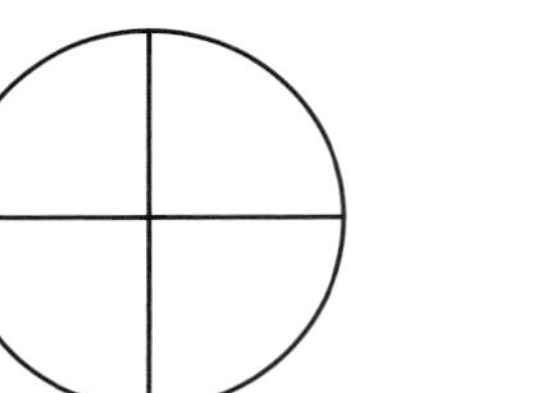
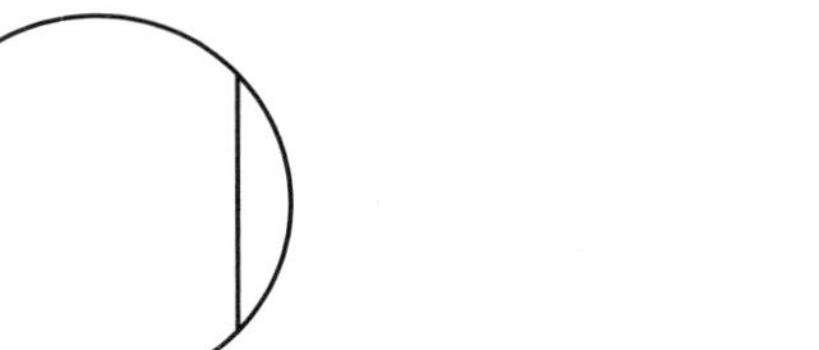

yes no	yes no	yes no	yes no
yes no	yes no	yes no	yes no

Draw lines to show **2 equal parts**.

Draw lines to show **4 equal parts**.

Bonus: Draw a pizza. Draw lines to show 4 equal parts.

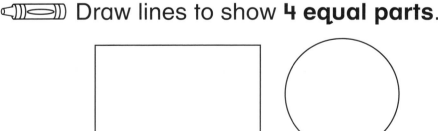

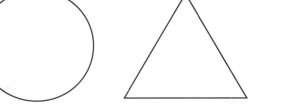

Name ____________________

Cat's Castle

  Look at Cat's Castle. Count.

Color the graph.

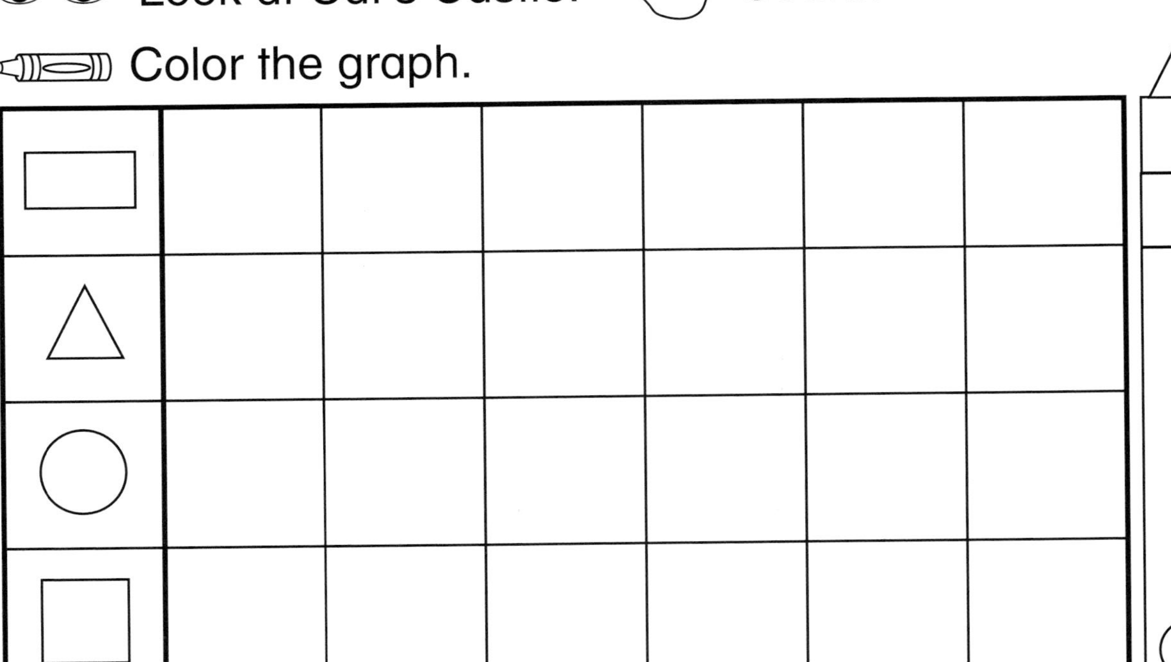

Bonus: Which two shapes have the same amount?

Write about the graph. Use the words **more** and **less**.

____

____

____

Name ______________________________ Addition (K.OA.A.2)

Fishy Addition

Write the missing number to solve each problem.

Draw dots to help you.

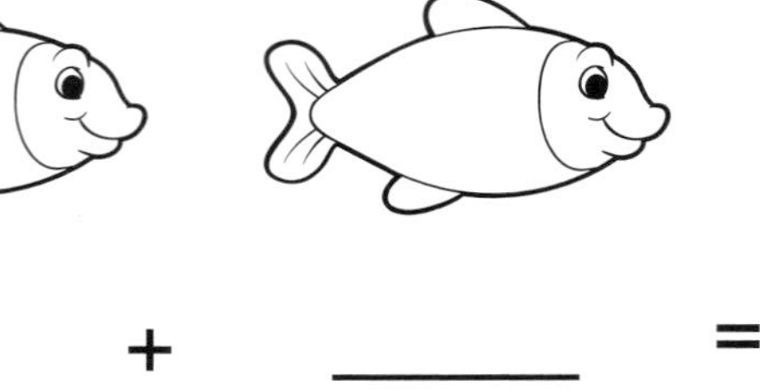

3 + 1 = 4

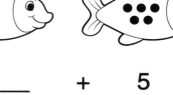

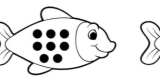

6 + ____ = 9

4 + ____ = 8

____ + 5 = 7

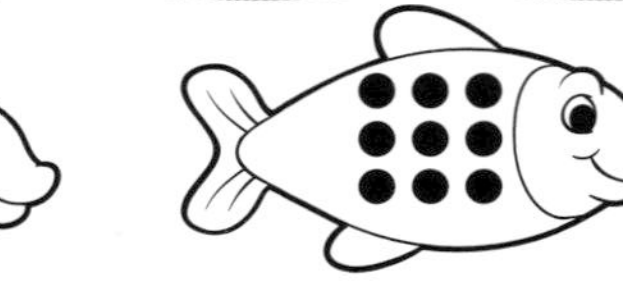

____ + 9 = 10

2 + ____ = 5

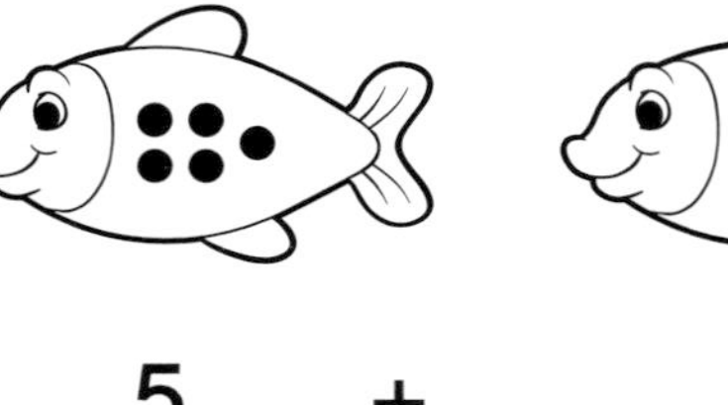

5 + ____ = 6

8 + ____ = 10

Classroom Displays

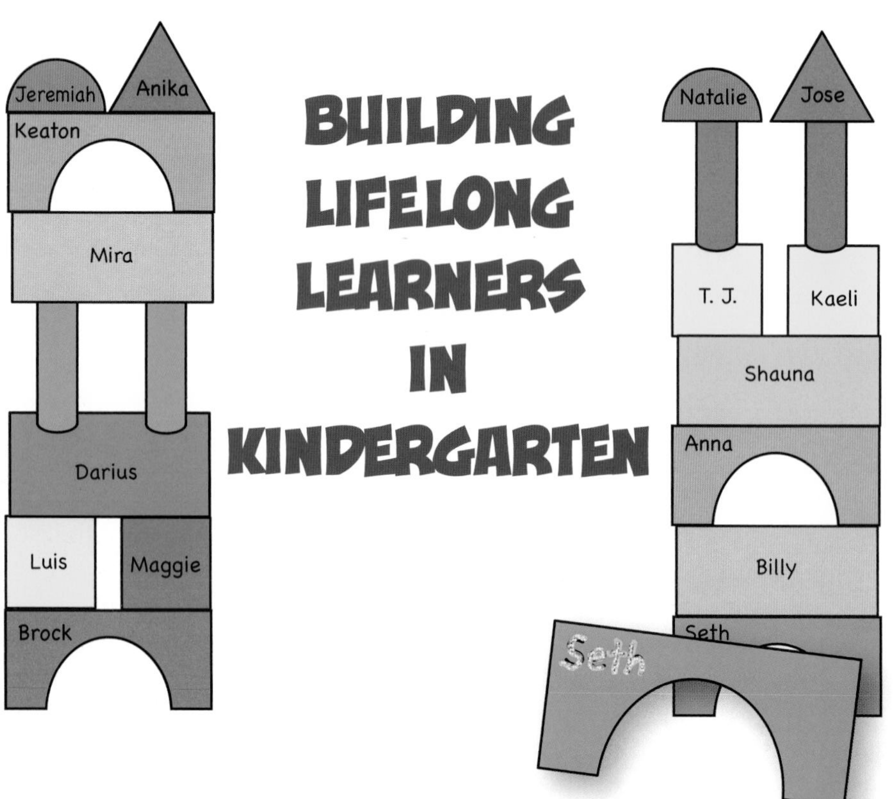

Each child is sure to feel welcome when she sees her name on this wall display. Write students' names on separate building block cutouts. Have each child trace her name with glitter glue and set it aside to dry. Then tape the blocks to a wall with a title similar to the one shown. Encourage youngsters to find their names on the wall each morning and say, "I'm a lifelong learner!"

Dianne Neumann
F. C. Whiteley School
Hoffman Estates, IL

Painted plates are the perfect craft to make this cluster of fruit. Have each child sponge-paint a paper plate purple. After the paint dries, help students personalize their plates (grapes). Then assemble the grapes on a display with twisted green streamers (stems and vine) and a leaf cutout as shown. The completed display is sure to make every student feel included in the bunch!

Jodi Darter
Cabool Elementary
Cabool, MO

DISPLAYS That Welcome Kindergartners!

Students' assigned class responsibilities are on display with these cute catches! Write different jobs on copies of the net patterns on page 43. Also personalize a copy of the fish pattern (page 43) for each child. Arrange the display as shown and put fish on the nets to assign job tasks. To change the class responsibilities, simply move the fish!

Denise K. Clay
Kehoe France School and Camp
Metairie, LA

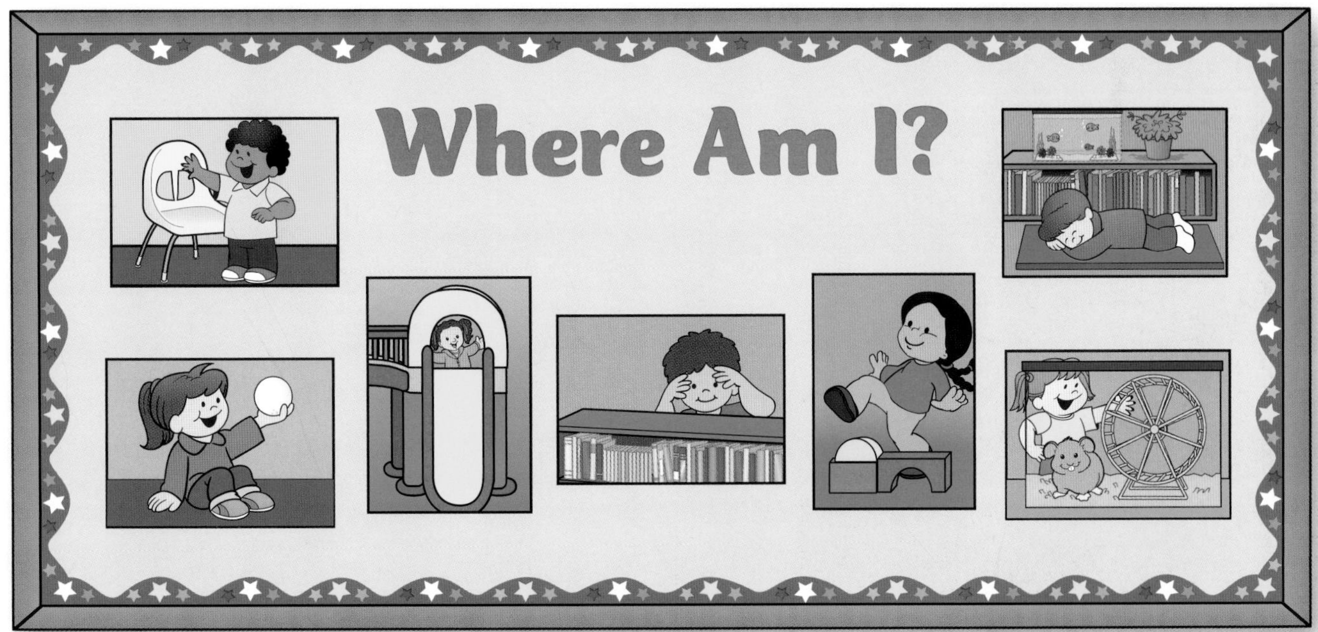

Welcome students and reinforce positional words! Take photos of your youngsters interacting with classroom objects in different positions around the room. When you have a suitable photo of each child, post the photos on a display. Then ask a question such as "Who is standing behind Harry Hamster's home?" Encourage youngsters to name the corresponding child and have the child point to her photo. **To extend the activity**, lead youngsters to form positional word phrases and record a caption to post with each photo.

Karla Barrow, Mount View Elementary, Brigham City, UT

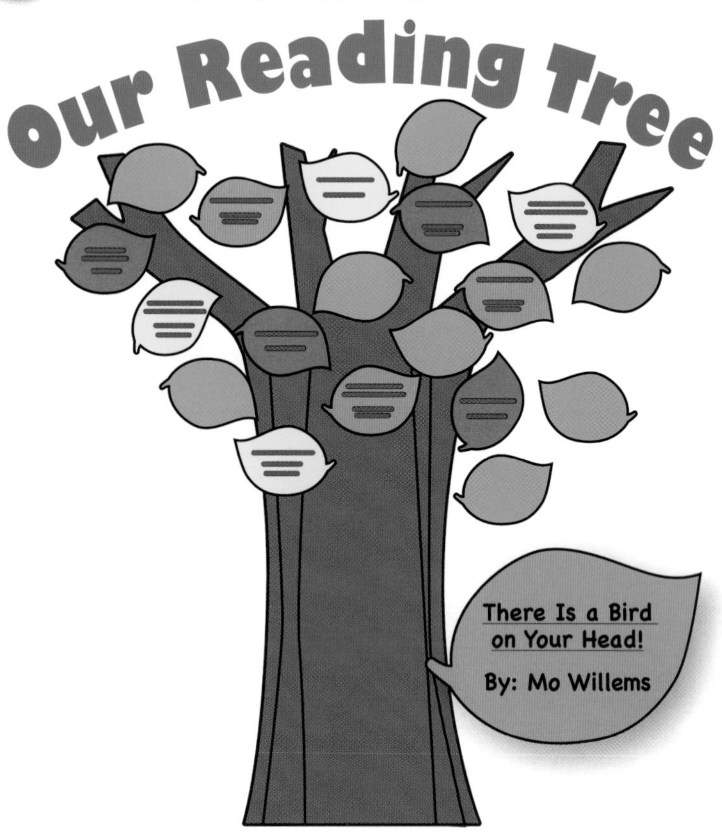

Youngsters read books to show the beautiful colors of fall on this wall display! Post a large tree trunk with several green leaves. Put a collection of red, orange, and yellow leaf cutouts nearby. After a child reads a book, help him write the title and author's name on a cutout. Then have him remove a green leaf and tape his leaf in its place. (Save the green leaves for similar use later in the year, posting them on a leafless wintry tree trunk.) Encourage youngsters to read in class and at home to see how full the tree can be by the end of fall!

Andrea Cornwell
Cornwell Academy
Lake Village, IN

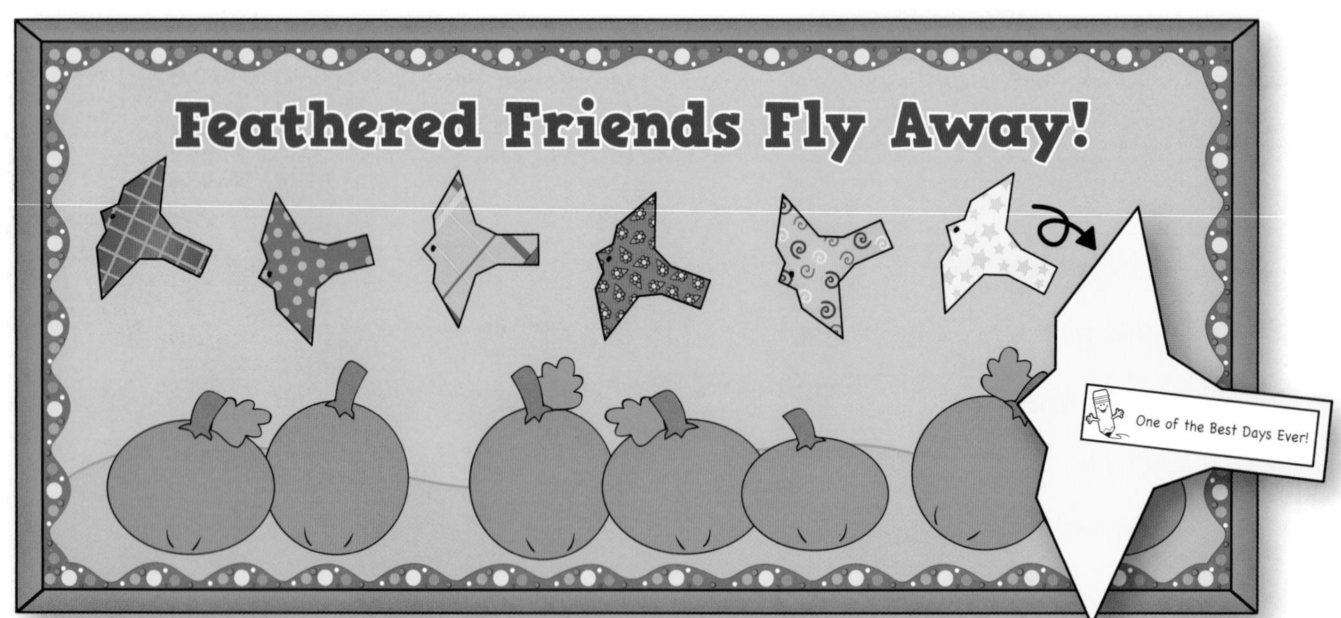

Feathered Friends Fly Away!
One of the Best Days Ever!

These beautiful birds prompt youngsters to write and mimic wintry habits! For each child, trace a bird template (pattern on page 44) on a magazine page or thin wallpaper covering and program a class supply of the cards from page 44 with different writing prompts. Have each child cut out her bird and tape a writing prompt card to the back. Staple the birds on a seasonal display. Each day, help a child read the prompt on the back of her bird and have youngsters respond to it. Then have the feathered friend "fly" home with the child, pretending to fly south for the season. If desired, feature a sign that shows how many birds in all have flown away. By wintertime, there will be fewer or no birds left on the fall display! *(W.K. 1–3)*

Stephanie Litwin, Mendham, NJ

These adorable penguins are sure to attract attention to this nonfiction display. Give each child a large black paper oval, a medium-size white paper oval, and paper scraps of black, white, and orange. Have her glue the white oval to the black oval to form the penguin's body. Next, have her use the scraps to make the eyes, wings, beak, and feet. Then help youngsters write different penguin facts on cloud cutouts. Display the clouds and penguins on a snowy board as shown.

Kiva English, Cato-Meridian Elementary, Cato, NY

What do these snowpals see in winter? A lot! Give each child a paper plate and craft materials to create a snowpal. Next, lead youngsters on a wintry walk with their snowpals, encouraging them to notice what their snowpals "see." Then help each child write on a speech bubble cutout to respond to the poem shown. Post the poem, snowpals, and speech bubbles. Lead youngsters to read the poem throughout winter. Each time, invite a different child to read what her snowpal had to say.

Felice Kestenbaum, Goosehill Primary, Cold Spring Harbor, NY

This display is perfect for both Valentine's Day and Presidents' Day! Take a photo of each child's profile. Position it on black paper and cut around it to make a silhouette. Have each child decorate the border of a personalized heart cutout and then glue his silhouette on the heart. Display students' crafts with silhouettes of George Washington and Abraham Lincoln. Then lead a discussion about each president's accomplishments.

Theresa Kutchey, Wilkerson Elementary, Warren, MI

Soaring With Writing and Reading

-at
-un
-ig
-ack
-ot
-ug
bug
rug
mug

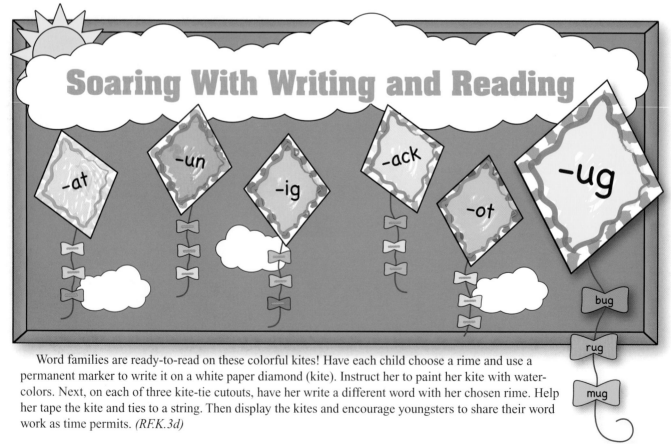

Word families are ready-to-read on these colorful kites! Have each child choose a rime and use a permanent marker to write it on a white paper diamond (kite). Instruct her to paint her kite with watercolors. Next, on each of three kite-tie cutouts, have her write a different word with her chosen rime. Help her tape the kite and ties to a string. Then display the kites and encourage youngsters to share their word work as time permits. *(RF.K.3d)*

Shannon Martin, Provena Fortin Villa Learning Center, Bourbonnais, IL

DISPLAYS That Are Super for Storybooks!

This herd of sheep can be used to embellish just about any sheep-related storybook display! Have each child complete a desired book-response activity on one side of a paper plate. Then, to make a sheep, have her glue a tagboard oval (head) and four paper rectangles (legs) to the blank side of the plate (body). Next, have her glue cotton balls to the body, glue pink paper scraps (ears) to the head, and draw facial details. Then use the sheep to decorate the display of your choice. **Book suggestions:** Nancy Shaw's *Sheep on a Ship*, *Sheep in a Jeep*, or *Sheep Take a Hike*

Barbara Preziosi, Hillcrest School, Morristown, NJ

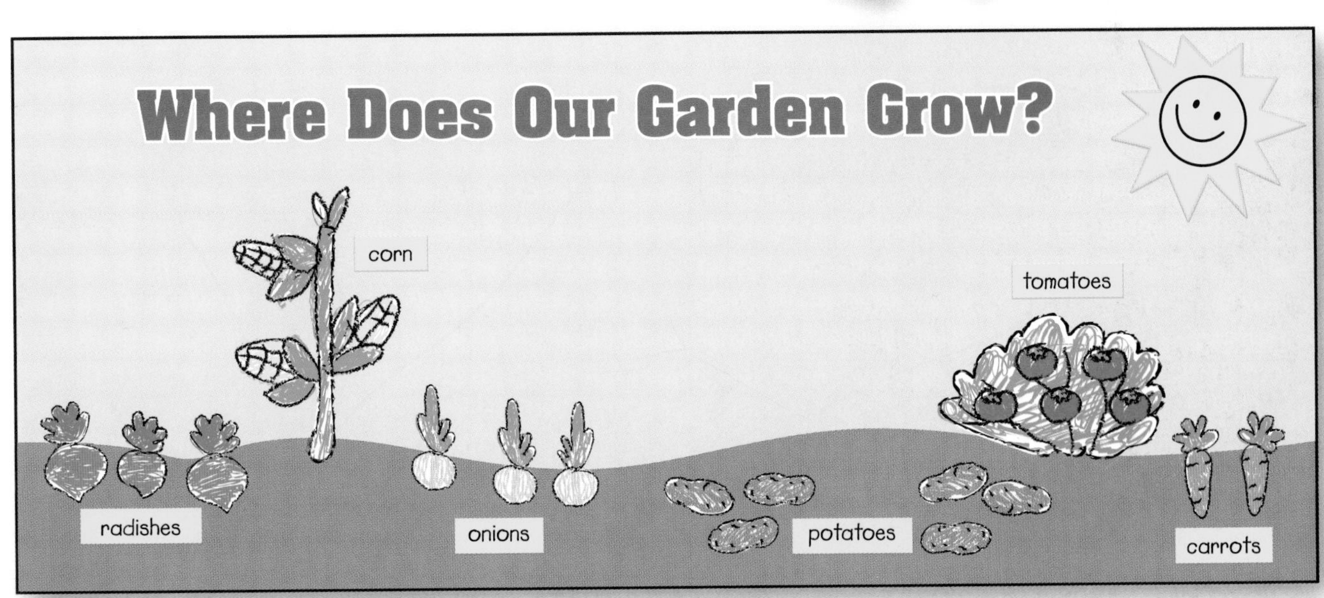

Students show where fruits and veggies grow with this class mural. Attach a length of brown paper to a blue background. Next, instruct students to draw and cut out different fruits and vegetables. Then name a fruit or vegetable and have each youngster with that food glue his cutout above or below the ground to show where it grows. Continue until all the cutouts are glued to the garden. Then add desired details to complete the display. **Book suggestions:** *Tops & Bottoms* by Janet Stevens or *The Vegetables We Eat* by Gail Gibbons

Susan Sisson, Glades Academy, Pahokee, FL

DISPLAYS That Are Excellent for the End of the Year!

Students are sure to enjoy revisiting interesting places they have explored throughout the year in storybooks! Set out several familiar books that have different settings. For each book, read the title and lead youngsters to provide details about where the story takes place. Then slide the books into separate resealable plastic bags and staple the back of each bag to a display with the title shown. Then have students draw and write about a favorite location, to compare two settings, or to make a minibooklet of amazing destinations. ***Identify settings (RL.K.3)***

adapted from an idea by Shannon Adams, Waxahachie Faith Family Academy, Waxahachie, TX

Look How We Have Grown!

Ann Smith

This "kinder-garden" features students' baby photographs with their end-of-the-year photos. Ask each child's family to submit a baby picture. Next, have each student write her first name and last name on separate leaf cutouts. Guide her to glue her leaves and a flower cutout to a paper stem. Then help her tape her baby picture at the bottom of the stem and tape a recent photo atop the flower. Showcase the completed flowers on a wall with the title shown. If desired, write on the back of each flower the child's name, grade level, and year and then send the project home as an end-of-the-year keepsake.

Stacey Abbott, St. Paul's Plus, Brooklandville, MD

Net and Fish Patterns

Use with "Our Job 'Net-Work'" on page 37.

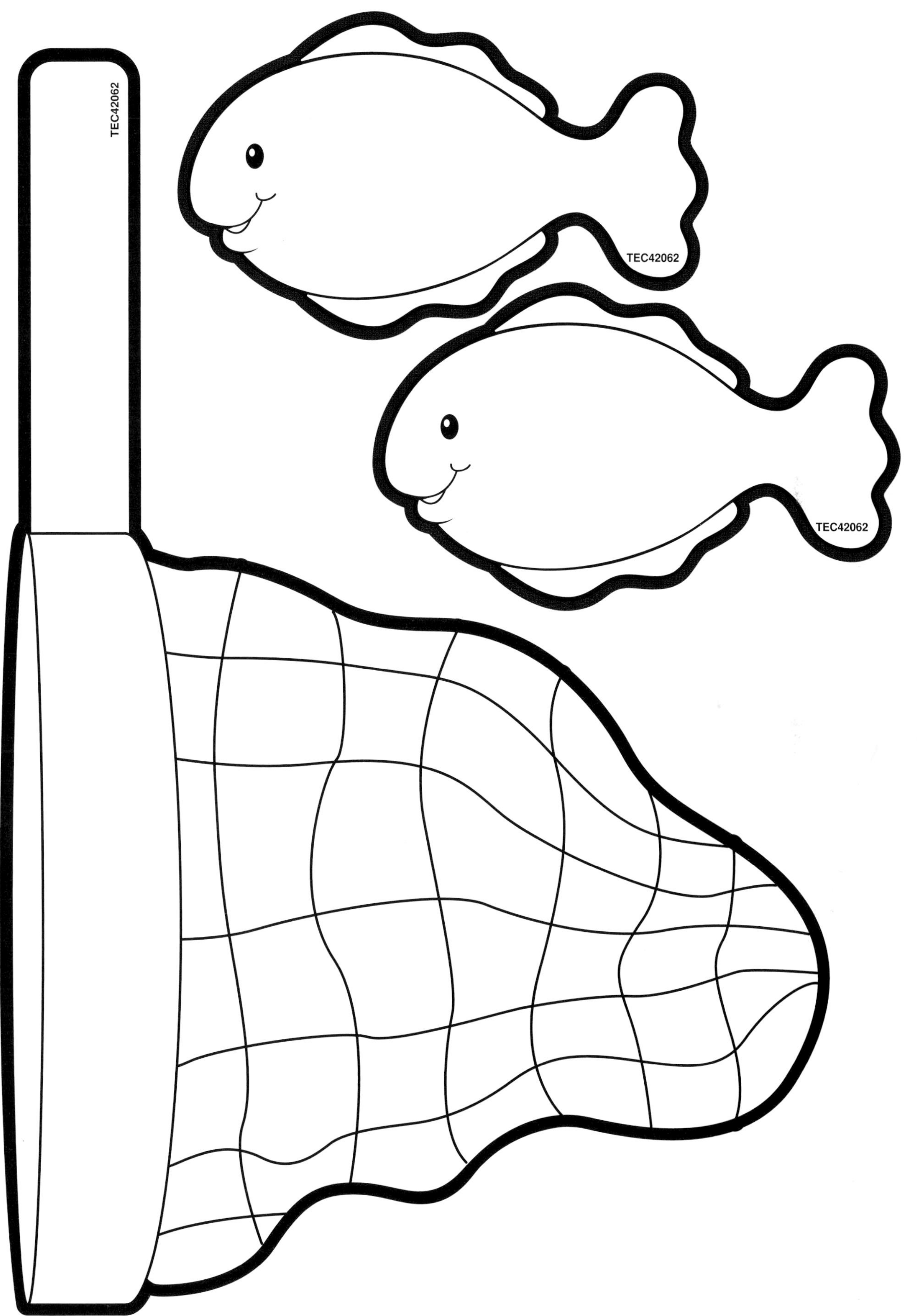

Bird Pattern and Writing Prompt Cards

Use with "Feathered Friends Fly Away!" on page 38.

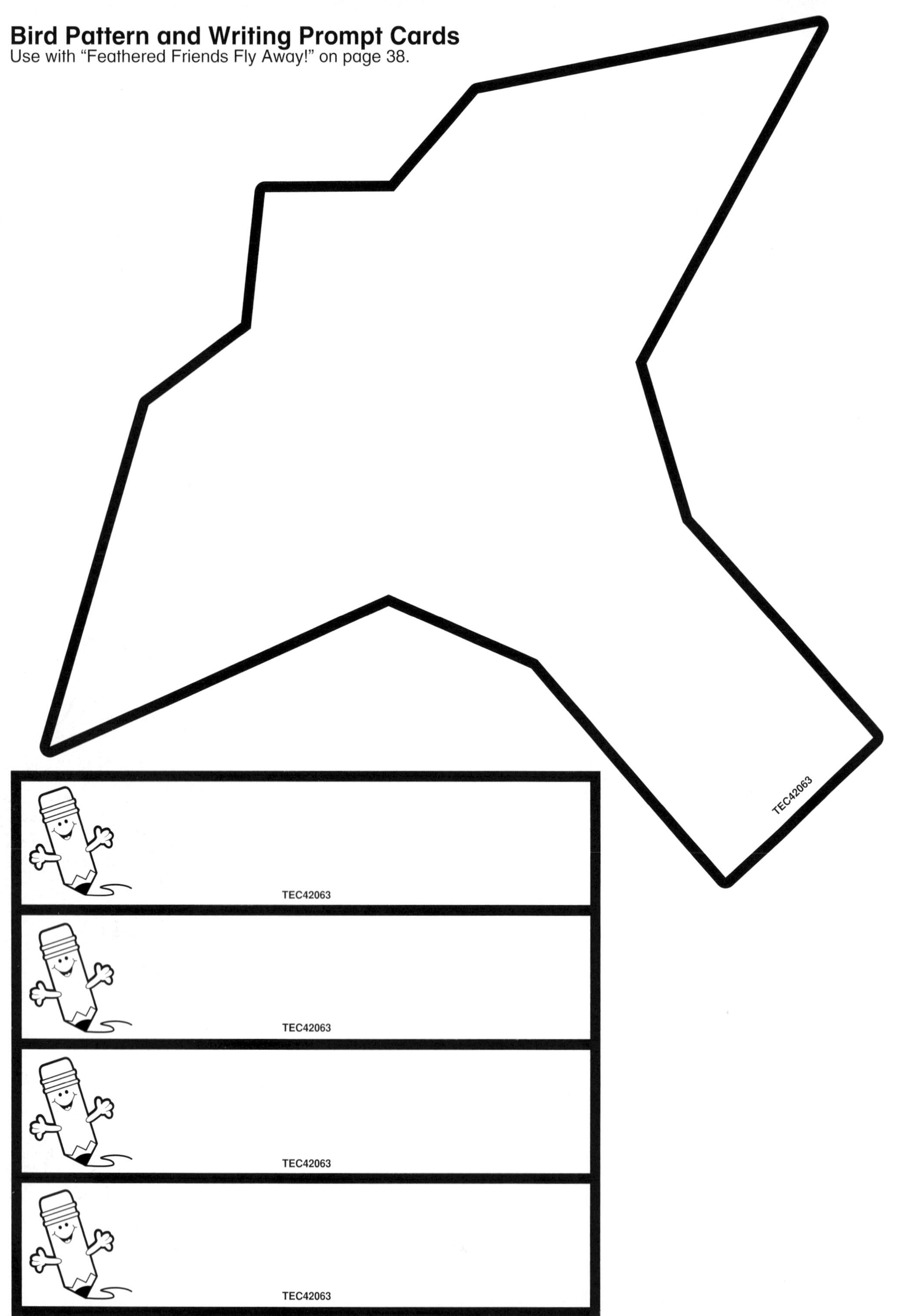

Learning Centers

Learning Centers

The Learning Tree

Literacy Center

Here's a seasonal display that can easily be adapted for other times of the year. Write a different uppercase letter on each of several red, yellow, and green apple cutouts (patterns on page 58). Display the apples on a simple tree cutout. Nearby, set out a set of matching letter cards and red, yellow, and green crayons. A child takes a letter card, finds the same letter on the tree, and uses the matching color crayon to write the letter. He continues with each remaining letter card. Later in the year, replace the apples with other seasonal shapes—such as leaves, holiday ornaments, and blossoms—and label them to review different skills. **For an easier version**, provide a recording sheet with the matching letters for students to trace. ***Letter matching (RF.K.1d), letter formation (L.K.1a)***

Marcia Cochran
Kalamazoo Christian West Preschool
Kalamazoo, MI

Grocery Shopping

Math Center

Exposure to environmental print is an added benefit of this counting center. Make several paper shopping carts by gluing circles to trimmed construction paper as shown; write a different number on each cart. Then cut out easily recognizable logos from grocery store–item labels. Set out the prepared shopping carts and logos. A child chooses a shopping cart, reads the number, and places the correct number of items on the cart. He repeats the process with other carts. **For extra support to recognize numbers**, put a matching number of sticky dots on the back of each cart. ***Counting (K.CC.A.3)***

Jill Davis, Kendall-Whittier Elementary, Tulsa, OK

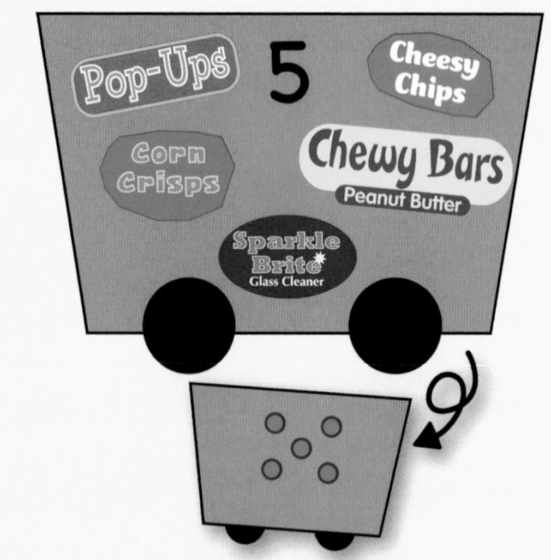

Spell and Smell

Literacy Center

This fragrant center is sure to be a favorite of your youngsters. Personalize a paper plate for each child. Place at a center, the plates, glue, and flavored gelatin powder. A center visitor finds her plate and traces each letter in her name with glue. Encourage her to name each letter as she traces it. Then she sprinkles gelatin powder on the glue and sets the plate aside to dry. When the glue is dry, she shakes off the excess gelatin powder. ***Writing one's name (RF.K.1d)***

Andrea Singleton, Waynesville Elementary, Waynesville, OH

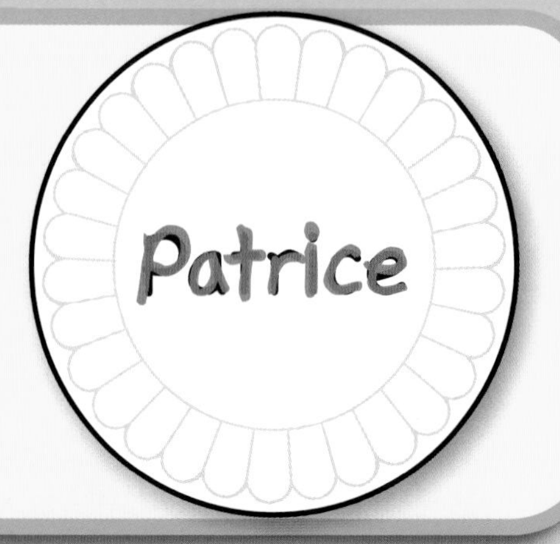

Learning Centers

Roll and Build

Math Center

How tall are the towers? A student must roll the dice to find out! Set out Unifix cubes, a pair of dice, and paper at a center. A child rolls the dice and stacks the matching number of cubes to form a tower. He continues to roll and build to form five towers. Next, he lines up the towers along the short edge of his paper in ascending or descending order. Then he traces each tower, writes the total number of cubes per tower, and labels his paper to compare the structures. **For a different skill**, have youngsters pretend the linked cubes are worms and compare the lengths of five worms! ***Ordering objects by height***

Jaclyn Bzibziak
Potters Road Elementary
West Seneca, NY

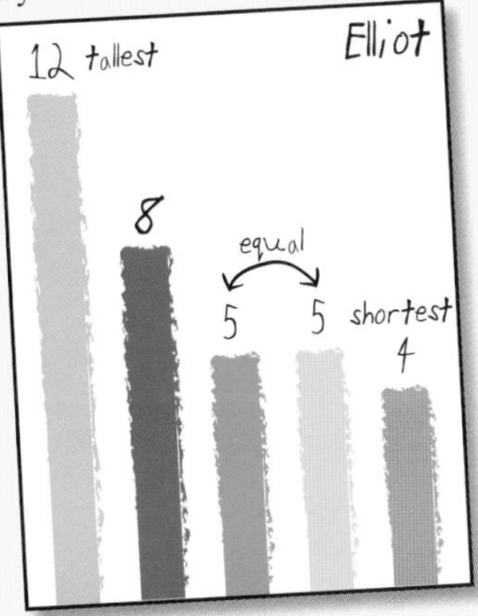

Feed the Birds

Math Center

Here, birdie, birdie! Students are sure to enjoy feeding these birds! Cut apart a copy of the labels on page 59. Attach each label to a separate paper cup. Put the cups, a sign similar to the one shown, and small pom-poms (seeds) at a center. A child reads the sign and puts the corresponding number of seeds per bird in each cup. Then he counts the total number of seeds in each cup. To make the activity self-checking, program the bottoms of the cups with the matching number of seeds to match the sign. ***Counting***

Stephanie Litwin
Mendham Township Elementary
Mendham, NJ

Jack and Jill

Literacy Center

This familiar nursery rhyme is sure to help students match beginning sounds to letters. Color and cut out the copy of the center mat on page 60. Write the matching inital consonant on the back of each card to make the activity self-checking. Then color and cut apart a copy of the center cards on page 61. Store the cards in a resealable plastic bag. Place the bag and mat at a center. To complete the activity, a student stacks the cards faceup. He names the picture on the top card, identifies the initial consonant, and puts the card in the corresponding space. After he sorts the remaining cards, he flips the cards to check his work. ***Initial consonants (RF.K.3a)***

Karin Bulkow, Washington School for Comprehensive Literacy, Sheboygan, WI

Super Simple Center Set out calendar numbers for students to ***order numbers***, sort into ***even and odd numbers***, or use as a reference to practice ***writing numbers***. Jennifer Frankle, Michael C. Riley ECC, Bluffton, SC

Easy Center Formats for a Variety of Skills (CCSS)

Students are sure to become familiar with these center formats and will get to work on the featured skill right away!

Setup: On a poster board, make several one-inch slits across two rows. Slide two paper clips through each slit so that one points up and the other points down. Turn over the poster and tape the clips in place for added stability. For added appeal, embellish the board with details as desired.

Activity: Gather sets of cards for youngsters to match into pairs for desired skills. Put the sets in separate resealable plastic bags. A child empties a bag, finds a matching pair of cards, and slides each card under one of two paper clips paired together. **For an easier version**, clip one card from each pair on the board for students to find the match.

Jackie Wright, Summerhill Children's House, Enid, OK

Setup: Draw lines to make six columns on a sheet of paper. Write different letters, numbers, or words at the top of each column to make headings and set out a copy of the paper for each child. Then program each side of a cube with letters, numbers, or words that correspond with the featured headings. For example, write six different uppercase letters as headings and write the matching six lowercase letters on the cube.

Activity: A child rolls the die and writes the letter, number, or word under the matching column on her paper. She continues to roll and write until one column wins with five recordings.

Sandy Petersen, Gifford Elementary, Racine, WI

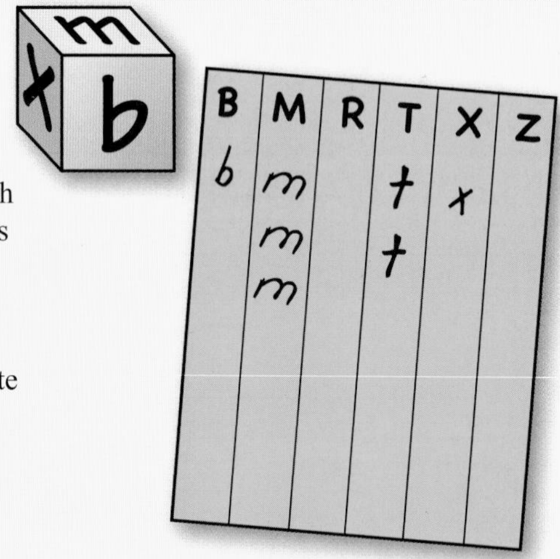

Setup: On a copy of page 62, program the pumpkin cards to form matching pairs when cut apart. For example, write different high-frequency words to make matching card pairs or write an addition problem on six cards and their sums on the other six. Then cut apart the cards and glue each set side by side in random order on a length of paper. Laminate the paper.

Activity: A child connects the matching pairs by drawing lines with a wipe-off marker. To extend the activity, he records the matching pairs on a sheet of paper. When finished, he wipes away the lines with a cloth to ready the activity for the next center visitor.

Laurie Gibbons, Huntsville, Alabama

Learning Centers

Make a Pair

Literacy Center

For this partner center, set out two small whiteboards, two markers, and an alphabet chart. One child writes an uppercase letter on his whiteboard and shows it to his partner. Without looking at the alphabet chart, the partner writes the matching lowercase letter on her whiteboard. Then the twosome uses the alphabet chart to check for accuracy. To continue, partners erase their boards and switch roles. ***Matching uppercase and lowercase letters (RF.K.1d)***

Suzanne Moore
Tucson, AZ

How Many Cookies?

Math and Literacy Center

Reinforce counting and number words with this matching activity. Cut apart a copy of pages 63 and 64. A child counts the cookies in a jar and places the matching number word beside the jar. He continues with each remaining card. To make the activity self-checking, program the backs of each matching pair of cards with the corresponding numeral. If desired, have a student write on paper the number of cookies in each jar and its number word. ***Counting and number words (K.CC.B.5; RF.K.3c)***

Jackie Wright
Summerhill Children's House
Enid, OK

Snowball Scoop

Literacy Center

Label each of several Ping-Pong balls (snowballs) with a different high-frequency word and place the balls in a plastic bucket. Put the bucket, an ice cream scoop, and blank paper at a center. A child scoops out a snowball, reads the word, and then writes it on her paper. She continues with the remaining snowballs. When time permits, she reads her list to a classroom adult. **For an added challenge**, have youngsters write sentences using the words listed. ***High-frequency words (RF.K.3c)***

Sheila Freeman
Southern Tier Catholic School
Olean, NY

Tip To easily organize and store writing paper options at a center, glue a sample of each paper choice to separate manila envelopes. Laminate the envelopes, slit to reopen the pockets, and put matching paper in each envelope. ***Vanessa Rivera, La Luz Elementary, La Luz, NM***

Learning Centers

Weighty Comparisons
Math Center

Set out a balance scale, small stuffed animals, Unifix cubes, teddy bear counters, and blank paper. A child chooses a stuffed animal and places it on one side of the scale. Next, she places Unifix cubes, one at a time, on the other side of the scale until the scale balances. On her paper, she draws the stuffed animal and writes how many Unifix cubes she put on the scale. In the same manner, she then uses the bear counters to measure and record the weight of the stuffed animal. Finally, she writes a sentence to compare the two measurements. ***Nonstandard measurement***

Suzanne Moore
Tucson, AZ

The Poetry Corner
Literacy Center

A poetry center is the perfect place to reinforce a variety of literacy skills. Put copies of a familiar poem at the center along with cards labeled with directions such as "Highlight the high-frequency words," "Circle each word that begins with [*f*]," and "Underline the rhyming words." A child performs each task as described on the direction cards. Next, he glues the poem on a sheet of paper. Then he writes and illustrates a sentence that tells how the poem relates to him or whether he liked the poem. ***Skill review (CCSS)***

Carolyn Scardina
Linthicum Elementary
Linthicum, MD

Snow is falling
All around.
A fluffy white blanket
Covers the ground.
I like to play in
the fluffy snow.

Collect students' papers for several poems to make individual poetry books!

How Many Shoes?
Math Center

To prepare for this partner game, color a copy of the envelope label on page 65, the center mats on page 66, and the cards on page 67. Attach the label to the front of a manila clasp envelope. Cut apart the mats and cards. To make the activity self-checking, write the matching number on the back of each card. Then put the cards and mats in the envelope.

To begin the activity, each partner picks a mat and helps stack the cards faceup on the envelope label. When it is his turn, a partner takes the top card. To find out how many shoes he has, he solves the problem or names the number represented on the shoebox. Next, he flips the card to check; then he places the card in an empty space on his mat below the critter with the same number of feet. If there is not an empty space, he puts the card on the bottom of the card stack. The first player to fill his center mat is the winner. ***Number sense***

Karin Bulkow, Washington School for Comprehensive Literacy, Sheboygan, WI

Learning Centers

Rolling and Sliding

Math Center

Try this simple-to-set-up geometric sort. Write "rolls," "slides," and "rolls and slides" on separate cards. Put the cards and three-dimensional objects at the center. A child takes an object and tests it to see if it rolls and slides. Then he places the object under the matching card. He continues with the remaining objects. If desired, have him photograph his work with a classroom camera to review his sort at a later time. ***Attributes of three-dimensional shapes (K.G.B.4)***

Suzanne Moore
Tucson, AZ

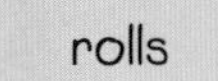

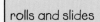

rolls and slides

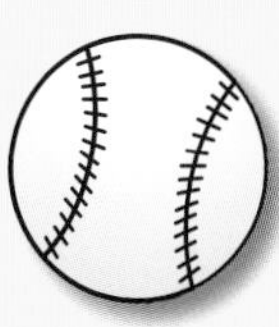

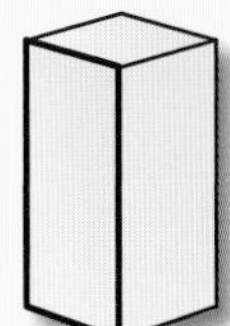

Digging for Words

Literacy Center

When your youngsters dig up these bones, they apply their puzzling skills to make new words. Laminate and then cut apart a copy of the bone patterns on page 68. Bury the bone parts in a tub of brown paper shreds (dirt). Set out the tub and blank paper. A child digs up bones and puts them together to make words. Then she reads the words, writes them on paper, and draws pictures to match. ***Reading words (RF.K.3)***

Jean Gerth
Houston, TX

Select a Shoe

Math Center

Students explore with measurement at this center. Set out a collection of shoes that vary in size and style along with a ruler, a few different types of manipulatives to be used for measuring, and blank paper. A child chooses a shoe and makes a tracing of it on her paper. Then she measures the shoe two different ways and records the measurements. She continues with different shoes as time permits. ***Measurement***

adapted from an idea by Lisa Cohen
Laurel Plains Elementary
New City, NY

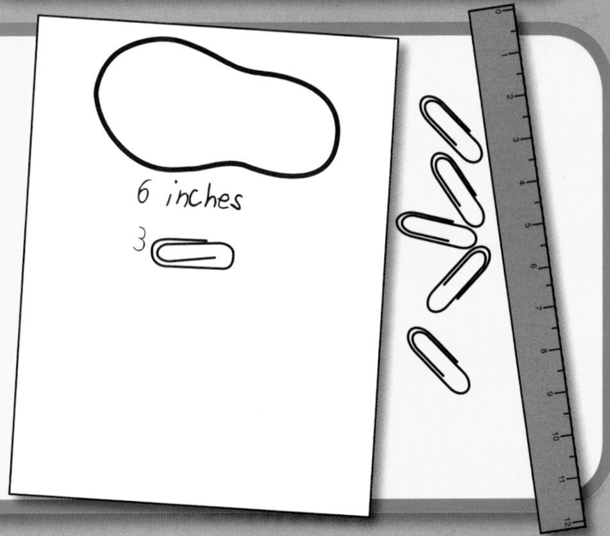

To keep interest high in your **writing center**, regularly change the writing instruments or types of paper. Youngsters are sure to enjoy the surprise of using gel pens and note cards or colored pencils and notepads. ***Laura Johnson, South Decatur Elementary, Greensburg, IN***

Learning Centers

Faces on a Roll!

Math Center

Reinforce two important math skills with this quick-to-prepare center. Draw a smiley face on each of three sides of a cube and sad faces on the other sides. Set out the face cube, a die, a supply of Unifix cubes, and blank paper. Then choose one of the tasks below for youngsters to complete.

Comparing sets (K.CC.C.6): For this partner center, each child makes a tower with ten Unifix cubes. Next, each player takes a turn rolling the die and the face cube. If she rolls a smiley face, she adds cubes to her tower to match the number on the die. If she rolls a sad face, she removes cubes to match the number on her die. Then players use vocabulary such as *less*, *more*, *taller*, *shorter*, and *equal* to compare and describe the towers. They continue as time permits.

Addition and subtraction equations: A child makes a tower that is at least six cubes tall and draws it on a sheet of paper. Next, he rolls the die and face cube. If he rolls a smiley face, he makes a tower of cubes to match the number on the die. Then he draws the tower, combines his towers, and writes a number equation to match. If he rolls a sad face, he removes the number of cubes indicated on the die, crosses out the cubes on his paper, and writes a subtraction equation to match.

Karin Bulkow
Washington School
for Comprehensive Literacy
Sheboygan, WI

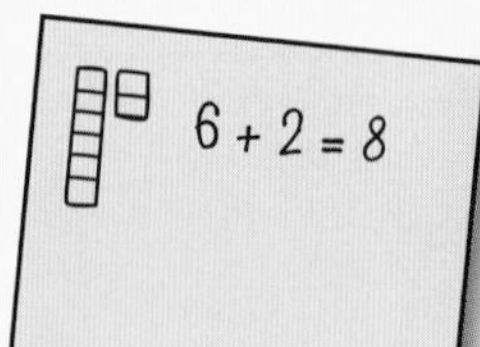

Ladybug Race

Literacy and Math Center

Reinforcing counting skills is an added benefit of this number word partner game. Color a copy of the gameboard on page 69. Then decorate a small red and a small orange paper circle so they resemble ladybugs. Put the gameboard, ladybugs, and a bag of number word cards at a center. Each player places a ladybug on START. Then Player 1 takes a card, reads the number word, and moves his ladybug that many spaces. After Player 1 returns the card to the bag, Player 2 takes a turn. The first ladybug to reach the flower garden wins! ***Number words (RF.K.3c), counting (K.CC.A.1)***

adapted from an idea by Laurieann LeDoux
Park Lane Elementary
Broken Arrow, OK

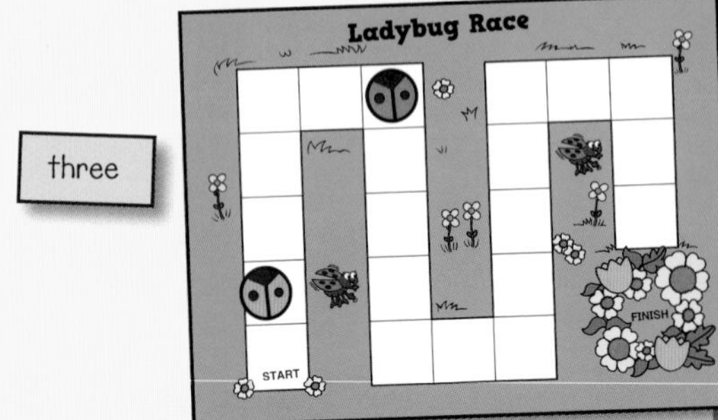

Read-O!

Literacy Center

This two- to four-player game makes reading high-frequency words monstrously fun! Color and cut out a copy of the lotto game cards on page 70, back them with construction paper, and store them in a resealable plastic bag. Also color and cut apart a copy of the gameboards on pages 71 and 72. Place the bag, the gameboards, and 24 game markers at a center. Each player takes a gameboard. One player shuffles and stacks the cards facedown. To take a turn, a player flips the top card in the stack and reads the word aloud. If she finds the word on her gameboard, she covers it with a marker. If she does not, her turn is over. If she turns over a monster card, she reads aloud any uncovered word on her gameboard and then covers it with a marker. The first player to cover four words in a row wins. ***High-frequency words (RF.K.3c)***

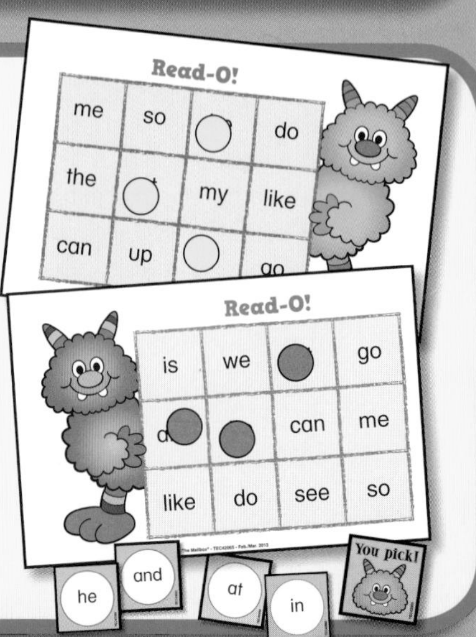

Learning Centers

Working With Words

Literacy Center (RF.K.3)

Using thematic notepads is an inexpensive way to add a little flair to your centers. Obtain a notepad of your choice and prepare one or more of the options below.

High-frequency words: Program several notes with different high-frequency words. Set out the notes, letter manipulatives, and paper. A child takes a note, uses the manipulatives to spell the word, and writes a sentence on her paper using that word.

CVC words: Write a different CVC word on each of several notes, leaving space between the letters. Puzzle-cut the notes between the letters and place the pieces in a small container. Set out the container and blank paper. A child assembles the word puzzles. Then she writes each word on her paper and draws pictures to match.

Word families: Program several notes with different rimes. Set out the notes, letter manipulatives (consonants only), and paper. A child writes a rime at the top of a paper. Then he uses the manipulatives to form words with the rime and writes each real word on his paper.

Jeanne-Marie Peterson
Charlottesville, VA

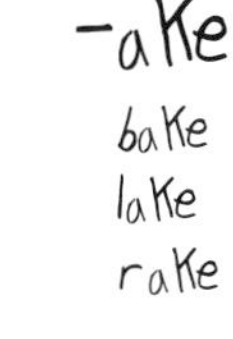

-ake
bake
lake
rake

Cool Combos!

Math Center

How can an empty tissue box spark interest in exploring number combinations? Check this out! Use adhesive Velcro fasteners to attach five cubes to a tissue box. Set out the box and paper. A child writes the number 5 on her paper. Next, she drops a desired number of the cubes into the box and writes number-related combinations on her paper. For example, she may drop two of the five cubes into the box and write "5 = 2 + 3" and "5 = 3 + 2." She continues to explore other combinations for five. If time permits, she writes combinations for a different number of cubes. For added fun, decorate the box so it looks like a silly character named The Cube Muncher and have youngsters feed it cubes! ***Exploring number combinations (K.OA.A.3)***

Doria Owen
William Paca Old Post Road Elementary
Abingdon, MD

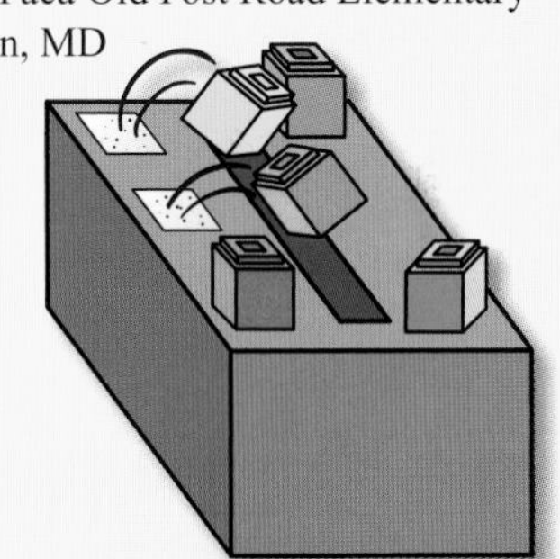

Sticker Stories

Literacy Center

Encourage creative writing with this quick-to-prepare center. Set out a variety of stickers, story paper, and crayons. A child chooses a sticker, places it on his paper, and then draws a scene around it. Next, he writes a story related to his picture. ***Writing (W.K.3)***

Allison Hernandez
Deasy Elementary
Glen Cove, NY

Learning Centers

Shopping Spree

Math Center

To prepare for this partner center, cut apart a copy of the cards on page 73. Place the cost cards on one side of a pocket chart and the coin cards on the other side. To begin, a child turns over a card from each side of the pocket chart. If the total amount of the coins matches the cost card, she removes the cards. If the cards do not match, she turns the cards over and her partner takes a turn. Play continues until all the cards are removed. ***Counting coins***

Vanessa Rivera, La Luz Elementary, La Luz, NM

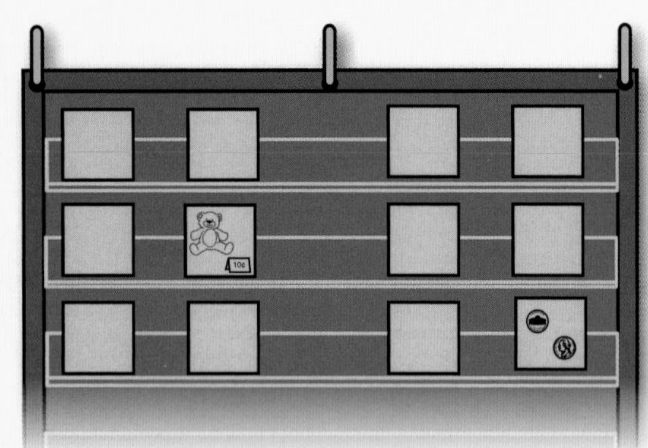

Hot Pots

Literacy Center

Cook up hands-on spelling practice with this adorable center! Color and cut apart a copy of the workmat and word cards on page 74. Gather a letter manipulative for each of the following letters: *c*, *d*, *g*, *h*, *l*, *n*, *o*, *p*, *r*, and *t*. To complete the activity, a youngster puts a word card on the first pot and reads the word. She uses the letter manipulatives to form the word on the second pot and spells the words aloud. Then she clears the mat and continues with the remaining cards in the same manner. If desired, have her write each word on paper as she goes. ***Word family* -ot *(RF.K.3)***

Bananas for Monkeys

Math Center

Looking for a different approach for students to work with math problems? Try this! Color a copy of the center mat on page 75. Color and cut apart a copy of the center cards on page 76. Write the matching number on the back of each card to make the activity self-checking. Store the cards in a resealable plastic bag. Place the bag, mat, and ten counters at a center. To complete the activity, a student puts the center cards in faceup rows. Next, he takes seven counters to decompose the number 7 into pairs (1 + 6, 2 + 5, and 3 + 4) and puts the matching cards on the corresponding space on the mat. He continues in this manner for each remaining number. Then he flips the cards to check his work. **For a different skill,** have students add to solve the problems and put each card on the mat below the matching sum. ***Decompose numbers into pairs (K.OA.A.3)***

Barbara Mason, Deposit Elementary, Deposit, NY

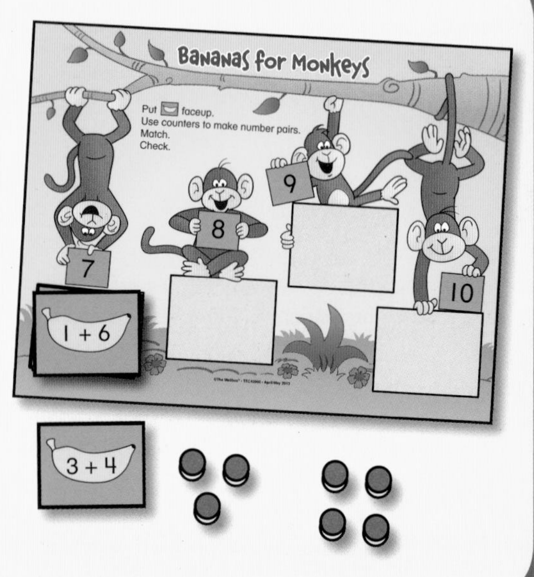

Learning Centers

Word Worms

Literacy Center

The word family ending with the most spins is the winner of this independent game. To make a spinner, attach a paper clip with a brad to a copy of the spinner pattern on page 77. Write *-ack*, *-ap*, *-uck*, and *-ug* words on separate cards to have five words per rime. Set out the cards and spinner along with four paper ovals (worms) per center visitor. A child puts the word cards in faceup rows. On each worm, she draws an eye and a mouth and then copies a rime from the spinner as shown. Then she spins the spinner, reads a word card with that rime, and writes the word on the matching worm. She continues until one worm wins with five words in its word family. ***Word families (RF.K.3d)***

adapted from an idea by Catherine Broome-Kehm
Melbourne Beach, FL

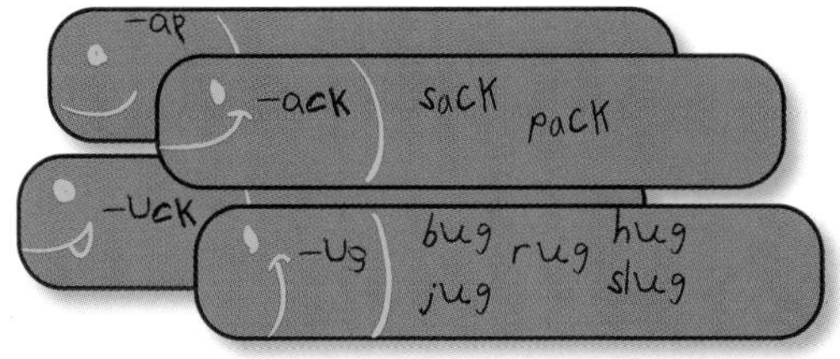

Roll and Add

Math Center

Bowling and number sentences go hand in hand at this center. Set out ten plastic soda bottles (bowling pins), a ball, paper, and crayons. A child sets up the pins, walks five steps away, and bowls. On his paper, he draws the pins, standing or fallen, to match his roll. Then he writes an addition equation and a subtraction equation related to his drawing. He continues as time permits. ***Addition and subtraction (K.OA.A.2)***

Nicole Furaro
St. Paul Catholic School
Guelph, Ontario, Canada

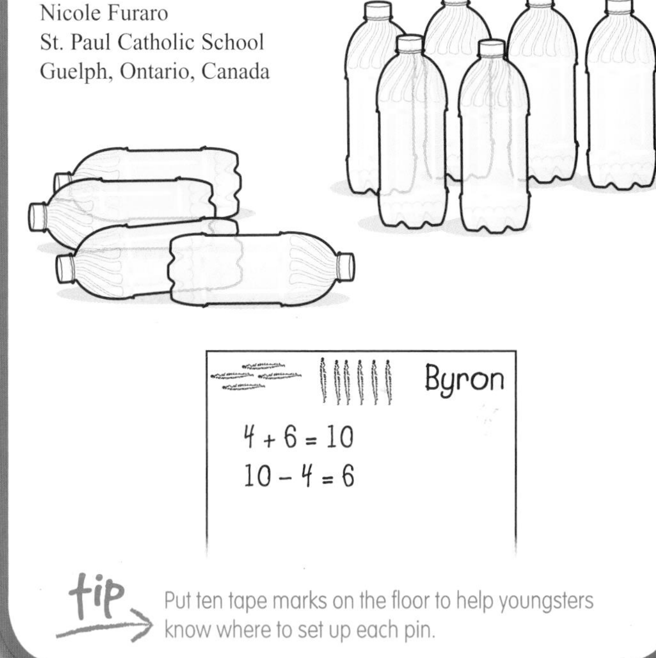

tip Put ten tape marks on the floor to help youngsters know where to set up each pin.

Make and Write

Literacy Center

Students form and illustrate silly or realistic sentences when they order these words. Cut apart a copy of the word cards on page 78. Set out the cards, story paper, and crayons. A child uses the cards to form a complete sentence, starting with a word that has a capital letter. Next, he writes the sentence on his paper and adds the punctuation. Then he reads his writing and draws a picture to match. To continue, he flips his paper over to write and illustrate a different sentence. **For more detailed sentences,** provide additional word cards, such as *fast*, *slow*, *brown*, and *yellow*. ***Writing sentences (L.K.1f; L.K.2a, b)***

Patrice Clynes
Plantsville Elementary
Plantsville, CT

The pig and the frog are on a boat.

Learning Centers

Balance That!

Math Center

Reinforce counting and measurement skills with this quick-to-prepare center. Set out a balance scale, Unifix cubes, number cards from 1 to 20, a variety of small classroom objects, and blank paper. A child takes a card and makes a tower with a matching number of cubes. She places the tower on one side of the scale. Then she places combinations of objects on the other side until the scale balances. She draws a picture to show the results of the balanced scale, labeling each side with the matching number of objects. ***Counting (K.CC.A.3), measurement***

Suzanne Moore
Tucson, AZ

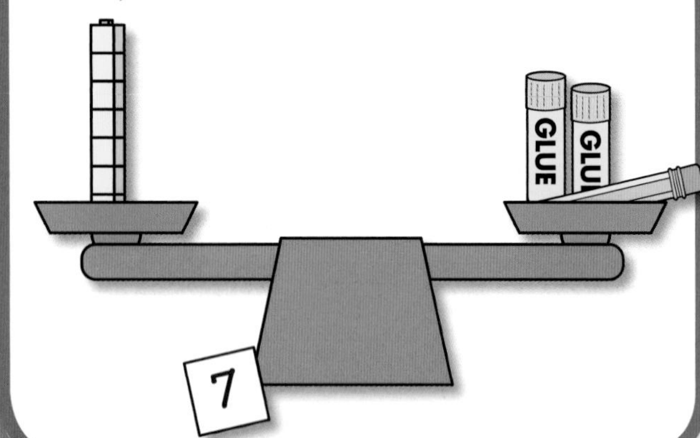

In the News

Literacy Center

Can your students read parts of the newspaper? Sure they can! Laminate sheets of newspaper to make them reusable. Set out the newspapers along with wipe-off markers and paper towels. A child reads and circles familiar words on a sheet of newspaper. At a later time, he reads the circled text to you. To reuse the newspaper, simply wipe it clean and put it back at the center. For added fun, provide small pointers, fun sunglasses, and magnifying glasses for youngsters to use as props while reading the paper. ***Print concepts (RF.K.1)***

Michelle Jenkins
Apple Pie Ridge Elementary
Winchester, VA

Fishing for Ten

Math Center

Youngsters "catch" some practice making ten with this summery activity. Cut apart a copy of the fish cards on page 77. Attach a paper clip to each fish and place the cards on blue paper (water). Place a magnetic toy fishing pole, blank paper, and crayons nearby. A child goes fishing and pretends to reel in a fish. He reads the number on his catch and determines how many more make ten. On his paper, he writes or draws to show his thinking and then writes the corresponding equation. He continues until each fish has been caught. **For added support**, set out fish-shaped crackers or paper fish for students to use as manipulatives. ***Making ten (K.OA.A.4)***

Marcy Satkoski
Slate Run Elementary
New Albany, IN

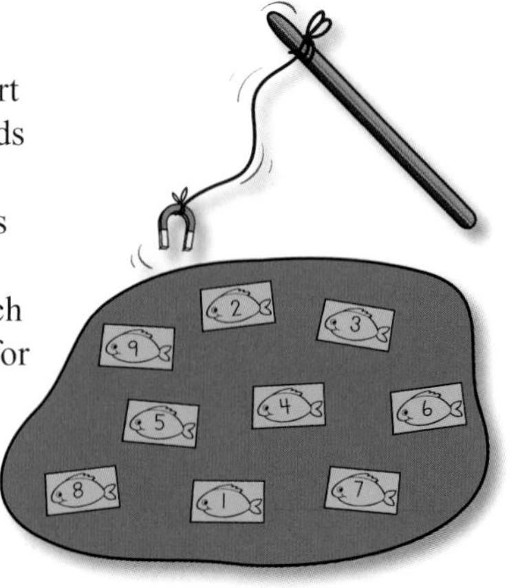

Find **ready-to-use centers** on pages 80 and 81 and pages 82–84!

Alphabet Centers
From sorting letters to ABC order, your youngsters are sure to be wild about these zoo-themed centers!
ideas contributed by Katherine Fisher, Indialantic, FL

On the Loose!

Sorting uppercase and lowercase letters (RF.K.1d)

Zoo animals have escaped, and it is up to your center visitors to help round them up! Program copies of the zoo animal cards on page 79 with different uppercase and lowercase letters. Cut apart the cards and spread them out in your center area. Also label two sheets of construction paper, as shown, to make zoo sections and put them at the center. A child looks at the letters and moves each animal to the matching zoo section.

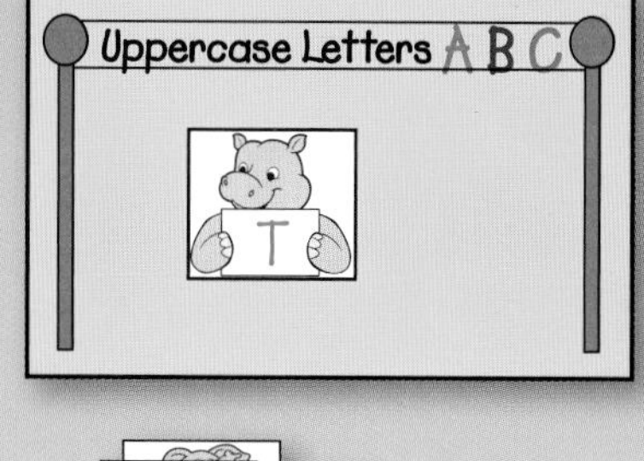

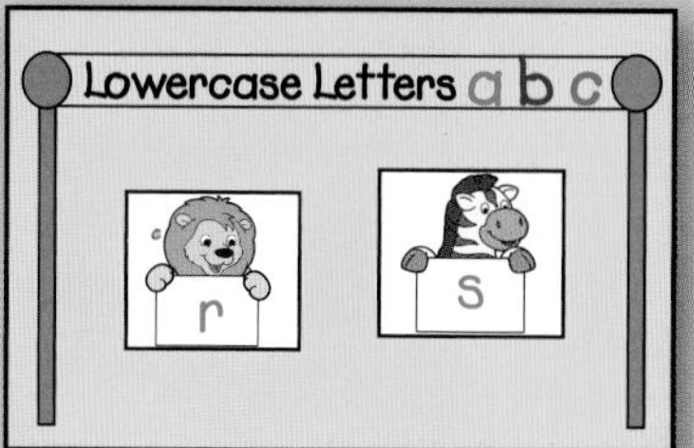

Zoo Crew

Matching uppercase and lowercase letters (RF.K.1d)

Students pair letters to put this puzzle together. Obtain a zoo-themed puzzle with 26 pieces or less. Cut a paper at least the size of the assembled puzzle to make a puzzle backing. Write a different uppercase letter, in random order, on the back of each puzzle piece. Then remove one piece of the puzzle and, on that section of the backing, write the corresponding lowercase letter. Continue with each puzzle piece. Place the unassembled puzzle and backing at a table. Invite a small group of students to pair matching letters, flip each puzzle piece picture-side up, and lay it on the backing. Soon, the picture will be revealed!

tip To make your own puzzle, cut a zoo-themed poster into puzzle pieces for students to assemble.

All in a Row

ABC order, writing letters (L.K.1a)

Invite your little zookeepers to create an animal lineup. Write the alphabet letters on separate zoo animal cards (cards on page 79). Place the cards in a shoebox (zoo). For added fun, decorate the box so it resembles a zoo-themed environment. A child lines up five animals and then arranges them to put them in alphabetical order. Then he copies the letters onto a sheet of paper. He continues with different animal lines as time permits. **For added support**, provide an alphabet strip for youngsters to use as a guide.

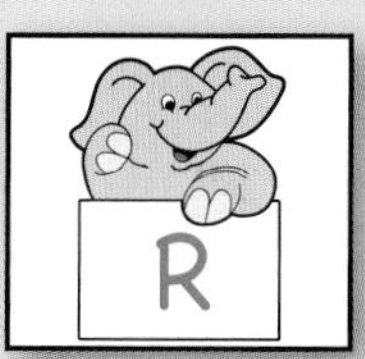

Apple Patterns

Use with "The Learning Tree" on page 46.

Bird Labels

Use with "Feed the Birds" on page 47.

TEC42063

TEC42063

TEC42063

TEC42063

TEC42063

TEC42063

TEC42063

TEC42063

TEC42063

TEC42063

Jack and Jill

Put ☐ to match.
Check.

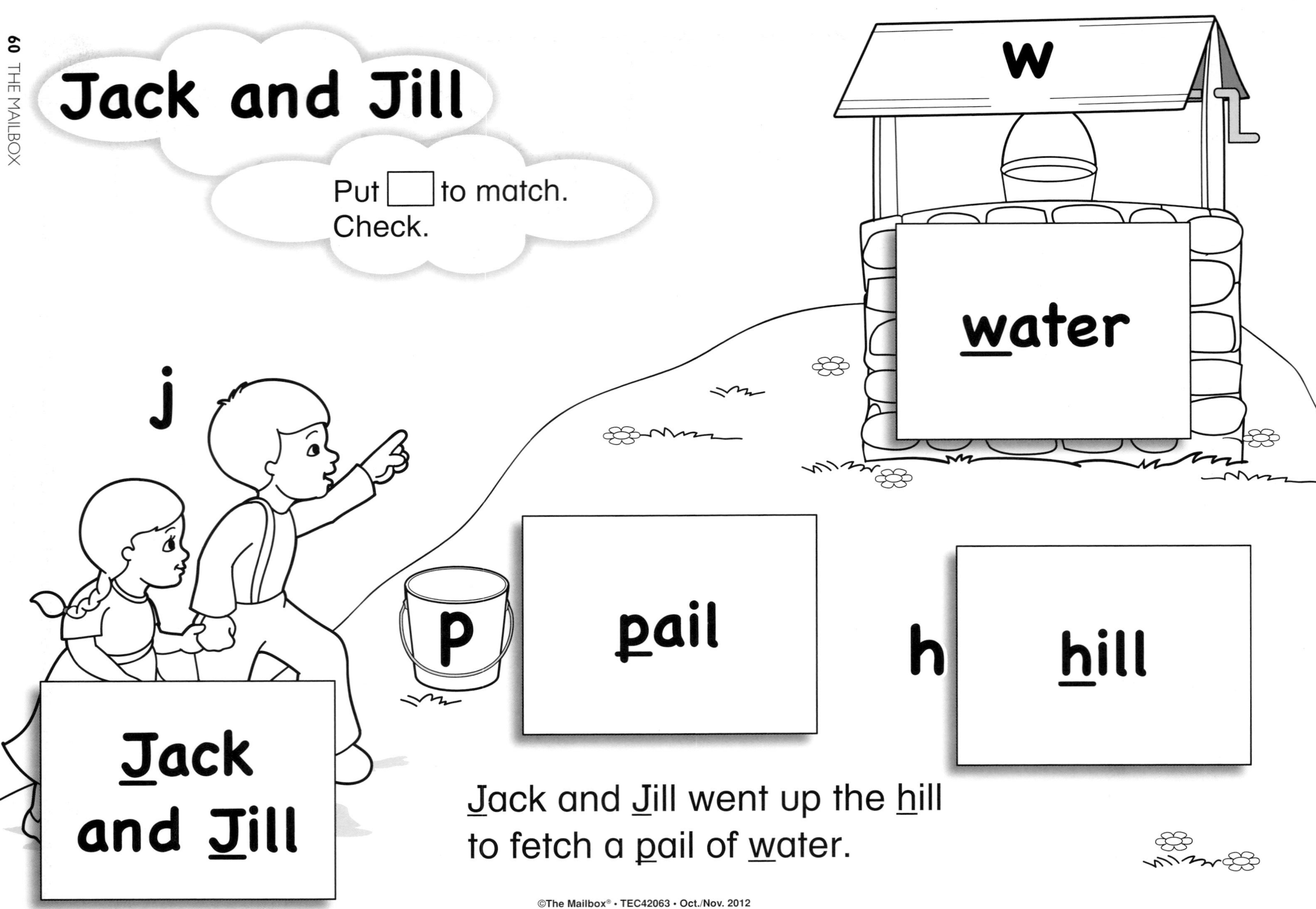

Jack and Jill went up the hill
to fetch a pail of water.

beginning sounds J, P, W, H

Center Cards

Use with "Jack and Jill" on page 47.

Pumpkin Cards

Use with the third center on page 48.

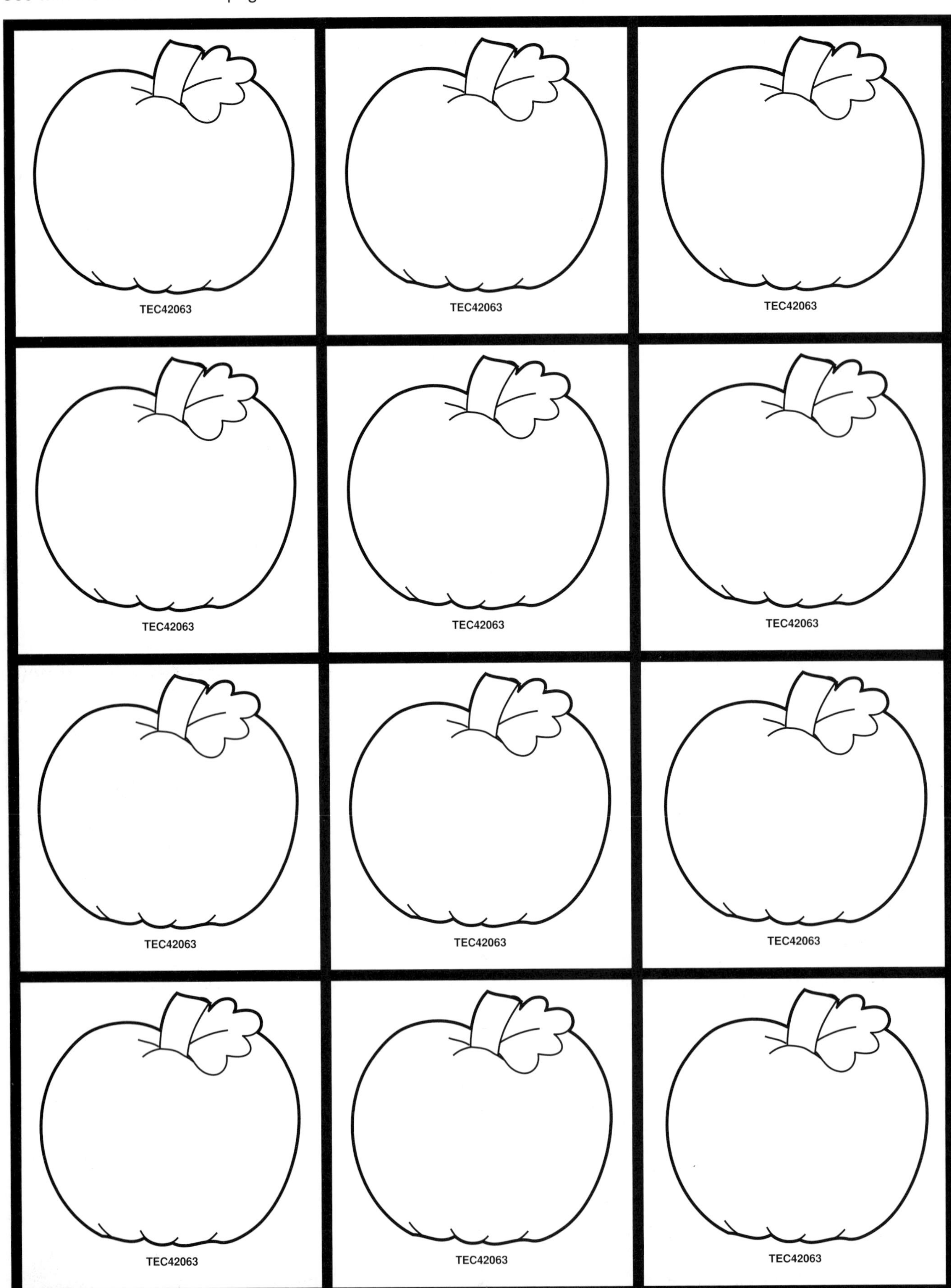

Cookie Jar Cards

Use with "How Many Cookies?" on page 49.

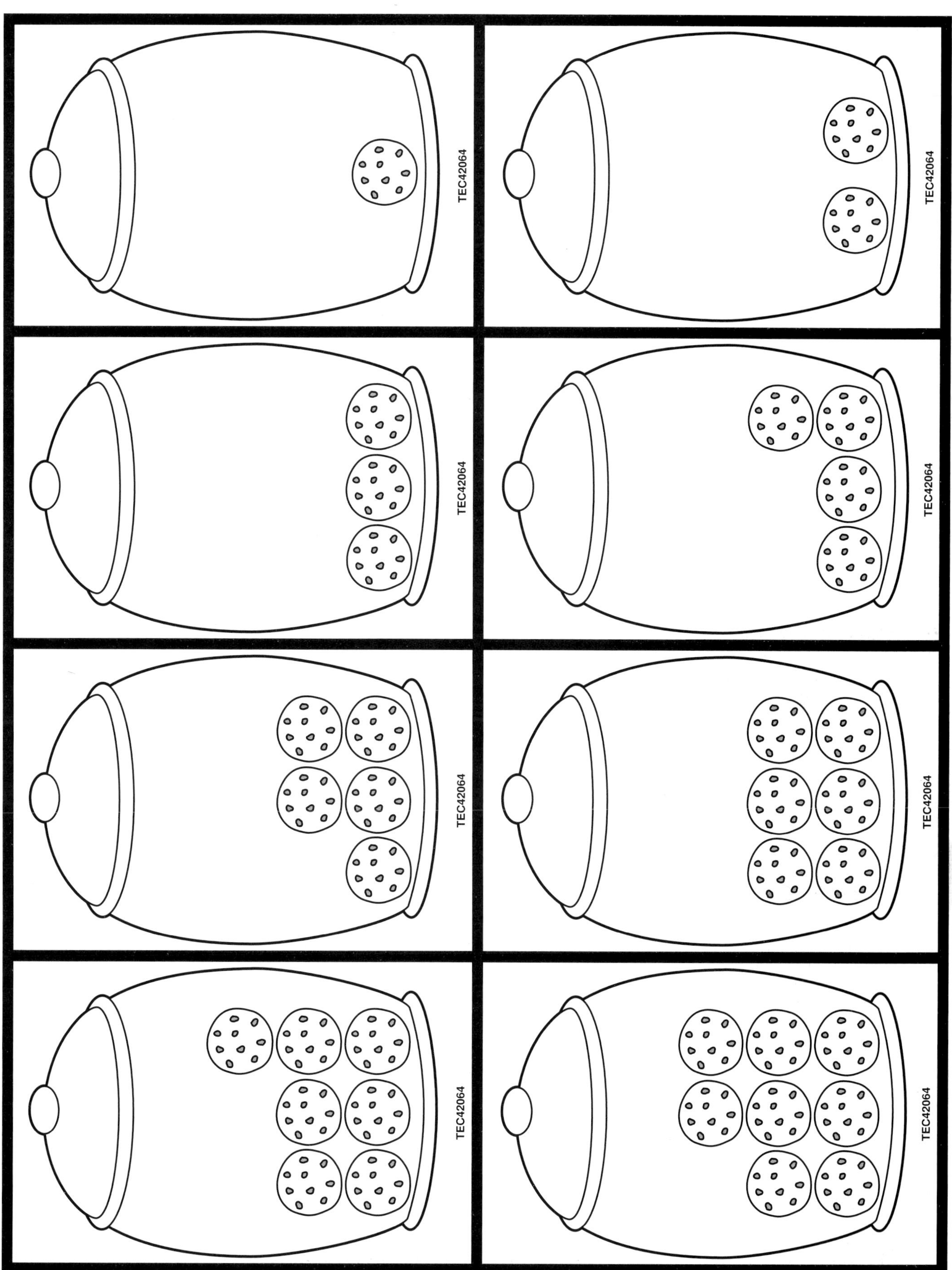

Cookie Jar and Number Word Cards

Use with "How Many Cookies?" on page 49.

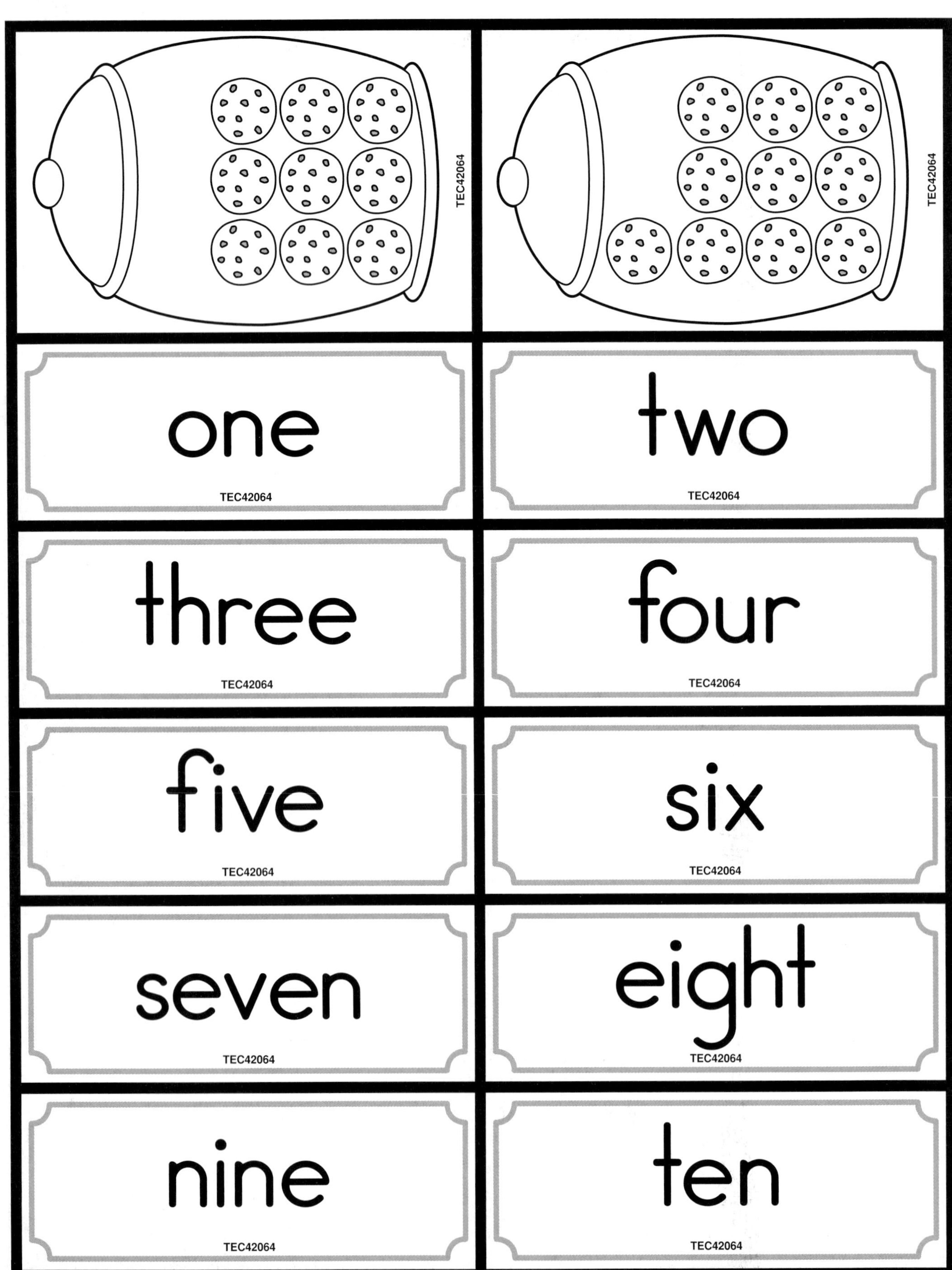

How Many Shoes?

Partner game

What to do

1. Pick a 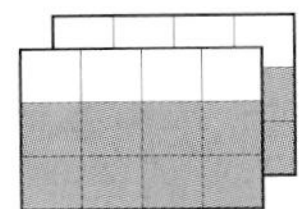. Stack the .
2. When it is your turn, take a .

   Name or solve; then flip to check. 

   Put on 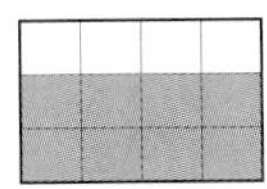. If you cannot, put here .
3. Play until a 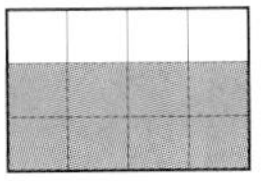 is filled.

Center Mats

Use with "How Many Shoes?" on page 50.

 4 shoes	 6 shoes	 8 shoes	 10 shoes
			TEC42064

 4 shoes	 6 shoes	 8 shoes	 10 shoes
			TEC42064

Use with "How Many Shoes?" on page 50.

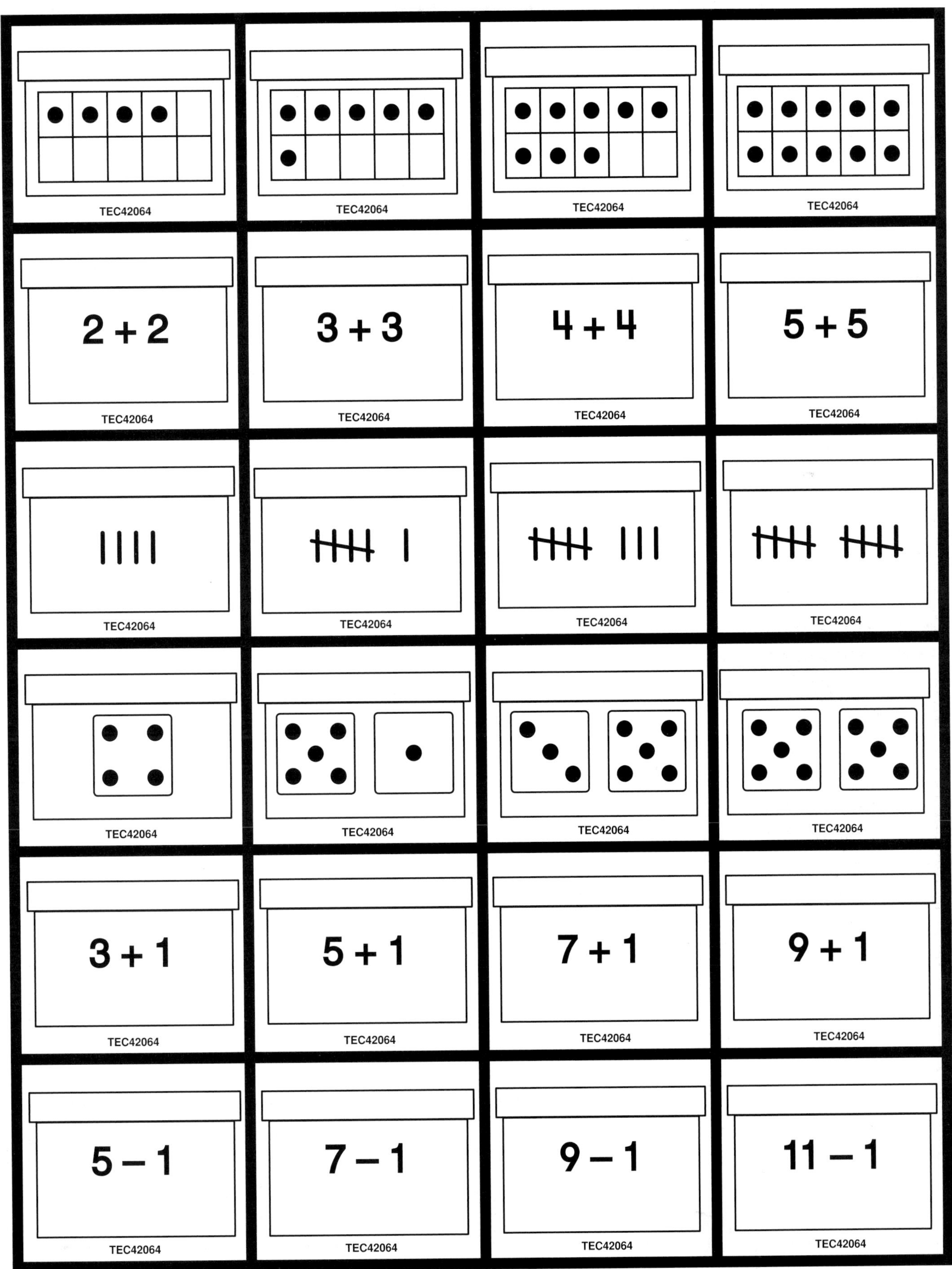

Bone Patterns

Use with "Digging for Words" on page 51.

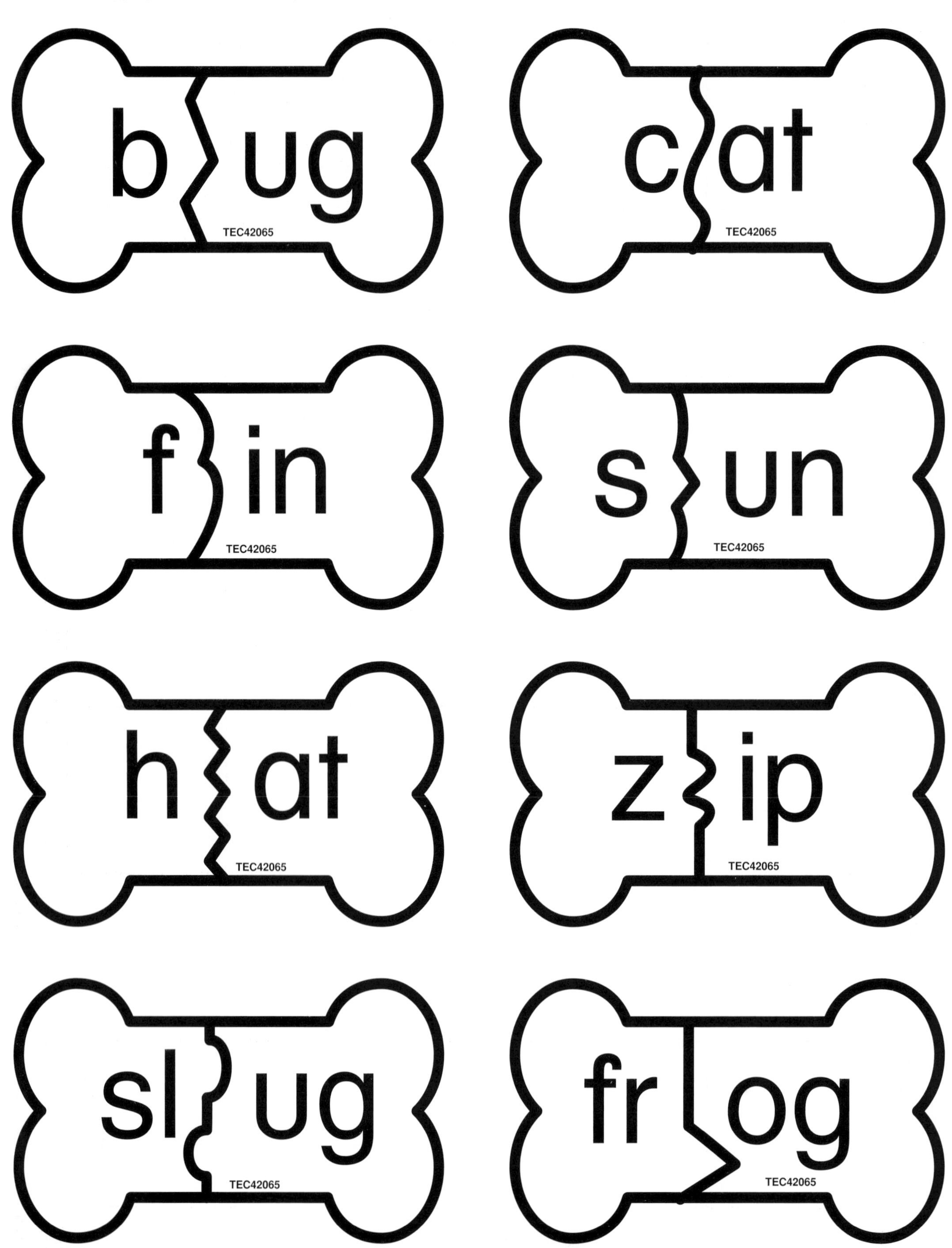

Ladybug Race

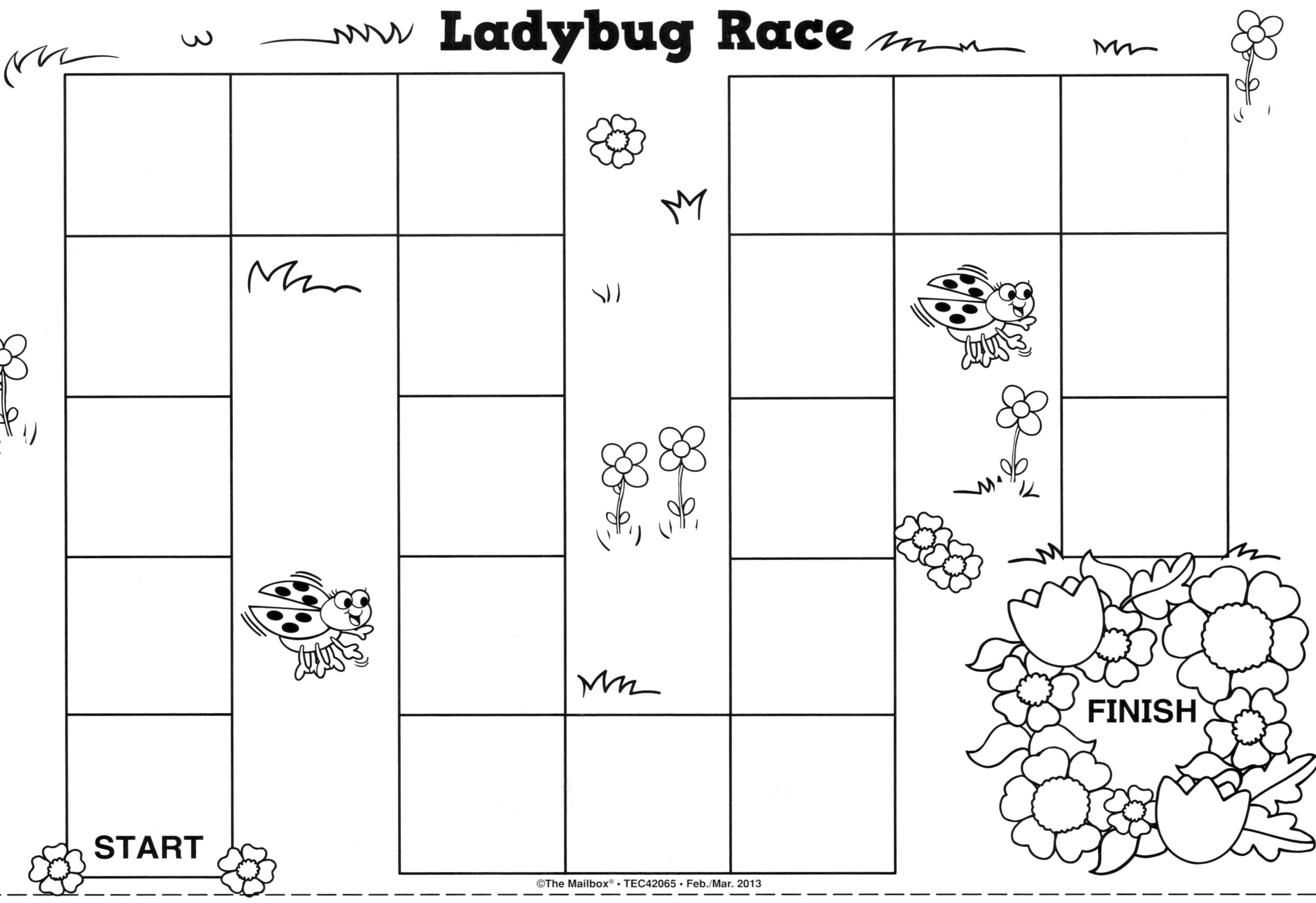

Note to the teacher: Use with "Ladybug Race" on page 52.

Lotto Game Cards

Use with "Read-O!" on page 52.

at TEC42065	and TEC42065	can TEC42065	do TEC42065
go TEC42065	he TEC42065	in TEC42065	is TEC42065
like TEC42065	me TEC42065	my TEC42065	we TEC42065
see TEC42065	so TEC42065	the TEC42065	up TEC42065
You pick! TEC42065	You pick! TEC42065	You pick! TEC42065	You pick! TEC42065

Read-O!

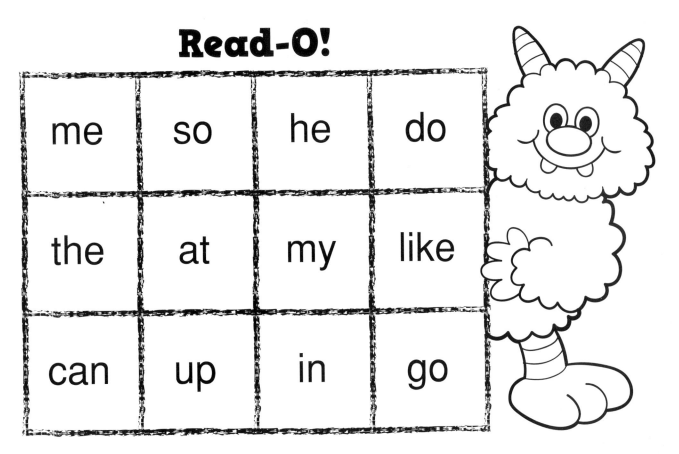

me	so	he	do
the	at	my	like
can	up	in	go

Read-O!

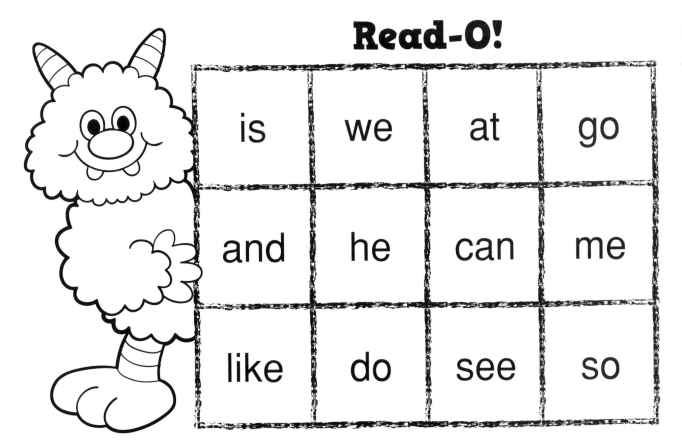

is	we	at	go
and	he	can	me
like	do	see	so

 Use with "Read-O!" on page 52.

Read-O!

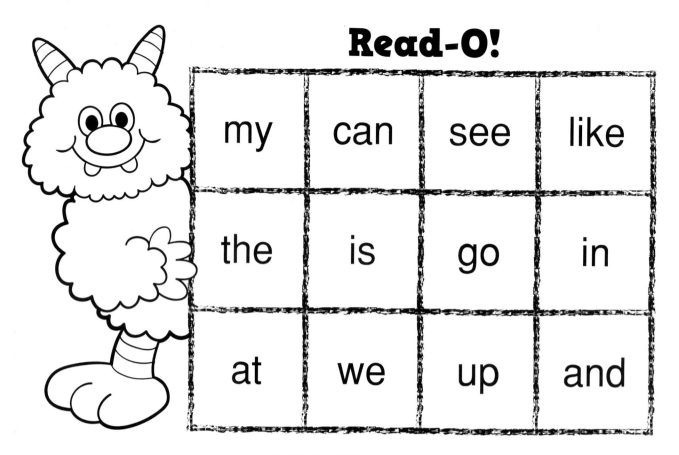

my	can	see	like
the	is	go	in
at	we	up	and

Read-O!

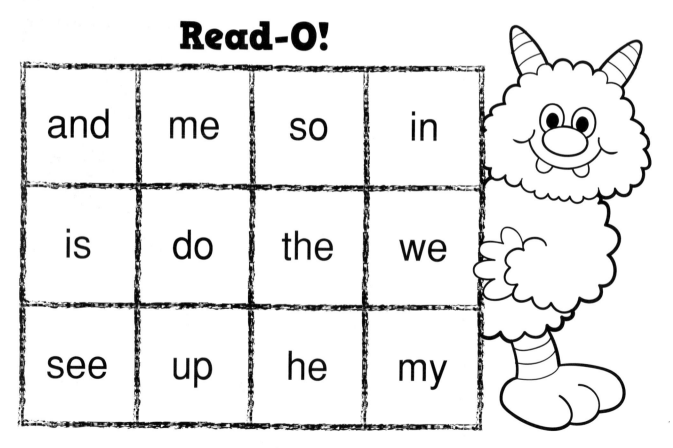

and	me	so	in
is	do	the	we
see	up	he	my

 Use with "Read-O!" on page 52.

Cost and Coin Cards

Use with "Shopping Spree" on page 54.

cot TEC42066	dot TEC42066	got TEC42066	hot TEC42066
lot TEC42066	not TEC42066	pot TEC42066	rot TEC42066

Note to the teacher: Use with "Hot Pots" on page 54.

Bananas for Monkeys

Put  faceup.
Use counters to make number pairs.
Match.
Check.

Center Cards

Use with "Bananas for Monkeys" on page 54.

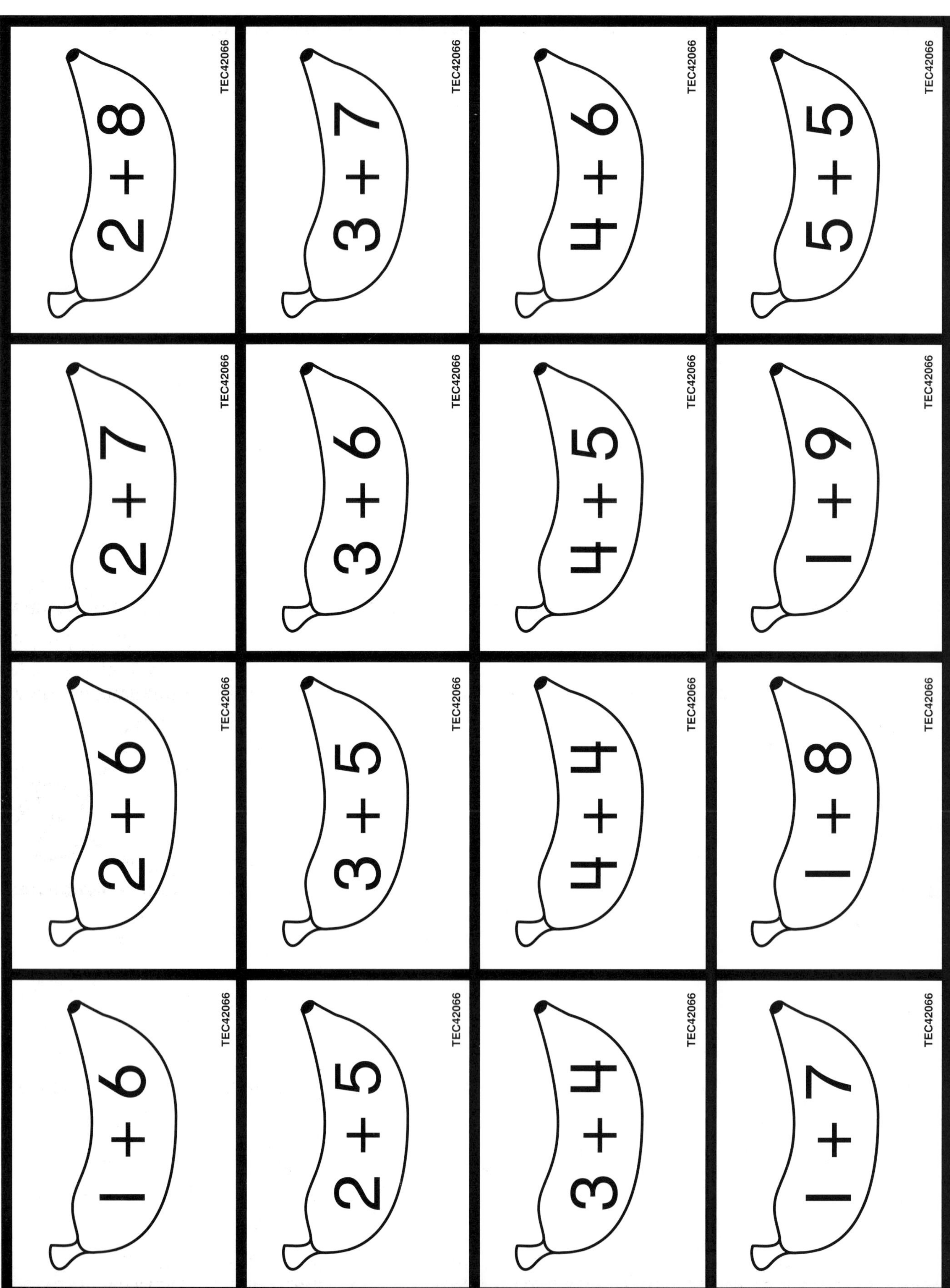

Spinner Pattern

Use with "Word Worms" on page 55.

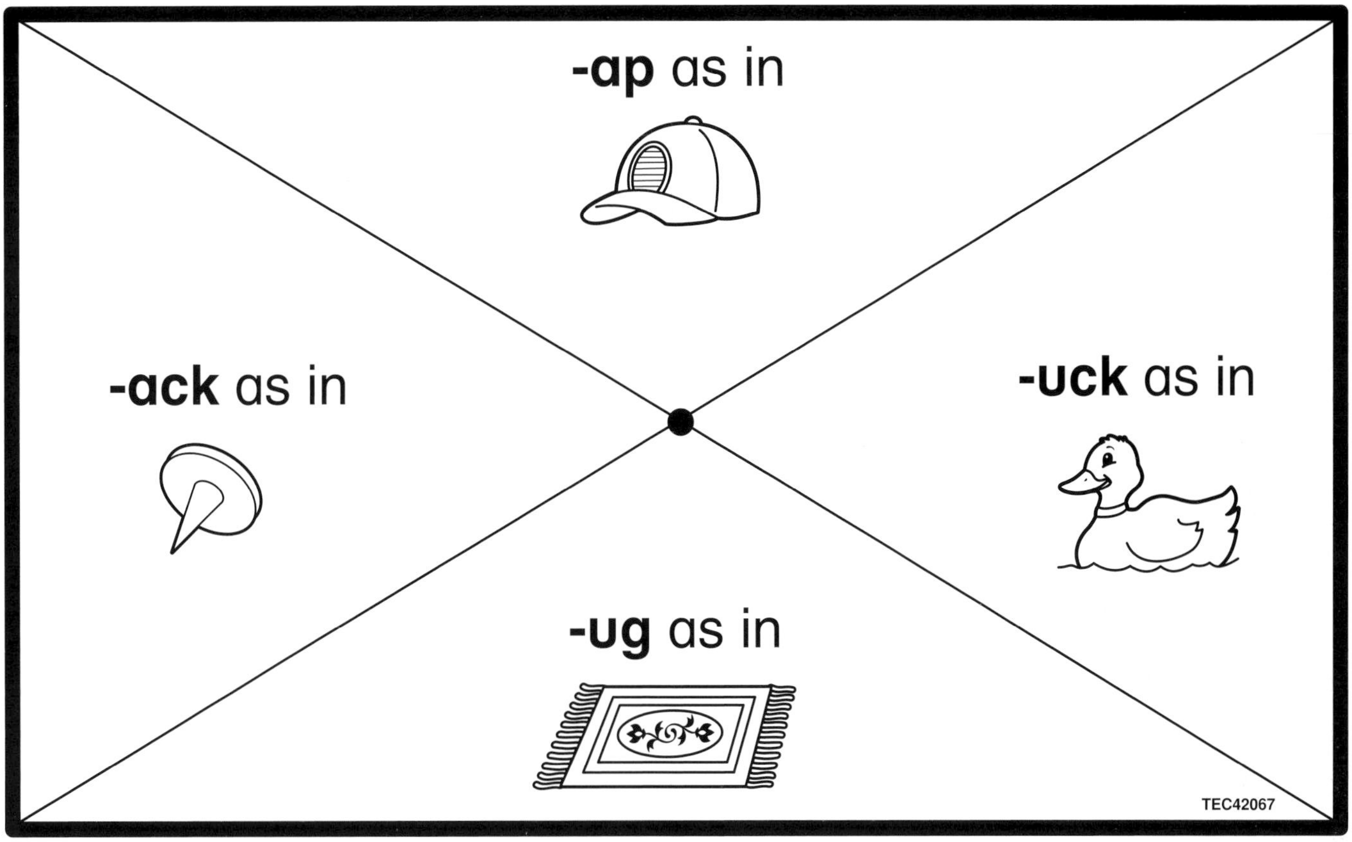

-ap as in

-ack as in

-uck as in

-ug as in

TEC42067

Fish Cards

Use with "Fishing for Ten" on page 56.

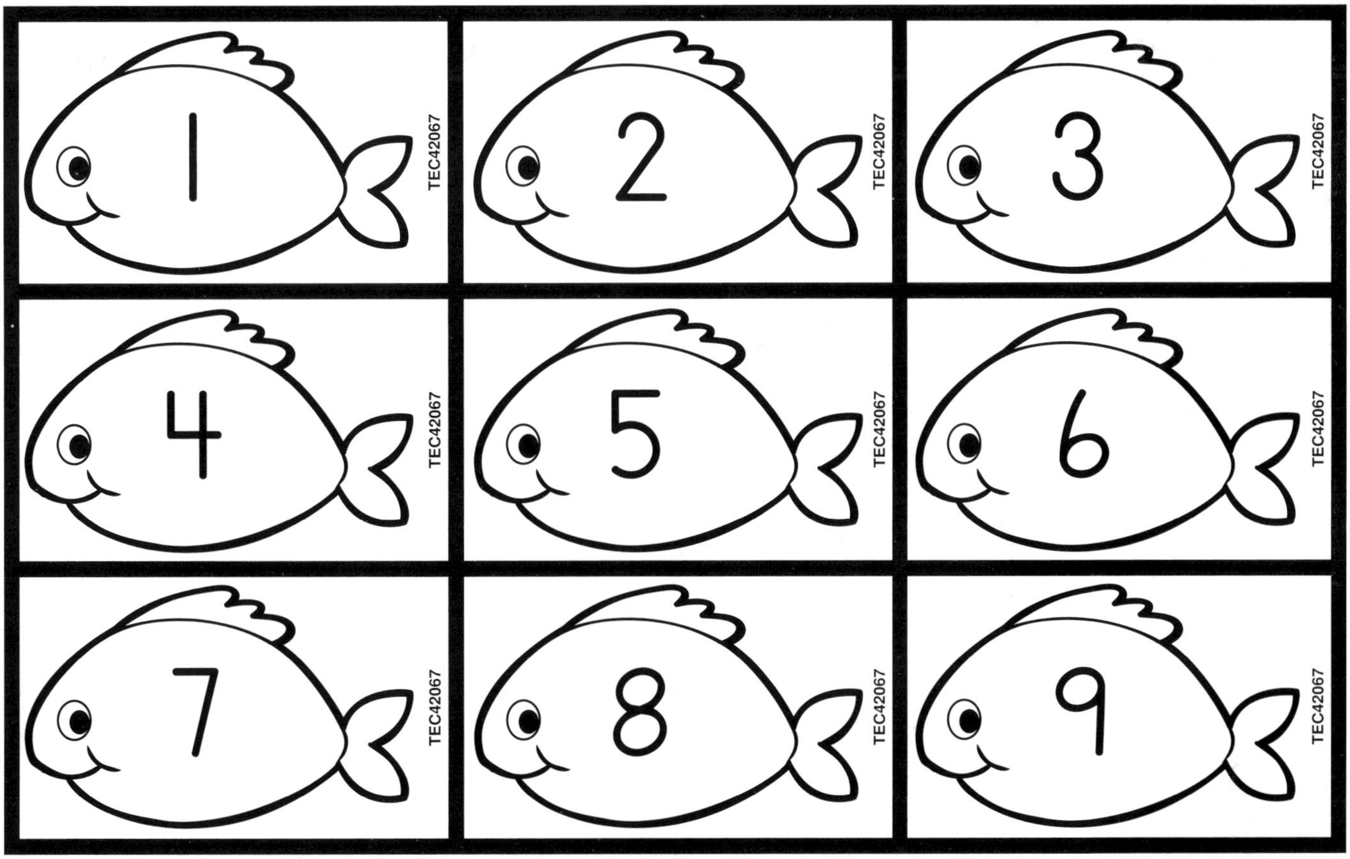

1 TEC42067	2 TEC42067	3 TEC42067
4 TEC42067	5 TEC42067	6 TEC42067
7 TEC42067	8 TEC42067	9 TEC42067

Word Cards

Use with "Make and Write" on page 55.

There TEC42067	I TEC42067	The TEC42067	the TEC42067
a TEC42067	and TEC42067	is TEC42067	on TEC42067
are TEC42067	see TEC42067	big TEC42067	little TEC42067
cat TEC42067	dog TEC42067	pig TEC42067	lion TEC42067
bug TEC42067	frog TEC42067	bus TEC42067	boat TEC42067
house TEC42067	car TEC42067	hat TEC42067	book TEC42067

Zoo Animal Cards

Use with "On the Loose!" and "All in a Row" on page 57.

Center

Build the Words Activity

To prepare this center activity, color and cut apart a copy of the center mats on page 81 and cut out a copy of the picture and letter cards on this page. For each set (CVC and CVCC), store the mat, picture cards, and letter cards in a resealable plastic bag. A child takes a set, puts a picture card on the mat, and uses the letter cards to spell the word. She continues with each remaining picture card. To make the activity self-checking, label the back of each picture card with the matching word.

a d

Set 1: CVC words (L.K.2c, d)

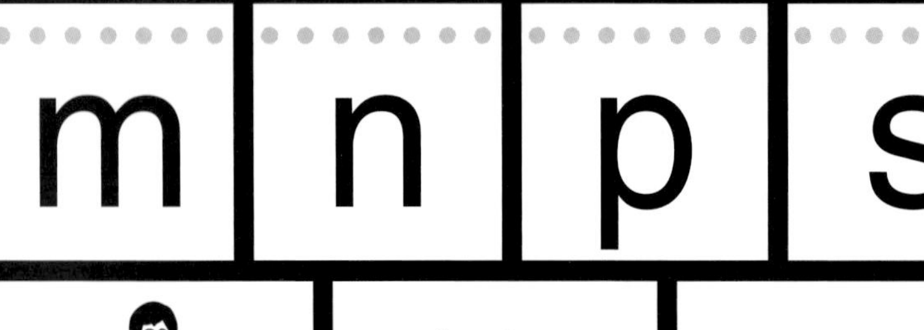

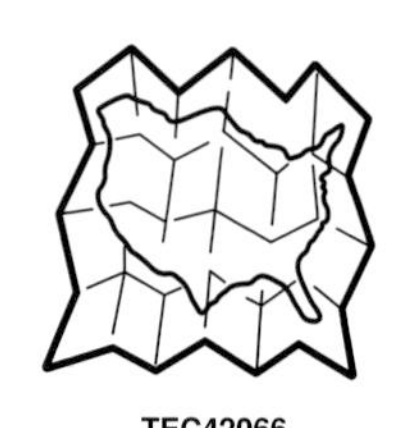

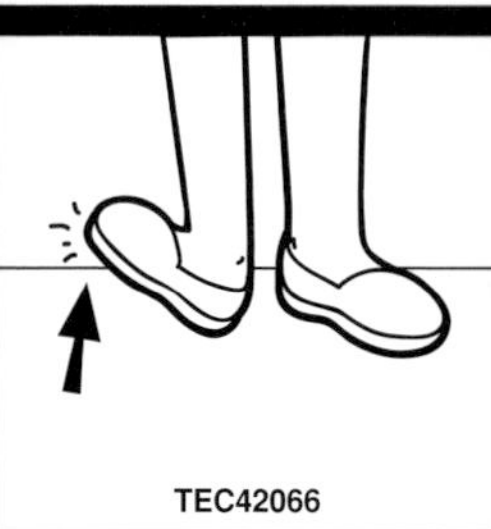

Set 2: CVCC words (L.K.2c, d)

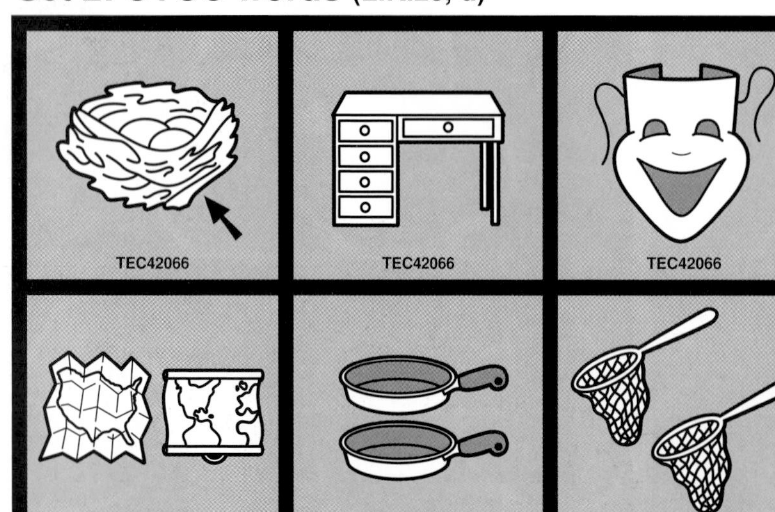

a e d k m n p s t

Build the Words!

CVC words (L.K.2c, d)

Build the Words!

CVCC words (L.K.2c, d)

Note to the teacher: Use with the directions on page 80.

Center Activity Cards

Make a class supply (plus an extra copy for your files) of the recording sheet on page 84. Color and cut apart a copy of the cards on this page and page 83; store them in a resealable plastic bag. A child matches each word with a long vowel to its picture to assemble the pail puzzles. Then she writes each word next to the correct picture on her recording sheet. ***CVCe words (RF.K.3b)***

Use with the directions on page 82.

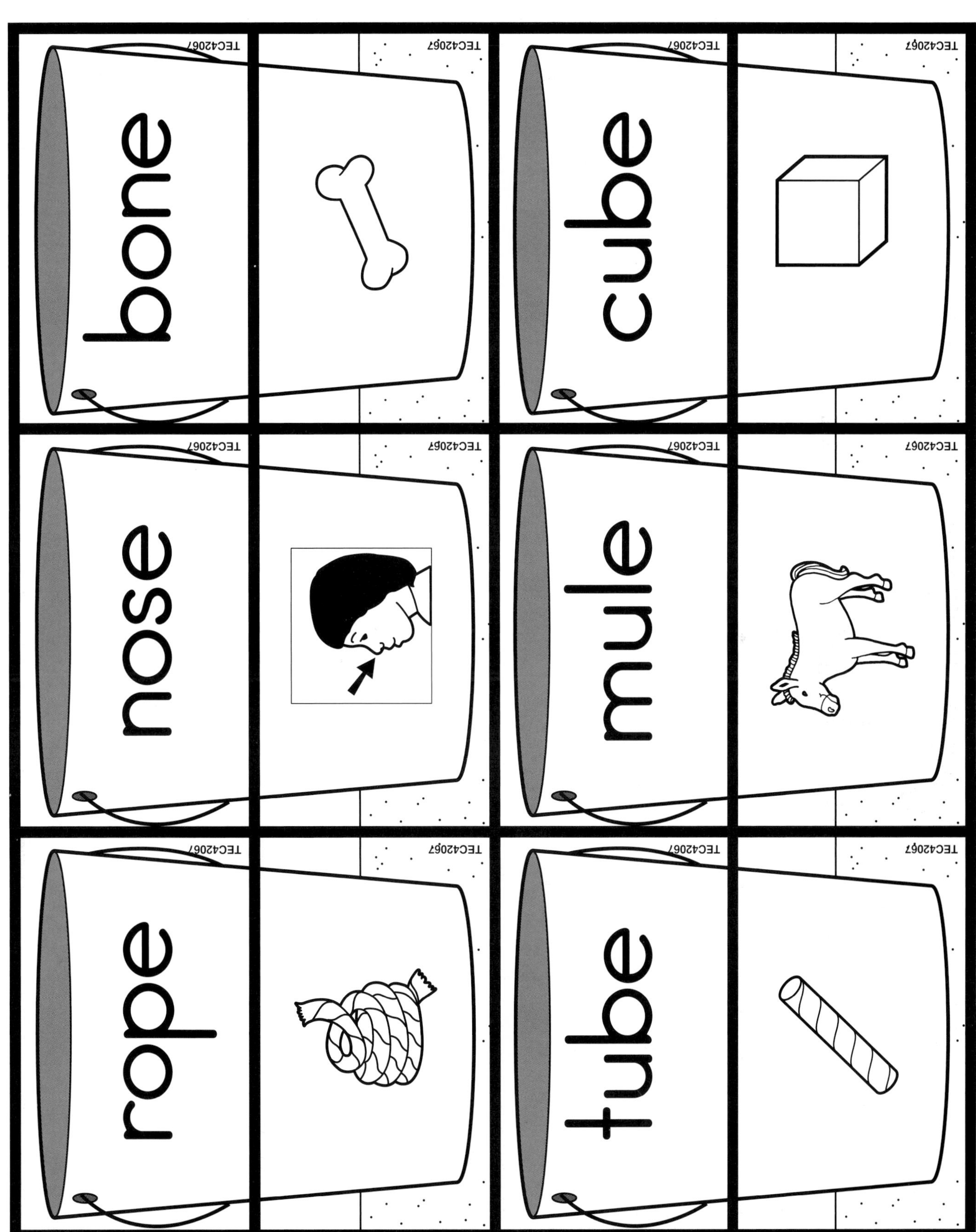

Name ____________________

CVCe words (RF.K.3b)
Recording sheet

Pail Puzzles

Write the word to match each picture.

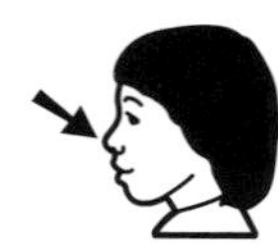
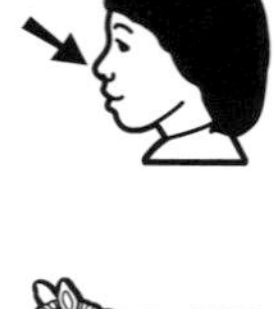

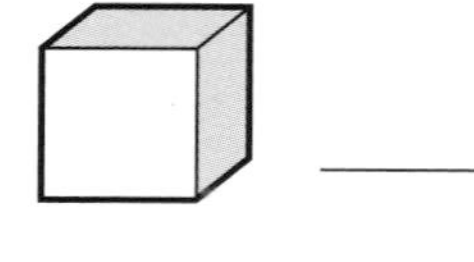
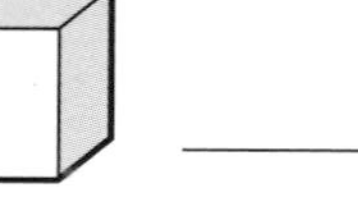
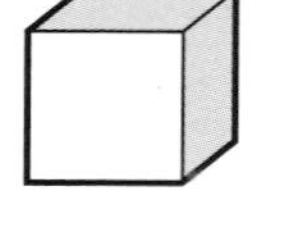
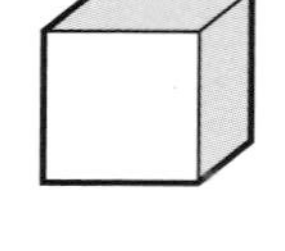

Pick two words from above.
Write a sentence using each word.

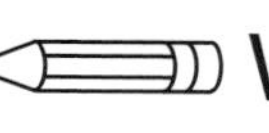

1. ____________________

2. ____________________

Note to the teacher: Use with the directions on page 82.

Management Tips & Timesavers

Management Tips & Timesavers

A Marvelous Mailer

Important mail can travel between home and school in this special mailer! For each child, attach a copy of page 89 to a large personalized manila envelope. Laminate each resulting mailer and gently slit the crease to reopen the envelope. Now it's ready to travel in the child's backpack carrying important notes and papers!
Ann Nowac, Immaculate Heart of Mary School, Cuyahoga Falls, OH

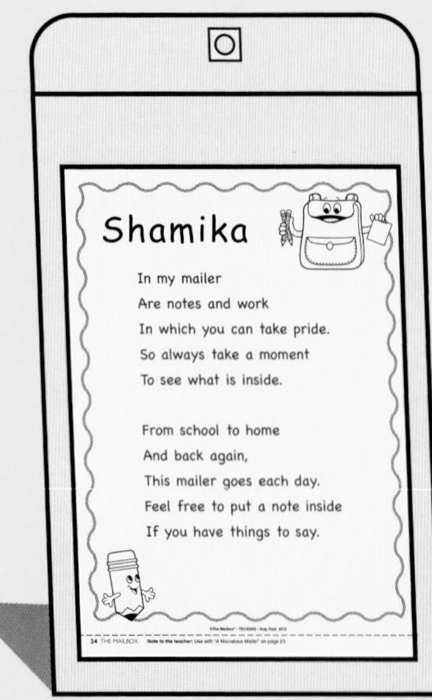

Shamika
In my mailer
Are notes and work
In which you can take pride.
So always take a moment
To see what is inside.
From school to home
And back again,
This mailer goes each day.
Feel free to put a note inside
If you have things to say.

Grouping Is a Snap!

Oversize interlocking blocks are perfect for grouping students quickly! Use a permanent marker to write each child's name on an individual block and then snap the blocks together according to desired groups. To designate where each child sits, simply put each resulting tower at a different table. ***Suzanne Ward, Caledonia Centennial Public School, Caledonia, Ontario, Canada***

Simple Center Organization

For this space-saving center routine, place a different activity in each of several numbered buckets (or tubs). For example, one bucket may contain writing paper and a prompt, another may have a phonemic awareness activity, and a third may contain packets of letter cards for spelling practice. When a student is ready for a new task, he goes to his assigned bucket and completes the activity. ***Ashley Ortega, Somerset Academy of Emerson, Las Vegas, NV***

Whisper Music

To remind students when to use quiet voices in the classroom, simply turn on a recording of whisper music (classical music played at a low volume). Students know that when the whisper music is on, their voices should not be heard above the music. ***Christine Labrasca, Chestnutwold Elementary, Ardmore, PA***

Help Needed!

No classroom job chart is complete without a substitute! The substitute's job is to fill in for any child who is absent. What a great idea! ***Denice Hatch, Atwood Primary School, Oakland, ME***

Management Tips & Timesavers

Who's Ready?

Find out who is ready to start the day and later who is ready to go home with this simple poster. Personalize a card for each child. Laminate the cards and a large backpack cutout. Then use adhesive Velcro fasteners to attach the name cards to the backpack. Post the backpack in a student-accessible location and set the name cards in a basket nearby. After a child settles in upon arrival, she finds and puts her name card on the backpack. Later, after she completes the tasks associated with preparing for dismissal, she returns her name card to the basket. ***Paula Staffeld, Westwood Elementary, Wellington, OH***

In the Bag

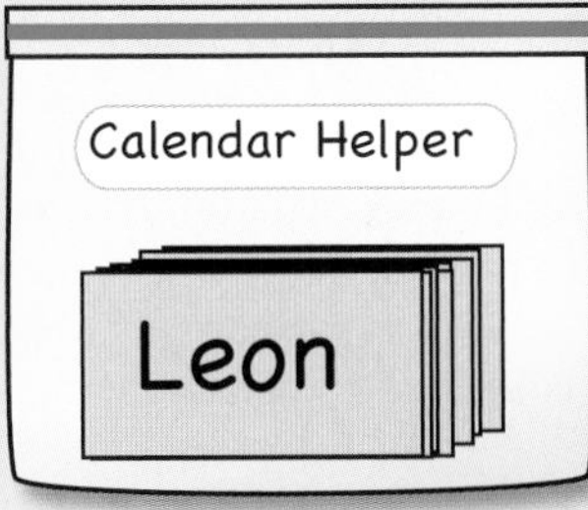

Here's a simple way to assign class jobs and make sure everyone gets a turn at each job. Write job names on separate resealable plastic bags. Then place a complete set of your students' name cards in each of the bags. To assign jobs, simply remove a card from each bag and post it with the corresponding job on your job chart. Continue to reassign jobs in this manner, setting the cards used aside. When a bag is emptied, return a class set of cards to the bag to begin a second round of responsibilities for that task. ***Jessie Roberts, Mt. Bethel Elementary, Marietta, GA***

Monthly Binders

Organizing teaching materials is a snap with these three-ring binders! For each month, place divider pages labeled with subject areas, themes, and topics in a three-ring binder. Gather the materials for that month and punch holes in the pages. For project samples, punch holes in a large resealable plastic bag and slip the project inside. Store the monthly materials behind the appropriate divider pages in that month's binder. Then the materials will be easy to find, and the binders look great on a bookshelf. ***Ashley Brumbaugh, Rock Island Academy, Rock Island, IL***

Supply Tubs

Distributing supplies is quick and easy with this tip. Attach a different decorative cutout to each table (work area). Then, for each table, attach a matching cutout to a tub containing that table's supplies. Store the tubs in a student-accessible location. To distribute the supplies, ask a child to deliver each tub to the table with the matching cutout. ***Tammy Shanks, Stepping Stones Learning Academy, Fruitland, MD***

We're All Smiles

What do students' behavior choices and ten-frame math have in common? Read this! Display a large laminated ten frame. At the end of the day, lead the class to assess its behavior to earn one or two smiley faces. Use a wipe-off marker to draw the matching number of faces on the ten frame. Next, have youngsters determine how many more faces are needed to fill the frame. When there are ten smiley faces on the frame, reward the group as desired. Then erase the faces to ready the board for the following day. ***Sara Fox, Franklin Monroe Elementary, Arcanum, OH***

Tip Check out the parent-teacher conference form on page 90!

Management Tips & Timesavers

Work It Out

Students take ownership of getting along and decision making with the help of this negotiation basket. Put in a basket dice, sand timers, and a two-sided counter labeled "*A*" on one side and "*Z*" on the other. Then have youngsters use the props to settle debatable issues. For example, to take turns sharing an item, encourage youngsters to use a sand timer for fair-share timing. To decide who will go first in an activity, have students roll the dice (the child with the higher number goes first) or flip the counter (the child whose name is closer to the letter in alphabetical order goes first). The possibilities are endless. ***Nicole Snyder, Parkway Elementary, Paramus, NJ***

Now What?

Looking for a quick directive for early finishers? Try this! Give each youngster a small notebook and special pencil to keep in his pencil box or cubby. When he completes his work, he takes out his notebook and pencil and journals as desired. ***Teresa Aten, Elm Creek School, Elm Creek, NE***

Password Pockets

Here's a fun way to individualize assessment. Personalize a library pocket for each child and post the pockets under the title "Password Pockets." In each pocket, place a task card appropriate for that child. To start the day or to transition from one activity to another, have the child say his password by doing the task on his card. Once he has mastered that task, change the card to establish a new password! ***Amanda Grudzien, Bristol Grade School, Bristol, IL***

Read the words.

the like am
are was

Welcome Aboard!

Students' positive behavior causes this bus to move from the bus depot to a special destination. Divide a tagboard strip (bus route) into a desired number of sections; write "bus depot" on the leftmost section and write the name of a special reward, such as extra recess time, on the other end. Then glue a bus cutout to a clothespin and clip it to the bus depot. When the group displays a particular behavior, move the bus to the next stop on the route. Continue until the bus reaches its final destination. For personalized goals, make bus and bus route props for each child to monitor skill-based or behavioral progress. ***Julie Keb, Madison Primary Center, South Bend, IN***

Feeding the Fish

Ensure that your pet fish are properly fed with this tip. Use a pill organizer to ration the correct amount of fish food for each school day. Then your fish keeper simply opens the compartment for that day and feeds the fish! ***Leigh Shumate Branham, Waynesboro, VA***

In my mailer
Are notes and work
In which you can take pride.
So always take a moment
To see what is inside.

From school to home
And back again,
This mailer goes each day.
Feel free to put a note inside
If you have things to say.

Note to the teacher: Use with "A Marvelous Mailer" on page 86.

Parent-Teacher Conference Notes

Student ______________________ **Date** ____________

Attending ______________________

Strengths

Areas of Need

Helpful Suggestions

At School

At Home

____
parent/guardian

____
teacher

Let's Do Social Studies!

Let's Do Social Studies!

Read the Roof!

Recognizing one's address

Students match their home addresses to these three-dimensional projects. For each child, personalize one side of a folded paper rectangle (roof) with his name and address. Have each child decorate a paper bag, keeping the opening at the top, so it resembles a home. If desired, set out construction paper scraps for him to cut out and glue on details such as windows and a door. Next, instruct him to stuff the bag with paper scraps. Then help him fold down the top of the bag and staple it closed. Finally, guide each child to find and say his address and set the roof atop his home craft. **For more practice**, simply remove the roofs for youngsters to match day after day.

Marilyn Dais Machosky
Sylvania Franciscan Academy
Sylvania, OH

We the People

Constitution Day and Citizenship Day

Celebrate Constitution Day and Citizenship Day with these patriotic headbands. Give each child a paper strip sized to fit her head and three cards labeled as shown. Discuss with youngsters who "We the People" refers to. Next, have each child glue the cards, in order, in the center of her strip. Encourage her to decorate the strip with red, white, and blue drawings, an assortment of stars, and patriotic stickers. Then tape together the ends of each strip to form headbands for youngsters to wear and read throughout the day.

Angie Kutzer
Garrett Elementary
Mebane, NC

Tools of the Trade

Community helpers

Encourage critical thinking with this hands-on activity. In advance, collect a variety of objects that represent different jobs and place them in a large container. Discuss with students different workers and the objects they use to help them work. Next, invite a child to randomly choose an object from the container and identify it. Then guide youngsters to name workers associated with the object and have them explain how it might be used. Continue in this manner with each remaining object.

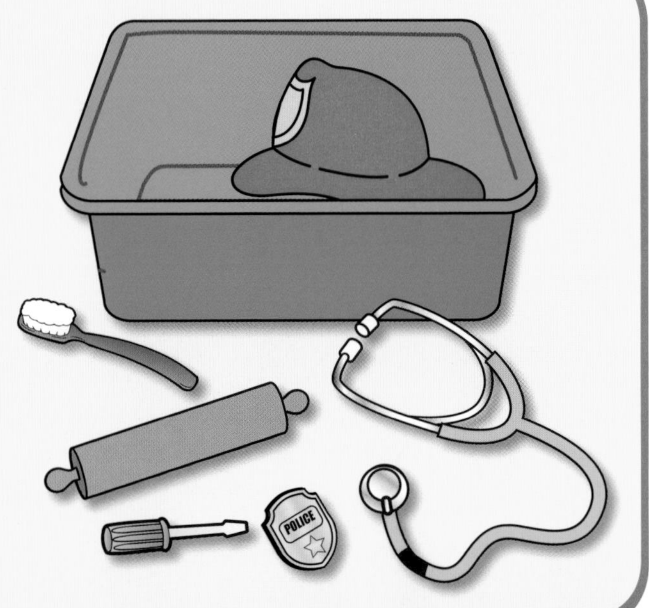

Let's Do Social Studies!

A Different Life

Past and present

Provide students a peek into the past with this home-school activity. Assign students the task of asking a parent, a grandparent, or an adult friend to describe something they now have that they did not have growing up. Send home with each child a recording sheet for him to draw a related picture and write a sentence to match, getting help as needed. When the papers are returned to school, invite each student to take a turn sharing his work with the group. Throughout the sharing, lead youngsters to compare and contrast present-day life to life in the past. ***(SL.K.5)***

Cecelia Granholm, Grenada Elementary, Grenada, MS

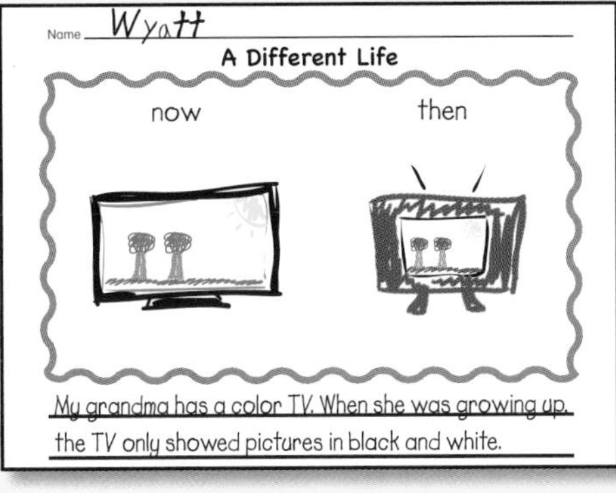

Hail to the Chief!

Presidential responsibilities

What ideas do your students have about being the leader of a country? Find out with this writing project that doubles as an adorable display! Lead youngsters to discuss the roles and responsibilities of a president or other country leader. To make a personal connection, have each child respond to a prompt such as "If I were president, I would..." and write his response on a sheet of paper. Next, have him pose while saluting or holding a patriotic flag, take his picture, and attach the photo to his paper. Display students' papers with the title "Presidential Possibilities." ***(W.K.2)***

Teresa Aten, Elm Creek Public School, Elm Creek, NE

Cast Your Ballot

Understanding the election process

Hold a class vote in honor of Election Day! Decide what students will vote on, such as their favorite books, favorite ice cream flavors, or favorite outdoor games. To create a "polling place" in your classroom, place a voter sign-in sheet, a class supply of ballots, and a ballot box on a table. Invite each child, in turn, to go to the polling place. Here she signs her name on the sign-in sheet, marks her choice on a ballot, and puts her ballot in the box. After each child votes, make a tally chart that shows the class favorite.

Jennifer Martin, Francis L. Stevens Elementary, Ballston Lake, NY

What is your favorite ice cream?

chocolate ☐ vanilla ☒ strawberry ☐

Let's Do Social Studies!

Helping Hands

Kwanzaa

This partner activity is a perfect way to reinforce the Kwanzaa principle of *Ujima* (working together or helping each other). After explaining *Ujima*, give each of two students a large hand cutout. Guide the student pairs to position the cutouts so they resemble a handshake as shown. Instruct each child to write or draw on his cutout to show how he can help his partner. Invite each twosome to share its work with the group. Then display each handshake project on a board titled "Helping Hands."

Land Comparisons

Landforms

Display pictures of landforms, such as a mountain, hills, an island, a peninsula, and a volcano. Guide students to notice characteristics of each landform. Next, have each child make a landform of her choice using colorful play dough. Then invite student pairs with different landforms to take turns sharing one way their landforms are alike and one way they are different. ***(SL.K.1a)***

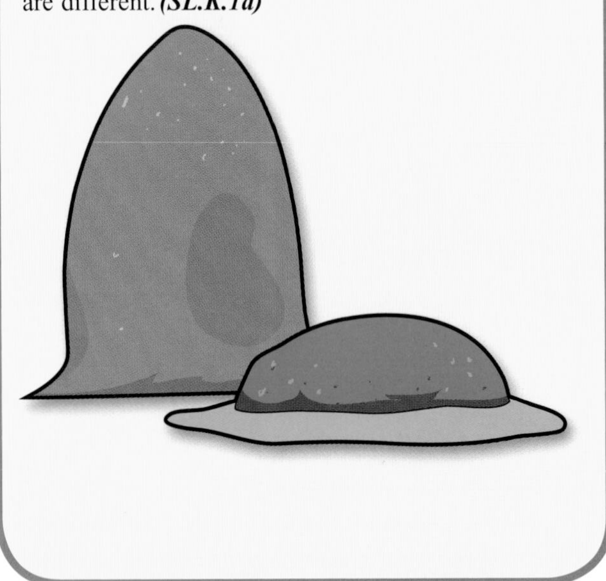

Peaceful Art

Martin Luther King Day

Celebrate Dr. King's dream of all people living together peacefully with this beautiful display. During a peace-related discussion, tell students that a dove is a symbol of peace. Next, give each child a copy of the recording sheet on page 97 and have him color the dove as desired. Guide him to complete the sentence on his paper and draw a picture to match. Display students' completed pages. To reinforce positive behavior, refer to the display each time youngsters are caught living peacefully. ***(W.K.2)***

adapted from an idea by Shannon Riddle
Montgomery Early Learning Center
Wynnewood, PA

Let's Do Social Studies!

Share and Discuss

Black History Month

Spark students' interest in the achievements of famous African Americans. Periodically during the month of February, place in a container a few objects or pictures related to a famous African American without naming the person. (See the list for suggestions.) Share the objects and encourage students to discuss why they think that person is famous. Then, with great fanfare, reveal the person's identity and explain how each item relates to the person. If desired, follow up the activity by reading aloud a book about the person's life. ***(SL.K.2)***

Famous African Americans

George Washington Carver (peanut, soap, picture of a farmer): scientist who made more than 300 products from the peanut plant

Rosa Parks (toy bus, toy police officer's badge): civil rights leader who was arrested for refusing to give up her seat on a public bus

Michael Jordan (basketball, basketball shoes, gold medal): basketball star who played in the Olympics

Mae Jemison (toy stethoscope, toy astronaut, toy spaceship): physician and first female African American in outer space

To the Park

Map skills

Youngsters practice using map symbols as they navigate their way through this booklet project. Have each child cut apart the booklet strips and backing on page 98. Then direct her to stack the strips in order and staple them atop the booklet backing. Lead students in reading each strip and tracing the named map symbol to match the text. ***(RI.K.7)***

Karin Bulkow
Washington School for Comprehensive Literacy
Sheboygan, WI

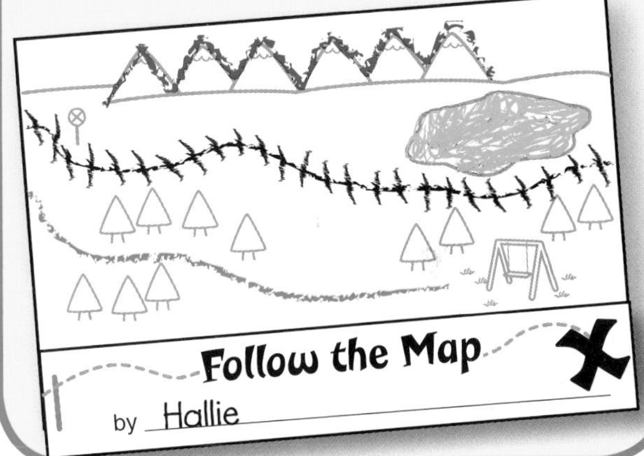

All About Abe

Presidents' Day

Sing this toe-tapping tune with youngsters to review facts about Abraham Lincoln's life. If desired, guide students to create other verses of the song using facts they know, such as he always wore a tall hat or he was a lawyer.

(sung to the tune of "The Mulberry Bush")

Where did Lincoln live as a boy?
Live as a boy, live as a boy?
Where did Lincoln live as a boy?
In a cabin made of logs.

Lincoln really liked to read,
Liked to read, liked to read.
Lincoln really liked to read
When he was just a boy.

Lincoln became the president,
President, president.
Lincoln became the president
Of America.

Lincoln wanted to free the slaves,
Free the slaves, free the slaves.
Lincoln wanted to free the slaves
So he fought the Civil War.

adapted from an idea by Andrea Singleton, Waynesville Elementary, Waynesville, OH

Go to page 99 for a **writing activity** related to Presidents' Day.

Let's Celebrate the Earth!

Encourage earth-friendly attitudes and actions with this selection of special activities!

Did you know it can take 450 years for some plastic bottles to break down in a landfill? Oh my!

Give Our Earth a Hand

Citizenship: responsibility

Lead students in singing this simple action song, encouraging them to clap to the beat during the final line of each verse. Then encourage students to name other ways they can be kind to the earth.

(sung to the tune of "Mary Had a Little Lamb")

[Let's reduce the trash we make],
[Trash we make, trash we make],
[Let's reduce the trash we make],
We'll give the earth a hand.

Continue with the following: *Pick up litter when you can, Please recycle and reuse, Plant a tree to show you care*

Sarah Hibbett
Henderson, TN

Container Comparison

Comparing sets (K.CC.C.6)

Gather a variety of clean plastic containers with recycling symbols. Make a simple index card sign for each recycling number. To begin, give each child a container. Explain that each container has a recycling symbol with a number. Instruct each student to identify the number on his container. Then help children sort the containers by number, placing them next to the appropriate signs. Encourage youngsters to compare the groups using the words *more*, *less,* and *equal.* If desired, explain that containers with numbers 1 and 2 can be easily recycled in several communities.

Suzanne Moore
Tucson, AZ

Love the Earth

Writing (W.K.1)

To make these colorful earth projects, ask youngsters why they love the earth and encourage them to write their thoughts on a heart cutout. Next, have each child fold a white construction paper circle in half. Instruct her to unfold the circle and drizzle slightly diluted green and blue paint on one half. Prompt her to refold the circle and gently press down on the paper. When she unfolds the circle, have her press her prepared heart in the middle and then set her project aside to dry. Display the projects on a wall with the title "Who Loves the Earth? We Do!"

I love the earth because the trees are nice and green. I also love the lakes. They are fun to swim in.

Debra Bousquet
Edward Fenn Elementary
Gorham, NH

See page 100 for an earth-friendly **reproducible**!

Name ______________________________ Recording sheet (W.K.2)

Peace is ______________________________

______________________________.

Note to the teacher: Use with "Peaceful Art" on page 94.

Booklet Strips and Backing

Use with "To the Park" on page 95.

Follow the Map

by ______________________________

First, go up and down the purple mountains. 1

Then cross the blue lake. 2

Next, ride on the black railroad. 3

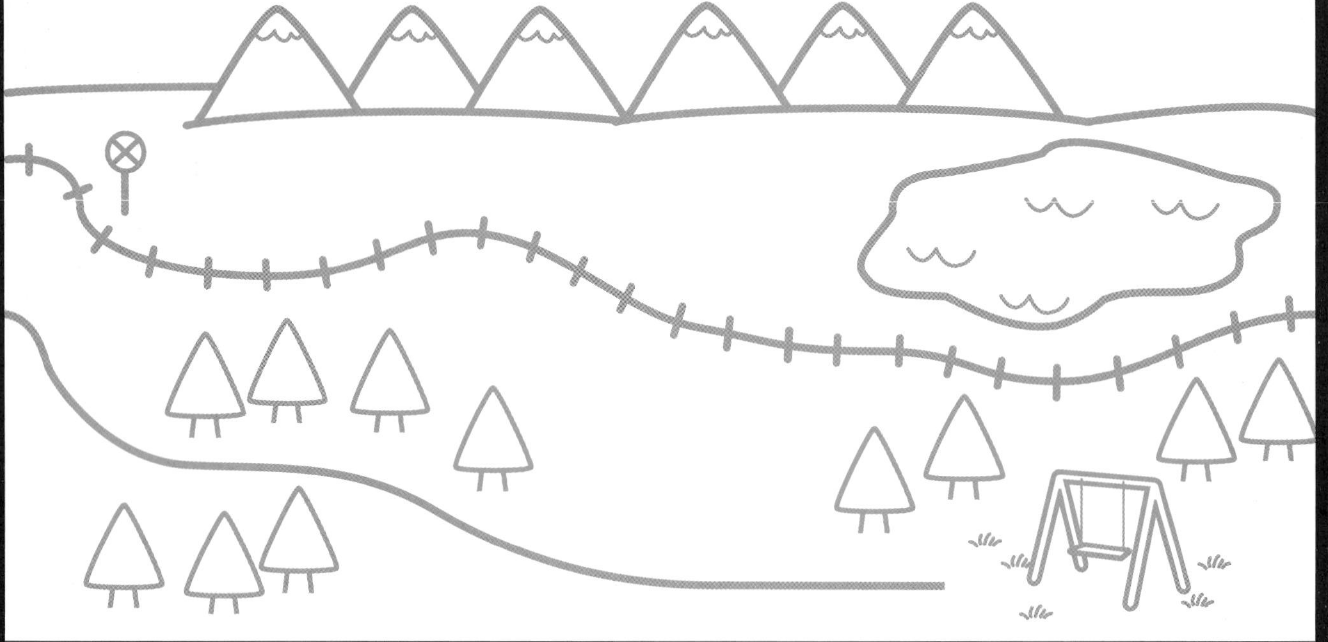

Finally, drive on the red road to the park. 4

Name ____________

President for a Day!

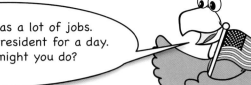

The president has a lot of jobs.
Imagine you are president for a day.
What three jobs might you do?

Listen and do.

Note to the teacher: Give each child a copy of this page. Then guide him to draw and write where indicated to respond to the prompt.

Name ____________________

Help the Earth!

Write an X for each activity you do.

Activity	Monday	Tuesday	Wednesday	Thursday	Friday	Saturday	Sunday
Pick up litter.							
Turn off the water while brushing my teeth.							
Help recycle.							
Turn off lights when not in use.							

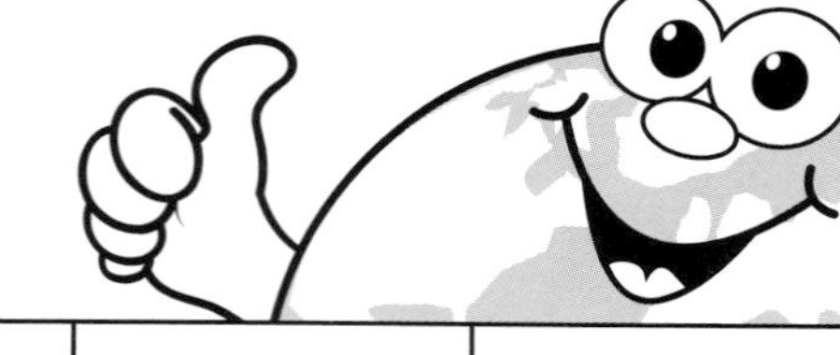

Note to the teacher: Have each child take home a copy of this page and have them return it completed by a specific date. Then have students discuss their results and how they might further help the earth.

Our Readers Write...

Our Readers WRITE...

(and EMAIL and BLOG and TWEET and POST)

"I have been teaching for 26 years and *The Mailbox* has been a part of my classroom for most of those years!—*Debbie Fodrie via Facebook*

Photo Blocks

I take a photograph of each child and use clear Con-Tact covering to attach each photo to a wooden block. The blocks are perfect for getting-acquainted activities, name matching, graphing, designating cooperative groups, and more. My students even use them in the block center! ***Debbie Nemo, George Washington Elementary, Marion, OH***

FIRST DAY FAREWELLS

Here's a polite way to encourage parents to drop off their children and quickly move on with their day. I simply post for parents a list of instructions like the ones shown. Students get settled in while I continue to greet each child when he arrives, and it also lets parents know I appreciate their help and quick departure. ***Bonnie Bahr, Lackland City Elementary, San Antonio, TX***

Here's how you can help this morning!

1. Help students find their cubbies and hang up their backpacks.
2. Help students put on their nametags.
3. Encourage students to begin the morning activity.
4. Kiss your child goodbye and have a good day!

Alphabet Tip

My class studies a different letter each week. To mark our progress, I cover the weekly letter with yellow plastic wrap. (Cellophane squares work too.) To save time and money, I leave the highlighted letters on the chart for the following year. Then I simply remove the covering when a letter is introduced. ***Jeanne Pinkman, Cathedral of the Risen Christ School, Lincoln, NE***

"Opening *The Mailbox* magazine and books is like Christmas for me. I can always count on finding fresh twists for teaching traditional concepts."—*Marcia Snarski Wuest via Facebook*

Stoplight Days

To help reinforce the time concept of yesterday, today, and tomorrow, I label a paper stoplight as shown, laminate it, and post it near my calendar display. Each day, we wipe away yesterday's information and use a wipe-off marker to update the days accordingly. ***Amy Hart, Saint Sylvester School, Pittsburgh, PA***

Seasonal Sight Words

I display each sight word I introduce on a seasonal cutout and use a different cutout for each month. The monthly cutouts tell how long my students have been exposed to the words. For example, if a child is struggling with a word in March and it is written on an apple cutout, I know he has been exposed to the word since September. It's an easy and informative reference point! *(RF.K.3c)* ***Angela Farley, North Side Primary Center, Herrin, IL***

"*The Mailbox* makes a difference in the lives of so many people every day!—*Laura Mihalenko via The Mailbox Blog*

Daily Memories

Revisit the day's events with this simple rhyme. I insert a different child's name each time I say, "Hey, hey, what do you say? What did [child's name] do at school today?" Then the named child tells something she did at school that day. This also reminds students of daily events to share with their parents when they get home. For a variation, I substitute *learn* for *do* in the second line. *(SL.K.4)* ***Brook Baglini, Main Elementary, Athens, PA***

"*The Mailbox* helps to keep my class running."—*Nancy G. Askew via Facebook*

A Birthday Mystery

At the beginning of the school year, I give each child a large paper programmed with his name. I have him cut out magazine pictures of favorite things and activities he likes and then glue them to his paper. I encourage him to draw added details as desired. Then I collect the completed collages. On a child's birthday, I name some of his favorite things from his collage and encourage classmates to guess who it is. Then I display the collage and ask the birthday child to tell about it. ***Michele Agri, Tampa, FL***

Our Readers WRITE...

(and EMAIL and BLOG and TWEET and POST)

How many days in a week?
Question Box

Question and Answers

I review concepts throughout the year with this transition tool. I decorate a large box that I call the question box. When we finish a unit of study, I write related questions on separate slips of paper and put them in the question box. I also add questions related to calendar time, math, and literacy concepts. Then, to switch activities or get students to line up, I first pose a question. If the group answers correctly, I signal to them to move as expected. My question box also serves as a great time filler! ***Denise Bessemer, Stillwater Township Elementary, Stillwater, NJ***

CLIP IT

I use personalized clipboards to switch out students' best writing samples. I tack the clipboards to a display and clip each child's writing to her board. When it is time to change the writing samples, I can quickly take the old piece out and clip the new one in. ***Kate Searing, College Park Elementary, Greendale, WI***

Noelle
The big dog licked me.

A Message From Your Teacher

Looking for a unique way to remind students about your expectations when there is a substitute in your classroom? Try this! I prepare a short video for my substitute to view with students at the beginning of the day. In the video, I encourage youngsters to make the substitute feel welcome. Also, I remind them of the rules and my expectations for them while I am out. I explain that the substitute will leave a note to let me know about the day. This video is especially helpful when my absence is unexpected. *Lindsey O'Conner, Braintree Public Schools, Braintree, MA*

"I don't know what I'd do without *The Mailbox*® magazines! I love the easy, practical, and relevant activities in each magazine. My students always love the activities, and the magazine saves me a ton of time!"—*Danielle Hudson via Facebook*

Our Readers WRITE...
(and EMAIL and BLOG and TWEET and POST)

ALL TIED UP

Here's a cute and fun way for my kindergartners to practice tying shoes during their free time. I purchase an inexpensive pair of children's shoes and stuff the toe area of each shoe. Then I pull a pair of children's socks over two tall plastic containers with wide openings. I place a container in each shoe so it resembles a leg and slide the leg under a table leg. The table legs keep the shoes from moving, and my students enjoy tying the table's laces! ***Mary Baumann, Sandstone Elementary, Billings, MT***

Snazzy Spiderwebs

These webs add a cool effect to any spider-themed art project or display. For each child, I place a copy of a web pattern in a large resealable plastic bag. Then I have him squeeze glue to trace over the web. (For added fun, use colored glue.) When the glue is dry, I guide each child to carefully peel his web from the bag. ***Carrie Johnson, Stone Elementary, Crossville, TN***

I love using *The Mailbox*® ideas and activities as a curriculum supplement. Many of the activities are great for creating portable centers. I put the activities in resealable plastic bags, baskets, or recycled shoeboxes so students can complete the activities anywhere!—*Charisse Audra Collier via Facebook*

A Handy Tip

During the year, I do several projects that use cutouts of each child's hands. To save time, I make a tracing of each child's hands and store it for safekeeping. When I plan a project that requires hand cutouts, I use a copier to make the needed number of construction paper copies of each child's tracing. ***Jodi Darter, Cabool Elementary, Cabool, MO***

Tooth Tales

Losing a tooth is an important event for a kindergartner. I have a tote bag filled with tooth-related books that I call "Tooth Tales." To celebrate a child's lost tooth, I invite him to take the "Tooth Bag" home. He can read some or all of the books with his family before returning the bag to school the next day. Near the end of the year, I give each child who has not lost a tooth the opportunity to take the bag home in anticipation of the big event. *Cheryl Ladd, Mesnier Primary, St. Louis, MO*

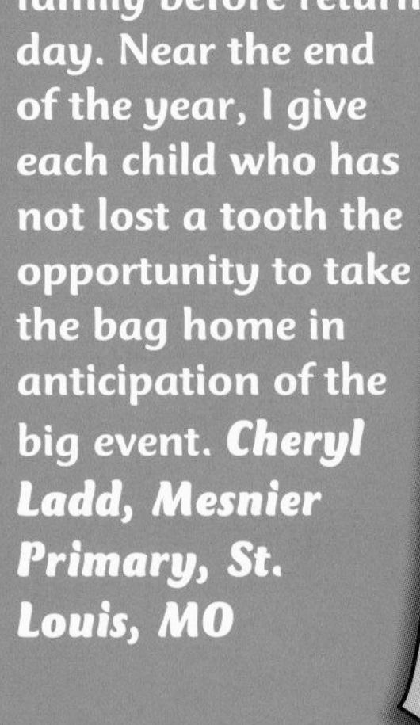

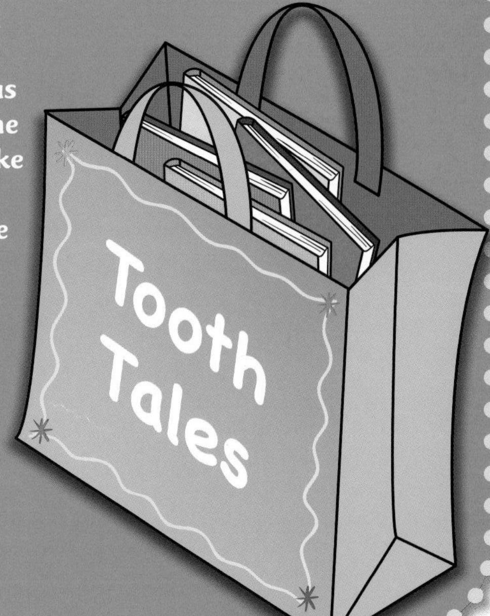

Our Readers WRITE...

(and EMAIL and BLOG and TWEET and POST)

6				
5				
4				
3				Alexis
2	Jessie		Victor	Alexis
1	Jessie	Tomas	Victor	Alexis
	Jessie	Tomas	Victor	Alexis

Gift Tag Graphing

Here's how I promote responsible behavior and incorporate graphing skills during December. In advance, I gather inexpensive packages of self-adhesive gift tags and make a graph that has a column labeled for individuals or small groups. When I post the graph, I explain how students can earn gift tags for the graph, such as being kind to others or using free time wisely. When a youngster earns a gift tag, I help her label the tag and stick it on the graph. Every few days, I guide students to interpret the data collected thus far. ***Litsa Jackson, Covington Integrated Arts Academy, Covington, TN***

"I have used *The Mailbox* for 28 years! I love everything about the magazine and can't wait to read it once it arrives...Keep up the good work!"—*Rhonda Mann via The Mailbox® Blog*

SNAZZY SNOW SCENES

To give winter art projects a snowy 3-D effect, I mix together equal parts of glue and nonmentholated shaving cream (snow). After each child creates a winter scene on construction paper, I invite him to brush some snow onto his scene. To add extra dazzle to the projects, I allow students to sprinkle clear glitter on the snow before it dries. In a day or two, the projects are ready to display. ***Susan Smith, Bascomb Elementary, Woodstock, GA***

tip To embellish other projects with a different-color 3-D effect, use food coloring to tint the mixture.

Quick Quiz

I write on individual cards tasks that relate to previously learned skills. I place the cards in a decorative bag labeled "Quiz Cards." To jump-start learning each morning, I pull a few cards from the bag. I read aloud each card and have the group or a different volunteer complete each task. It is a quick way to review skills each day and get my students quickly focused on learning. ***Teresa Aten, Elm Creek Public School, Elm Creek, NE***

"I like how practical the ideas are for the grade-level skills and how easy the reproducibles are for the activities and learning centers."—*Jeanine Bulber via Facebook*

Our Readers WRITE...

(and EMAIL and BLOG and TWEET and POST)

A COOL CARRIER

My students love sharing class-made books with their families. I have discovered that a plastic bag with handles (the kind comforters and quilts are often sold in) is perfect for transporting the precious cargo. ***Judy Fickler, Beth Israel Preschool and Kindergarten, Eagle, PA***

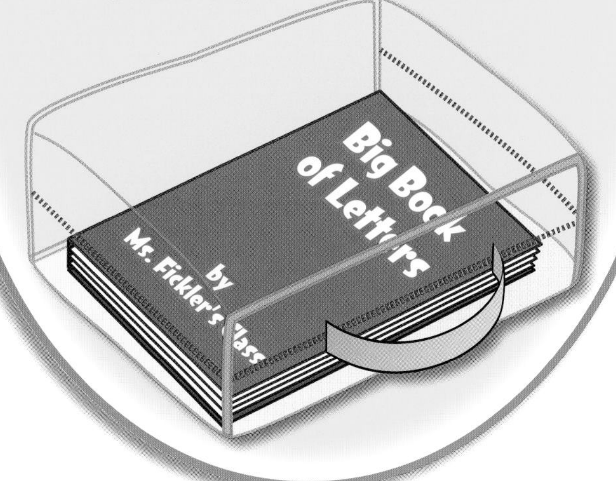

Hooked!

I have found a quick and economical way to connect the pieces of mobile-style art projects. Each year during after-holiday sales, I stock up on ornament hooks. When a child is ready to assemble a mobile, I give her the number of hooks she needs. Then I help her punch holes in the project pieces, and she "hooks" the pieces together. This method is so much easier than using yarn! ***Jodi Darter, Cabool Elementary, Cabool, MO***

"The Kindergarten magazines are my curriculum (and mindset) rejuvenators! I LOVE, LOVE, LOVE getting those! They fire me back up for the month/theme ahead and give me new ideas."*—Suzanne Denecke via The Mailbox® Blog*

100 Days

On the 100th day of school, we have a Miss Bindergarten-style celebration! We wear hats and goggles as we count to 100 in a variety of ways. I also invite youngsters to take turns sharing 100-item collections made at home for the special occasion. It's grand fun! ***Melissa Barker, San Antonio, TX***

Sign Your Name

A	l	y	s	s	a	N	o	e	l
l	e	J	o	h	n				

For a 100th day of school activity, I give each child a blank hundred chart for collecting signatures. To begin, each child signs her paper. To do this, she starts in the first open space and writes each letter of her name in a separate space. Then she invites different classmates to sign her paper until she collects 100 letters. For added fun, I award a special prize to each child who gathers a final signature that has the exact number of letters as the remaining open spaces on her paper. *(L.K.1a) Jodi Darter*

Praiseworthy Email

My best tip for working with parents is to send them a quick email about something specific their child said or did in class. The biggest hit is to send a photo of their child working on something. ***Jill Exe, Harold Kaveolook School, Kaktovik, AK, via The Mailbox® Blog***

Our Readers WRITE...

(and EMAIL and BLOG and TWEET and POST)

Animal Valentine Holders

Clean, empty disinfecting wipe containers are perfect for making valentine holders. I help each child wrap a container with a personalized piece of construction paper sized to fit. Next, I provide paper scraps and encourage her to draw and cut out bunny, bear, or dog details and glue them to the container. Then her cute critter card holder is ready to receive valentines! ***Iris Avila, Ramirez Burks Elementary, Cotulla, TX***

Ready to Roll!

I use a fishing tackle box to sort and store my collection of dice. I put one style of die in each section, and now my dice are supereasy to find! *—Jamie Walker via The Mailbox® Blog*

Magnificent Math

Pancakes are a tasty way to learn about equal and unequal parts! I give each child a pancake cut in halves, fourths, or unequal parts. Then I ask youngsters to form two groups: those with equal-part pancakes and those with unequal-part pancakes. After comparing the pancake parts, youngsters are invited to drizzle syrup and enjoy their yummy treat. *Helen McClernon, St. Matthew's Catholic School, Jacksonville, FL*

I've been teaching for 20 years and subscribe to the kindergarten version of *The Mailbox®*. The entire magazine is always wonderful, and I always find something I want to create to use in my classroom. From cooking, science, and math to writing and reading: I love all the ideas!*—Ella Stroupe via Facebook*

A LETTER GAME

This version of tic-tac-toe is perfect for practicing letter formation. Youngsters simply play the traditional game, but instead of using *X*s and *O*s, they practice writing an uppercase and lowercase letter pair of an assigned letter! ***(L.K.1a) Pam Szeliga, Relay Elementary, Baltimore, MD***

Our Readers WRITE...

(and EMAIL and BLOG and TWEET and POST)

SEND A HUG

I help my youngsters mail Valentine's Day wishes! In advance, I ask students' families to send me the address of someone to whom their child would like to send a Valentine's Day hug. Next, I have each child make two handprints, cut them out, and write a message similar to the one shown. We attach the message to a length of yarn long enough to "hug" an adult and tape a hand cutout to each end. The child puts his hug in an envelope, and then I help him address it, stamp it, and drop it in the mail! ***Shannon Riddle, Montgomery Early Learning Center, Wynnewood, PA***

Family Reading Night

For a family literacy event, our school invites parents and students to a special evening of fun! All the teachers select a story to read (some act it out and get dressed up in costume!), and groups of families rotate among reading stations to hear all the stories. Pajamas are welcome, and we serve milk and cookies for a grand finale. It's always a hit! —*Cheryl Ener via The Mailbox® Blog*

The Riddle Box

This quick-to-prepare idea reinforces writing, reading, and listening skills. I decorate an old lunchbox to make a Riddle Box. I place an object inside the box and send it home with a child. With the help of his family, the child writes a riddle that contains three clues about the object. When he returns the box to school, he reads his riddle to his classmates. Then they guess the name of the object. —*Lorna Kearns via The Mailbox® Blog*

Ruler Rhyme

This rhyme will help youngsters remember how to measure an object with any type of ruler. ***Karin Bulkow, Washington School for Comprehensive Literacy, Sheboygan, WI***

Measuring objects is supercool!
So get out your ruler or other tool.
Match the edge, and you can begin
To find out how long, short, wide, or thin!

Name That Category!

When welcoming students, I name different items of a particular category, such as breakfast foods, articles of clothing, or animal names. I encourage youngsters to repeat the word or, if they think they know the category, provide different words in that category. Later in the day, I ask youngsters to name that category. Several teachers on our hallway participate, and it has become a great educational greeting our kindergartners look forward to! **(L.K.5) *Jennifer Nelson, Woodleaf Elementary, Woodleaf, NC***

Waffles, pancakes, omelets,...

Our Readers WRITE...

(and EMAIL and BLOG and TWEET and POST)

Warm Fuzzies

This cute creature reminds my youngsters to make good choices. I glue a pom-pom creature to a container and place colorful pom-poms (warm fuzzies) nearby. When an adult compliments the class or an individual for positive behavior, I add a warm fuzzy to the container. When the container is full, we celebrate with a special treat! *Anne Frost Hawker, Green Valley Elementary, Hoover, AL*

Super Organized!

I use magazine holders to store my games and center activities. On each holder, I write the time of year and list specific standards that I cover during that time. I store games and center activities in the corresponding holders so, when I need them, they are easy to find and ready to go! *Ashley Cahill, Olympic View Elementary, Lacey, WA, via The Mailbox® Blog*

Window Watchers

I have so many windows in my classroom that I decided to use them as learning spaces! I use a window marker or dry-erase marker to write a letter, word, or number on a designated window. Each day of the week, I write on a different window. By Friday, we review the week's window work. My students are always eager to read the windows! *Denice Yost Hatch, Atwood Primary, Oakland, ME*

Tell a Story

Here's an entertaining approach to practicing word problems. I invite two volunteers to each show a number card. Then I create a word problem using the volunteers' names and their numbers. Seated youngsters use drawings or manipulatives to solve the problem. Then the volunteers reveal the answer by drawing on the board to show how they would solve the problem. *Marianne Carstensen, Walworth, WI*

GREAT GIFT!

This 3-D flower project is marvelous for Mother's Day or any other occasion to present a heartfelt greeting to a loved one. I have each child cut out a copy of the poem shown so it resembles a cloud. I also instruct her to cut paper scraps to form a stem, leaves, and a flower center. Next, I guide her to glue the cloud and flower parts to a paper. Finally, I provide plastic bottle caps for her to dip into glue and use as petals. ***Jackie Wright, Summerhill Children's House, Enid, OK***

This little flower is special, you see,
Because it was made for you by me.
I carefully glued each flower part
To show that I love you with all my heart!

"I look forward to the learning centers in *The Mailbox*® magazine. My kindergartners use them daily in small-group learning centers and for partner and independent practice."—*Linda Wasemann-Phillips via Facebook*

Sort or Store

Whenever someone brings a clear fruit or vegetable tray to a gathering, I clean and save the empty tray and lid. Then I have my students sort objects into the empty sections. Since the tray parts are clear, it is also great for storing small objects because you can see at a glance what is inside! ***Sara McKrill, Milford Elementary, Wolcottville, IN***

SPRING PAINTINGS

I have my students paint with pastel colors! I mix a small amount of paint—such as red, blue, purple, green, or yellow—into separate cups of white paint. Youngsters use the pastel paints to create spring scenes. For added fun, I set out egg, raindrop, flower, and bunny cutouts on which students can paint. ***Virginia Zeletzki, The Villages, FL***

From Caterpillar to Butterfly

Save leftover laminating film for this cute science activity. I guide each child to make a line of fingerprints in the center of a five-inch tagboard square. Next, I have him draw a face and antennae on the top print to complete a caterpillar. Then I lay a five-inch square of film atop each student's tagboard and tape them together along one edge. Finally, I have him use permanent markers to draw wings on the film to transform the caterpillar into a butterfly. My students love to lift and lower the film to see the caterpillars and butterflies! ***Louise Garrison, St. Anne School, Rock Hill, SC***

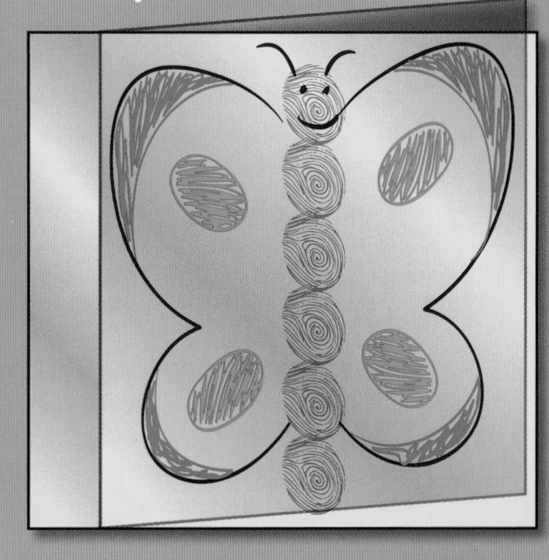

Simple Storage

To keep supplies close but not on my desk, I glue magnets to plastic canisters and spice jars. Then I put various supplies in separate jars and attach them to the filing cabinet beside my desk. ***Peggy Watson, Kid's Academy, North Little Rock, AR, via The Mailbox® Blog***

Our Readers WRITE...

(and EMAIL and BLOG and TWEET and POST)

RECYCLED CRAYONS

At the end of the school year, I ask for crayons that my students and fellow teachers are throwing away. I peel the paper from the crayons, break them into smaller pieces, and drop the pieces into seasonal-shaped trays suitable for baking. I put the trays in the oven at 220 degrees for about ten minutes or until the crayons melt. Then I remove the trays and let the crayon liquid cool. Soon after, the shapely crayons are ready for use. I like to give my crayon creations to my students as gifts throughout the next school year. ***Tammy Willey, Pine Street Elementary, Presque Isle, ME***

Classy Memories

On the inside of my classroom closet, I have a photo posted of each class I have taught. Late in the school year, I add my current class's photo to the collection. Then I invite a couple of students at a time to look at the photos. They always enjoy looking for siblings; for friends; and, of course, to see how much I have changed over the years. ***Barbara Mason, Deposit Elementary, Deposit, NY***

"I truly love your magazines, especially the ones with ready-made colorful centers. My whole kindergarten grade level has bought so many books from The Mailbox we could open our own store. Now this should tell you how much I love them. My centers look great." *—Frinzetta Boman via Facebook*

Sticker Storage

This great organizational tool keeps my stickers organized! I laminate sheets of construction paper to make dividers and label each divider with a different theme. Then I put the dividers in a basket and file all my stickers thematically. When I need a sticker, it's right there! *Kelly Childers, Starr Elementary, Starr, SC, via The Mailbox® Blog*

Free-Time Friend

Our Free-Time Friend is a great visual reminder for students to work together and have great days. After the first great day, students earn the head without any features. Each successful day thereafter, I add one more detail—such as an eye, a nose, an eyebrow, or another eye—until our friend is complete. Then I reward the class with 20 minutes of free-play time. It works like a charm! ***Sheryl Keseian, Avon, MA***

Partner Games

Name ____________________

Rhyming pictures (RF.K.2a)

Pizza by the Slice

Partner Game Use with the directions and spinner pattern on page 115.

Spinner Pattern and Directions

Use with "Pizza by the Slice" on page 114.

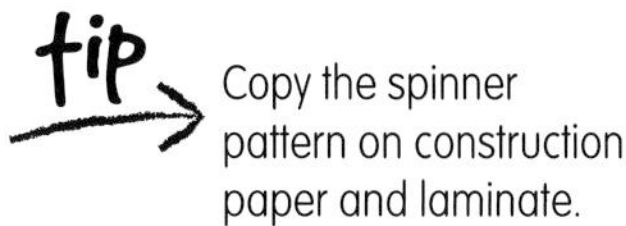

Copy the spinner pattern on construction paper and laminate.

Pizza by the Slice

Skill: Rhyming pictures (RF.K.2a)

What You Need

2 gameboards
spinner card
2 red crayons RED RED
paper clip
pencil

How to play:

1. Play with a partner.
2. When it is your turn, spin the spinner. Name the picture.
3. Look for a rhyming picture on your pizza slice.
   - If you find a rhyming picture, color it.
   - If you do not find a rhyming picture, your turn is over.
4. Play until each picture on one player's pizza slice is colored or time runs out. The player who colors more pictures wins. If both players color the same number of pictures, the game is a tie.

Name____________________

Number order to 20 (K.CC.A.3)

Happy Hoppers!

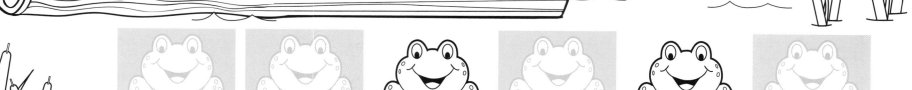

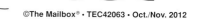

Partner Game Use with the cards and directions on page 117.

Game Cards and Directions

Cut apart a copy of the game cards. Use the cards and directions with "Happy Hoppers!" on page 116.

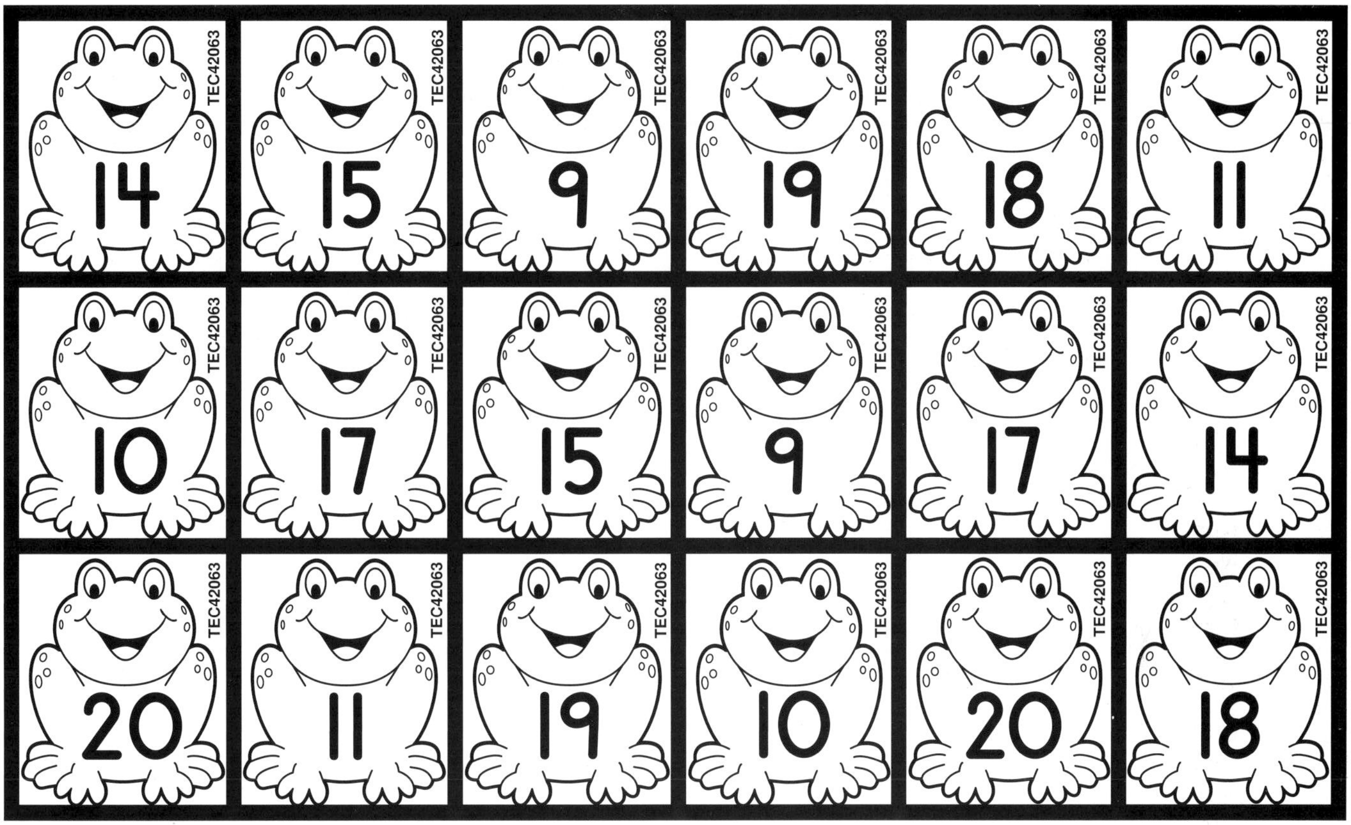

14 TEC42063	15 TEC42063	9 TEC42063	19 TEC42063	18 TEC42063	11 TEC42063
10 TEC42063	17 TEC42063	15 TEC42063	9 TEC42063	17 TEC42063	14 TEC42063
20 TEC42063	11 TEC42063	19 TEC42063	10 TEC42063	20 TEC42063	18 TEC42063

Happy Hoppers!

Skill: Number order to 20
(K.CC.A.3)

What You Need

2 gameboards
paper bag with game cards inside

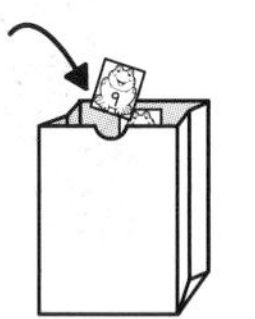

How to play:

1. Play with a partner.
2. When it is your turn, take a card from the bag. Say the number.
3. Put the card on your gameboard. If you cannot, put the card back in the bag.
4. Play until one player's gameboard spaces are all covered or time is up. The player who has more frogs wins.

Names ________________ and ________________

Color and number words
(RF.K.3c)

Reading Speedway

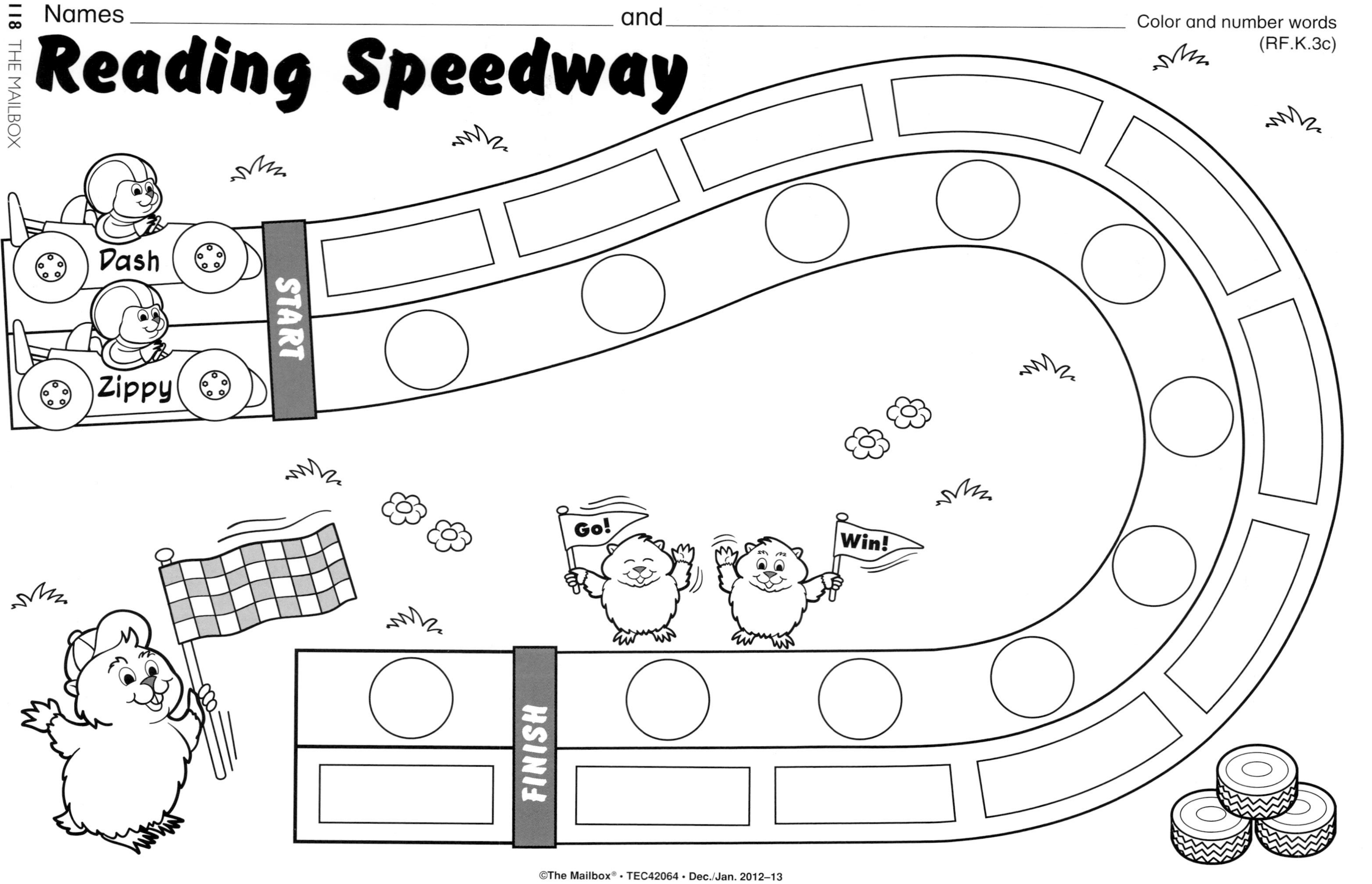

Partner Game Use with the directions on page 119.

Game Cards and Directions

Cut apart a copy of the game cards. Use the cards and directions with "Reading Speedway" on page 118.

nine TEC42064	yellow TEC42064	two TEC42064	green TEC42064
four TEC42064	purple TEC42064	three TEC42064	red TEC42064
eight TEC42064	one TEC42064	blue TEC42064	black TEC42064
five TEC42064	orange TEC42064	brown TEC42064	six TEC42064
pink TEC42064	ten TEC42064	seven TEC42064	zero TEC42064

Reading Speedway

Skill: Color and number words (RF.K.3c)

What You Need

gameboard

paper bag with game cards inside

crayons

pencil

How to play:

1. Play with a partner. Choose a game path.
2. When it is your turn, take a card from the bag. Read the word.
   - If the word is a number word, write that number in the next open space on your game path.
   - If the word is a color word, use that color crayon to color the next two open spaces on your game path.
3. Play until both players cross the FINISH line!

Win!

Names ______________________ and ______________________

Short *a* words (RF.K.3)

Bubble Blast!

Partner Game Use with the directions on page 122.

Names ______________________ and ______________________

Hop to the Top!

Left path	Flowers	Right path
5 – 0		9 – 3
10 – 5	10	5 – 3
9 – 6	9	7 – 0
6 – 2	8	4 – 2
4 – 3	7	6 – 3
8 – 5	6	10 – 4
2 – 1	5	9 – 5
3 – 2	4	3 – 1
6 – 4	3	8 – 4
7 – 2	2	6 – 1
5 – 1	1	2 – 2
	0	
START		START

Partner Game Use with the directions on page 122.

Bubble Blast!

Skill: Short *a* words (RF.K.3)

What You Need

gameboard
labeled counter S B
two different-color crayons

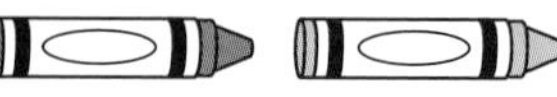

How to play:

1. Play with a partner. When it is your turn, toss the counter.
2. Use the Bubble Code. Find a matching-size bubble that is not colored.
3. Read the word; then color the bubble. If there are no bubbles left in the matching size, your turn is over.
4. Play until all the bubbles are colored or time runs out. The player who colors more bubbles wins.

Hop to the Top!

Skill: Subtraction from ten

What You Need

gameboard
2 game markers
labeled counter 1 2
two different-color crayons

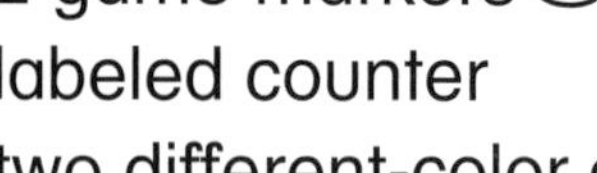

How to play:

1. Play with a partner. Pick a frog.
2. When it is your turn, toss the counter and move that many spaces.
3. Read the problem and solve it. Use the flowers to help you. Color the space.
4. The first player to reach FINISH wins.
5. Play until both players reach FINISH. For extra practice, trade crayons with your partner and go back down the hill! When it is your turn, read and solve the first problem on your path that is not colored. Play until both players have a fully colored path.

 Note to the teacher: Use with the gameboards on pages 120 and 121.

Names ______________________ and ______________________ Addition (K.OA.A.5)

Fresh-Cut Hay

Partner Game Use this gameboard with the spinner pattern and game directions on page 124.

Spinner Pattern and Directions

Use with "Fresh-Cut Hay" on page 123.

5 2
3 4

TEC42067

Fresh-Cut Hay

Skill: Addition (K.OA.A.5)

What You Need

gameboard
spinner card 
paper clip 
pencil 
2 different-color crayons

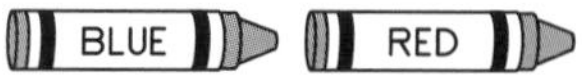

BLUE RED

How to play:

1. Play with a partner. Choose a crayon.
2. When it is your turn, spin the spinner. Name the number.
3. Look for an addition problem that makes this number.
   - If you find a problem, circle it.
   - If you do not find one, your turn is over.
4. Play until all the problems are circled or time runs out. The player who circles more problems wins.

Problem Solved!

Problem Solved!

Your Solutions to Classroom Challenges

What is your best tip for a great *kindergarten lineup*?

To help students **make a straight line**, I tie knots at regular intervals in a length of rope (or several jump ropes). Then I hold one end of the rope, and each child holds a different knot—away we go!

Patty Henderson, Early Childhood Learning Center, Titusville, PA

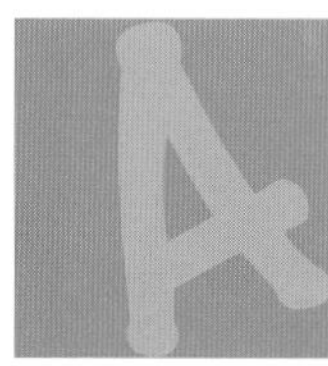

I line up different **number cards** on the floor (one for each student) and then cover the cards with Con-Tact covering. To line up, a child simply stands on his assigned number card!

Marilyn Wagner, Carleton Elementary, Milwaukee, WI

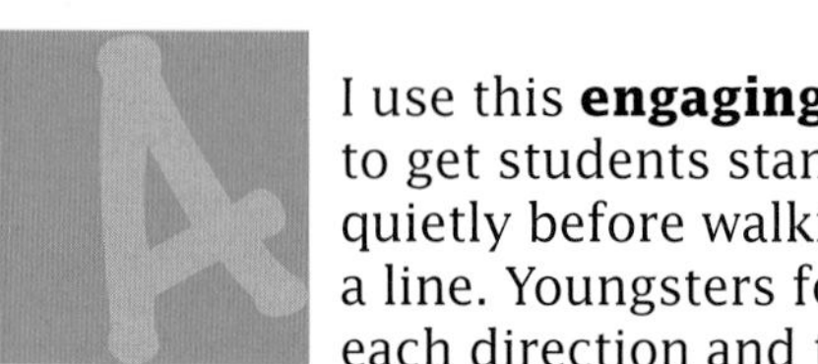

I use this **engaging chant** to get students standing quietly before walking in a line. Youngsters follow each direction and then repeat the last line after me in a whisper, signaling they are ready to go!

Clap your hands.
Check your feet.
We're ready to walk
To a hallway beat.
We face forward
And keep our hands down low.
We stand quietly.
We're ready to go!

Lisa Carlson, Ridge Hill Elementary
Hamden CT

"The most crucial variable associated with student achievement is good classroom management.... We know that effective teachers create and maintain an orderly, stimulating, and motivating learning environment."
—Institute of Child Education and Psychology

I have a few **students model** how to walk in a line correctly. Next, I invite several students to model incorrect line behavior. (I whisper mischievous acting ideas in their ears first.) After classmates identify what's wrong, I have a third group of students model the correct behavior again.

Adrienne Hugo, Washington School, Mundelein, IL

I have students line up. Then I close my eyes (peeking a little bit for safety) and recite the **chant** shown. When I open my eyes, students are in a perfect line!

I'm going to close my eyes and count to three;
What kind of line do you think I'll see?
Will it be quiet? Will it be straight?
Come on, kindergartners—make it great!

Patti Gehring, St. Mary's School, Bryantown, MD

It's your turn! Share your ideas.
themailbox.com/submitideas

Problem Solved!

Your Solutions to Classroom Challenges

How do you manage your *learning centers*?

For **easy organization**, I store my center activities in shoeboxes (or plastic containers). I place the materials and directions for each center in a separate box. To color-code the boxes by subject area, I use different-color boxes or box lids. Then I label the outside of each box with the center's name and target skill and stack the boxes by subject area for easy access.

Rebecca Landreth, Wyndmoor, PA

To help students **transition** quickly and easily from one center to another, I signal cleanup time by slowly counting backward from ten. By the time I reach "one," each center should be ready for the next visitors and each child should be standing quietly, ready to move to the next center.

Sarah Newsome, Enterprise Learning Academy
Jacksonville, FL

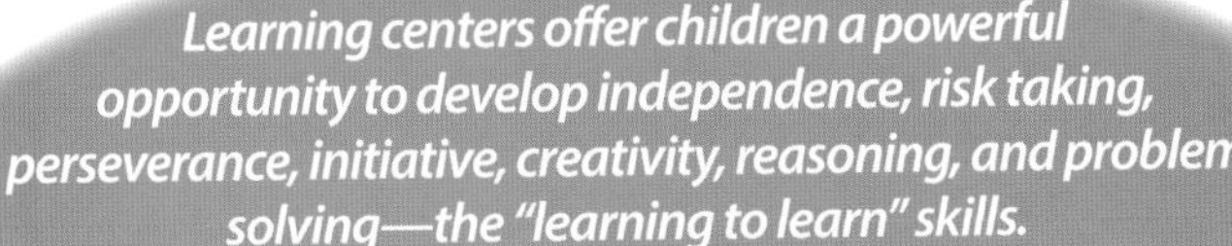

Learning centers offer children a powerful opportunity to develop independence, risk taking, perseverance, initiative, creativity, reasoning, and problem solving—the "learning to learn" skills.

—National Association for the Education of Young Children, K Today, "Teaching and Learning in the Kindergarten Year"

I **set up** my centers using trifold boards! I label the board with the activity name or skill and then clip instructions to it. I add pockets for storing papers or other center materials. For center time, I stand each board on a different table or desk. After center time, I fold and stack the boards for easy storage.

Martha Tully, Fleming Island Elementary
Fleming Island, FL

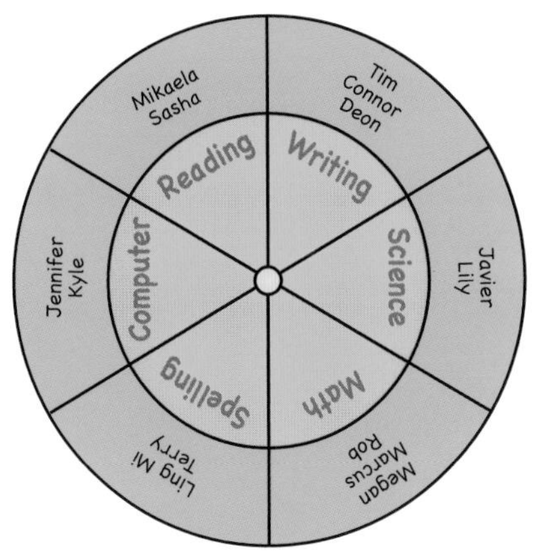

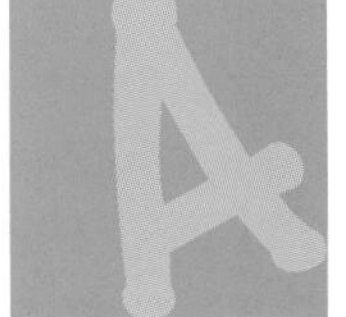

I use a rotating wheel to **assign students** to centers. I cut one large circle and one small circle from poster board and laminate them. I fasten the circles together with a brass fastener and divide the circles according to the number of centers I have. I use a wipe-off marker to label each of the outer sections with student names and each inner section with a different center name. Then I assign students to different centers by simply spinning the inner wheel. When I am ready to change the centers or student groupings, the wheel is a cinch to clean and reprogram!

Teresa Phillips, Belle Terre Elementary, Palm Coast, FL

It's your turn! Share your ideas.
themailbox.com/submitideas

Problem Solved!

How do you *strengthen* *communication* with students' families?

Your Solutions to Classroom Challenges

I post a **large colorful calendar** outside my classroom and mark important dates for parents, volunteers, and school personnel. Next to the calendar, I put a paper titled "Coming Next Month" with a list of upcoming dates to remember. The families of my students appreciate this handy reference!

Erin Ohanlon, Marion T. Academy Charter School, Wilmington, DE

To keep track of notes parents have sent to school, I personalize a **sheet protector** for each student and store the sheets in a three-ring binder. Any note or communication I might need to refer to is stored in that child's sheet protector.

Vanessa Rivera, La Luz Elementary, La Luz, NM

"Parents want to know what is going on for their child in school. They prefer informal contact that is positive, regular, private, planned, nonintrusive, two-way, and early enough to make a difference."

—Sue Roffey

A **parent binder** is a wonderful way to keep families up-to-date! On top of our cubbies, I keep a three-ring binder. In it, I place every note, letter, reminder, and monthly calendar I send home. The binder is a handy reference for parents, and it gives me a running dialogue of my entire year!

Parent
Binder

AnnaLisa R. Damminger, West Jersey Child Development Center, Voorhees, NJ

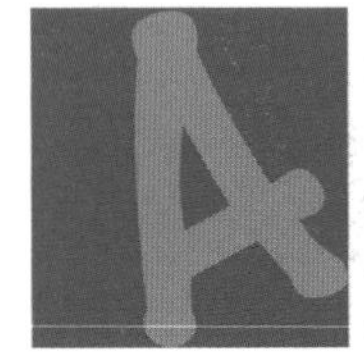

If I have something I absolutely need parents to see that day, I make **bracelet notes**! I print a class supply of the note, cut the notes apart, and then tape one around each child's wrist. My students love them!

Jamie Slack, Chavez Elementary, Little Elm, TX

I prepare batches of colorful **quick notes** with information I know I'll need to send home periodically, such as a standard thank-you note, a quick-to-program "supply needed" note, or a little checklist such as the one shown. Then I simply grab the appropriate note when I need it, insert necessary details, and pop it in the youngster's backpack!

Toni Gardiner, Lincoln Park Elementary, Muskegon, MI

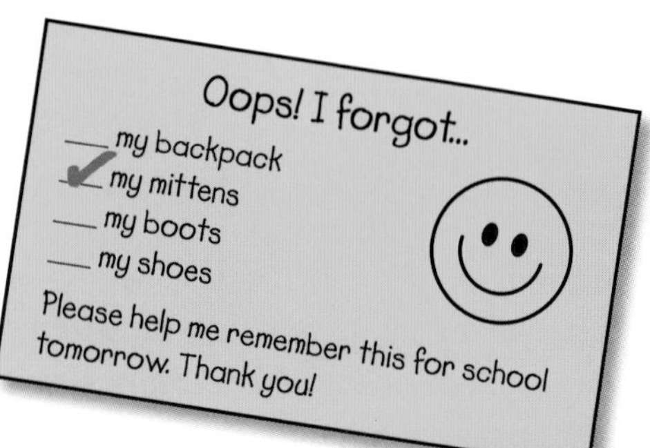
Oops! I forgot...
my backpack
my mittens
my boots
my shoes
Please help me remember this for school tomorrow. Thank you!

It's your turn! Share your ideas.
themailbox.com/submitideas

Problem Solved!

How do you help a substitute teacher *have a successful day?*

Your Solutions to Classroom Challenges

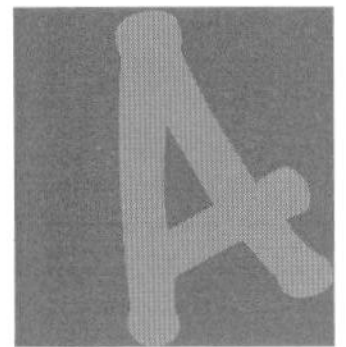

These **nametags** are really helpful for my substitutes! I purchase clip-style plastic name badges and slide a student name card into each one. Then each student simply clips on his sturdy name badge for easy identification.

Kelly Lu, Berlyn School, Ontario, Canada

I help a substitute teacher **locate supplies and manipulatives** by taking a photo of each area in my room. On the back of each photo, I label the items that can be found in that area. For example, the math area contains math workbooks, number magnets, dice, counters, and linking cubes. This has been really helpful!

Clare Cox, Homer Davis Elementary, Tucson, AZ

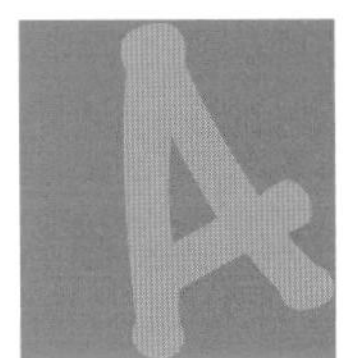

I show youngsters a **stuffed toy lamb** and mention that the lamb is watching them anytime a substitute is called to cover class. I explain how the lamb will report any positive happenings as well as any concerns. I display the lamb in the room and leave a feedback sheet, such as the one shown, for the substitute. My youngsters always try to behave for the lamb.

Keeping My Eyes on "Ewe"!
Substitute Report

Highlights of the day: ____________

Concerns: ____________

Teacher: ________ Date: ______

Janice Burch, Tri-Valley Elementary, Downs, IL

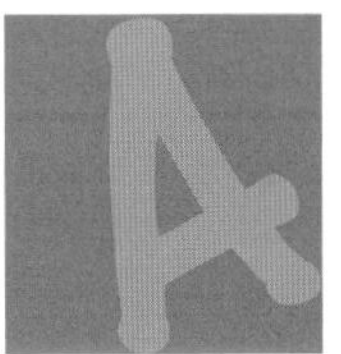

I put all my **daily songs** on one CD. I use a permanent marker to label the CD with the song order, and then I place it in the folder with my sub plans. This makes it simple for the substitute to find each song needed.

Joni Shuler, Catlettsburg Elementary, Sevierville, TN

"There was a time when substitute teachers were considered hired babysitters, but those days are gone. With today's focus on standardized test scores, schools are taking a closer look at who's teaching children when the permanent teacher is out."

—Reg Weaver, Former National Education Association President

It's your turn! Share your ideas.
themailbox.com/submitideas

Problem Solved!

Your Solutions to Classroom Challenges

How do you challenge youngsters who *finish their work early*?

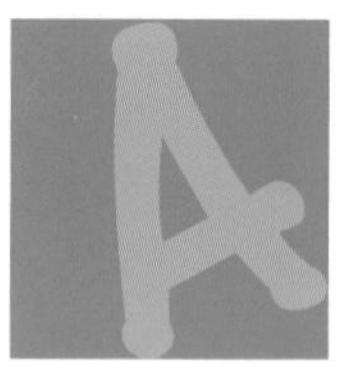

I cut out and laminate **comic strips**. Then I cut the individual frames and place each set in a resealable plastic bag. When a child finishes his work early, he chooses a bag and sequences the frames.

Suzanne Moore, Tucson, AZ

I create **Busy Bee Books**! For each child, I stock an inexpensive three-ring binder with writing paper, drawing paper, and skill sheets that relate to our current focus. If a child finishes his work early, he gets his Busy Bee Book and chooses one of the options.

Donna Buck, Bowers Elementary
Harriman, TN

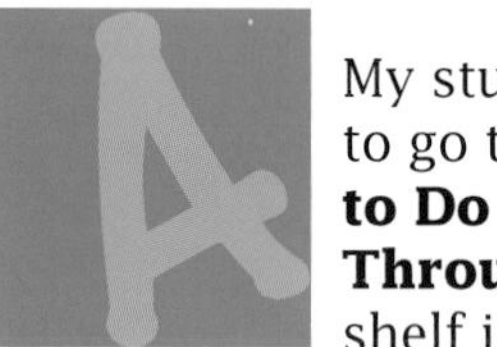

My students know to go to the **"What to Do When I Am Through" shelf**. This shelf is stocked with baskets containing picture books, individual whiteboards, writing paper, art supplies, dominoes, and other items. A child chooses a basket and takes it to his desk to complete an activity. I make sure I switch the items in the baskets frequently to keep interest high and to focus on our current skills.

Suzanne Moore

"Anchor activities are classroom learning opportunities for students at the beginning of class, when a lesson finishes early, or when individual students have completed their work....Anchor activities should give students an opportunity to be challenged by the curriculum material or receive exposure to it in a low-stress format."

—Catherine Lovering

I put extra skill sheets in a box that I refer to as our **"Dig It" box**. When students have extra time, they dig through the sheets to find one they would like to complete for extra practice.

Alisha George, Haley Elementary, Chandler, AZ

Early finishers in my class have the option of adding to a **classroom mural**. At the beginning of the week, I tape a length of white paper to a wall and announce a theme, such as friendship, dinosaurs, or insects. When a child finishes his work, he uses markers and crayons to add drawings and text to the interactive mural.

Marianne Cerra, St. Ignatius R.C. Elementary, Sinking Spring, PA

It's your turn! Share your ideas.
themailbox.com/submitideas

Reading Tips & Tools

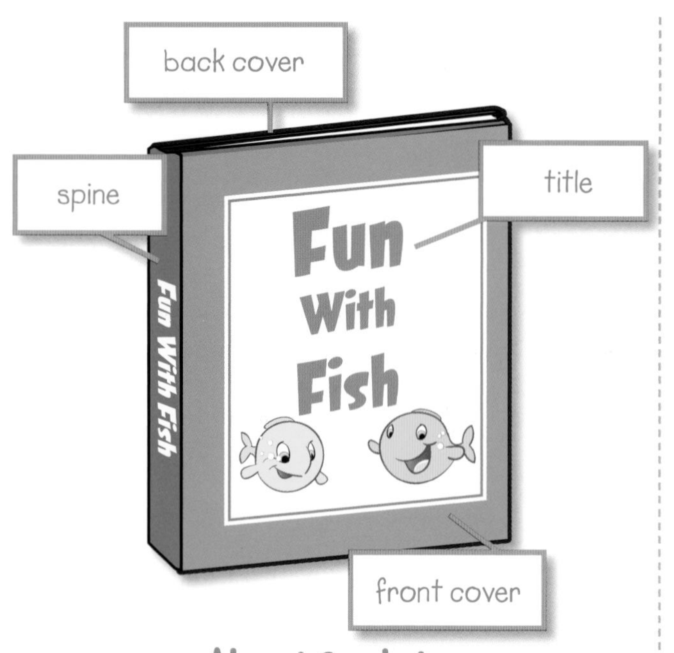

About Books!

Concepts of print (RI.K.5)

Students point to different parts of a nonfiction book while singing this little ditty. Give each youngster a book. Before singing, have each child point to the front cover, back cover, title on the cover, and spine. Then guide him to turn to the title page and point to the title, author, and illustrator. Explain that if an illustrator is not specified, the author is also the illustrator. Then lead students in singing the song shown and pointing to the corresponding parts of the book.

(sung to the tune of "Ten Little Indians")

Front cover, back cover, title, and spine,
Front cover, back cover, title, and spine,
Front cover, back cover, title, and spine—
We know the parts of a book.

Title page, title, author, and illustrator,
Title page, title, author, and illustrator,
Title page, title, author, and illustrator—
We know the parts of a book.

Donna Williams
River Ridge Elementary
Moore, SC

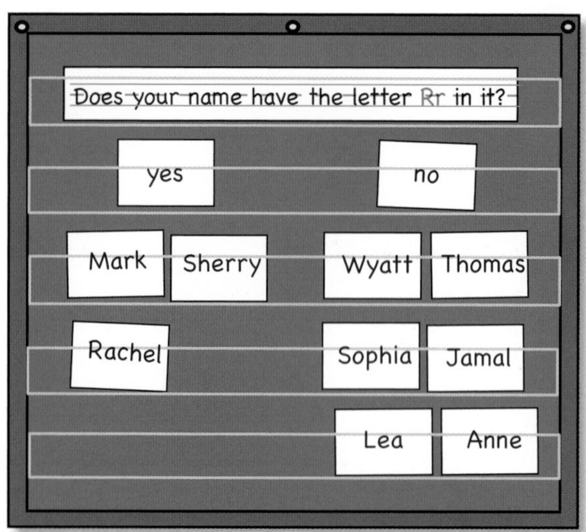

Letter of the Day

Letter recognition (RF.K.1d)

Students' names are on display with this pocket chart activity. To prepare, put "yes" and "no" cards in the second row of a pocket chart and set students' name cards nearby. Write the question prompt on a sentence strip, leaving a space to feature a letter, and laminate the strip. To begin, use a wipe-off marker to write a letter in the space and post the strip in the top row of the chart. Have each child put her name card under the corresponding heading. Then lead youngsters to recognize the placement of the featured letter in each child's name and any names that have more than one of that letter. To feature a different letter, simply wipe off the strip and begin again!

Amy Kerrigan
Frostick Elementary
Croswell, MI

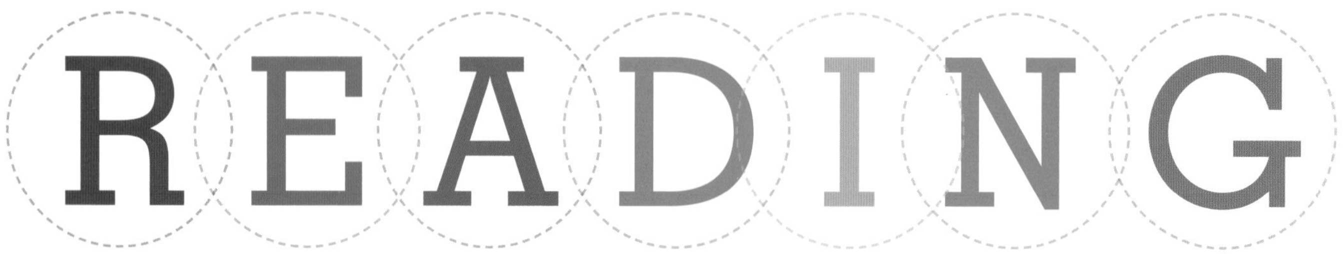

tips & tools

What's Missing?

Letter knowledge (RF.K.1d)

Practice ABC order and letter recognition with this small-group activity. Place several magnetic letters in order on a cookie sheet. Hold it up for the group to see and then secretly remove one letter. Then show the sheet again and invite your young detectives to solve the case of the missing letter! When the letter is correctly named, line up different letters for more practice. **For a whole-group alternative,** cover several letters on your classroom alphabet strip and have youngsters name the missing letters.

Nicole Liversage
Associazione Culturale Linguistica Educational
Via Roma, Sanremo, Imperia, Italy

Singing Sounds

Segmenting words (RF.K.3a, b)

Here's a song that will help youngsters review a vowel sound and isolate each sound in a word. Write a CVC word on the board and draw a simple picture to match. Have youngsters use the picture to help them read the word. Then lead youngsters in singing the song shown and pointing to the corresponding letters as you sing. Continue with different words as time permits.

(sung to the tune of "Where Is Thumbkin?")

Teacher: Here's a short [a].
Students: There's a short [a].
Teacher: [/a/, /a/, /a/].
Students: [/a/, /a/, /a/].
Teacher: Let's all read the word now.
Students: We can read the word now!
All: [/b/, /a/, /t/].

adapted from an idea by Abby Beahan
Zela Davis Elementary
Hawthorne, CA

Curtain Call

High-frequency words (RF.K.3c)

These little swimmers are sure to capture students' attention! Write different high-frequency words on theme-related cutouts, such as pond or ocean critters. Then tape the cutouts to a blue shower curtain. To begin, signal students to move to the curtain by saying "Bath time!" Then invite a child to use a long-handled scrub brush as a pointer to lead the class in reading the words. **For added fun,** provide a bathrobe and a pair of slippers for the youngster to wear.

Amy Hart
Saint Sylvester School
Pittsburgh, PA

See page 148 for a skill sheet on high-frequency words.

Favorable Fingerprints

Concepts of print (RF.K.1a, c)

These fingerprints help students practice reading from left to right, develop the concept of word, and improve fluency. Give each child in a small group a reproducible booklet and an ink pad. As you lead each youngster in reading the text, have her use her ink pad to make a fingerprint under each word. Then have her wash her hands and return to reread the story, pointing to a fingerprint as she reads each word.

Kate Szyszko
American School of Warsaw
Konstancin-Jeziorna, Poland

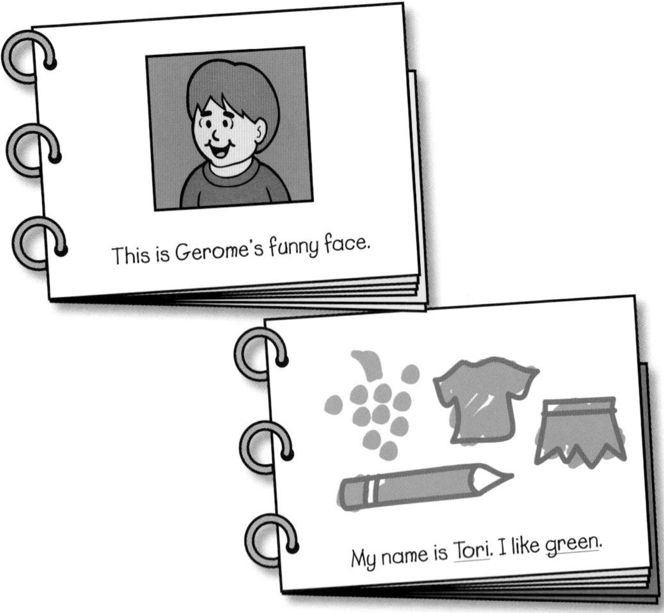

Personalized Pages

High-frequency words (RF.K.3c)

After making and reading these class books, students are sure to recognize the words *this*, *is*, *my*, *I*, and *like*; their classmates' names; and basic color words! For each book, follow the directions below to have students create the pages. Then bind the completed pages between construction paper covers. If desired, provide each child the opportunity to take a turn taking the book home to read to family members.

- **Funny Faces:** Take a photograph of each student while he makes a funny face. Glue the photos on separate sheets of paper (book pages). Then guide each child to write on his page to complete the sentence "This is ________'s funny face."
- **Color Preferences:** Have each child select a favorite basic color. Guide her to write the sentence shown on a sheet of paper (book page), filling in the blanks with her name and a color word. Then have her use the matching-color crayon to draw pictures on her page.

Amy Lloyd
Neary Elementary
Haverstraw, NY

tips & tools

Singers on the Move

High-frequency words (RF.K.3c)

Students will find reading reminders all around the school with this idea! Write different high-frequency words on separate bus cutouts (pattern on page 156). Display one bus in the classroom and post the remaining buses around the school where your youngsters will see them. Next, point to the bus in the room, name the featured word, and lead youngsters in singing the song below. Then tell youngsters to be on the lookout for other buses as they travel around the school. When a bus is spotted, encourage the group to quietly sing the song using the appropriate word. Go!

(sung to the tune of "The Wheels on the Bus")

The word on the bus is [go, go, go],
[Go, go, go, go, go, go].
The word on the bus is [go, go, go]
All around the school.

Wendy Wellman
Tri-Center Community Schools
Neola, IA

Seek the Sticky Dots!

Letter-sound associations (RF.K.3)

Students will see several words with the same beginning letter after this classroom scavenger hunt. Put a sticky dot on each of several classroom objects whose names begin with the same sound and letter. To begin, instruct youngsters to look around the room for the sticky dots. For each movable object, encourage the child who finds it to place it in a designated area. Next, gather youngsters and ask different volunteers to point to and name the objects found. Write each response on the board. Then read the resulting list and lead youngsters to make connections between the featured beginning sound and the first letter of each word.

Margi Saks
Park East Day School
St. Bronx, NY

The Doctor Is In

Sentence structure (L.K.1f)

Gather a small group of students (sentence surgeons) for this unscrambling activity. Write different sentences on separate paper strips so there is one for each student. Then cut between the words to make word cards. Put each set of word cards in a separate resealable plastic bag. Instruct each sentence surgeon to arrange a set of cards to form a sentence. Guide him to use the capital letter and punctuation as clues. After writing the sentence, encourage group members to trade bags and begin again. **For added fun**, write the words on bone cutouts for surgeons to line up bone to bone.

tip: Write each sentence on different-color paper for easy management.

See page 150 for a **practice page** on ending sounds.

Save the Princess!

Rhyming (RF.K.2a)

The child who stacks seven rhyming steps is the hero of this partner game. Make a copy of pages 157 and 158. Cut apart the cards and put them at a center with the game mat. The two players stack the cards facedown, and each youngster chooses one side of the tower. To take a turn, a player names the pictures on a card. If the words rhyme, he puts the card (step) on his side of the tower. If the words do not rhyme, he sets the card aside. Play continues until one player has seven steps and saves the princess!

Janice Burch
Tri-Valley Elementary
Downs, IL

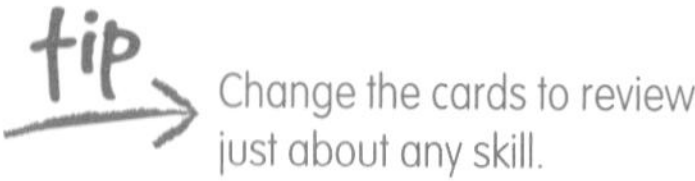

Change the cards to review just about any skill.

Read the Flapjacks

High-frequency words (RF.K.3c)

Who wants to read words? Set out this pancake serving center and find out! Write a different high-frequency word on each of several paper plates. Write the same words on separate small felt circles (pancakes). Put the plates, the pancakes, a spatula, and a pan at a center. A child sets out the plates and puts the pancakes word-side up in the pan. Then she reads a word, scoops up that pancake with the spatula, and serves it on the matching plate. She continues with each remaining pancake. If time permits, she rereads the words and pretends to eat the pancakes.

Luann Baker
Redcliffe Elementary
Aiken, SC

tips & tools

Gingerbread Comparisons

Comparing and contrasting storybooks (RL.K.9)

Your favorite versions of a familiar tale are perfect for this whole-group activity. Select a gingerbread-character story—such as *The Gingerbread Man*, *The Gingerbread Cowboy*, *Gingerbread Baby*, or *Gingerbread Friends*—to read aloud. After reading the story, have youngsters name the characters, setting, problem, and solution. Record the story element responses on a poster or graphic organizer of your choice. Later, read a different version of the tale and repeat the follow-up activity. Then use the posters to discuss the similarities and differences between the stories. Continue with additional stories and posters as desired.

Vicky Morgan
Kathleen Elementary
Lakeland, FL

Sing That Lesson

Letter-sound associations (RF.K.3)

This little ditty can be adapted for any vowel or consonant. Sing the first two lines of the song. Then signal youngsters to join you in singing the rest of the song. Continue singing different verses, inserting words, letters, and sounds where needed.

(sung to the tune of "Bingo")

There is a [vowel] whose name is [A],
And [A] is for [*apple*].
[/a/, /a/, /a/, apple].
[/a/, /a/, /a/, apple].
[/a/, /a/, /a/, apple].
This letter is a [vowel].

Elizabeth White
Forest Ridge Elementary
Laurel, MD

Read, Roll, and Repeat!

Comprehension (RL.K.10; RI.K.10)

Students are sure to be alert during storytime when they see this question cube! Write a different reading response prompt on each side of a cube. Keep the cube nearby as you begin to read a story aloud. When desired, roll the cube and have youngsters respond to the prompt that lands faceup. Continue to read and roll, calling on different volunteers to participate throughout the story. Students will not only be on their toes to talk, they will also gain plenty of practice answering comprehension questions.

Lori Dworsky
Richardson Park Learning Center
Wilmington, DE

See page 151 for a **practice page** on reading and writing sentences.

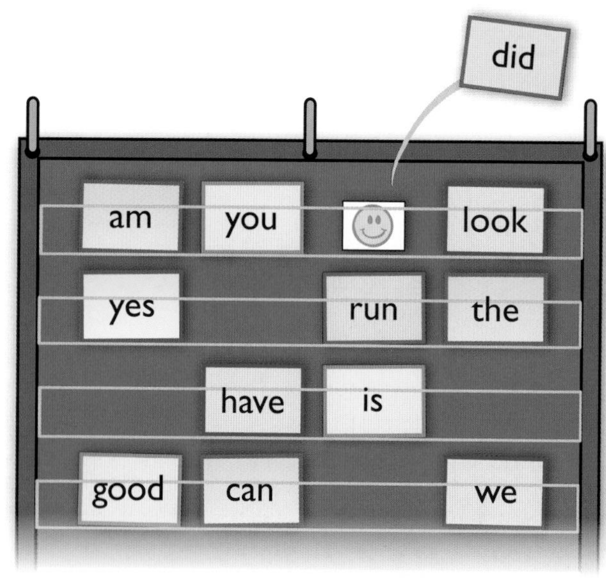

Read and Do!

Skill review (CCSS)

These file folders provide ready-to-use reading activities at your fingertips. To make one, write the text of a leveled reader or other student book on an open file folder and write the title of the book on the tab. Laminate the folder. Then write on a card a task, such as underlining high-frequency words, highlighting punctuation, or circling vocabulary. Put the card and the book in the file folder. A child takes the file folder, reads the book, and then uses wipe-off markers to write his name on the folder and complete the task. When time permits, it is easy for you to check his work, make notes to monitor his progress, and then wipe the folder clean for reuse!

Linda Edwards
Brinson Memorial Elementary
New Bern, NC

Find the Smiley Face!

High-frequency words (RF.K.3c)

Teams of students read words to reveal the winner of this partner game. Put different high-frequency word cards in your pocket chart. Secretly slide a smiley face card behind one of the words. Then invite each of two teams to sit by the chart. To play, a child from Team 1 takes a turn reading a word. If she is correct, she removes the card and sits with it. If she is not correct, her turn is over. Then Team 2 takes a turn. When the smiley face card is revealed, that team gets a point. To continue, return all the cards to the pocket chart and hide the smiley face card for the next round. The first team to get five points wins.

Kiva English
Cato-Meridian Central School
Cato, NY

tips & tools

Silly Soup

Initial consonants and sounds (RF.K.3)

Sing this little ditty and prompt your young chefs to name interesting ingredients! Sing the first two lines of the song to gather students near a pot containing letter tiles of your choice. As youngsters sing the third line, show a letter from the pot for students to name in the last line of the song. Then draw a pot outline on chart paper and label it as shown. Invite volunteers to share different food names that begin with the featured letter and list the foods on the pot. Continue with different letters on other days as time permits.

(sung to the tune of "Short'nin' Bread")

Teacher: Lots of ingredients make a silly soup.
Will you make this soup with me?
Students: Yes, we'll help you make a silly soup.
[*P*] is the letter that we see!

adapted from an idea by Marie E. Cecchini
West Dundee, IL

Silly Pp Soup
peas
pickles
popcorn
peanuts
pasta
pancakes
potatoes

What's the Word?

Syllables (RF.K.2b), word meanings (L.K.5c)

No materials are needed for this whole-group activity! Simply give two clues for a chosen word: the first clue tells the number of syllables in the word, and the second clue relates specifically to that word. For example, for *tractor*, say, "It is a two-syllable word. It is something you can drive on a farm." Then encourage youngsters to guess the mystery word, guiding them to make connections to the clues for each guess. For added support, provide extra clues. When the correct word is named, discuss how each clue relates to the chosen word. Continue with different words.

Jodi Darter
Cabool Elementary
Cabool, MO

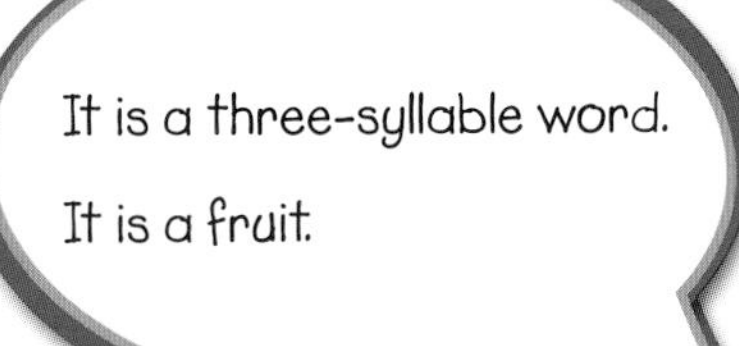

It is a three-syllable word.
It is a fruit.

Act It Out!

Story elements (RL.K.3), retelling (RL.K.2)

Three houses, three pigs, and a wolf are the perfect props to reenact the story of the *Three Little Pigs*! After sharing your favorite version of the tale, guide youngsters to identify the story's characters, its setting, the problem, and the solution. Next, have each child color and cut out a copy of the story cards on page 159. Instruct him to glue the house of straw and the house of sticks to separate paper tents. Have him glue the brick house to a tagboard tent. Then encourage him to use his props as he retells the story, gently blowing on each of the houses for the wolf.

adapted from an idea by Donna Pollhammer
Charles Carroll Elementary
Westminster, MD

Don't miss the **skill sheet** on page 152.

On the Nose!

High-frequency words (RF.K.3c)

This clown craft makes reading words tons of fun! Give each child a copy of the clown patterns on page 160 along with a large paper plate and six paper circles (noses). Instruct each child to write a different high-frequency word on each of the noses; help him stack and staple the noses to the center of the plate. Next, have him color, cut out, and glue his patterns on the plate so it resembles a clown. Then encourage pairs of students to take turns reading their noses. For added fun, encourage youngsters to use a variety of silly clown voices while reading their words.

Kim Power
Houston, TX

Tune In!

Reading foundational skills

These two little ditties are perfect for a phonics review! Put letters in a box and sing the first little ditty below, which prompts youngsters to name different letters and corresponding sounds. For a word-reading version, put word cards in a box and check out the second variation of the tune.

Jackie Wright
Summerhill Children's House
Enid, OK

Letter identification (RF.K.1d), letter-sound relationships (RF.K.3a)
(sung to the tune of "Mary Had a Little Lamb")

Pick a letter from the box,
From the box, from the box.
Pick a letter from the box.
Please say its name and sound!

Reading words (RF.K.3)
(sung to the tune of "Mary Had a Little Lamb")

Pick a word card from the box,
From the box, from the box.
Pick a word card from the box.
Please read and say that word!

Read a Row

Word families (RF.K.3d)

With this variation of bingo, the matching rimes in the columns serve as helpful hints for students to read words. Choose five word families. Write six or more words for each word family on separate craft sticks and put them word-side down in a container. Using the same words shown on the craft sticks, prepare gameboards similar to the one shown for a small group of students.

To begin, give each player a gameboard and 20 game markers. Then play as in the traditional game of bingo until one child has five game markers in a row and says, "I can read a row!" After confirming accuracy, have youngsters clear their boards to begin a new round.

Jeanne-Marie Peterson
Crozet, VA

-an	-ap	-ug	-in	-op
can	map	bug	fin	mop
pan	tap	rug	win	top
man	lap	mug	pin	hop
fan	nap	hug	tin	pop

Eat the /a/ Words!

Short-vowel discrimination (RF.K.2)

Students pretend to be anteaters for this /a/, /a/, activity! Give each child a toy party blower and have her pretend that it is an anteater's tongue. Tell her that when she hears a word with /a/ as in *ant*, she should flick her tongue, pretending to eat that /a/ word! If she does not hear /a/, have her rub her tummy to show the anteater is still hungry. Then announce words, most of which have a short *a*, and encourage youngsters to respond as directed. **For an added challenge,** have youngsters repeat the vowel sound and name that letter for each word.

Brenda McGee
The Goddard School
Allen, TX

Fun fact! An anteater's tongue is about two feet long and is used to lick up lots of ants!

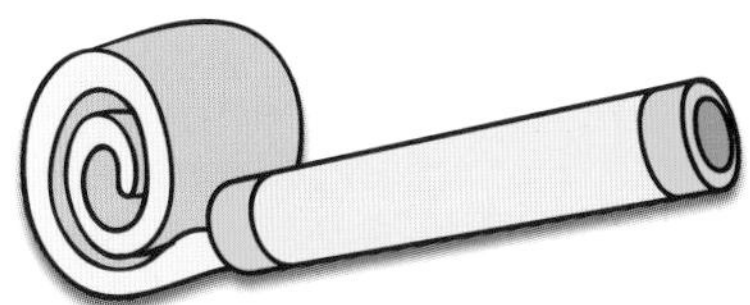

Day-by-Day Caterpillar

Following directions (SL.K.2), word recognition (RF.K.3)

How do listening skills, days of the week, and colors lead to a cool buggy project? Take a look! Provide each child a copy of the caterpillar patterns on page 161. Then give directions such as "Use a yellow crayon. Color the circle with the word *Thursday*." and "Find the circle with the word *Saturday*. Color that circle with a green crayon." Continue with different directions until the caterpillar patterns are colored. Then have each child cut out her patterns and order the days of the week to the right of the head. If she is correct, instruct her to glue her critter together and add construction paper legs.

For a literature-related extension, read aloud *The Very Hungry Caterpillar* by Eric Carle. When a day of the week is named in the story, encourage each youngster to point to that word on her caterpillar.

adapted from an idea by Diane Flohr Henderson, Kentwood, MI

A-E-I-O-U!

Long and short vowels (RF.K.2)

This little ditty prompts youngsters to name the sound of a chosen vowel and name words that begin with that sound! Sing the first two lines of the song, inserting the long- or short-vowel name of your choice. Then lead youngsters to sing the remainder of the song, pointing to different students to name words that begin with the featured sound in the fifth line. Repeat the same verse for more practice or change the featured vowel to review other vowels.

(sung to the tune of "Old MacDonald Had a Farm")

If you know the [short *a*] sound,
Sing it now for me!
Yes, we know the [short *a*] sound!
[/a/, /a/, /a/, /a/, /a/].
With an [apple] here and an [alligator] there,
Here an [/a/], there an [/a/], everywhere an [/a/, /a/].
Yes, we know the [short a] sound!
[/a/, /a/, /a/, /a/, /a/].

adapted from an idea by Andrea Batten
Yorktown Elementary
Yorktown, VA

Lucky Ducky

High-frequency words (RF.K.3c)

Students are sure to be eager to read the right high-frequency word with this little duck display! Write a different high-frequency word on each of several duck cutouts (patterns on page 162) and post them in a child-friendly location. To begin, chant the rhyme shown and then ask a volunteer to point to the duck that shows the word named in the third line. If she is correct, encourage her to waddle around the room one time, "quacking" the word along the way; if she is not correct, give a classmate the opportunity to find the word. Continue with different words when time permits for a great skill-based time filler!

I'm a lucky ducky
As anyone can see.
If you find the word [are],
You can point to little me!

Kim Power
Houston, TX

READING

tips & tools

Reading Race

Reading words (RF.K.3)

The object of this whole-group game is for students to beat their best time reading words. Have youngsters stand in a row facing the words and pass the pointer to one child. To start the game, check the time and have the child point to a word, read it, and prompt the class to repeat the word. Then have her hurry back to the row, pass the pointer to a classmate, and quickly sit down. Play continues until each child is seated. Record the stop time and announce the time to beat for the next round of reading. For added support, if a child gets to the display and cannot read a word, encourage her to return to the row, pick a classmate to be a helper, and have the twosome read a word together.

Cheryl Lee
Messiah Christian School
Reynoldsburg, OH

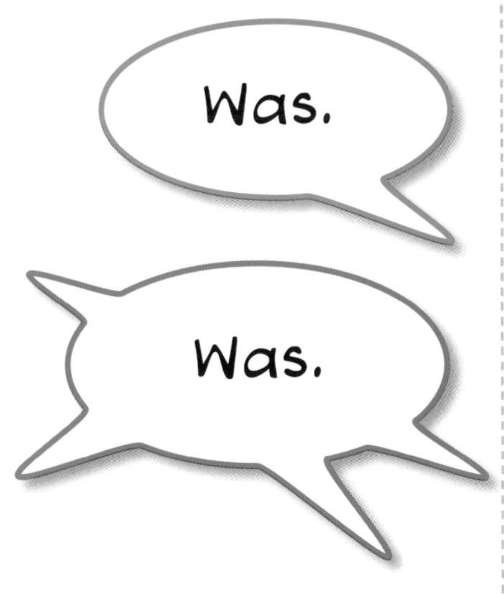

Time to Blend!

Word family: *-ock* (RF.K.3d)

This clock is the perfect tool to form an *-ock* word family. For each member in a small group, label a narrow paper strip with different onsets that form real words with *-ock*. Prepare a paper-plate clock for each child as shown, cutting each plate so the child can easily slide the prepared strips. Next, lead youngsters to read and write the *-ock* words. Then challenge each child to choose a word and use it in a sentence. If desired, have him draw a picture to match his writing.

Laura Del Prete
H. Russell Swift School
Egg Harbor Township, NJ

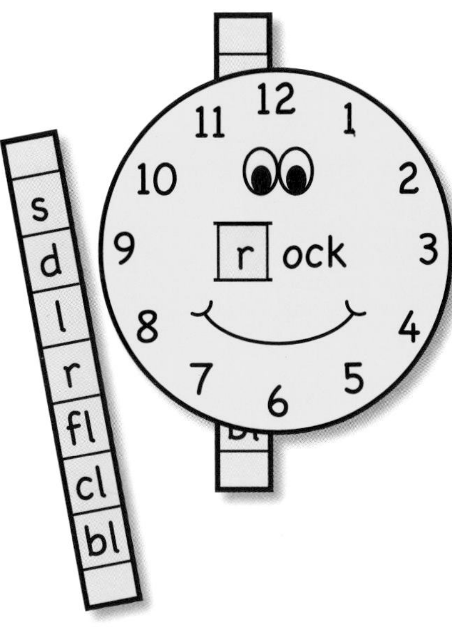

Side by Side

Word family review (RF.K.3d)

Add a little action to word work with this whole-group activity! Write onsets and rimes (see the suggestions below) on separate cards and write the matching rimes on the board as word family column headings. Then give each child a card. Name a word and invite the youngsters holding the corresponding word-part cards to stand side by side to form the word. Lead youngsters to blend together the word parts and have students tell you under which column the word belongs. Continue with different words until each child has had a turn to form a word.

Jennifer Willis
Oneco Elementary
Bradenton, FL

Card suggestions:
ack, ick, ock, uck, b, d, k, l, p, r, s, t, bl, cl, fl, sl, cr, tr

Resulting word list suggestions:
back, buck, dock, duck, kick, lack, lick, lock, luck, pack, pick, puck, rack, rock, sack, sick, sock, suck, tack, tick, tock, tuck, black, block, clack, click, clock, cluck, flick, flock, slack, slick, crack, track, trick, truck

Check out the **book report** form on page 155.

Sorting Activity

Each child cuts out a copy of the first card set below. On a copy of page 145, he places a different letter card at the top of each column. Then he sorts the remaining cards on the paper to match. **For more sorting practice**, he cuts out and sorts a copy of the second card set. ***Initial consonants (RF.K.3a)***

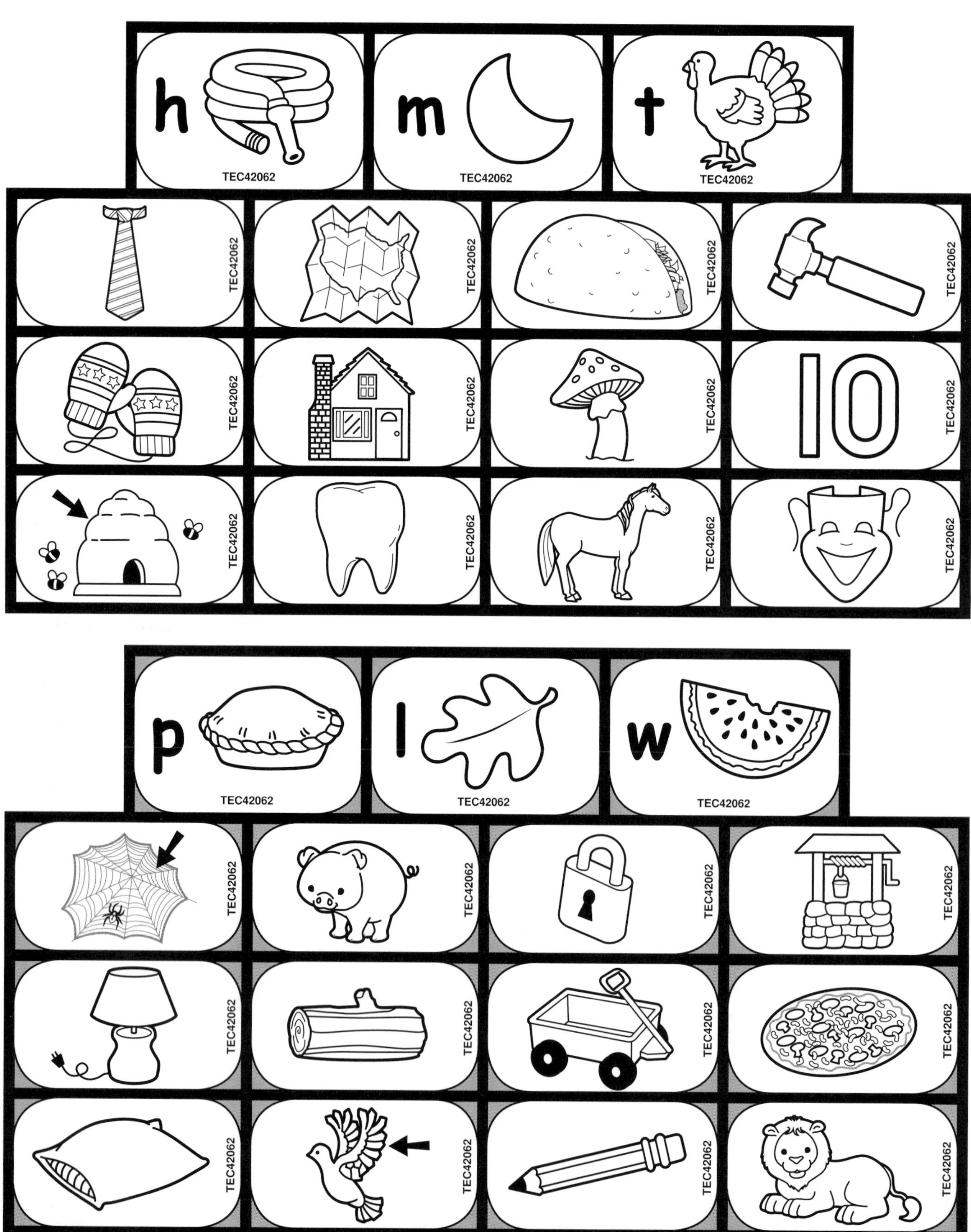

Name ______________________________

Initial consonants (RF.K.3a)

Meow!

Bonus: Name one more word that begins with each letter shown.

Bubble Bath

Note to the teacher: Use with the sorting activity on page 144.

Sorting Activity

Each child cuts out a copy of the first card set below. On a copy of page 147, she places an "ends like" card at the top of each column. Then she sorts the remaining cards on the paper to match. **For more sorting practice**, she cuts out and sorts a copy of the second card set.

Ending sounds /g/, /k/, /l/ (RF.K.2d)

ends like TEC42064	TEC42064	TEC42064	TEC42064
ends like TEC42064	TEC42064	TEC42064	TEC42064
ends like TEC42064	TEC42064	TEC42064	TEC42064

Ending sounds /n/, /p/, /t/ (RF.K.3)

Name ______________________________ Ending sounds (RF.K.2d)

Perfectly Popped!

Note to the teacher: Use with the sorting activity on page 146.

Name ____________________ High-frequency words (RF.K.3c)

Busy Bees

Trace. Cut.

Glue to match.

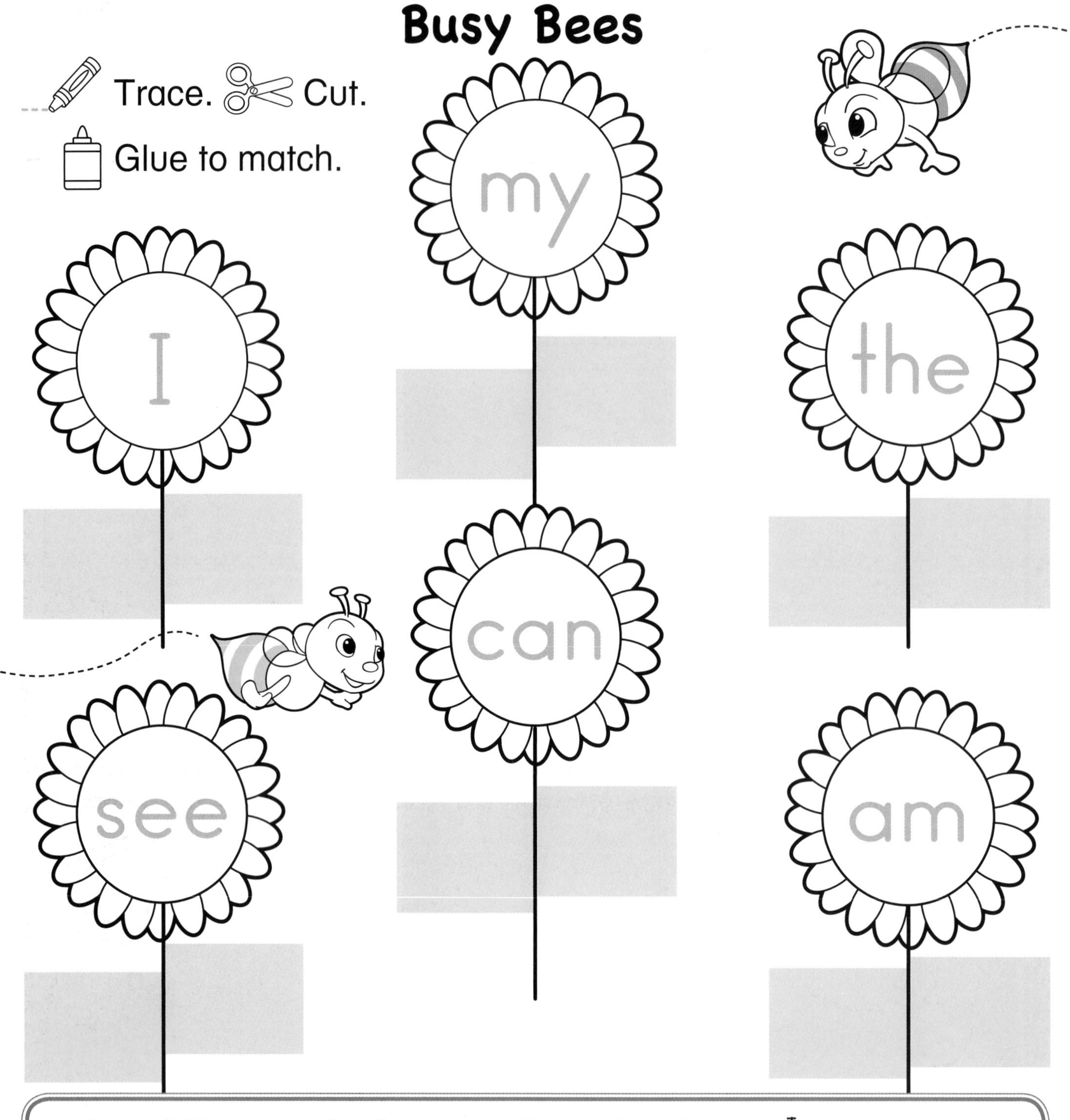

Bonus: Write and complete the sentence. Draw a picture to match. I see *my* ________.

my	the	see	am	I	can
see	can	I	my	the	am

For instant small-group skill review, keep a die and a copy of each card handy. Use the hot-air balloon card to reinforce phonological awareness. Use the rocket card for comprehension of literature. Invite each group member to take a turn rolling the die. Then read aloud the corresponding task for the child to complete, supplying a word when needed. (RF.K.2; RL.K.1–3)

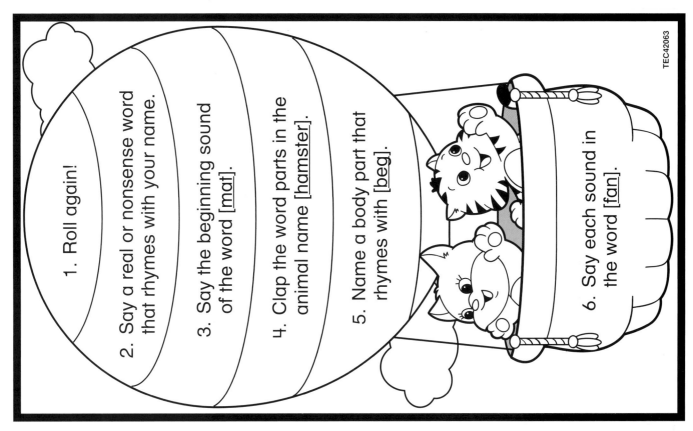

1. Roll again!
2. Say a real or nonsense word that rhymes with your name.
3. Say the beginning sound of the word [mat].
4. Clap the word parts in the animal name [hamster].
5. Name a body part that rhymes with [beg].
6. Say each sound in the word [fan].

TEC42063

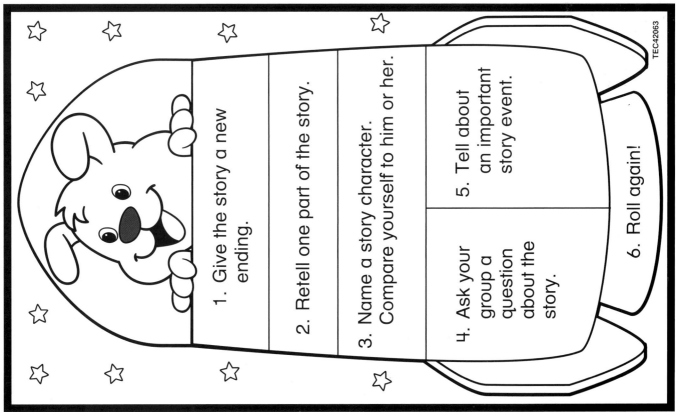

1. Give the story a new ending.
2. Retell one part of the story.
3. Name a story character. Compare yourself to him or her.
4. Ask your group a question about the story.
5. Tell about an important story event.
6. Roll again!

TEC42063

Name ______________________ Ending sounds (RF.K.2)

Munching Popcorn

Cut.

Glue to match ending sounds.

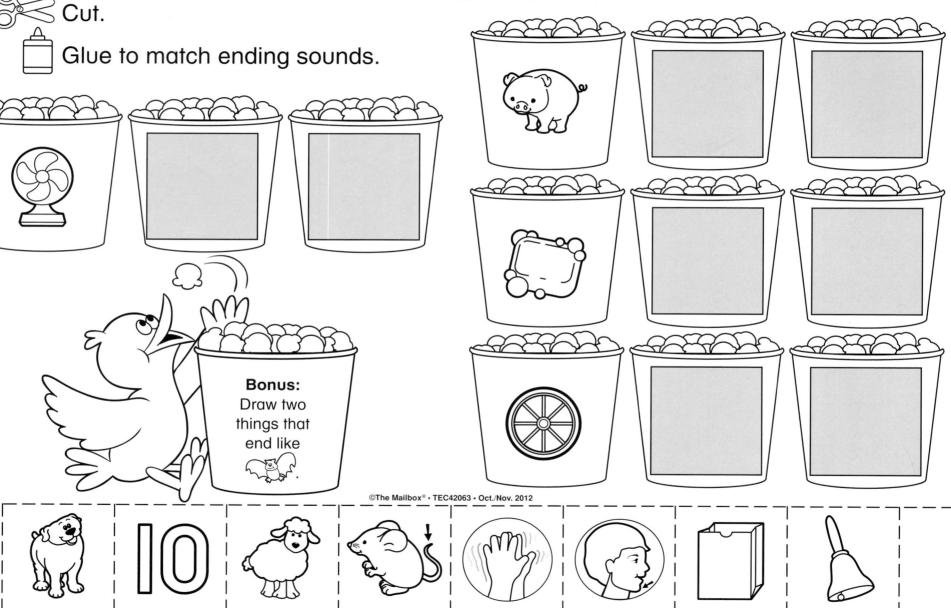

Bonus:
Draw two things that end like .

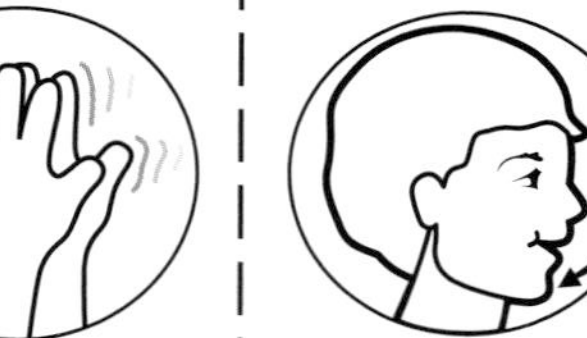
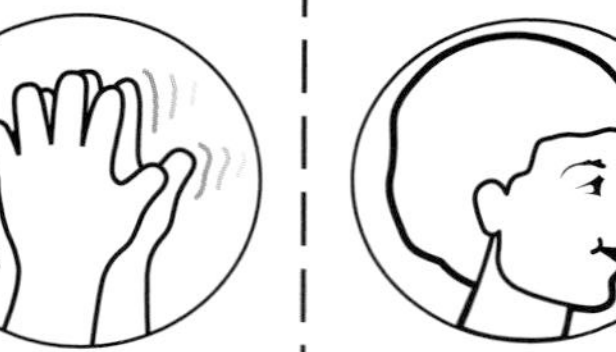
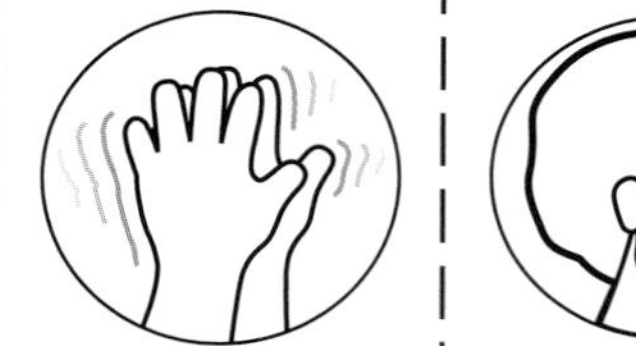

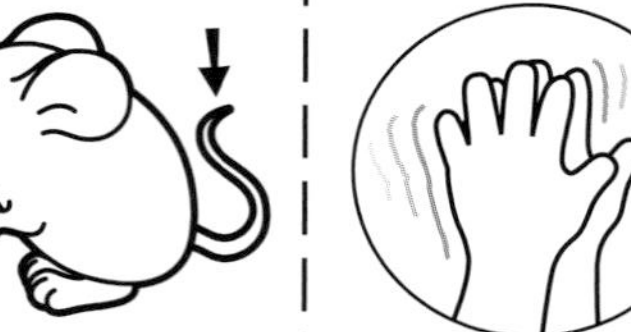

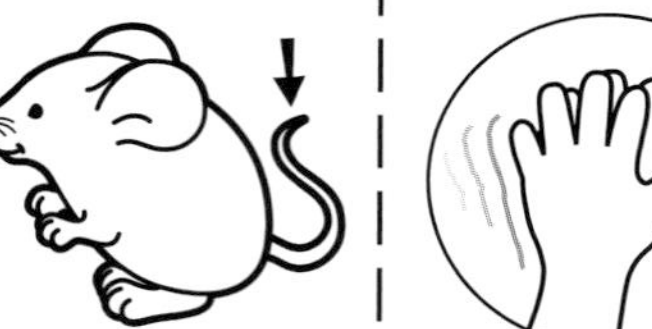
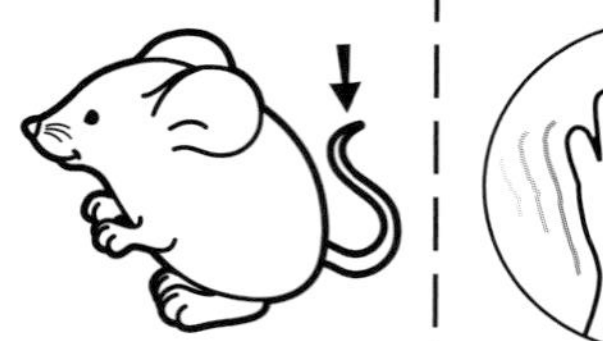

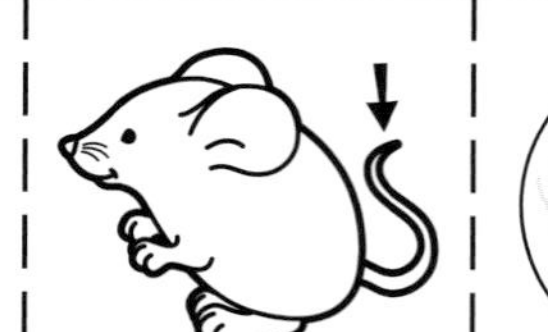
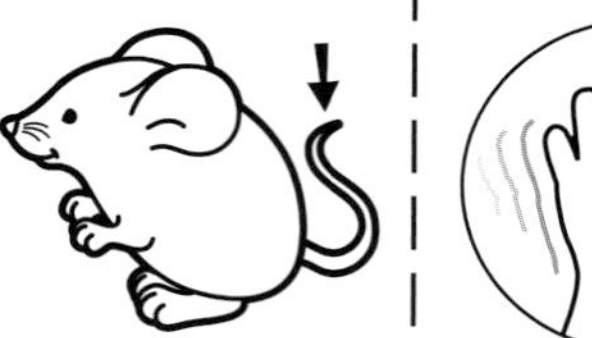
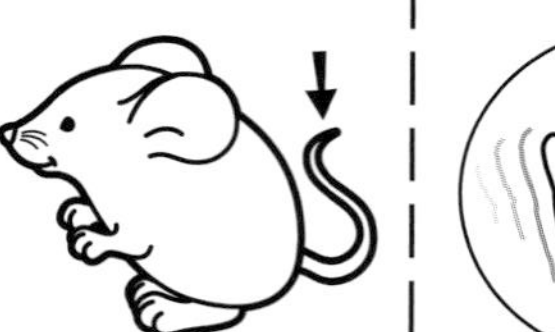
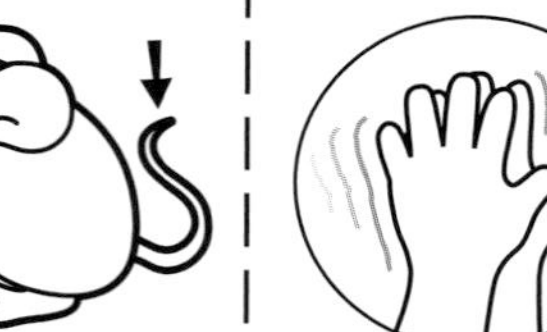

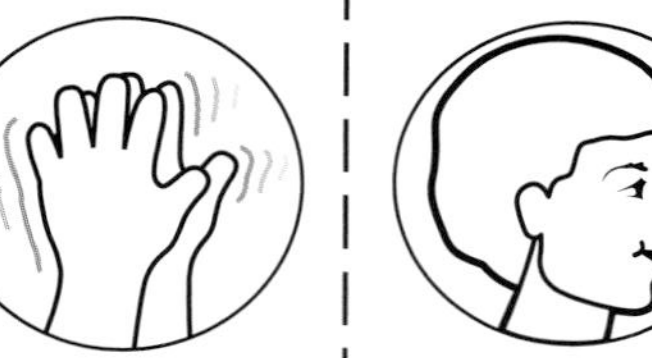
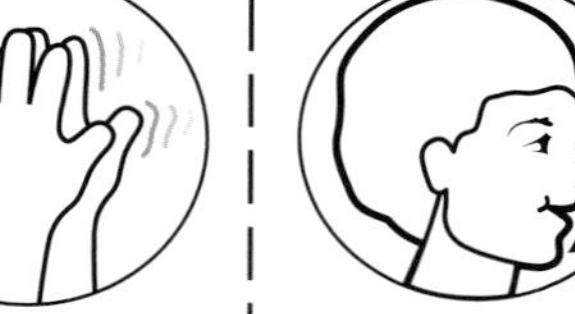

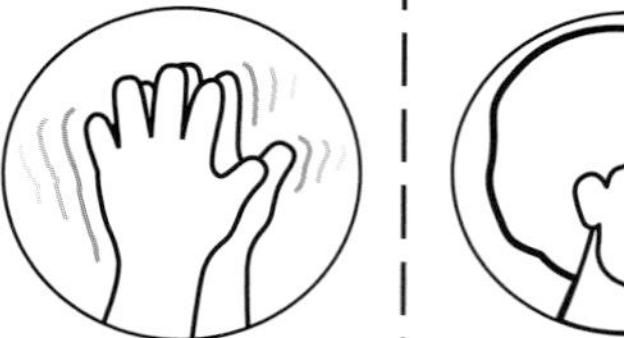
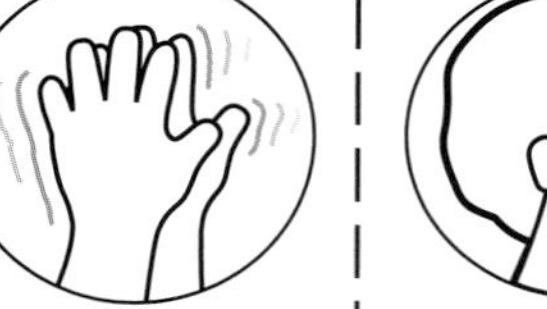

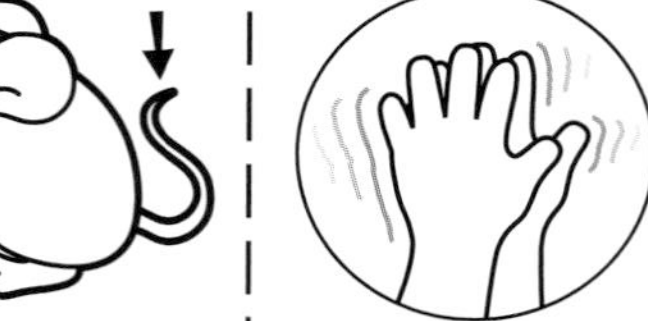

Name ________________________________ Reading and writing sentences (RF.K.3, L.K.2)

Max Can!

Write a sentence for each picture.
Use the words on the bone.

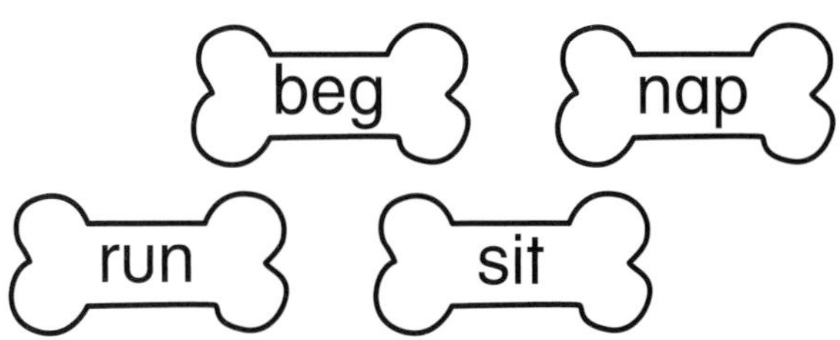

Max can run.

Max can ________________

____

____

Bonus: Write a different sentence about Max. Draw a picture to match.

Name ____________________ Color words and number words (RF.K.3c)

Fern's Flower Shop

Read and do.

A Color three red.
B Color two yellow.
C Color nine orange.
D Color one blue.
E Color five purple.
F Color six pink.
G Color two yellow.
H Color four red.

Bonus: Find the flowers that are not colored. Color them green. Write how many.

Name ______________________________ Making words (RF.K.3d)

Hide-and-Seek!

Change the last letter.

Write the word that matches the picture.

cat cap	pop	wet
bun	pig	dot

Bonus: Write the word **bat**. Change the last letter to **g** and write the new word. Draw pictures to match.

Name ______________________

Spelling words with short vowels: *a, i, u*
(RF.K.3b; L.K.2c)

Pigeon's Pails

Cut. Sort. Glue. Write each matching word.

ă as in hat	ĭ as in pig	ŭ as in sun

Bonus: Draw a picture to match each word. Label your drawings. **bat** **fun** **bug**

Name ______________________________ Book report (RL.K.3)

Book Buddy

Draw or write.

Beginning	Middle	End

Did you like the book? Circle. **yes** **no**

Write to tell why.

____

____

Bus Pattern

Use with “Singers on the Move” on page 135.

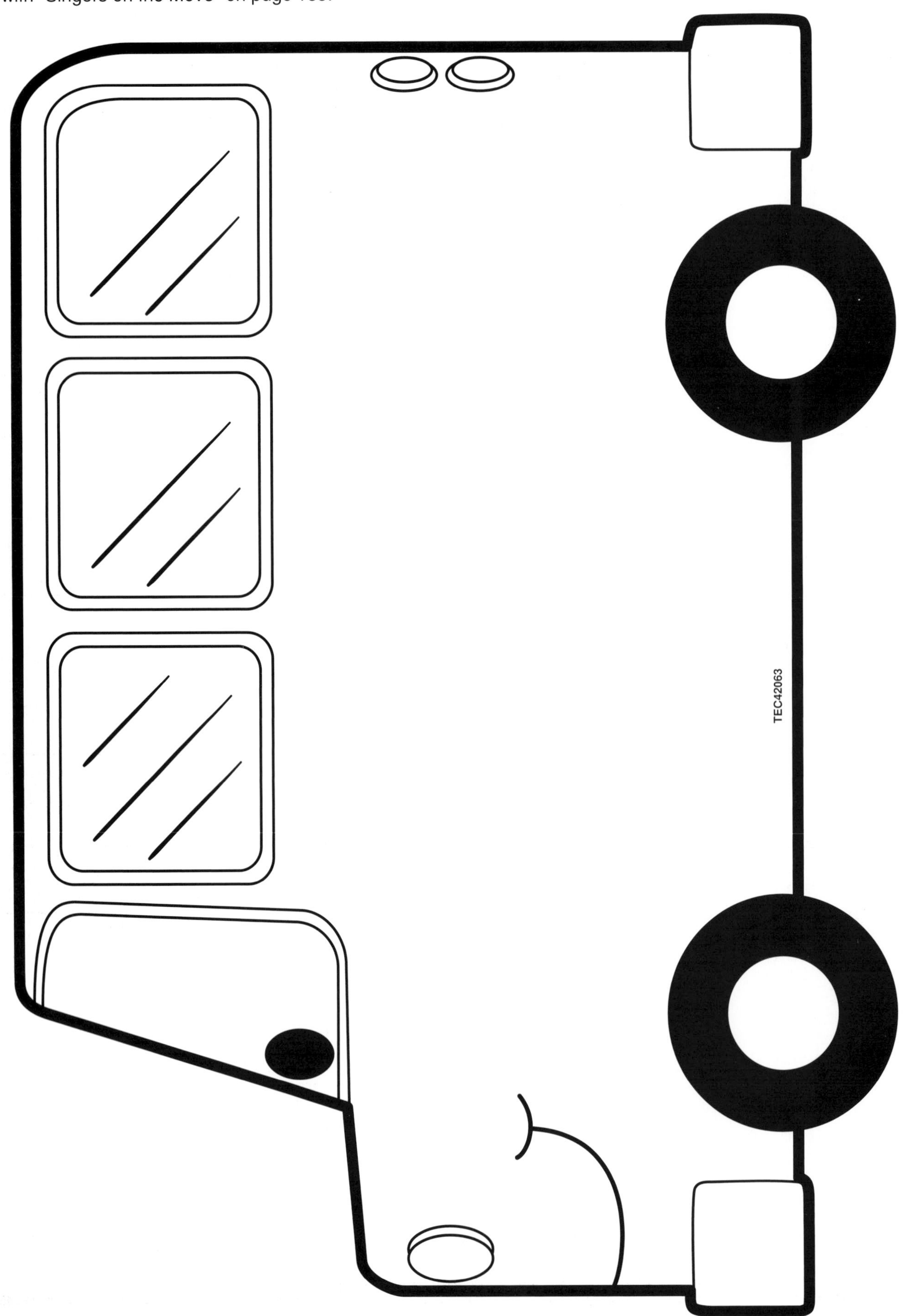

Note to the teacher: Use this game mat with "Save the Princess!" on page 136.

Game Cards

Use with "Save the Princess!" on page 136.

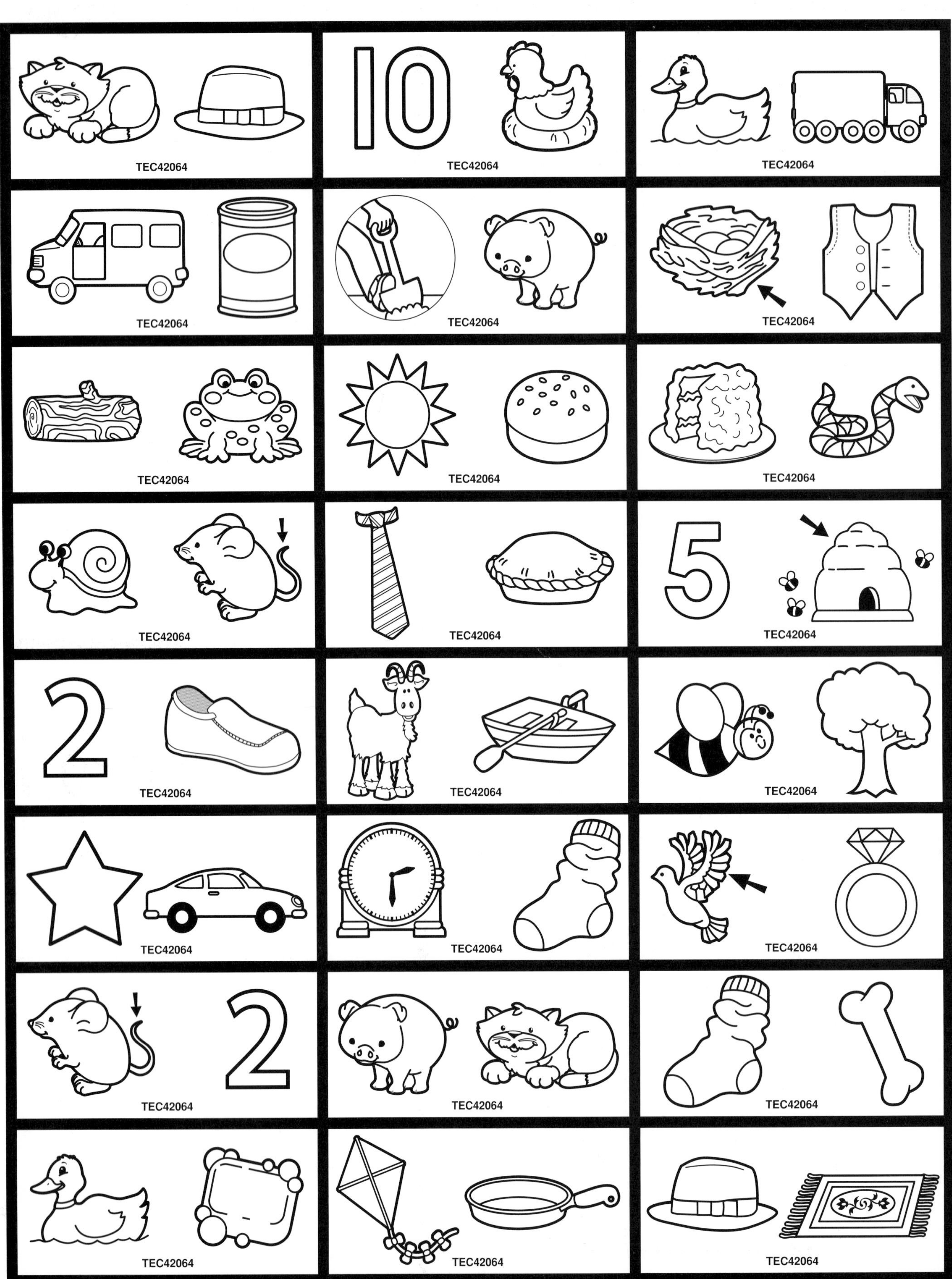

Story Cards

Use with "Act It Out!" on page 139.

Clown Patterns

Use with “On the Nose!” on page 140.

Use with “On the Nose!” on page 140.

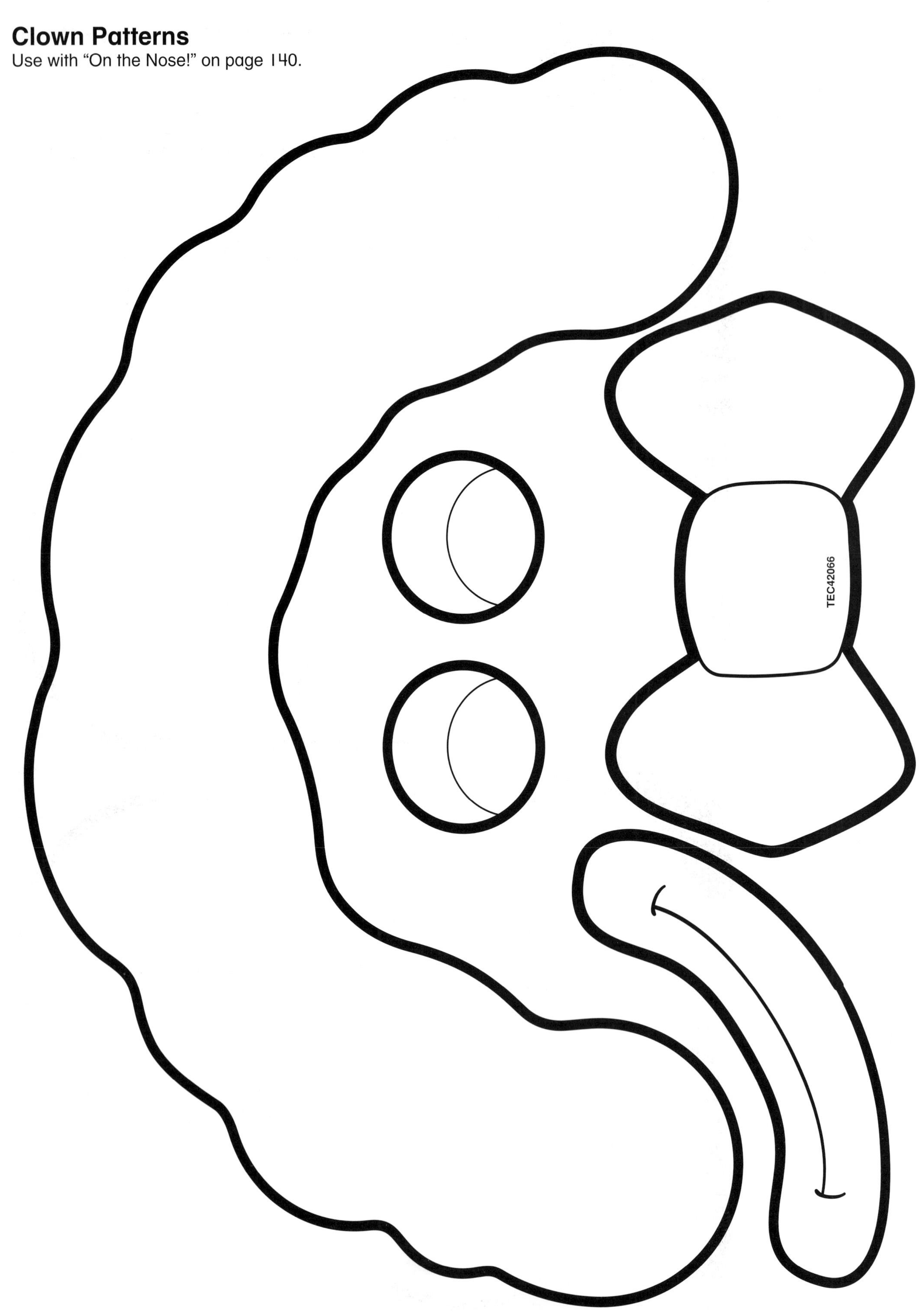

Caterpillar Patterns

Use with "Day-by-Day Caterpillar" on page 141.

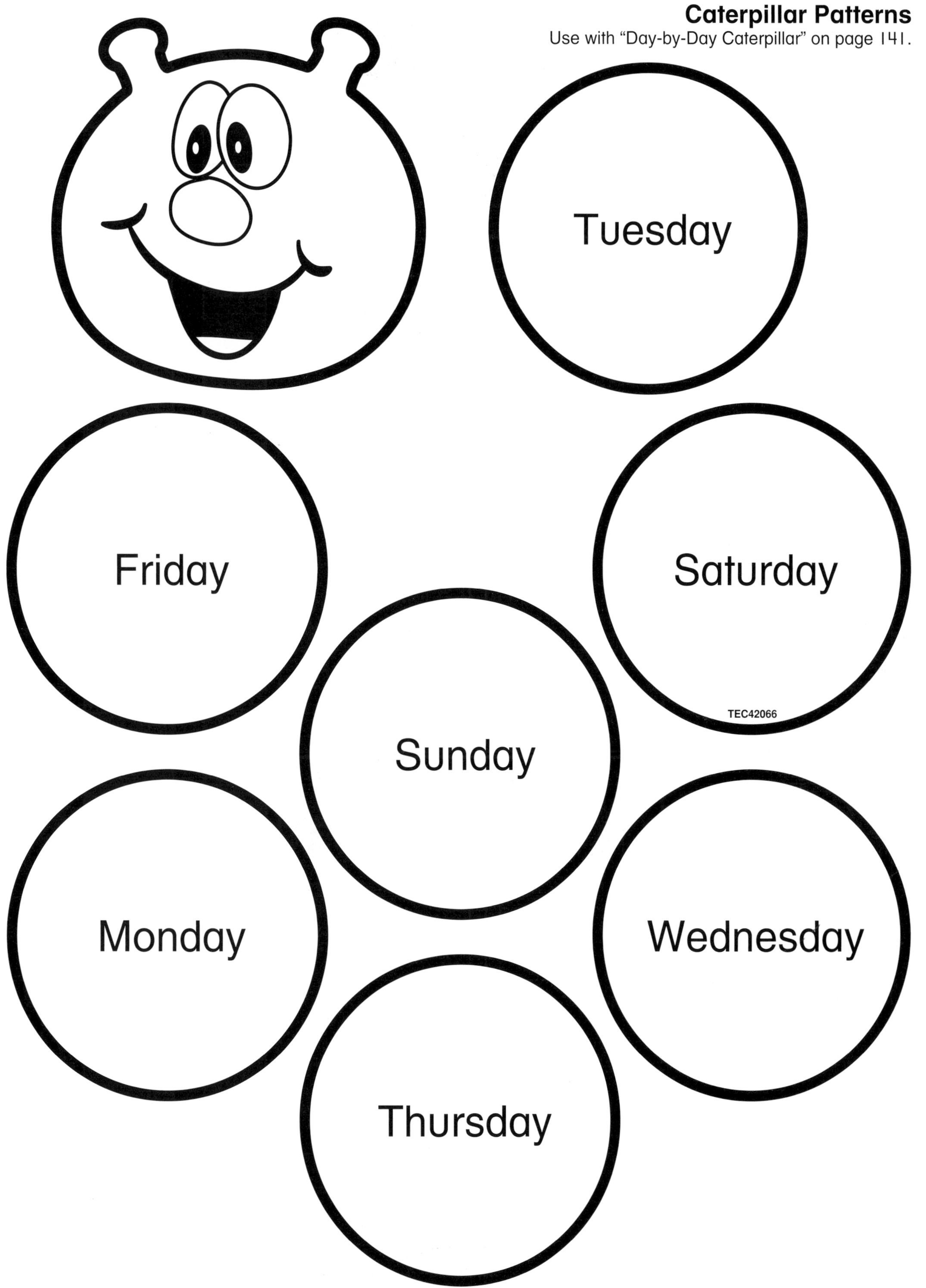

Duck Patterns

Use with "Lucky Ducky" on page 142.

Simple Science

simple SCIENCE

Sorting Supplies

Classifying objects by physical properties

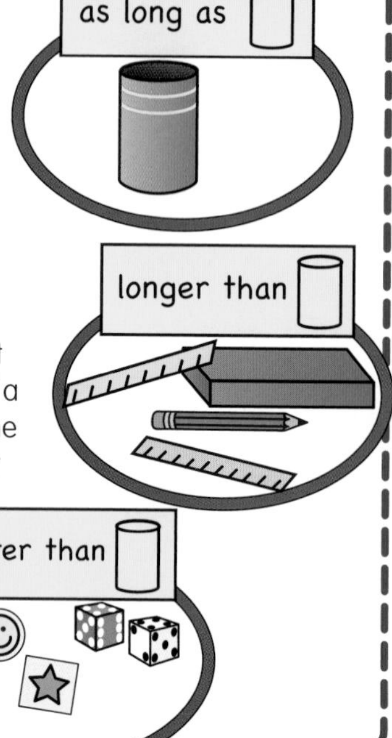

getting ready

- Use yarn to make three large loops in an open area.
- Place a supply of blank cards and a writing utensil near the loops.

activity

Have each child choose a school supply from his materials and then sit with it by the yarn loops. Invite students to share their chosen supplies; then have them brainstorm ways the items can be sorted. Next, label three heading cards for a desired sort and put a card in each loop. Direct each child to place his object in the corresponding section. (If a child's object does not correspond with any of the headings, have him place it outside the loops.) Then lead students in discussing the results. If desired, have students collect their objects and then sort them in a different way. **For a center activity**, have students sort small school supplies into three different pencil boxes.

Janice Burch
Tri-Valley Elementary
Downs, IL

Examination Station

Observing and describing objects using the senses

getting ready

- Place different objects, each of which can relate to several of the five senses, in a container.
- Display a copy of page 169 (four senses) or page 170 (five senses). Nearby, place the container of objects, magnifying glasses, and a class supply of blank paper.

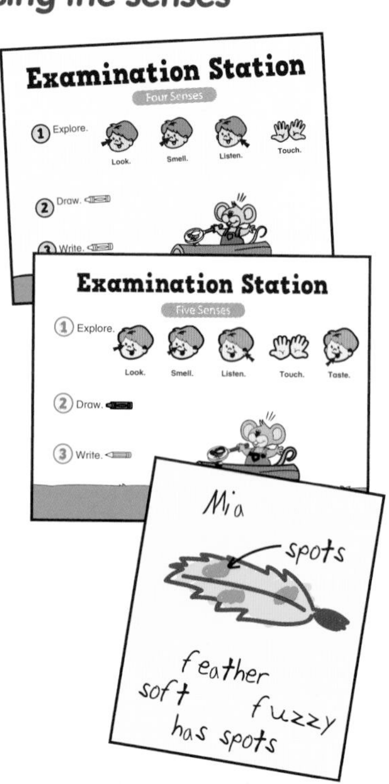

activity

Guide small groups of students to explore with different objects. Call attention to the featured "Examination Station" poster and lead students to use their senses, as is appropriate, to share detailed descriptions for each object. Then have each child draw and write about a desired object. If time permits, have her draw and write about a different object on the back of her paper. ***(SL.K.4; W.K.2)***

Kim Barnhill
Elm Grove Elementary
Elm Grove, LA

Make a science discovery box for a center activity! Hot-glue yogurt cups inside a plastic shoebox to feature specific items and to keep small objects organized. Periodically change the contents for fresh and inspiring explorations.

simple SCIENCE

Does It Attract?

Exploring magnetism

getting ready

- Get a large magnet and each of the following objects: a paper clip, crayon, metal ring, wooden block, bolt, and plastic game marker.
- Partially fill a plastic tub with rice or sand.
- Make a class supply of the recording sheet on page 171 (for use at a center).

activity

Discuss with youngsters how a magnet attracts certain objects and does not attract others. Then invite a child to gently push one object from your collection into the rice. Instruct him to hold a magnet over the object for classmates to observe any magnetic attraction. Continue with different volunteers and objects. Lead youngsters to make connections between the similarities and differences of objects that are and are not affected by the magnetic force.

For independent center exploration, a child gently nestles the six objects in the rice. Then he uses the magnet to determine which objects are magnetic and which are not. He records his observations by coloring the matching face on his recording sheet for each object.

Linda Rasmussen, Donner Springs Elementary
Sparks, NV

All About Acorns

Investigating attributes of acorns

getting ready

- Put the following items at different workstations: tongs, magnifying glasses, a balance scale, and a shallow container of water.
- Put acorns at each of the four stations.

activity

Have small groups of students perform different exploratory tasks with the acorns at each station. For example, have students use the tongs to sort the acorns by physical attributes, such as size, color patterns, or the presence of a cap; use the magnifying glasses to explore shells and caps of acorns; weigh the acorns on a balance scale to observe how the size of an acorn may affect its weight; and use the container of water to investigate whether acorns sink or float. After a set amount of time, direct students to switch work areas until each group has spent time at every station. **To extend the activity**, put several acorns on damp paper towels and put them in a sunny location. Spray the acorns with water over time and have students draw observations as the acorns sprout.

Suzanne Moore
Tucson, AZ

Winter Weather

Animal behaviors

getting ready

- Cut an opening in a cardboard box and decorate the box to look like a cave. Place the cave where students can see it.
- Get cutouts of the following animals: a bear, a deer, and a bird.

activity

Discuss with students what different animals do in the winter. Explain that some animals migrate to warmer temperatures, some animals take long naps or hibernate, and some animals remain active. Display the animal cutouts and help students determine what each animal does during the winter months. Then have one volunteer place the bear in the cave for its nap and ask another volunteer to post the deer near the cave. Have another student "fly" the bird cutout to a predetermined place so it is out of sight. Leave the animals in their locations throughout the winter. At the beginning of spring, secretly place the bird near the cave and remove the bear. When students notice that the bird is back, ask them about the napping bear. Have a volunteer check inside the cave. Guide students to conclude that the bear awoke from its winter nap and left the cave.

adapted from an idea by Ann Steimle, The Homestead School, Glen Spey, NY

Changing Water

Exploring the states of matter

getting ready

- Partially fill a resealable plastic bag with water. Place the bag in the freezer to freeze the water.
- Blow air into a different resealable plastic bag and quickly seal it. Partially fill another resealable plastic bag with water.

activity

Show students the three bags. Then lead students in singing the song shown, inviting a volunteer to display the appropriate bag as each verse is sung. To conclude, discuss with students these states of matter and have them brainstorm how water changes its state.

(sung to the tune of "The Farmer in the Dell")

Liquid, solid, and gas.
Liquid, solid, and gas.
These are three states of matter.
Liquid, solid, and gas.

Water can be a liquid.
Water can be a liquid.
It can swoosh and swash around.
Water can be a liquid.

Water can be a solid.
Water can be a solid.
Frozen water turns to ice.
Water can be a solid.

Water can be a gas.
Water can be a gas,
In the air, we know its there.
Water can be a gas.

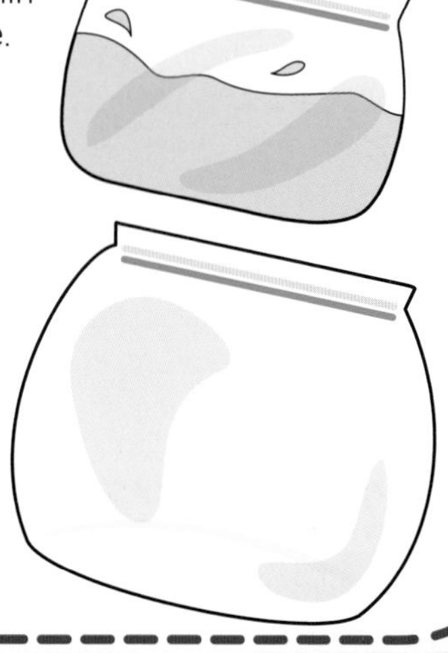

adapted from an idea by Jeanne-Marie Peterson
Charlottesville, VA

It's in the Bag!

Classifying as living or nonliving (L.K.5)

getting ready
- Label two lunch-size bags as shown.
- Gather a stack of blank cards.

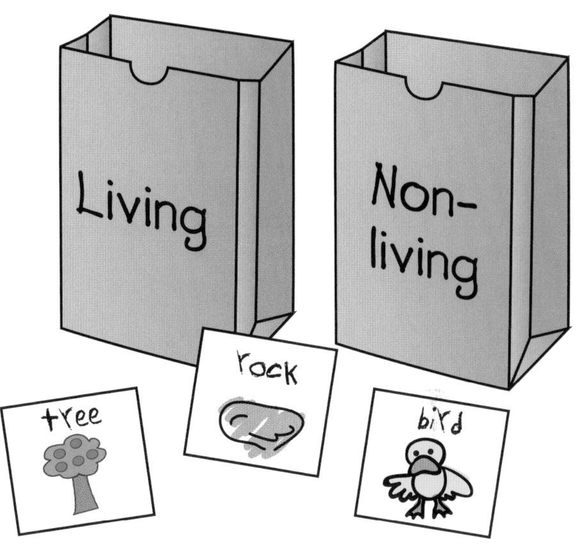

activity

Discuss the differences between living and nonliving things, emphasizing that living things need food, water, and air. Next, take youngsters outside for a walk and encourage them to notice living and nonliving things. After returning to the classroom, display the bags. Give each child a card and encourage him to draw and write the name of something he saw outside. Then invite a child to share what he has written, tell if it is living or nonliving, and place it in the appropriate bag. Continue with each remaining youngster.

Janice Burch
Tri-Valley Elementary
Downs, IL

What's the Weather?

Observing and comparing weather conditions

getting ready
- For each child, accordion-fold a 4" x 18" strip of paper to make six sections.

activity

This daily activity leads to a weekend follow-up. On a Monday, give each child a paper strip. Encourage her to write the days of the school week in the first five sections and "Weekend" in the final section. Then have her identify the weather for Monday and draw a corresponding picture in that section. Encourage her to continue throughout the week in the same way. After drawing a picture for Friday, have her take her strip home to observe the weekend weather and draw a picture in the final section. Instruct youngsters to return their completed strips to school to compare and contrast the weekend weather from different locations. Guide students to draw conclusions about consistencies and inconsistencies related to weather. If desired, flip the strip over and have students repeat the activity.

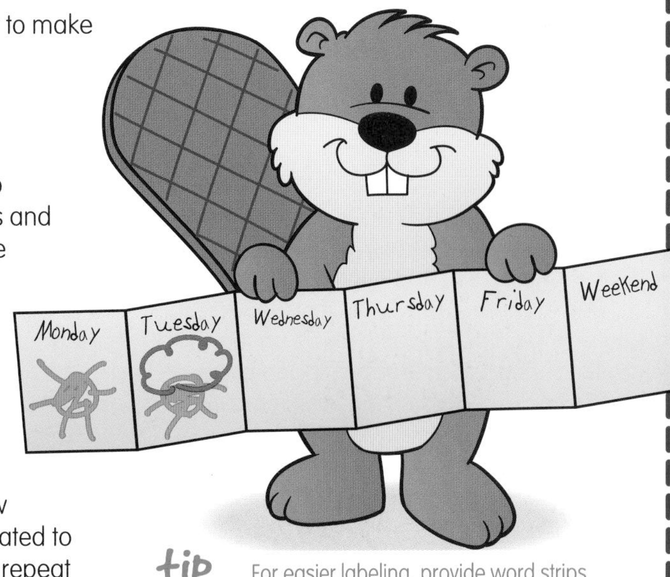

tip For easier labeling, provide word strips for youngsters to glue on their sections.

simple SCIENCE

Link by Link

Exploring a food chain

getting ready

- Give each child four 2" x 12" light blue construction paper strips.

activity

Discuss with students what different ocean animals eat. Explain that some ocean animals eat plants, some eat smaller ocean animals, and some eat both plants and animals. For visual support, draw and discuss a simple ocean food chain. Next, direct each child to draw each part of a similar ocean food chain on separate strips (leaving the ends blank). Guide him to loop the strip with the lowest member of the food chain and glue the ends together. Instruct him to continue looping the remaining strips, in order, to make a food-chain chain. Then discuss with students how the chain would be affected if it is broken in some way. **To extend the activity,** challenge youngsters to make a similar food chain for a different habitat.

Nancy Singelyn, Poway School, San Diego, CA

Where Does It Live?

Investigating habitat

getting ready

- Color and cut out a copy of the cards from page 172.
- Label a sheet of white, yellow, green, and blue construction paper as shown.

activity

Place the construction paper habitats in front of a small group of students and stack the cards facedown nearby. Have a child pick a card and name the animal. Ask a volunteer to name the habitat the animal lives in and give reasons why he thinks it lives there. Then guide the child to place the card on the correct habitat. Invite students to take turns placing cards on the corresponding animal habitats until all the cards are sorted.

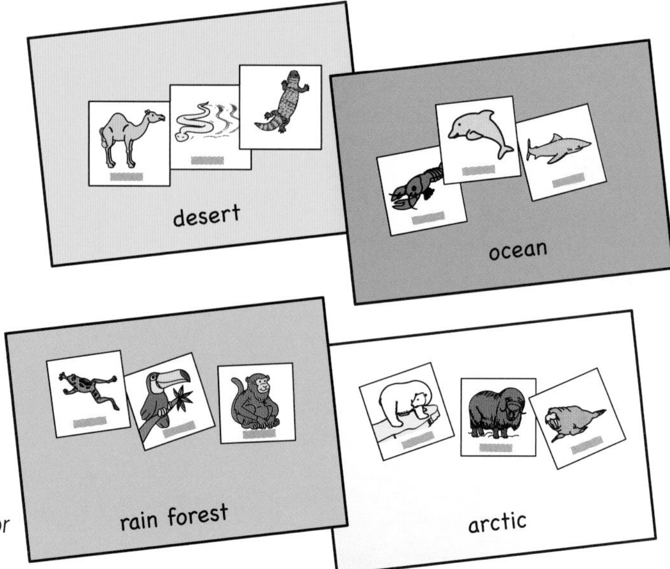

adapted from an idea by Karin Bulkow, Washington School for Comprehensive Literacy, Sheboygan, WI

Examination Station

Four Senses

Explore.

Look.

Smell.

Listen.

Touch.

Draw.

Write.

Note to the teacher: Use with "Examination Station" on page 164.

Examination Station

Five Senses

1. Explore.

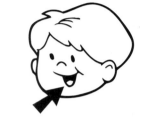

Look. **Smell.** **Listen.** **Touch.** **Taste.**

2. Draw. 

3. Write. 

Note to the teacher: Use with "Examination Station" on page 164.

Name ____________________ Recording sheet

Is It Magnetic?

Color the ☺ if it **is** magnetic.

Color the ☹ if it **is not** magnetic.

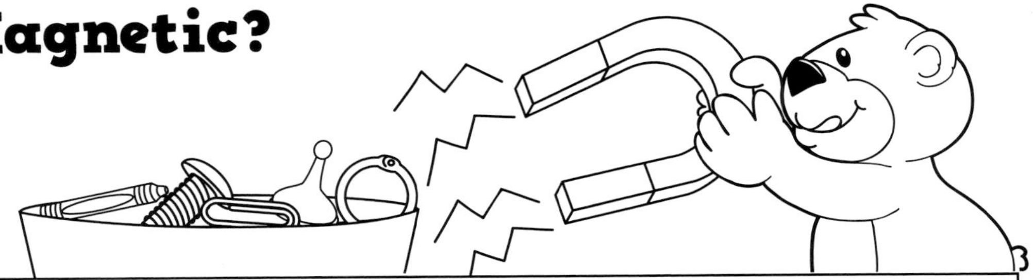

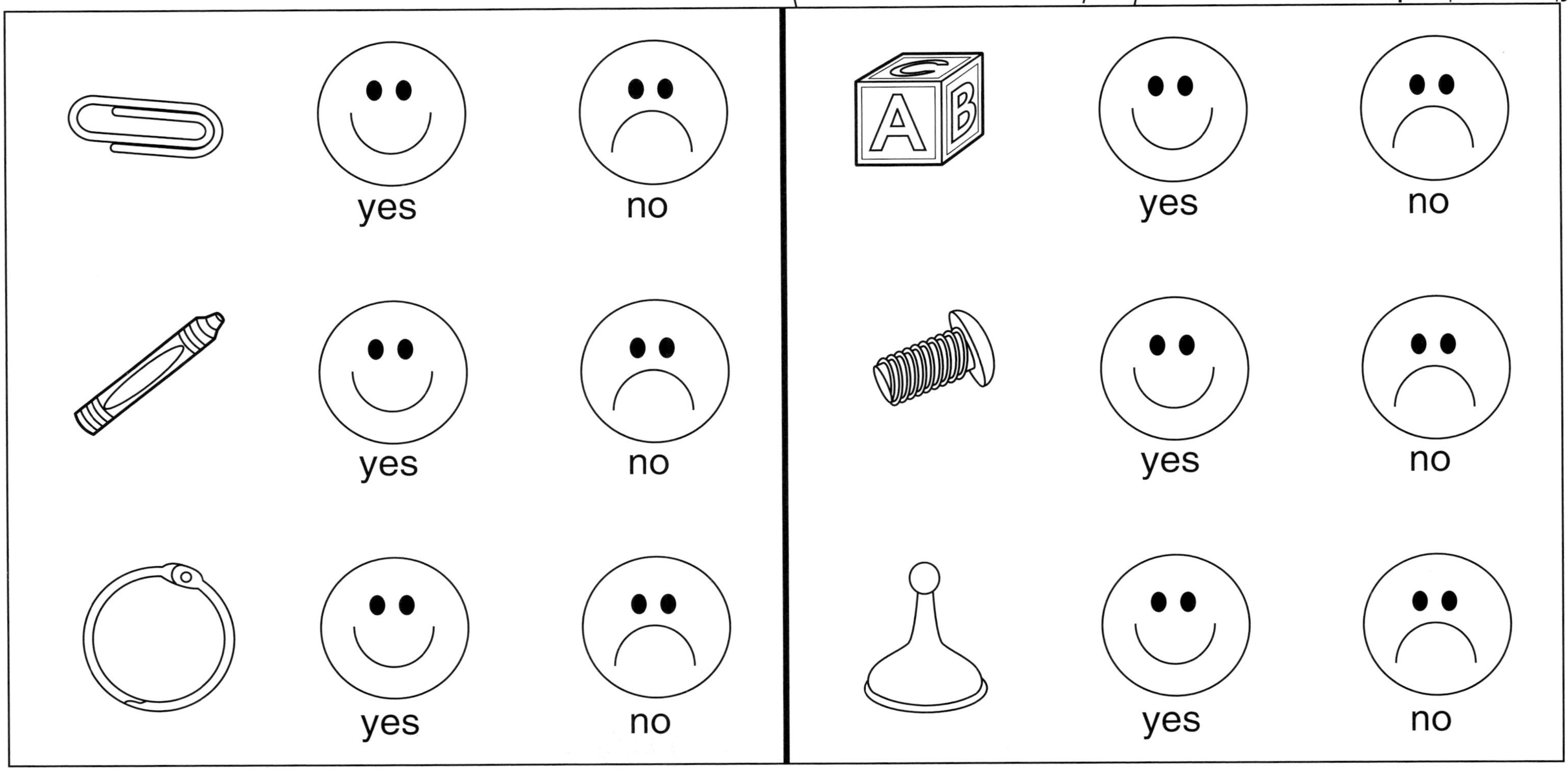

	yes	no		yes	no
	yes	no		yes	no
	yes	no		yes	no

Note to the teacher: Use with "Does It Attract?" on page 165.

Animal Cards

Use with "Where Does It Live?" on page 168.

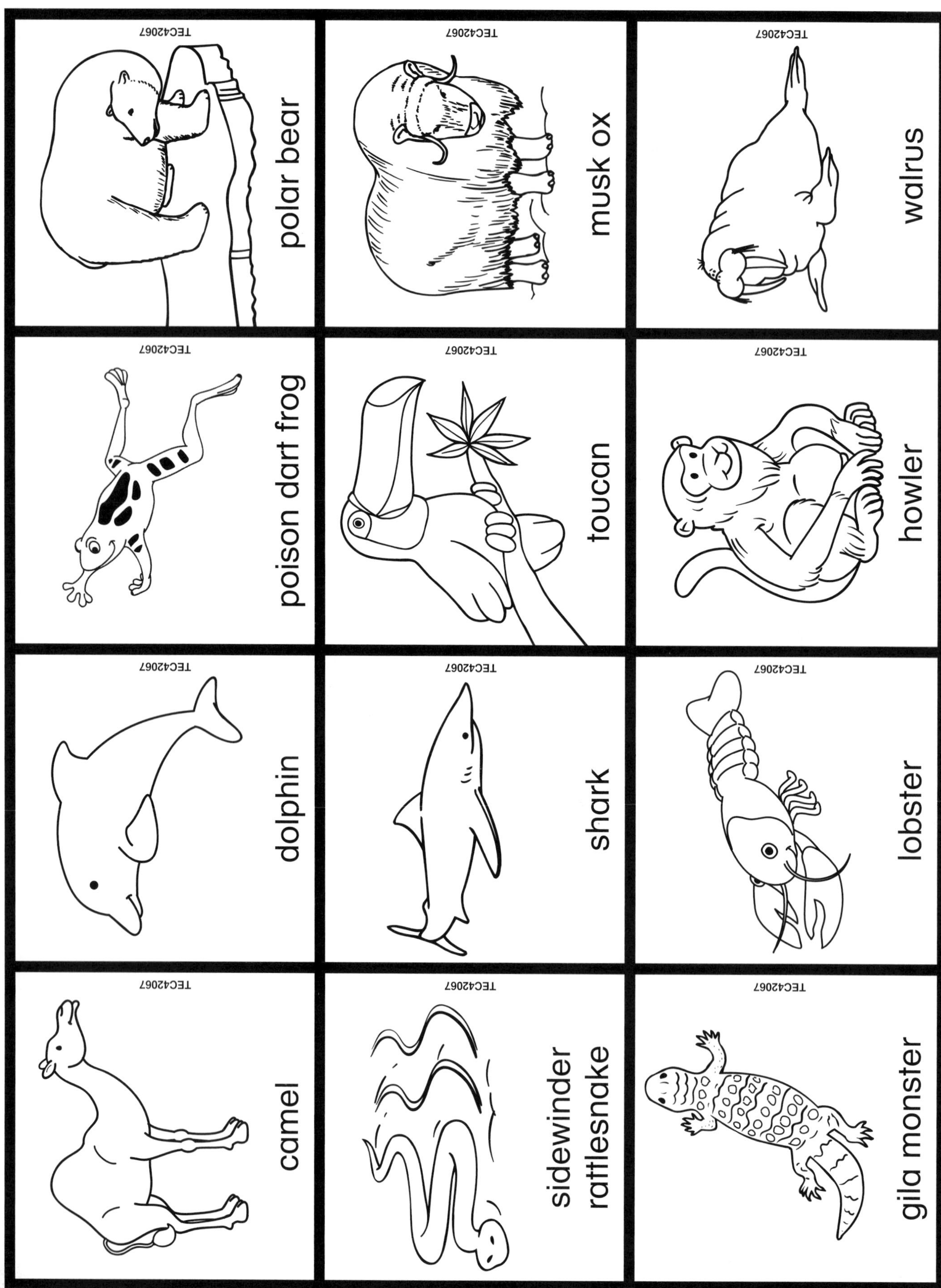

'Tis the Season

Summer Memories

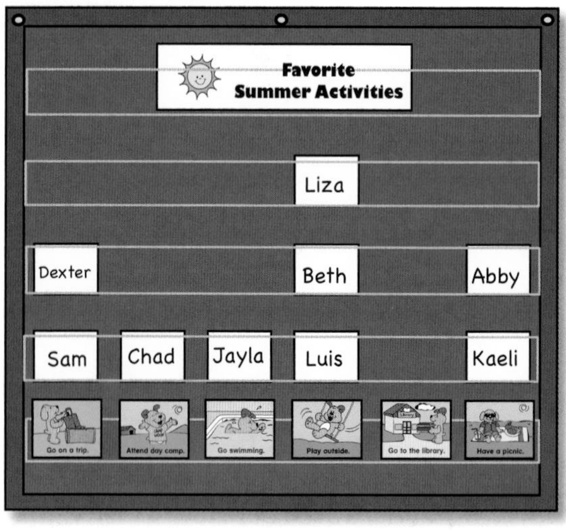

What are some of your students' favorite summer activities? Find out with this **graphing** idea. Place in a pocket chart a copy of the title and activity cards from page 175. Have each child show his favorite activity by placing a personalized card in the corresponding column. Then lead youngsters to determine most students' favorite summer activity by counting and comparing the number of cards in each column. **For a writing activity**, have each student draw a favorite summer activity on a sheet of paper. Then help him write and complete the sentence "During the summer, I ______." If desired, bind the completed pages to make a class book. ***(W.K.3)***

Janice Burch, Tri-Valley Elementary, Downs, IL

A Busload of Learning

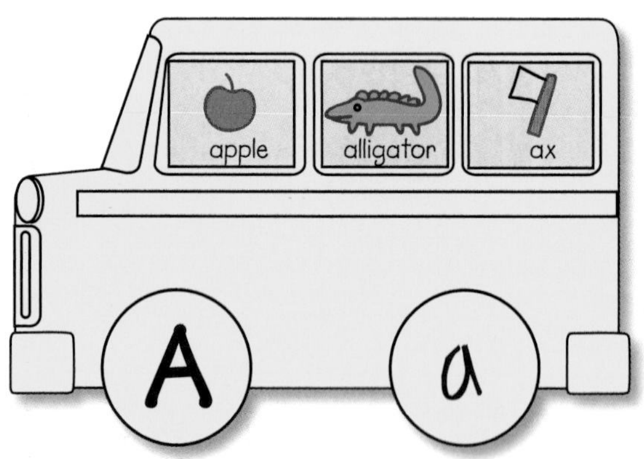

Use this entertaining song to foster **print concepts** and develop **reading readiness**. Display a laminated bus cutout in a student-accessible location and place a dry-erase marker, regular markers, and sticky notes nearby. To begin, write an uppercase letter on the left wheel and have a volunteer write the matching lowercase letter on the right wheel. Guide youngsters to name the letter and the corresponding sound(s). Next, invite students to name words that begin with the letter. Write and quickly sketch three students' responses on separate sticky notes and place them on the bus. Then lead youngsters in singing the song shown, three times, pointing to a different illustration for the second line each time. ***(RF.K.1d; RF.K.3)***

Jennifer Reidy
Halifax Elementary
Halifax, MA

(sung to the tune of "The Farmer in the Dell")

The [A] is on the bus.
The [apple] faces us.
/a/, /a/, /a/, /a/, /a/, /a/,
Yes, [A] is on the bus.

"A-peeling" Measurement

Explore **nonstandard measurement** with this apple-themed activity. Pass around three different-colored apples for youngsters to make observations about. Encourage students to pay particular attention to the size of each apple and have each child predict which apple peel will be the longest and which will be the shortest if the peels were lined up in a row. Then, as you peel the apples, encourage youngsters to share the reasoning for their predictions. Next, invite volunteers to put the matching-color peels in a line to observe the full length of each apple's peel. Compare students' predictions with the true measurement of each line of apple peels. **To extend the activity**, cut a matching-color length of yarn for each line of peels. Have youngsters compare the lengths of different objects to each strand of yarn. ***(K.MD.A.2)***

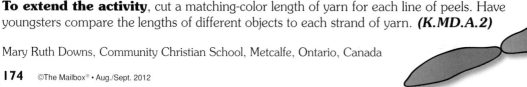

Mary Ruth Downs, Community Christian School, Metcalfe, Ontario, Canada

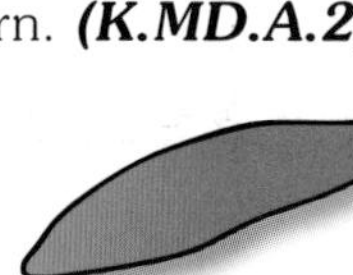

Use with "Summer Memories" on page 174.

Name ______________________

Math
Reading and writing numbers to 12 (K.CC.A.3)

Fido's First Day

Listen for directions.

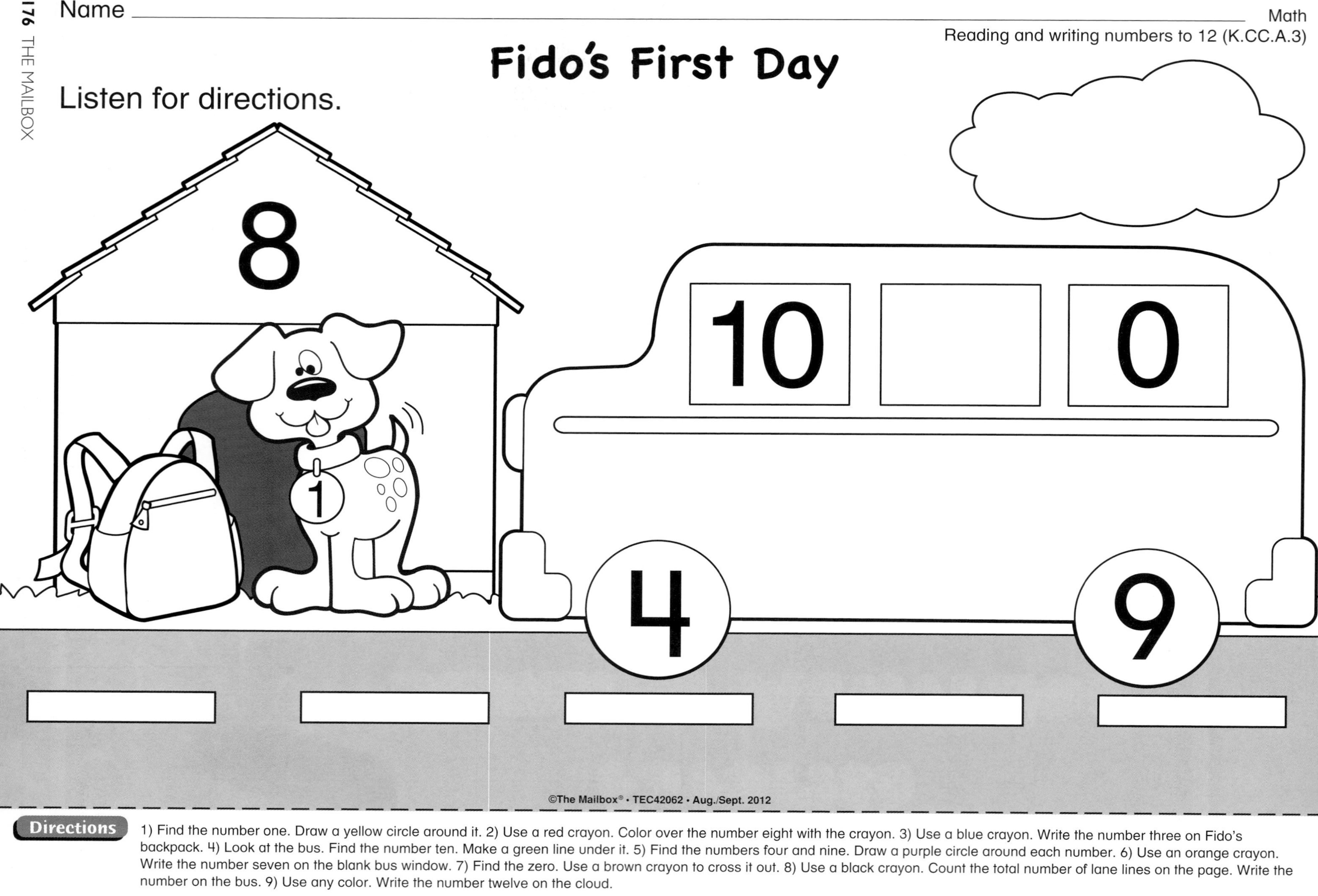

Directions 1) Find the number one. Draw a yellow circle around it. 2) Use a red crayon. Color over the number eight with the crayon. 3) Use a blue crayon. Write the number three on Fido's backpack. 4) Look at the bus. Find the number ten. Make a green line under it. 5) Find the numbers four and nine. Draw a purple circle around each number. 6) Use an orange crayon. Write the number seven on the blank bus window. 7) Find the zero. Use a brown crayon to cross it out. 8) Use a black crayon. Count the total number of lane lines on the page. Write the number on the bus. 9) Use any color. Write the number twelve on the cloud.

Name ______________________________ Literacy

Uppercase and lowercase letters (RF.K.1d; L.K.1a)

Ripe and Ready

Listen for directions.

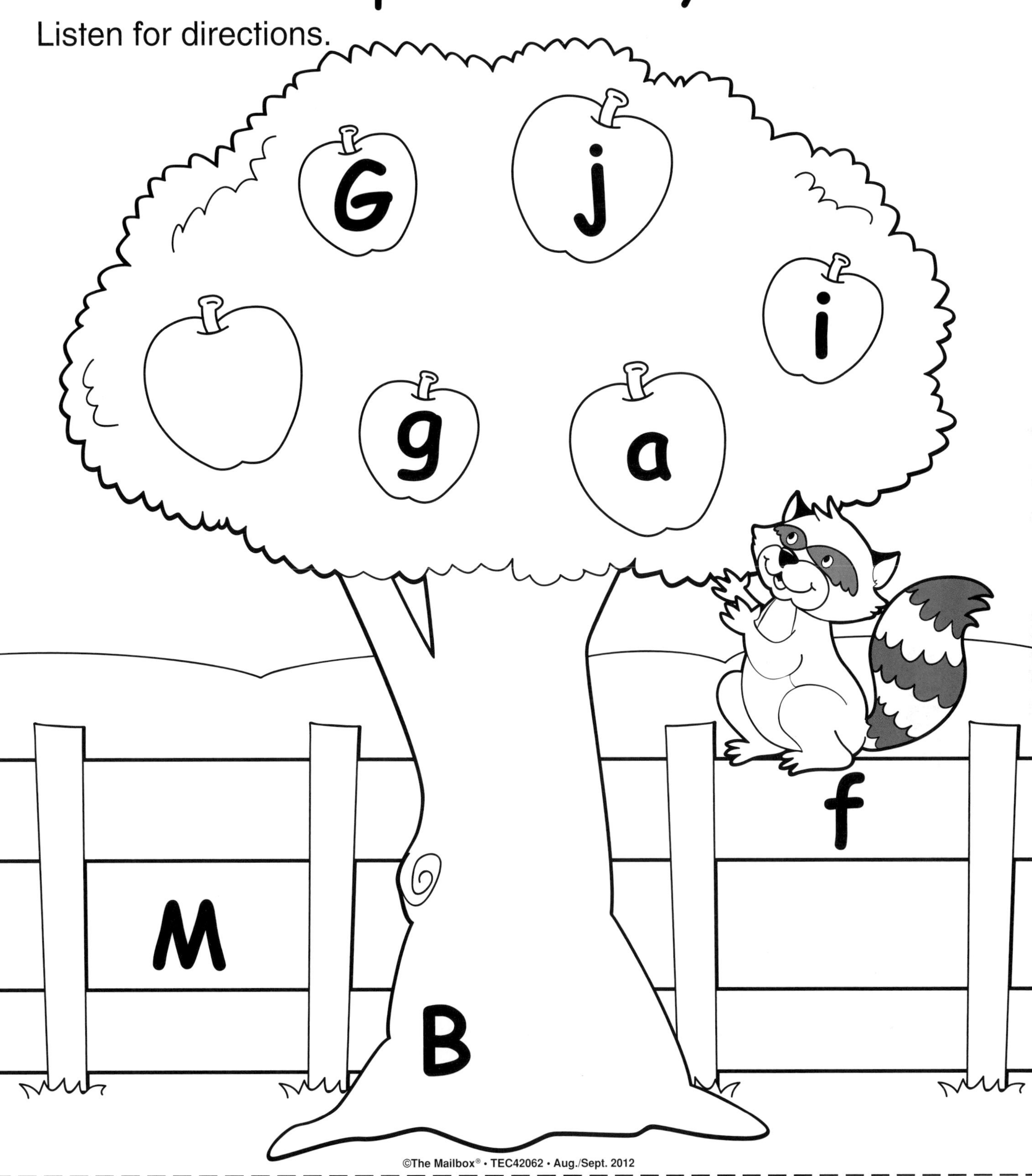

Directions 1) Look for the apple that shows the lowercase *a*. Color the apple red. 2) Find the lowercase *i* on an apple. Beside it, make a green uppercase *I*. 3) Use a purple crayon. On the blank apple, make an uppercase *T*. 4) Find two apples that make a matching letter pair. Color each apple yellow. 5) On the tree trunk, find the uppercase *B*. Beside the letter, write a brown lowercase *b*. 6) Look at the fence. Find the lowercase *f*. Below it, make a blue uppercase *F*. 7) Use an orange crayon. Above the uppercase *M*, make a lowercase *m*. 8) Use a black crayon. On the tree trunk, make an uppercase *H* and a lowercase *h*.

Name ______________________

Back-to-School
Sequencing (W.K.3)

Lunchtime!

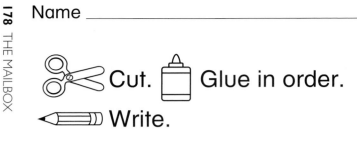

 Cut.  Glue in order.

 Write.

Word Bank

 juice  chips  apple

1 2 3

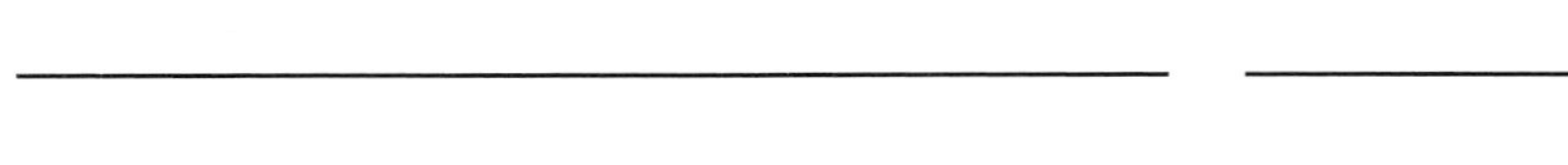

Name ______________________________

Look “Whoooo’s” Writing!

Write.

Practice:

Writing Center Make a copy of this page and write a letter pair on the owl’s board. Then, in the boxes on the writing lines, write the same uppercase letter on the top line, the matching lowercase letter on the middle line, and the same letter pair on the bottom line. Then have each student practice writing the letters on a copy of the prepared page.

Reproducible Booklet (RF.K.4)

Have each child cut apart a copy of pages 180 and 181. Then help her staple the booklet pages in order behind the cover. Guide youngsters to color the apples on booklet pages 5–7 to match the text and then answer the question on booklet page 7 by counting the total number of apples per page. **For additional skill reinforcement,** ask students to complete text-related tasks, such as underlining *apples* each time it appears or circling rhyming word pairs.

Apple Hunt
Name
©The Mailbox® • TEC42062 • Aug./Sept. 2012
Apples are in the trees.
1
Apples are under leaves.
2
Apples are on the ground.
3

Apples are all around.
4
Green apples are in a wagon.
5
Yellow apples are for a dragon.
6
Red apples—one, two, three.
How many apples do you see?
7

Note to the teacher: Use with the directions on page 180.

Spin, Count, and Cover

Reinforce youngsters' **number recognition and counting skills** with this five-person game. Cut apart a copy of the cards on pages 183 and 184; glue six cards on each of five sheets of paper to make a gameboard for each student. Make a tagboard copy of the spinner mat on page 185. Laminate the gameboards and mat for durability. On the mat, use brads to attach paper clips (spinners) where indicated.

To play, have each group member take a gameboard and six game markers. Then spin the spinners and call out the corresponding number and fall object. Guide the player with that combination to cover it on her board. If it is already covered, players do nothing. Play continues until one player covers all the spaces on her board. **For a whole-group alternative**, enlist students' help to make more gameboards and play as in the traditional game of lotto. ***(K.CC.B.4a,b)***

Tina Bellotti
George A. Jackson Elementary
Jericho, NY

Halloween Fashions

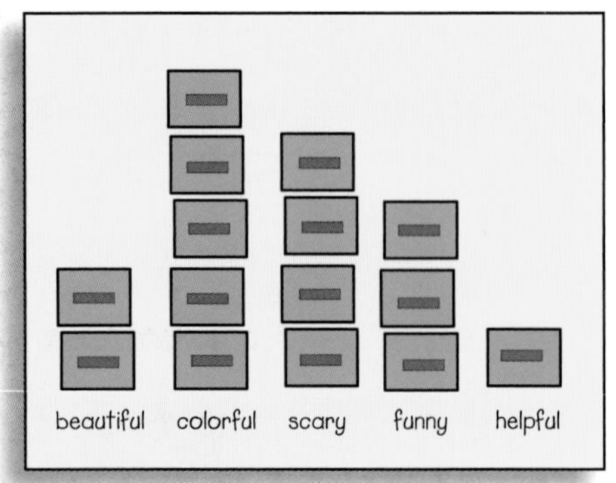

Here's a **graphing activity** that promotes students' **speaking skills** and fosters **vocabulary development** at the same time. Discuss with students different words that may be used to describe Halloween costumes. Write five of the adjectives across the bottom of a sheet of chart paper. Next, have each child write his name on a sticky note. Help him to place it above the word that best describes his costume or a costume he would like to wear. Then lead students to use the completed graph to answer data-related questions.

Shannon Riddle, Montgomery Early Learning Center, Wynnewood, PA

No Turkeys Here!

A farmer wouldn't recognize his flock of turkeys after this **home-school activity**! Send each child home with a turkey cutout and a note that invites the family to work together to create a clever costume for the turkey. (Set out craft materials for students to use if they are unable to complete the home activity.) When the projects are returned, invite each child to introduce her turkey and name its disguise. Write her response on a copy of the poem shown. Then help her glue her turkey and poem to a sheet of paper. Display the projects or bind them into a class book titled "No Turkeys Here!" ***(SL.K.6)***

Tina Bellotti

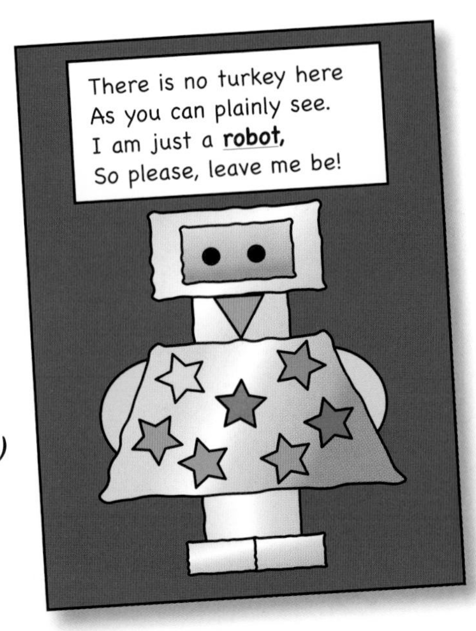

There is no turkey here
As you can plainly see.
I am just a robot,
So please, leave me be!

Game Cards

Use with "Spin, Count, and Cover" on page 182.

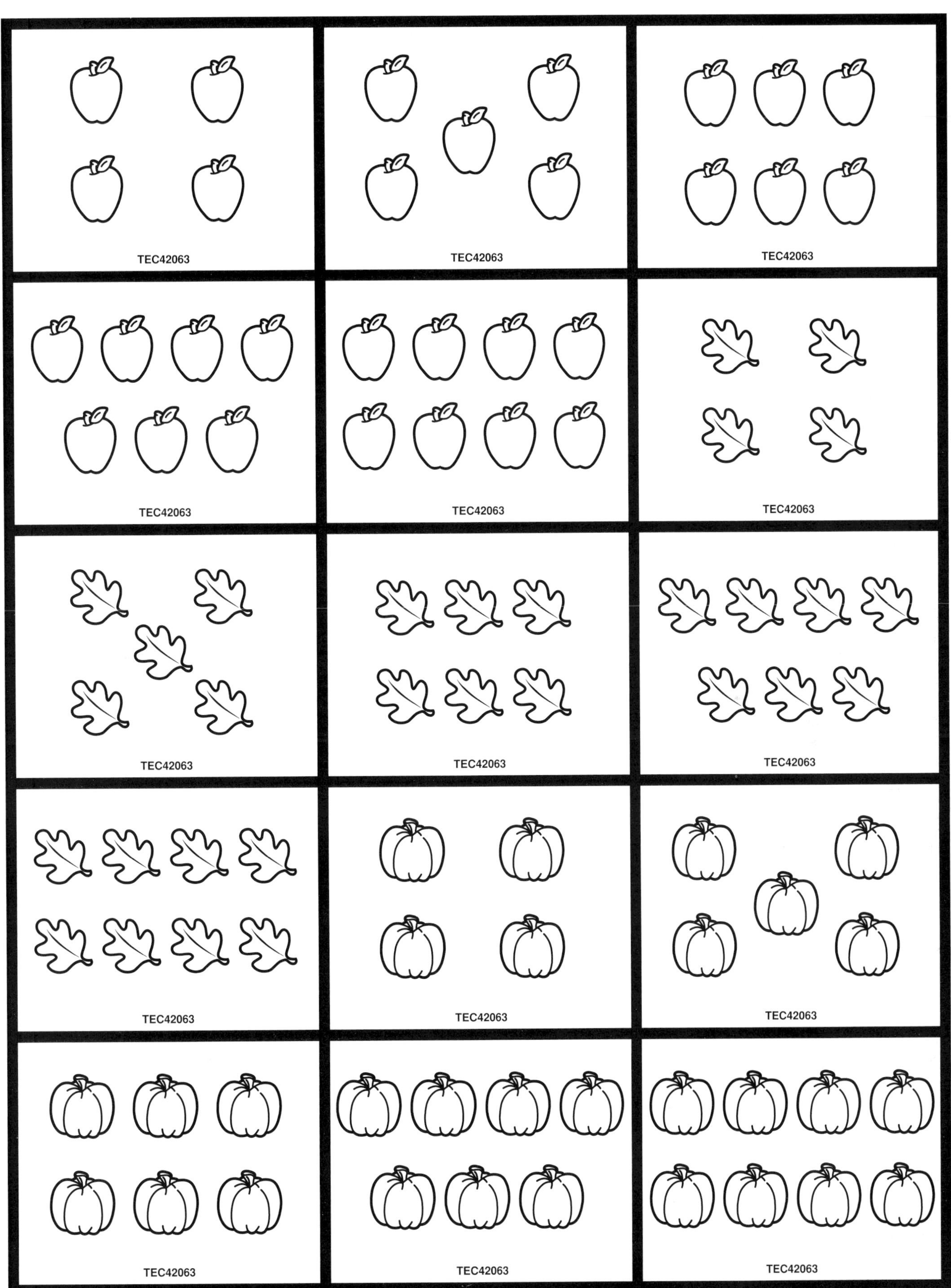

Game Cards

Use with "Spin, Count, and Cover" on page 182.

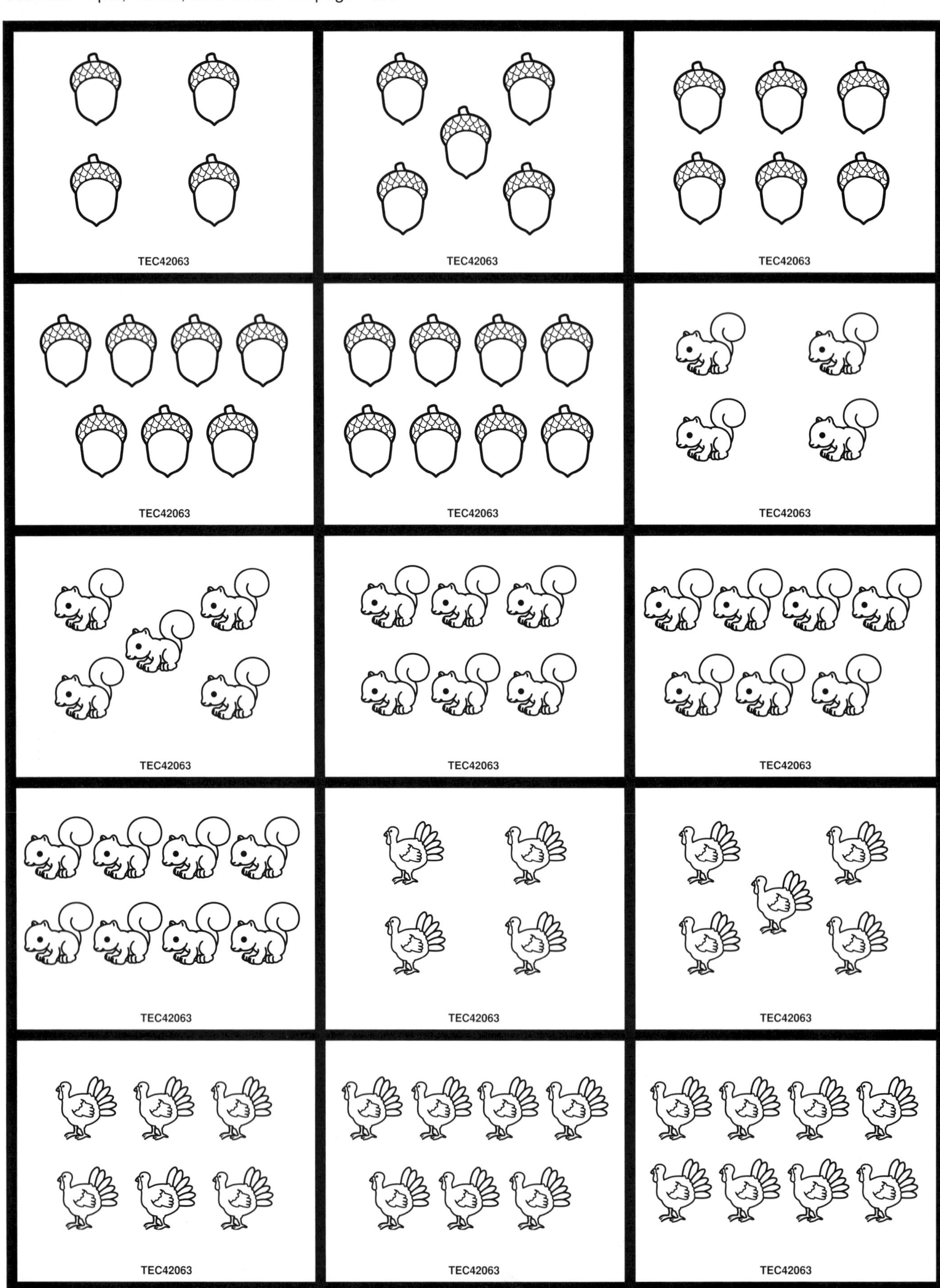

Fall Lotto

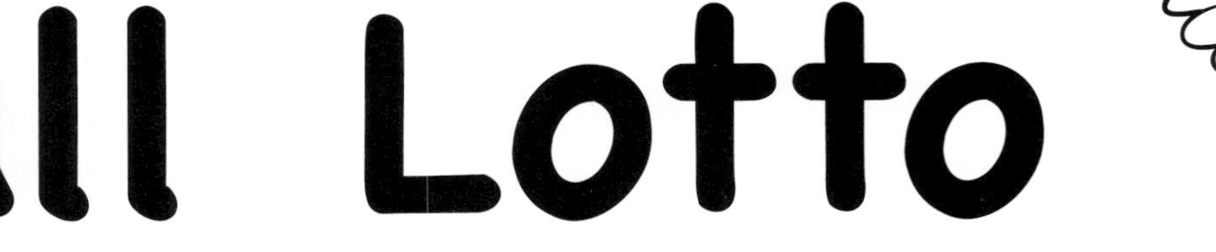

4

8 5

7 6

Note to the teacher: Use with "Spin, Count, and Cover" on page 182.

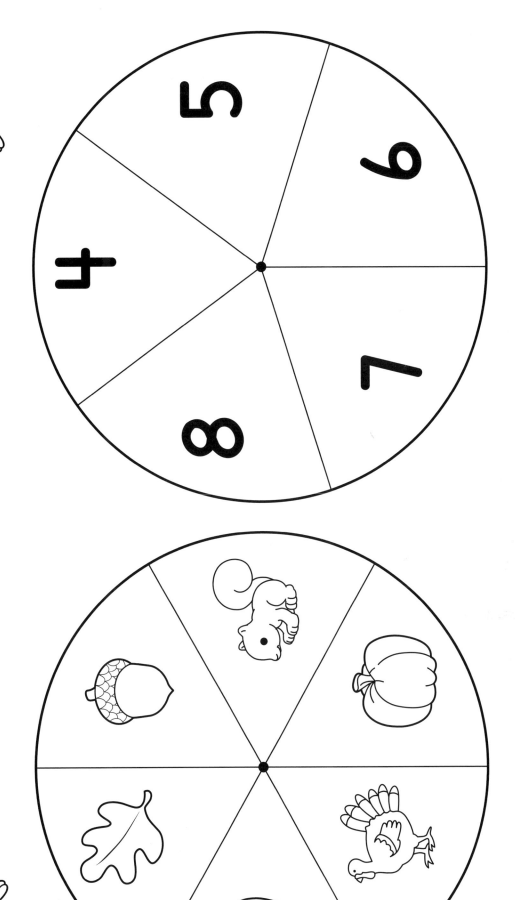

Name ______________________ Descriptive writing (W.K.3)

A Prize Pumpkin!

Think: What is each mouse thinking about doing with the pumpkin?

Draw.

Write.

Name ______________________________ Patterning

A Feast of Fruit

 Cut.

 Glue to finish each pattern.

1.     

2.  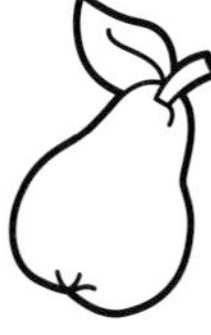   

3.     

4.     

5.     

Bonus: Color each row of fruit to make a color pattern.

Reproducible Booklet

Have each child cut apart a copy of this page and page 189. Then help him staple the booklet pages in order behind the front cover. Lead students in reading the booklet and underlining the social studies vocabulary. If desired, use the booklet pages to launch a more detailed discussion about events that led to the first Thanksgiving. *(RI.K.10)*

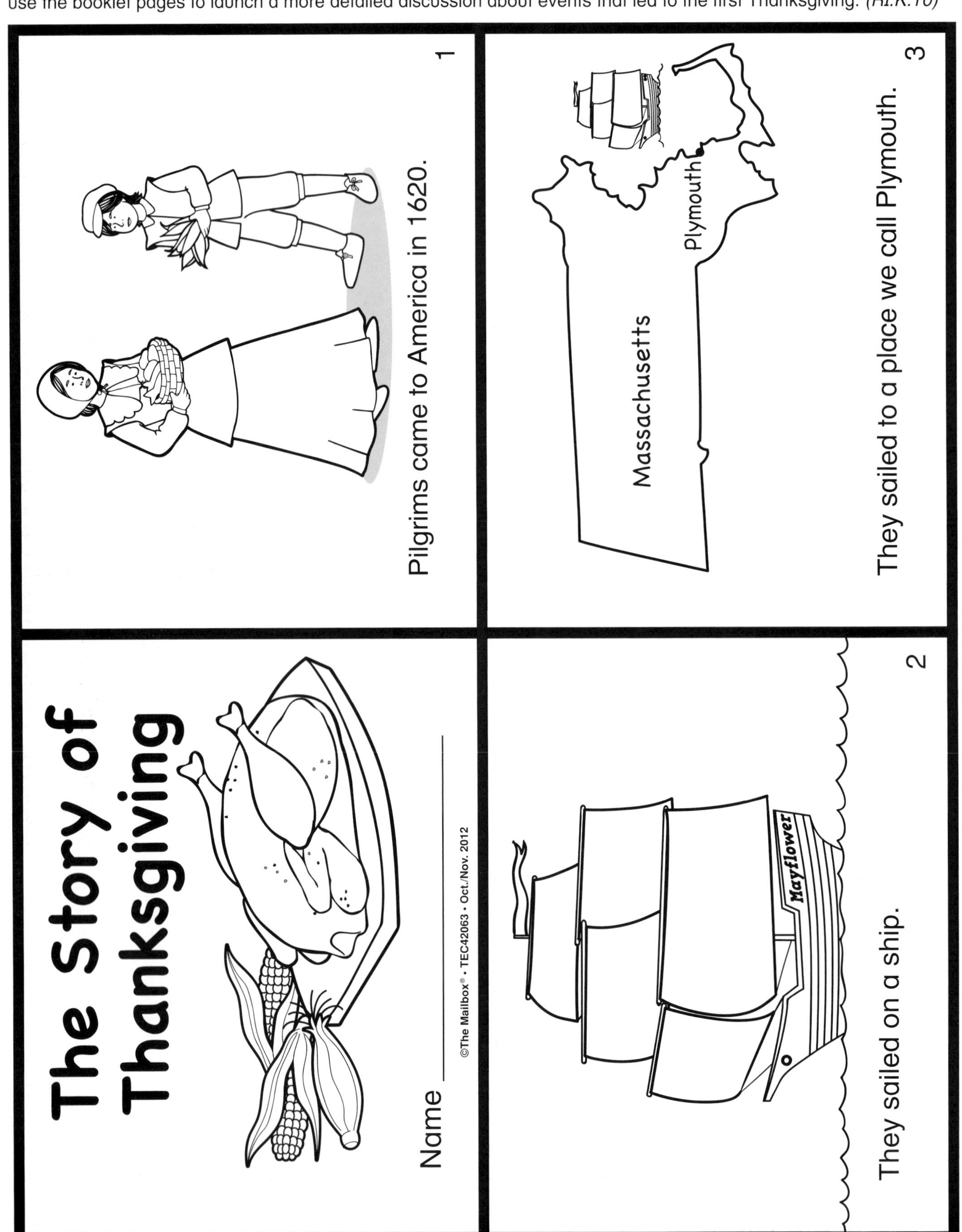

The Story of Thanksgiving
Name
©The Mailbox® • TEC42063 • Oct./Nov. 2012
Pilgrims came to America in 1620.
1
They sailed on a ship.
Mayflower
2
Massachusetts
Plymouth
They sailed to a place we call Plymouth.
3

The first winter was hard.
4
The native people helped the Pilgrims.
5
The Pilgrims were thankful and had a feast.
6
The feast lasted three days!
7

Note to the teacher: Use with the directions on page 188.

Gifts of Kindness

Invite youngsters to share ways to show kindness with this **writing** center. Wrap a box and lid and put a bow on the lid. Label the box with the question "How do you show kindness?" Put the box, lid, crayons, and a supply of large index cards at a center. A child writes or draws on a card to respond to the prompt and puts his card in the box. After each child has visited the center, invite youngsters to share their responses, in turn, to launch a **discussion** on ways they can share gifts of kindness this holiday season. ***(W.K.2; SL.K.1a, b)***

Kiva English, Cato-Meridian Central School, Cato, NY

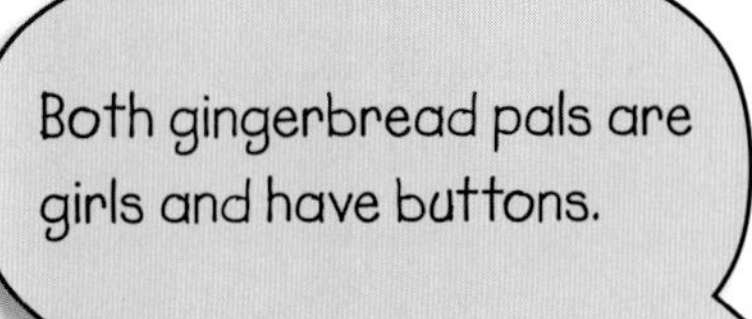

Both gingerbread pals are girls and have buttons.

Gingerbread Look-Alike

Youngsters **recognize and compare attributes** during this small-group game. To prepare, cut apart copies of the gingerbread pal cards on page 191 to have five cards per player plus one more. To begin, deal the cards and place the last card faceup. To take a turn, a child finds in his cards a gingerbread pal that has two attributes in common with the faceup card (excluding facial details). After you confirm accuracy, he places that card atop the faceup card. If he does not find a matching card, his turn is over. Play continues until a player matches all his cards and is declared the winner.

Mary Ann Craven, Fallbrook United Methodist Christian School, Fallbrook, CA

So Soft Snowflakes

Reinforce **word recognition** with this seasonal version of lotto. Give each child the same list of 15 high-frequency words, a snowpal cutout, a sheet of construction paper, and ten cotton balls (snowflakes). To make a gameboard, she glues the snowpal on her paper. Then she cuts her word list apart, glues ten words around the snowpal, and sets the remaining words aside. To play the game, read a word from the list and write it on the board. A child who has a matching word on her gameboard covers it with a snowflake. When a child covers all the words on her board, she alerts classmates with a phrase such as "Super Snowflakes." After confirming accuracy, instruct students to remove the snowflakes from their boards and prepare for another round. ***(RF.K.3c)***

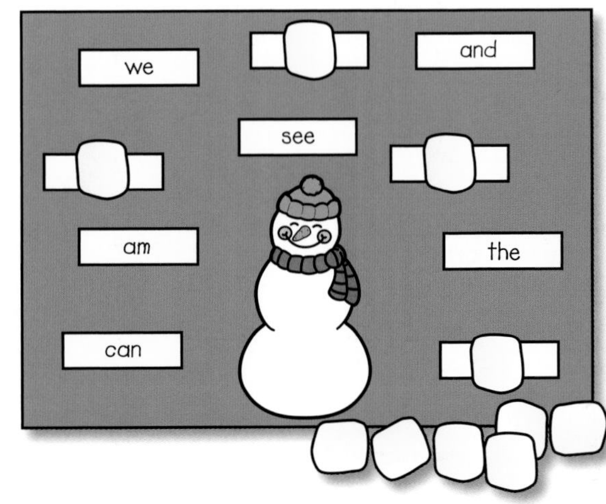

Kiva English

See page 192 for a **practice page** on graphing.

Gingerbread Pal Cards

Use with "Gingerbread Look-Alike" on page 190.

Name ______________________________ Graphing

Pretty Presents

Look at the [gift icons].

Color the graph to show how many.

Number of Presents

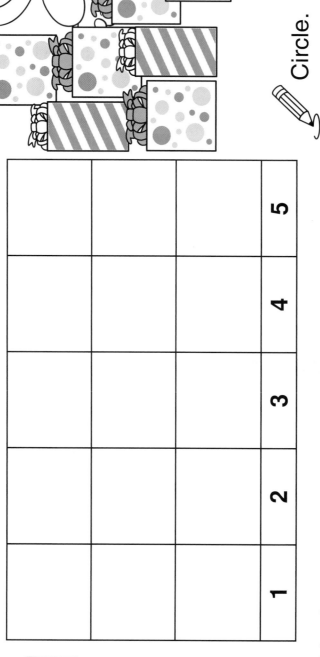

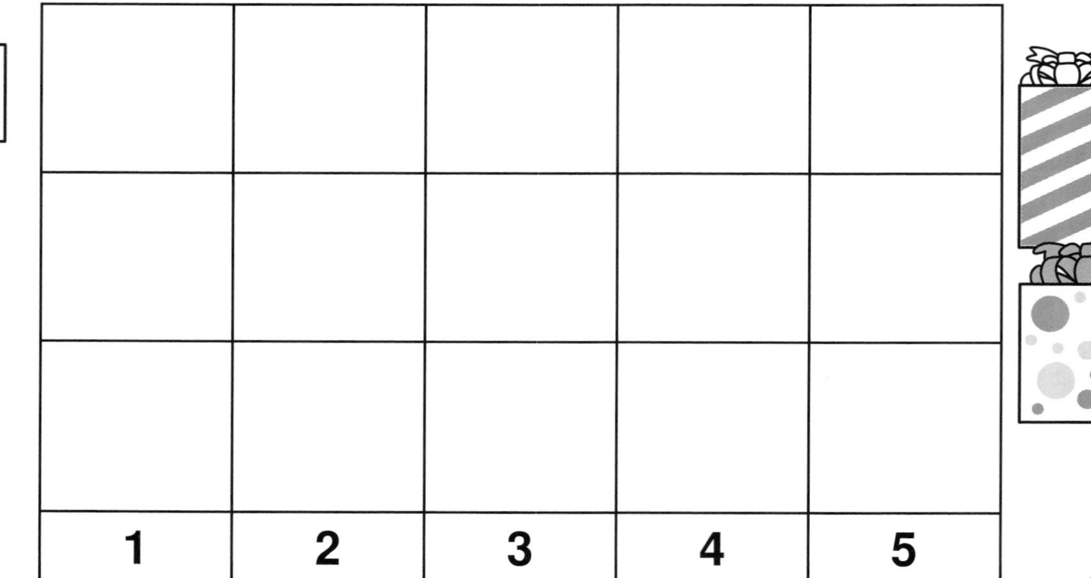

1	**2**	**3**	**4**	**5**

Write how many.

_____ _____ _____

Circle.

Which has the **most**?

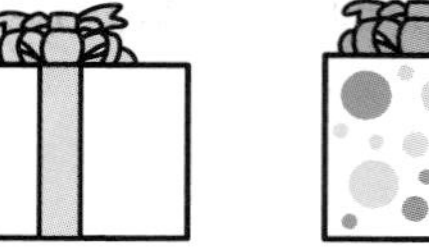

Bonus: Write the number of [gift icons] there are in all. Write or draw to tell how you know.

Name ______________________________

Wintry Writing

 A Fast Ride

 Crash!

 The Biggest Snowpal Ever

 My Friend, Sammy Snowpal

 How to Make a Snow Animal

 The Best Snow Fort

 I Found an Ice-Fishing Hole

 Slipping and Sliding on the Ice

 A Cozy Day Inside

 How to Make Hot Chocolate

Note to the teacher: Have each child keep a copy of this page in his writing folder. Have him respond to different prompts over several days.

Valentine Vocabulary

Youngsters **read holiday-related words** to play this partner game. Write five words on separate cards and then make a second set. Write the same words on separate heart cutouts for each player. Put the cards and hearts in a bag. To begin, players place the hearts faceup. Player 1 takes a card from the bag, reads the word, and takes a heart with the matching word. Then he sets the card aside and Player 2 takes a turn. If a player already has the featured word in her heart collection, she returns the card to the bag and her turn is over. The first player to collect five hearts with different words is the winner.

adapted from an idea by Marie E. Cecchini
West Dundee, IL

Golden Addition

This treasury of coins prompts youngsters to make **different combinations for the same sum**. Write the numbers from 5 to 10 on separate yellow paper circles (gold coins) to make a class supply. Put the coins in a pot and place it at a center along with counters and blank paper. A child takes a coin from the pot and glues it to the top of her paper. Next, she uses counters to form an addition problem that equals her number. She records the equation on her paper and draws a picture to match. She continues with different combinations as time permits. **For an added challenge,** encourage youngsters to include subtraction equations that equal the number on the coin. ***(K.OA.A.3)***

Stacie Stone Davis
Livonia Primary School
Livonia, NY

"Egg-cellent" Sentences

Hippity-hop! Students are sure to look forward to **writing** after this egg hunt. Cut a list of high-frequency words to have one word per student. Put each word in a separate plastic egg and place the eggs around the room. On your signal, instruct your students to pretend to be bunnies and hop around looking for eggs. When each child has one egg, have your youngsters return to their seats. Next, have each child open his egg, read the word, and write it on a sheet of paper. Then encourage him to write a sentence using that word and draw a picture to match. ***(L.K.1f)***

Allie Cornish
William Perry Elementary
Waynesboro, VA

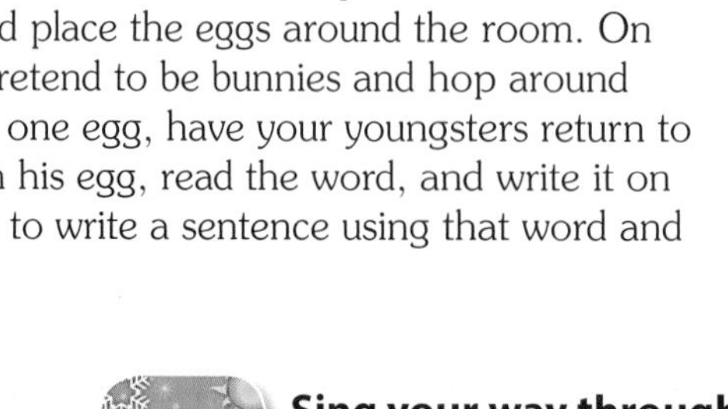

Name ____________________

Making words
(L.K.2d)

Look!

Change the first letter in each word to name the picture.

Write.

Bonus: Write **cat**. Change the first letter to make three new words. Draw pictures to match.

Reproducible Booklet

Have each child cut apart a copy of this page and page 197. Then help him staple the booklet pages in order behind the front cover. Lead students in reading the booklet and circling *yes* or *no* to answer each question on booklet pages 1 to 5. If desired, share with youngsters how some people believe that if a groundhog sees its shadow on Groundhog Day, there will be six more weeks of winter. *(RI.K.1)*

It's a Groundhog!

Name ______________________________

Groundhogs are brown and gray.

Are they purple?

yes no

1

Groundhogs are about two feet tall.

Are they taller than mice?

yes no

2

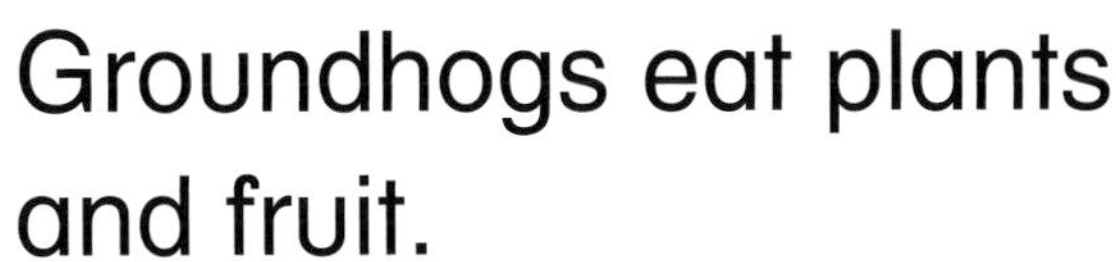

Groundhogs eat plants and fruit.

Do they eat pizza?

yes no

3

Groundhogs make their homes in the ground.

Do they live in tunnels?

yes no

4

Groundhog Day is on February 2.

Is Groundhog Day in February?

yes no

5

Note to the teacher: Use with the directions on page 196.

Name ______________________________ Writing to explain (W.K.2)

Shadow Play

Think: What game would be fun to play with your shadow? Why?

Draw.

Write.

Note to the teacher: Take students outdoors for a few minutes of shadow play, if possible, prior to introducing this writing activity.

Muddy Measurement

How many rain boots long? Find out with this **nonstandard measurement** activity. In advance, invite youngsters to use brown paint to fingerpaint a long length of white bulletin board paper. When the paint is dry, trim the paper so it resembles a mud puddle. Then invite a child to "pull on" her invisible rain boots and walk heel-to-toe across the mud puddle. As she walks, guide youngsters to count aloud to track her total number of steps and write that final number on the board. After several students have had a turn, lead youngsters to compare the recorded numbers and draw conclusions about the data. **For a center option**, have students use various objects to measure the length of the mud puddle. ***(K.MD.A.2)***

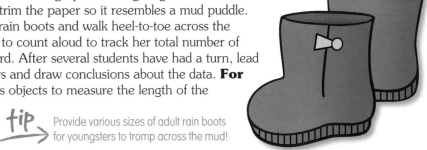

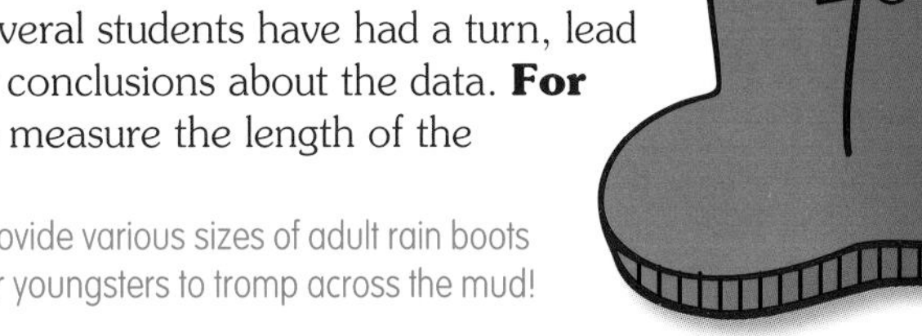

tip
Provide various sizes of adult rain boots for youngsters to tromp across the mud!

Eve Adams
Valparaiso, IN

Bunny Hopping for Gold

This entertaining small-group game is "egg-cellent" for encouraging youngsters to use their **problem-solving skills**. Display a row of ten egg cutouts, the rightmost of which is a golden egg, and place a stuffed toy rabbit or bird to the left of the first egg. Tell students that the object of the game is to land exactly on the golden egg. To begin, a child says "one," "two," or "three" and moves the rabbit that many spaces. Then another player takes a turn. Play continues until the rabbit reaches the golden egg. For increased math practice, after each player moves, ask a question such as "How many eggs away is the golden egg now?" or "If the next two numbers named are three and two, will the rabbit land on the golden egg?"

Jan Trautman, Poe Elementary, Raleigh, NC

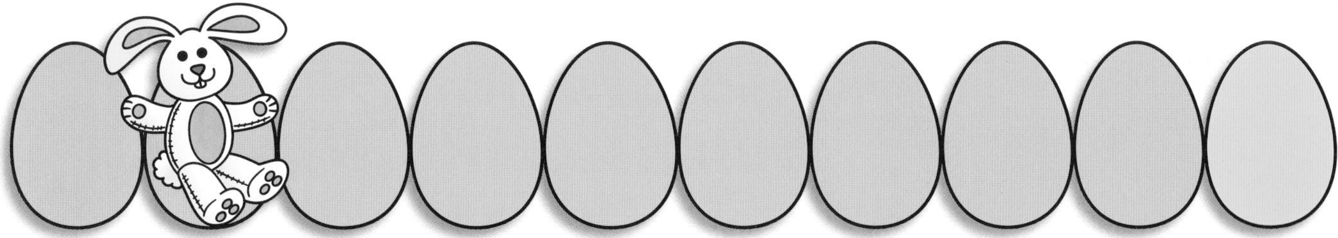

Drip, Drop!

Whether the sun is shining or students can hear the pitter-patter on a windowpane, **decomposing numbers** is a breeze with these raindrop scenes. Have each child fold and unfold her paper to make four boxes. After she traces the folds, instruct her to write a number from 10 to 19 in an umbrella shape as shown. Next, have her draw a matching number of raindrops. After recounting the raindrops to confirm accuracy, ask if she thinks she can make a group of ten and then have her circle a group of ten raindrops. Lead her to write the corresponding equation to show one ten and how many ones are in the two-digit number. Continue with different numbers for each remaining box. ***(K.NBT.A.1)***

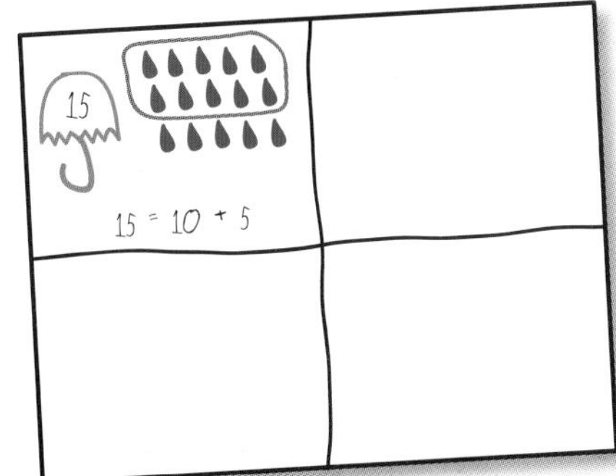

Name ______________________________ Spring

Frame Game

Literacy or Math

Free

Five in a row wins!

Lotto frame game: short-vowel words (RF.K.3) or time to the hour Cut out a copy of one set of cards from page 201 to make caller's cards. Give each child a copy of this page and a copy of the appropriate game cards. Ask each child to cut out the cards and glue each card to an empty board space. Then have students play the game like traditional lotto.

Game Cards

Use with "Frame Game" on page 200.

short-vowel words (RF.K.3)

gum	job	nap	lid	hen
dot	web	pup	jam	pig
bat	sit	nod	leg	bus

time to the hour

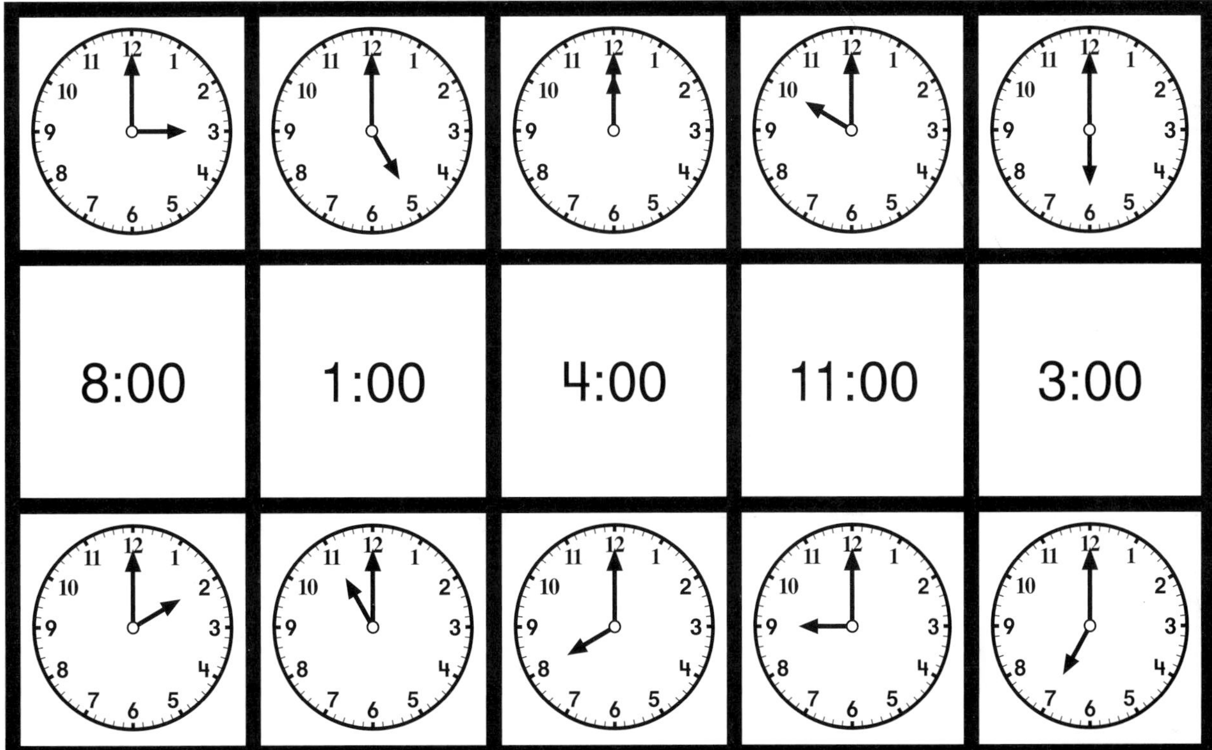

Write What You Think!

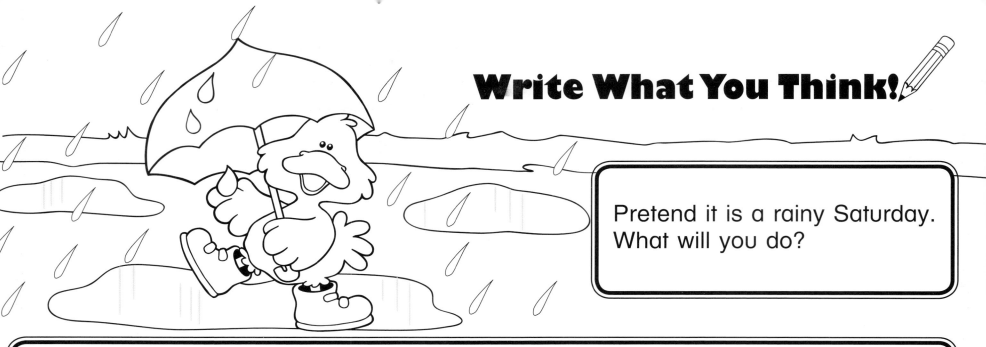

Pretend it is a rainy Saturday.
What will you do?

Word Bank

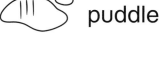

ball	car	dog	pizza
book	cat	hat	puddle
boots	coat	house	towel

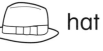

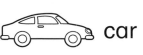

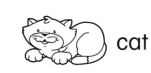

Writing Activity Card (W.K.3) Color a copy of this page and put it in a plastic page protector for durability. (To conceal the activity on the opposite side, slide construction paper into the plastic protector.) After you read and discuss this activity with students, set it out along with writing paper for students to complete.

Write What You Think!

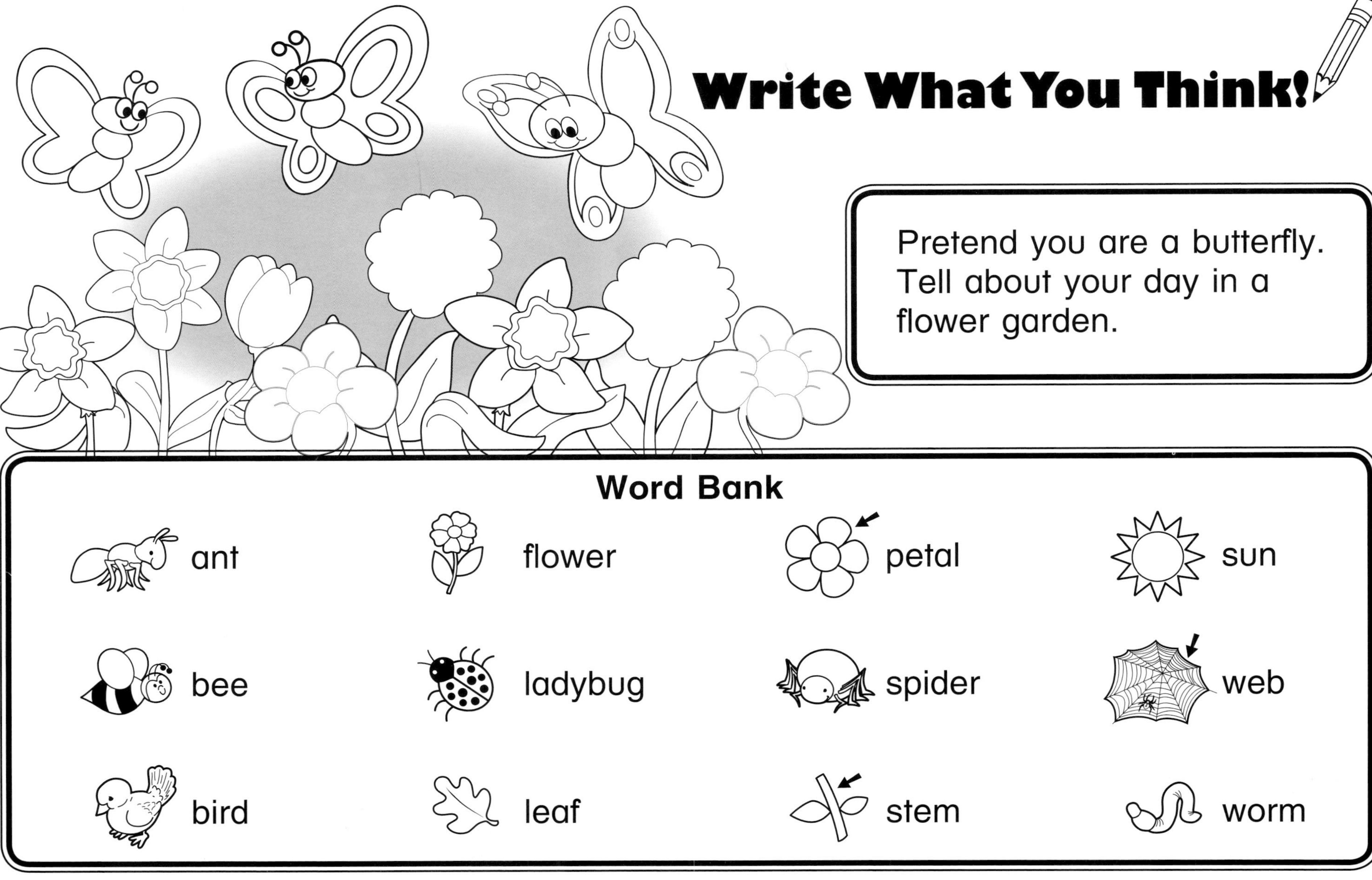

Pretend you are a butterfly. Tell about your day in a flower garden.

Word Bank

ant	flower	petal	sun
bee	ladybug	spider	web
bird	leaf	stem	worm

Writing Activity Card (W.K.3)

Color a copy of this page and put it in a plastic page protector for durability. (To conceal the activity on the opposite side, slide construction paper into the plastic protector.) After you read and discuss this activity with students, set it out along with writing paper for students to complete.

Reproducible Booklet

Have each child cut apart a copy of this page and page 205. Then help her staple the booklet pages in order behind the front cover. Lead students in reading the booklet. **For additional skill reinforcement**, have youngsters underline action words in the story, circle high-frequency words, or retell facts about ducks. ***Reading informational text (RI.K.10)***

Ducks in Spring
Name
©The Mailbox® • TEC42066 • April/May 2013
Ducks waddle on the ground.
1
Ducks fly in the sky.
2
Ducks play in the rain.
Happy ducks—do you see why?
3

Ducks splash with their webbed feet.
4
Ducks keep cool in the heat.
5
Ducks dive for food to eat.
6
Spring weather cannot be beat!
7

Note to the teacher: Use with the directions on page 204.

A Summery Scene

This picnic-themed display features your kindergartners' reviews of their favorite storybooks. Set out a collection of books that were read aloud during the year. Invite each child to select a book he enjoyed. Have him use the book to help him write the title and a **story summary** on a copy of the hot dog pattern on page 207. Then have him color and cut out the hot dog. Display the hot dogs on a board titled "Books That Hit the Spot!" When time permits, invite a writer to read his review aloud as you hold up the featured book. To include each student's favorite part of the story, have him write and draw on the back of his hot dog. ***(RL.K.2)***

Book: Llama Llama Mad at Mama
About the Story: Llama Llama goes to the store with Mama. He gets tired of shopping and gets mad. It gets better. Then they get ice cream!

tip A checked tablecloth makes a great background for this picnic scene!

Beth Marquardt
St. Paul's School of Early Learning
Muskego, WI

Dive In!

A swimming pool is perfect for introducing the **concept of area**. Cut from blue craft foam a few irregularly shaped swimming pools. Place at a center the swimming pools, a supply of Unifix cubes (children), and blank paper. A child chooses a swimming pool and traces it onto a sheet of paper. She places children side by side to cover the entire surface of the pool. Then she counts the children and writes the number inside the tracing. She repeats the process with other pools.

Suzanne Moore, Tucson, AZ

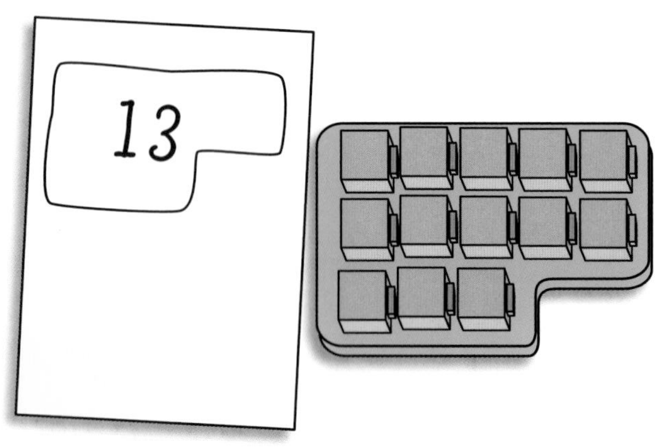

Ants, Bees, and Butterflies!

Students sing about **buggy behaviors** during a performance of this lively ditty! After students are familiar with the song, invite them to agree upon actions for each verse.

(sung to the tune of "Twinkle, Twinkle, Little Star")

Worker ants are in a nest,
Cleaning, fixing, and doing their best.
Take a look, and you will see;
Ants are like a family.
Worker ants are in a nest,
Cleaning, fixing, and doing their best.

Busy, buzzing, little bees,
How I hope you don't sting me!
Bees do fly from bud to bud.
They make hives from wax and mud.
Busy, buzzing, little bees,
How I hope you don't sting me!

Flitter, flutter, butterfly,
See my smile when you go by.
With colored wings, you paint the sky.
Up and down, you fly so high.
Flitter, flutter, butterfly,
See my smile when you go by!

adapted from an idea by Elizabeth Almy
Greensboro, NC

Hot Dog Pattern

Use with "A Summery Scene" on page 206.

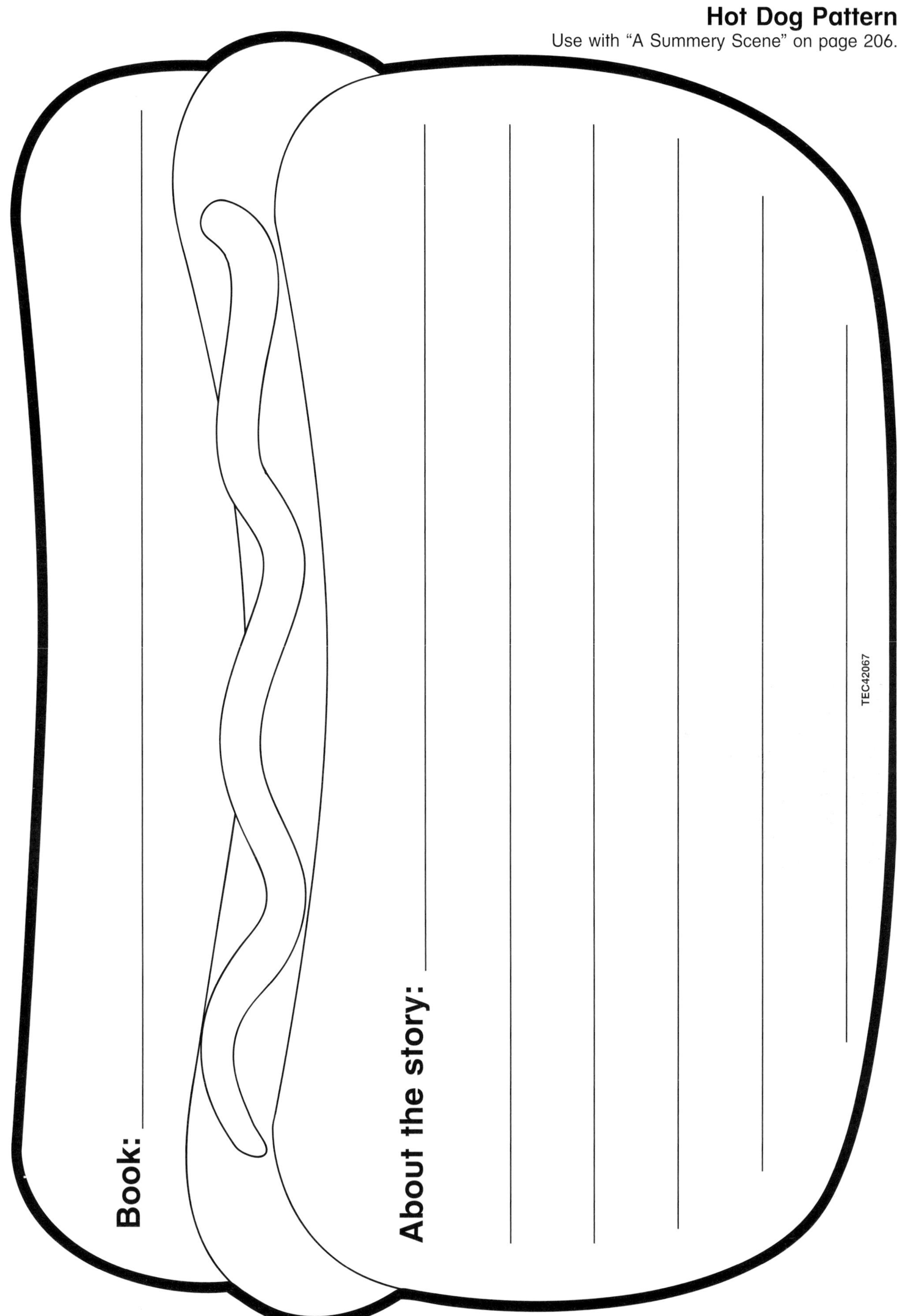

Fill the Pail!

Lotto game: high-frequency words (RF.K.3c) Cut out a copy of the game cards from page 209 to make caller's cards. Give each child a copy of this page and a copy of the game cards. Ask each child to cut out the game cards and glue each one to a blank board space. (Each youngster will have five extra cards.) Then choose a lotto version from the "Mix It Up!" card and have students play the game.

tip
Provide shell-shaped pasta for students to use as game markers.

Game Cards and "Mix It Up!" Card

Use with "Fill the Pail!" on page 208.

is	and	like	have	the
we	at	will	run	said
go	are	come	out	do
you	can	here	look	this

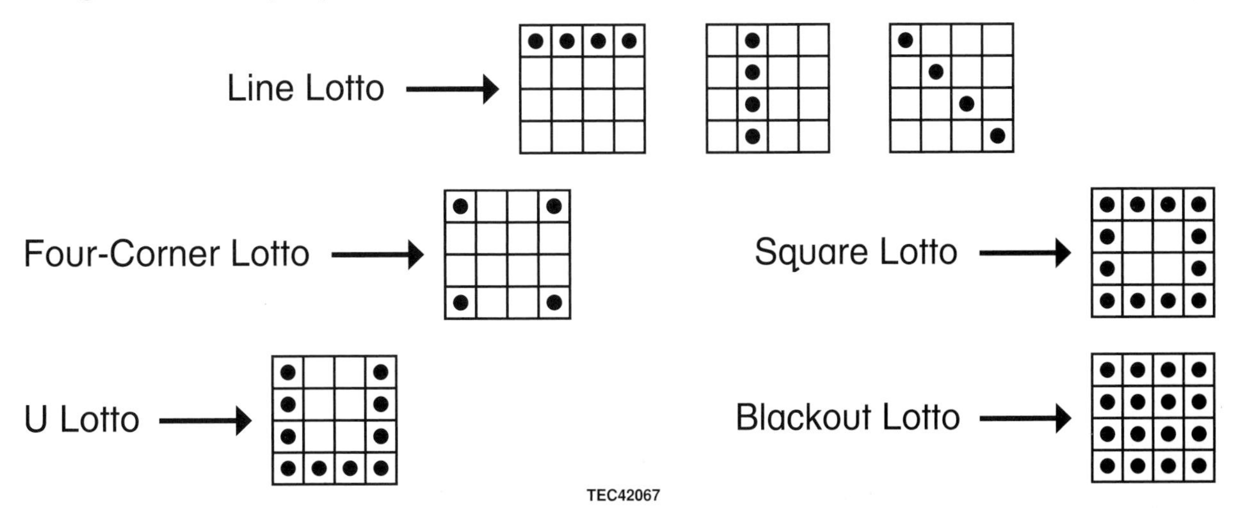

There's more than one way to play lotto! Before play begins, announce the game to be played and show students the winning pattern.
Line Lotto
Four-Corner Lotto
Square Lotto

Blackout Lotto

Reproducible Booklet

Have each child cut apart a copy of this page and page 211. Then help her staple the booklet pages in order behind the cover. Read the booklet with youngsters, guiding them to make connections with the pictures. Then have students read in pairs, each taking a turn as the reader, and respond to the prompt on the last page. ***Making connections with text and illustrations (RI.K.7)***

Animals in the Sea
Name ____________
©The Mailbox® • TEC42067 • June/July 2013
What animals live in the big, blue sea?
Turn the page and follow me!
1
A dolphin likes to jump and play.
It likes to jump and play all day.
2
Look! It is a big blue whale.
It's up to 100 feet long from head to tail!
3

Stay away from an **electric eel**.
Its shock will hurt you—it is real!
4
Sometimes hiding in the dark
You can see a hungry **shark**.
5
An **octopus** has eight arms, not
one or two.
It looks like it will wave at you!
6
A lot more animals live in the sea.
Can you name some more with me?
7

Note to the teacher: Use with the directions on page 210.

Name____ Sequencing and writing a story (W.K.3)

Bear Plays Golf

 Cut.  Glue in order. 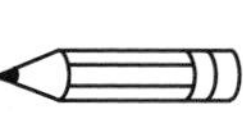 Write.

1	2	3

Literacy Units

That's So Predictable!

Print-Rich Activities

Make your kindergartners feel like great readers right away with these ideas!

Make class books!

The repetitive text, personalized sentences, and picture clues in these books make them easy to read!

Can-Do Hands

Connecting pictures to print (RI.K.7)

Students' hands are the main attraction of this class book. Give each child two skin-toned hand cutouts. (For more personalized handprints, make a photocopy of each student's hands.) Help him complete the sentence shown on a paper strip and glue it to a sheet of paper. Next, instruct him to glue the cutouts near the bottom of his paper. When the glue is dry, have him draw a picture that relates to his sentence. Then hole-punch students' completed pages and put them in a binder. For added fun, include a page that tells what the teacher's hands can do.

Linda Rasmussen
Domer Springs
Reno, NV

Mary said, "My hands can color."

This is Liza's backpack. I see blue and green stripes.

tip Change *backpack* to *toy, book,* or *stuffed animal* to feature a different object on the pages.

A Backpack Book

Connecting pictures to print (RI.K.7)

Take a photograph of each child wearing her backpack, posing in such a way that the photo will show both the child and the backpack. Glue each photo to a separate sheet of paper programmed as shown. Then invite each child to show off her backpack as you lead the group to complete the sentences. After each child has had a turn, bind the completed pages between construction paper covers with a title such as "This Is My Backpack—What Do You See?"

Janice Burch
Tri-Valley Elementary
Downs, IL

Perfect for pocket charts!

Rob the Reader

Concept of word (RF.K.1c)

Increase students' interest in just about any pocket chart activity with Rob the Reader! Decorate your chart so it resembles a reading buddy. Write the chant shown on paper strips, cut the words apart, and put them in the pocket chart. Lead youngsters in reading the sentences as you point to each word. Then continue with a reading activity of your choice.

Karin Bulkow, Washington School for Comprehensive Literacy
Sheboygan, WI

Read the Pictures!

Reading from left to right (RF.K.1a)

Reinforce the concepts of print with this picture card idea. Put a picture at the beginning of a row. Have youngsters "read" the picture as if reading the first word in a sentence. Continue to fill the top row with pictures. Then model how to drop down and move left to read the next line of pictures. At a later time, label each picture for youngsters to **connect words to pictures**. Then use the pictures in sentences to develop additional **sentence reading strategies**.

Karin Bulkow

Silly Sentences

Tracking print (RF.K.1a)

Display a line from a familiar nursery rhyme. Lead youngsters in reading the text, pointing to each word as it is said. Next, cover part of the sentence with a picture card and have youngsters read the new sentence. Continue with different picture cards as time permits.

Karin Bulkow

Sing It, Read It!

Recognizing names, tracking print (RF.K.1a)

Get students reading right away with this apple-related song! Stack students' name cards facedown in the top row and display the song shown. To begin, flip a name card and invite the child whose name is on the card to point to each word as she leads her classmates in singing the song.

(sung to the tune of "Row, Row, Row Your Boat")

Pick, pick, pick an apple
Gently from the tree.
Round and red and crunchy sweet,
It's tasty as can be.

Julie Granchelli
Lockport, NY

Chicka Chicka Names

Teach and take attendance at the same time! In advance, write students' names on separate cards and read aloud the story *Chicka Chicka Boom Boom* by Bill Martin Jr. and John Archambault. To begin taking attendance, say, "Chicka, chicka, boom, boom, look who is in our room!" and use an option below.

Name recognition (RF.K.1b): Put the name cards faceup in a pocket chart. Then name a child. Have the corresponding student remove her name card from the chart.

Alphabet knowledge (RF.K.1d): List three different letters on each of two header cards. Write "no" on a third card. Put the cards in the top row of the pocket chart. Invite each child to match the first letter in his name to a letter on a header card and put it in the corresponding column. If the letter is not featured, have him put his card in the *no* column.

Mona Suchocki, Handley School
Saginaw, MI

All Ears

Great Phonological Awareness Ideas

Encourage students to put on their listening ears for these fun-filled activities.

ideas contributed by Jennifer Reidy, Halifax Elementary, Halifax, MA

Please DO Feed the Elephants

Rhyming (RF.K.2a)

What kind of food will your center visitors feed these elephants? Rhyming peanuts! Cut out a tagboard copy of the elephant and peanut patterns on page 218. Thread a pipe cleaner (trunk) through each elephant at the X and hole-punch each peanut where indicated. Put the prepared pieces at a center. A child names the picture shown on a peanut and matches it to the elephant that shows a rhyming picture. To feed the elephant, she gently threads the peanut onto the elephant's trunk. She continues with each remaining peanut. Then she reads the rhymes for each elephant.

Rolling for Rhymes

Rhyming (RF.K.2a)

This picture cube is perfect for a large-group activity and can also be used for a small-group game. Put pictures that are easy to rhyme with on each side of a cube. Then use the suggestions below.

- **Whole group:** Gather youngsters in a circle and invite a child to roll the cube to a classmate. Have the child name the picture rolled and name a rhyming word. Then have her roll the cube to a classmate. Have this youngster generate a different rhyming pair of words. Encourage students to continue rolling and rhyming as time permits. **For added fun,** encourage youngsters to include nonsense words when naming rhyming word pairs.
- **Small group:** For this game, give each child three picture cards that rhyme with pictures shown on the cube. A player rolls the cube. If one or more pictures on her cards rhymes with the picture rolled, she chooses one and flips over the card. If a rhyming match is not made, her turn is over. Players take turns until one player turns over all her cards and is declared the winner.

Walk, Find, Draw!

See page 219 for a game on beginning sounds!

Beginning sounds (RF.K.2)

Student-drawn pictures are the center of attraction on these mini posters. Assign each student a different letter sound. Have each child draw on a large sheet of paper a picture whose name begins with the assigned sound. Then take youngsters on a walk. Invite students to draw additional pictures on their papers, making sure the beginning sounds match. After the walk, have each student take a turn naming the pictures drawn on her poster and encourage her classmates to name the corresponding beginning sound.

/b/-/a/-/t/. Bat!

Segmenting and blending words (RF.K.2d)

When students wear these headbands with bat ears, their hearing is sure to be enhanced! Have each child glue rounded triangles (bat ears) to a paper strip. When the glue is dry, size each child's headband to fit and staple it closed. Have youngsters sit in pairs. Ask one partner in each twosome to wear his headband (listener). Instruct the other partner to think of a word and slowly say each sound of the word in isolation. Next, have the listener blend the sounds to make a word. Then instruct partners to trade roles. **For added support**, provide picture cards for students to use rather than generating their own words.

To the Teacher!

Syllables (RF.K.2b)

This modified version of Red Light, Green Light invites youngsters to stomp the correct number of syllables in a word. Instruct youngsters to line up in a row facing you. Then name an article of clothing, such as a shirt, pants, sneakers, or overalls. Each child wearing the named item takes the number of steps equal to the syllables in the word. If she is not wearing the item, she stands still. When a child takes a step beyond your imaginary finish line, she sits. Continue until each child is seated.

Elephant and Peanut Patterns

Use with "Please DO Feed the Elephants" on page 216.

Name ______________________ and ______________________

Beginning sounds (RF.K.2)

Playing for Peanuts

Partner Game Each twosome needs a prepared copy of this gameboard and two different-color crayons. To prepare a gameboard, use a brad to attach a paper clip (spinner) to the elephant's nose. To take a turn, a player spins the spinner, names the picture in that section, and looks for a picture on a peanut with that beginning sound. If one is found, he colors the peanut. If one is not found, his turn is over. Play continues until all the peanuts are colored or time is up. The player who colors more peanuts wins.

Build Word Family Skills

1 Create Ladders

Draw a ladder and, on each space, write a different onset that forms a real word with a desired rime. Write that rime on a red paper circle (firefighter). A child slides the firefighter up and down the ladder to read the words. Then he records the word family list on a sheet of paper.

Michelle Elyea
Endeavor Elementary
Kentwood, MI

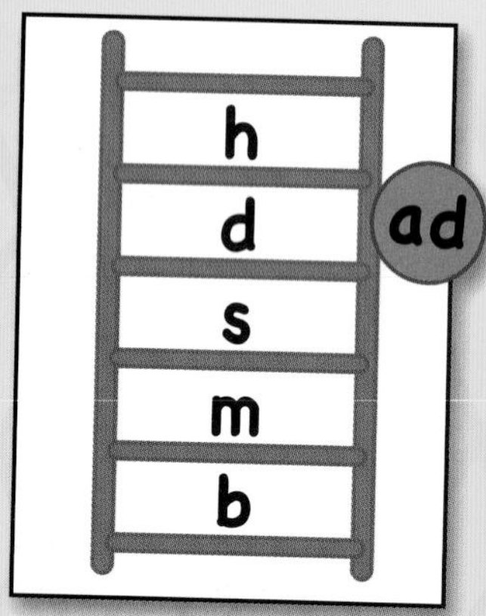

2 Sing a Song

Students will name, sing, and spell words with this little ditty. Write a word family ending on the board and then write a corresponding word. Next, lead youngsters to sing the song shown. Continue with four different words and, for the fifth word, change the last line to "That's a family!" Then invite volunteers to read the word family list.

(sung to the tune of "London Bridge")

I can spell [cat, C-A-T],
[C-A-T, C-A-T].
I can spell [cat, C-A-T].
Now try this word.

Suzanne Moore
Tucson, AZ

3 Plan a Partner Game

A tic-tac-toe board, two colored pencils, and two different rime cards are all partners need to play this game. Each player takes a card and a pencil. Then players play as in the traditional game, marking a game space by writing a word with her chosen rime. For an easier version, list words on each rime card.

Mary Davis, Keokuk Christian Academy, Keokuk, IA

big	fin	bin
win	dig	wig
pig	pin	tin

4 Use Picture Cards

Give each child a copy of page 222. Have her sort the cards and then write the words to form word family lists. For a partner game, have students use a set of cards and match word family words in a game of Concentration.

Alice Elizabeth Parry, Sterling Elementary, Charlotte, NC

Make Mats

Write a rime in the center of a sheet of paper (mat) and draw a box to its left for an onset card. On individual cards, write different onsets that form real words with the rime. Clip the onset cards to the mat. Make more mats for different word families as desired. To use a mat, a child places the onset cards faceup around the rime. Then he places a card in the box, reads the word, and records it on a sheet of paper. He continues with each remaining card and then reads the resulting word family.

Vanessa Rivera, La Luz Elementary, La Luz, MN

Bind Books

Looking for a way to reuse a word family chart? Try this! Put the chart and a star pattern at a center. A child traces the star and writes the rime in its center. Then she writes a word family word on each of the star's points, draws a face, and cuts out the star. Use a metal ring to secure the star behind a star-shaped cover featuring the title "Starring Word Families!" As different word families are introduced, have her add stars to her ring.

Ada Goren
Winston-Salem, NC

Use Technology

Create a slide show of word family words on the computer. Then play the slideshow anytime you have a few extra minutes or during dismissal. As it plays, have youngsters read the words.

Erin Green, Rosewood Elementary, Province, SC

Form Planes and Runways

Label each of two long paper strips (runways) with a different word family ending. Then label paper planes with different words that correspond with the runways. Put the planes and runways at a center. A child "flies" each plane onto the matching runway and then reads each runway of words.

Word Family Cards

Use with idea 4, "Use Picture Cards," on page 221.

Develop Sharp Writers!

Let's get to the point—are you looking for ways to encourage and improve students' writing skills? You found the "write" place!

Morning Mistakes

Your young editors correct writing errors with this daily activity. Write on the board or chart paper the date and a message with intentional mistakes, such as a missing word and a lowercase letter at the beginning of the sentence. Have youngsters read the message, find the errors, and tell you how to correct the writing. The lessons learned are quickly transferred into students' independent writing. ***(L.K.2) Margaret Philipson, Cayuga Heights Elementary, Ithaca, NY***

Check It!

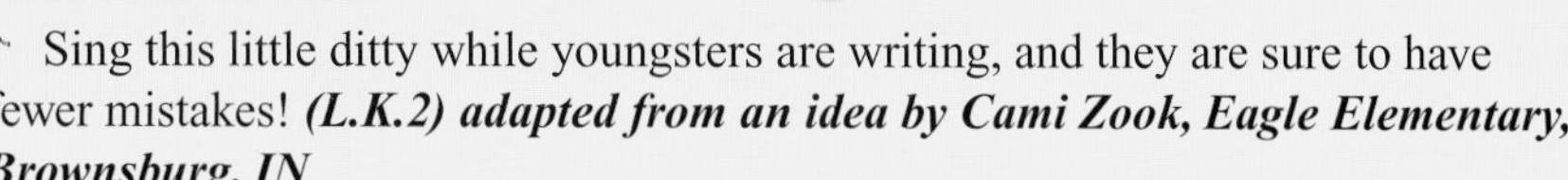

Sing this little ditty while youngsters are writing, and they are sure to have fewer mistakes! ***(L.K.2) adapted from an idea by Cami Zook, Eagle Elementary, Brownsburg, IN***

(sung to the tune of "If You're Happy and You Know It")

Don't forget to check your writing for mistakes.
Don't forget to check your writing for mistakes.
Capital letters, punctuation, and some space between your words—
Don't forget to check your writing for mistakes.

Hint: Red, Yellow, Green!

This visual aid fosters fabulous writing! Display a stoplight cutout and share with youngsters the meanings for each of the colors as described. Then keep the stoplight posted as a regular reminder for students to check their work. For added fun, keep a flashlight near the stoplight and "flash" a particular color, as needed, to guide your young writers. ***(L.K.2a–d) Karin Bulkow, Washington School for Comprehensive Literacy, Sheboygan, WI***

Stop.
End each sentence with punctuation.

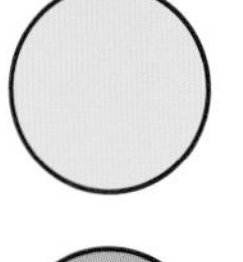

Slow down.
Make your writing easy to read and check your spelling.

Go.
Start each sentence with a capital letter.

Use Motion!

Put a little emphasis on punctuation marks with this active idea. When reading sentences, encourage youngsters to click one time for each period, tilt their heads in wonder and put a finger on one cheek for each question mark, and pump a fist in the air as a cheer for each exclamation point. ***(L.K.2b) Pamela Dwyer, John Brown Francis Elementary, Warwick, RI***

Fantastic Topics

Make students' ideas part of your lessons, and the writing experiences are sure to be tons of fun! Write student-generated writing topics on individual cards and put the cards in a decorative container. Before a lesson, remove a card and write sentences related to that topic to practice skills such as adding punctuation or writing and expanding sentences. ***Karin Bulkow, Washington School for Comprehensive Literacy, Sheboygan, WI***

Picture Prompts

Heighten students' interest to write stories with pictures they consider fascinating. Have youngsters cut from magazines pictures that are unique or would be fun to write about. Then store the pictures in a decorative box. When a child needs a writing jump start, have him go to the box for inspiration. ***Karin Bulkow***

Drawing a Story

This center activity leads to a fun twist for small-group story writing. Write the name of each student in a small group on a paper strip. Then fold the strip to make the same number of sections as there are students in the group. Make a similar paper for each small group of students. Put the papers at a center. A child finds her name on a strip and then draws in the leftmost blank section to begin, continue, or end a story. After each child has visited the center, gather each small group, in turn, and guide youngsters to use their drawings to write a story. ***(W.K.3) Deanna Greenwood, Columbiana, OH***

Simple Sequencing

A child transforms a sheet of paper into a graphic organizer with two simple steps! First, he folds a sheet of paper two times and unfolds it to make four equal sections. Second, he labels the sections in order: *First*, *Next*, *Then*, and *Finally*. Then he is ready to write and draw in the spaces about a topic of his choice. ***(W.K.2, 3) Karin Bulkow***

Nonfiction Fun

Inspire students to teach what they know with this writing activity. Instruct each child to draw and label a picture of her choice, such as a shark, an apple slice, or a volcano. Then have her write a fun fact about her topic and draw a decorative border around her writing. Encourage youngsters to share their work, in turn, to teach you and her classmates! ***(W.K.2) Karin Bulkow***

See page 225 for a **descriptive writing** skill sheet and page 226 for a **story organizer**.

Name ____ Descriptive writing (W.K.1–3)

Ready to Write!

Draw. Label your drawing.

Write.

Name ______________________________ Story organizer (W.K.3)

Oops!

Plan a story.

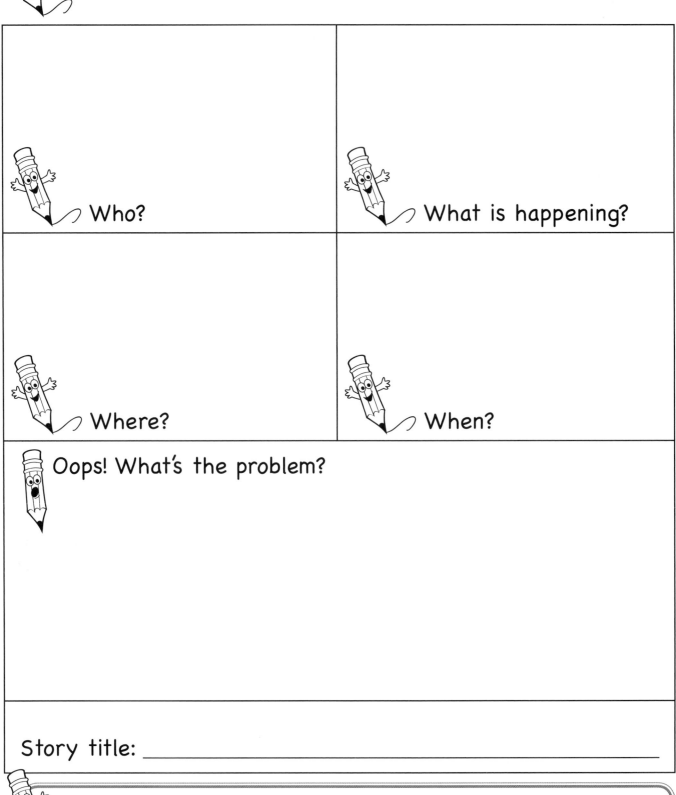

Who?	What is happening?
Where?	When?

Oops! What's the problem?

Story title: ______________________________

Write the story. Be sure to solve the problem.

Super Selections for Any Storybooks!

If you are looking for activities to use with a storybook of your choice, check out these fabulous options!

Ask Questions!

Story elements (RL.K.3)

This little ditty reminds youngsters to look for key parts of a story while they read!

(sung to the tune of "Do Your Ears Hang Low?")

When I read a story,
I ask questions here and there.
Who are the characters?
What is happening and where?
Is there a problem to be solved?
And how will the plot evolve?
Ask questions when you read!

Wonderful Word Work!*

Build vocabulary (L.K.6)

Prepare to introduce unfamiliar or interesting words in a book with this simple sticky note idea. Prior to reading a chosen story with students, skim the text for challenging vocabulary. Write the words on a sticky note and put it on the inside front cover of the book. To begin, write a word from the sticky note on chart paper and lead youngsters to discern its meaning. Continue with each remaining word. If desired, model using the words in sentences. During the read-aloud, instruct each youngster to respond with a predetermined signal, such as touching one's ear, each time she hears one of the featured words. Then encourage her to use her expanded vocabulary in her conversations and in her writing.

Barbara Mason, Deposit Elementary, Deposit, NY

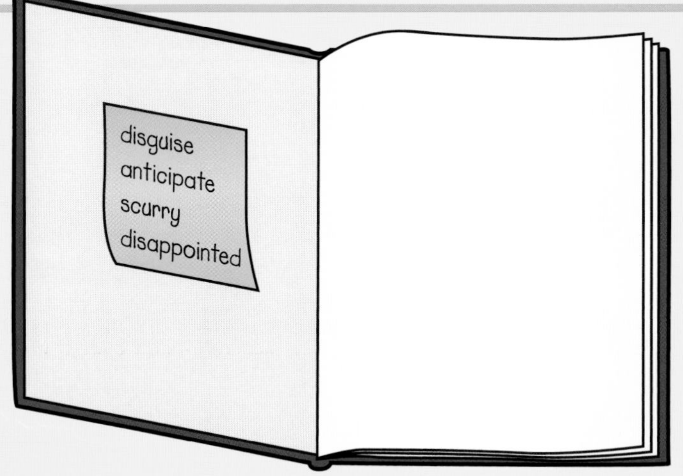

*This activity can be easily adapted for use with nonfiction books!

Puppet Possibilities*

Retelling a story (RL.K.2)

Student-made props are the center of attention for this partner activity. In advance, have each child in a twosome select a familiar book. Then have her draw the main characters or key topics for her book on paper, cut them out, and glue each one to a separate craft stick. Store each child's resulting puppets with her storybook. At a later time, a child gives her book to her partner to look at while she uses her props to retell the story or name the key topics. Then partners switch roles to review a different book. **For added fun,** provide a puppet theater for students to use during their performances.

adapted from an idea by Deborah Carlberg
Stewartsville Elementary
Goodview, VA

tip: An empty refrigerator box can be easily transformed into a perfectly pleasing puppet theater!

Storybook Sleuths*

Identify details in literature (RL.K.3)

Your young detectives are sure to want to solve this student-generated mystery! Showcase three or four familiar storybooks. Then invite a child to silently select his favorite book and prompt him to tell three key details from that story. Encourage his classmates to solve the mystery of the favorite storybook by identifying which of the featured books contains the named details. Continue with a variety of storybook selections on different days for more supersleuth practice!

The fish saw trouble. They used teamwork. The fish tricked a bigger fish.

adapted from an idea by Linda Rasmussen
Donner Springs Elementary
Reno, NV

After the Story*

Writing (W.K.1)

Youngsters use a combination of drawing and writing to share their opinions about a book with this follow-up activity. After reading a story aloud, give each child a copy of the book review on page 229. Guide her to write her name, the date, and the title and author of the book where indicated. Then have her color the face that is most fitting to share her opinion of the story, draw a related picture, and write to give reasons for her opinion. **For a home-school connection,** send each child home with a copy of the review for her to complete with a family member, using a book of her choice.

Name ____________ Date ____________ Book review (W.K.1)

Super Storybook?

Title ____________

Author ____________

My opinion of this book: ☺ ☹ 😐

Draw.

Write details to support your opinion.

adapted from an idea by Tonya Y. Wright
Baltimore, MD

Create Literature Journals!

Gather a collection of each child's completed book reviews; then staple the pages between construction paper covers to form a literature journal.

*This activity can be easily adapted for use with nonfiction books!

Name ______________________ Date ______________ Book review (W.K.1)

Super Storybook?

Title ______________________________

Author ______________________________

My opinion of this book:   

Draw.

Write details to support your opinion.

____

____

____

____

Note to the teacher: Use with "After the Story" on page 228.

Wild About Vocabulary!

Exploring meanings of words, word relationships, and more

What's the Word?

Add a little action to word work with this whole-group activity. Arrange youngsters into pairs and give each duo a card with a word that has two meanings, such as *duck*. Confirm that each twosome knows the meanings for their word. Next, instruct the duo to work together to plan actions that match each definition. When students are ready to perform, invite each twosome, in turn, to act out the different meanings for their assigned word. Then encourage classmates to guess the word and explain each of the meanings. ***Multiple-meaning words (L.K.4a)***

Bowl. One of you will demonstrate the word *bowl* as a container for food, and the other will show how to bowl, as in rolling a ball in the game of bowling.

Fur, Feathers, and Scales

One set of animal cards leads to a discussion for a variety of sorting opportunities! Give each of a small group of students a copy of the cards on page 232, cut apart. Encourage group members to work together to discuss categories that relate to their card collection, agree on a sorting rule, and then sort the cards accordingly. After each group has sorted the cards, lead a discussion to reveal students' final sorts and discuss the similarities and differences between the sorts. ***Sort objects into categories (L.K.5a)***

Karin Bulkow, Washington School for Comprehensive Literacy, Sheboygan, WI

Sorting possibilities include, but are not limited to, the following:
- fur, feathers, and scales
- two legs, four legs, no legs
- pets, not pets
- could or could not be seen in the backyard

Awesome Antonyms

Students go beyond naming the opposites of words with this sentence-centered activity. Think of a word for which students can easily name an opposite and use it in a sentence. Guide youngsters to use the opposite of one of the words to change the meaning of the sentence. For example, say, "The dog is asleep" for youngsters to generate the sentence "The dog is awake." Then discuss with youngsters how changing only one word changed the meaning of the sentence. Continue with different sentences. **For a more advanced version,** name a similar-style sentence that is false, such as "Turtles are fast." Encourage youngsters to use information about the topic (turtles) to prove why it is false and then use an antonym to make the sentence true. ***Opposites (L.K.5b)***

adapted from an idea by Karin Bulkow, Washington School for Comprehensive Literacy, Sheboygan, WI

The little elephant leads the line.

The big elephant leads the line.

Laugh, Giggle, Chuckle!

Students are sure to use a variety of words in their writing after this vocabulary sort. On chart paper, write "Emotions" and then list commonly used words expressing emotion. Then write synonyms for the featured emotions on cards and store them in a bag. To begin, read the words on the chart and tell youngsters there are many other words that are similar in meaning. Next, invite a child to take a card. Read the word and use it in a sentence to clarify its meaning. Guide youngsters to name the synonym written on the chart. Then have the volunteer tape the card in the corresponding column. Continue with each remaining card. Create other charts featuring words related to size, actions, and other categories when time permits. ***Synonyms (L.K.5)***

Karin Bulkow

Use That Word!

Inspire students to create imaginative sentences with interesting words from a read-aloud. During a reading, encourage youngsters to give a predetermined signal when they hear a new or unfamiliar word. Mark the word with a sticky note. After the story, go back to discuss the meanings of the identified words. Next, ask youngsters to make different real-life connections to the word. For example, if a character in a story thinks an apple is scrumptious, first talk about the meaning of *scrumptious* and then ask what someone or something else might think is scrumptious. Conclude by having each child write a sentence using one of the featured words and draw a picture to match. ***Use expanded vocabulary (L.K.6)***

Animal Cards

Use with "Fur, Feathers, and Scales" on page 230.

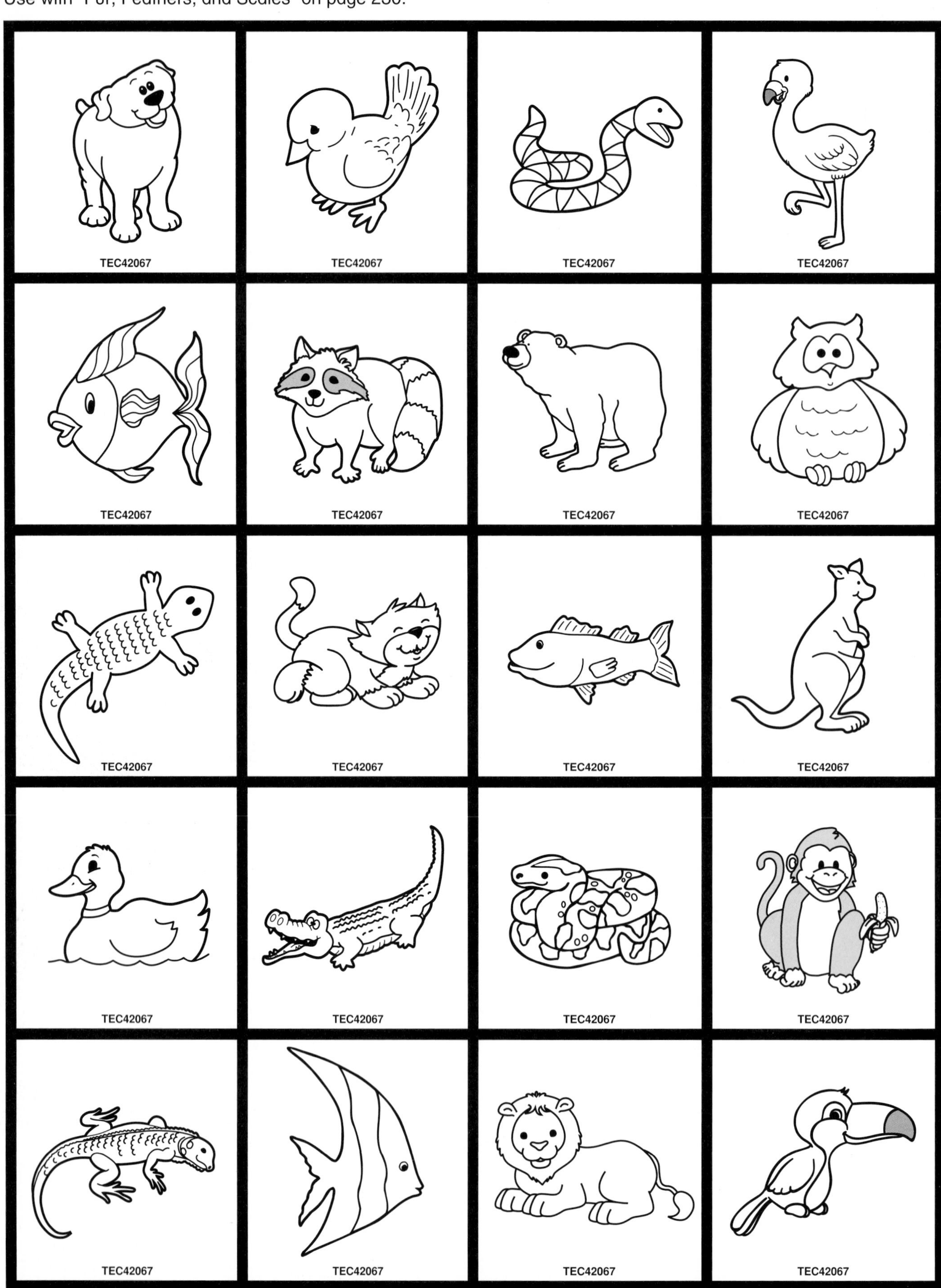

My favorite sea creature is a whale because it is gigantic! I like its spout too.
Emma

tip Sponge-painting with brown paint is a nice alternative to using sand for the ocean floor.

Animals at Sea

The result of this writing activity is an ocean mural of sea creatures. Ask youngsters to name and describe animals that live in the ocean and record their responses on chart paper. On writing paper, encourage each child to write the name of her favorite sea creature and two reasons that support her preference. Then help her glue her paper near the bottom of a large sheet of blue paper (ocean) and have her draw a picture of the animal above her writing. To complete the scene, have her trim the top of her ocean so it resembles waves and sprinkle play sand atop drizzled glue along the ocean floor. ***Sharing an opinion (W.K.1)***

Ada Goren, Winston-Salem, NC

My name is Malia. I like my laugh and my green eyes. I also like the way I run. I am special!

Me!

After reading aloud a story that focuses on personal characteristics, such as *I Like Myself!* by Karen Beaumont or *I Like Me!* by Nancy Carlson, ask students to respond to the prompt "What do you like about yourself?" Have each child write to complete the sentence "My name is _____." Next, have her write three or more details in sentences about things she likes about herself. Encourage her to conclude with a positive sentence, such as "I like me!" or "I am special!" Then invite youngsters, in turn, to share their work. If desired, invite classmates to offer what they like about the child that is sharing. ***Writing informative text (W.K.2)***

Jodie Smith, Melissa Independent School District
Melissa, TX

Page 234

Page 235

Page 236

Ready to Write!

Inspire students to write with these motivating ideas as well as with the writing helpers on pages 234-236.

Creative Pails

A sand pail is a great tool on a beach, but what other uses could there be for this shapely container? Showcase your students' responses with this summery display! Give each child a pail cutout. On one side, have him write about a fun way he might use a pail if he were not on a beach and tell why it is a good idea. On the other side, have him draw a picture to match his writing. Then help him attach a yarn handle to the pail. Hang the completed pails on a sunny scene with the title "Not at the Beach!" ***Writing explanatory text (W.K.2)***

Margie Rogers
Colfax Elementary
Colfax, NC

I could use my pail as a hat. I could march in a parade. I would look cool!
Wyatt

Kings and Queens

Find out what important decisions each of your students would make if he were ruler for the day. First, have him write to tell what location he would rule, such as a school or a country. Next, instruct him to write details about what he would do as a leader, about what he would change, and to give reasons to support his thinking. Help him glue his writing to a speech bubble cutout. Then have him draw and cut out a self-portrait in which he's wearing a crown and display the artwork with his writing. For added fun, have students embellish their crowns with foil, sequins, glitter glue, or other sparkly craft materials. ***Writing explanatory text (W.K.2)***

Lisa Cohen and Meredith MacCormick, Laurel Plains Elementary
New City, NY

Name ______________________ Responding to a prompt (W.K.2, 3)

Pick a Prompt!

Outdoor Fun

Cut.

Glue.

Write.

...18, 19...

How to Play Hide-and-Seek	Why Monkey Is Found	When I play outside with friends,...

Note to the teacher: Give each child a copy of this page. Read the prompts aloud. Then have each student cut out the prompts, glue one prompt to her paper, and respond to it.

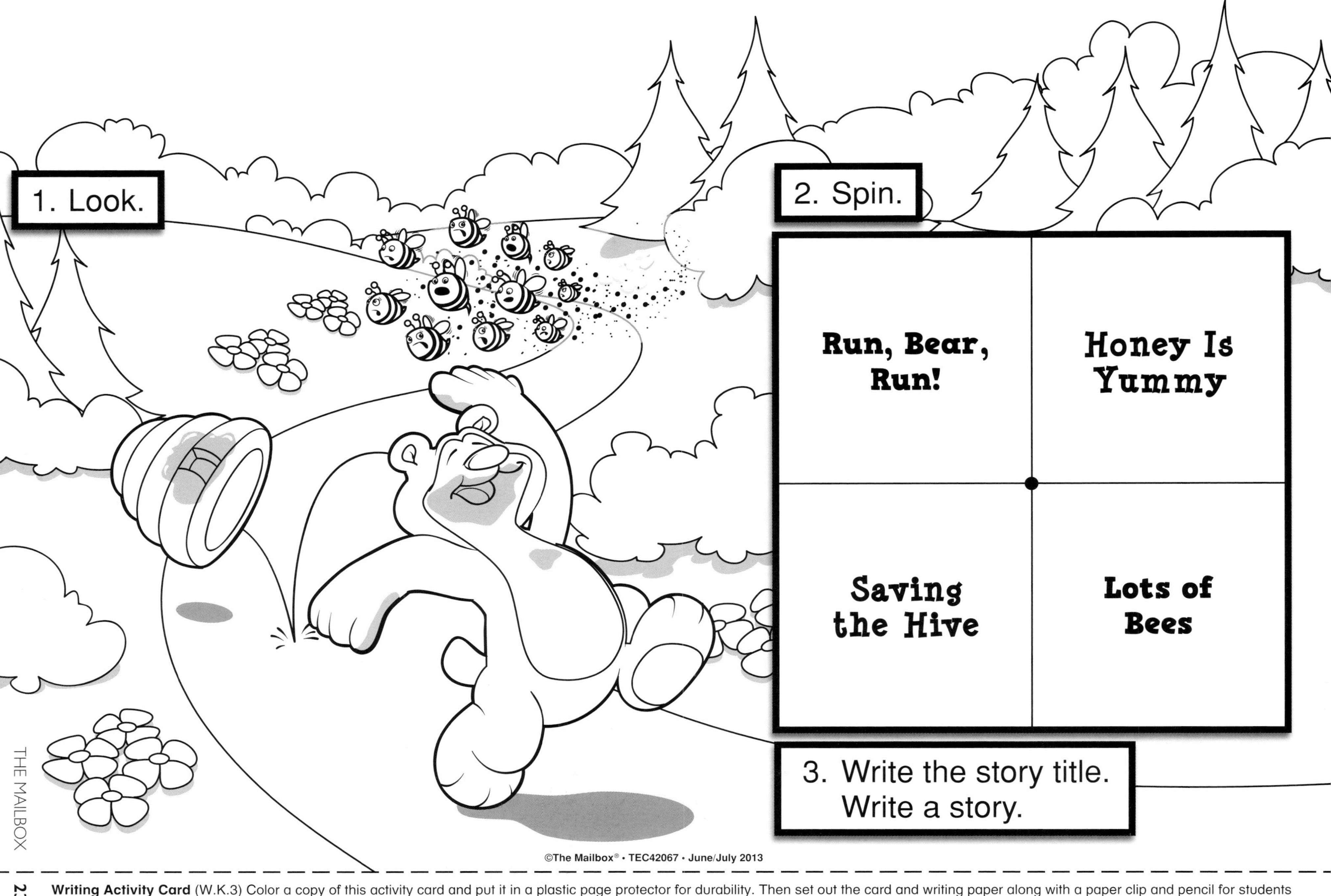

Writing Activity Card (W.K.3) Color a copy of this activity card and put it in a plastic page protector for durability. Then set out the card and writing paper along with a paper clip and pencil for students to use with the spinner.

Name______________________________ Using CVC words in sentences (L.K.2)

We Love to Shop!

Write sentences to tell what each animal **got**.
Use end marks.

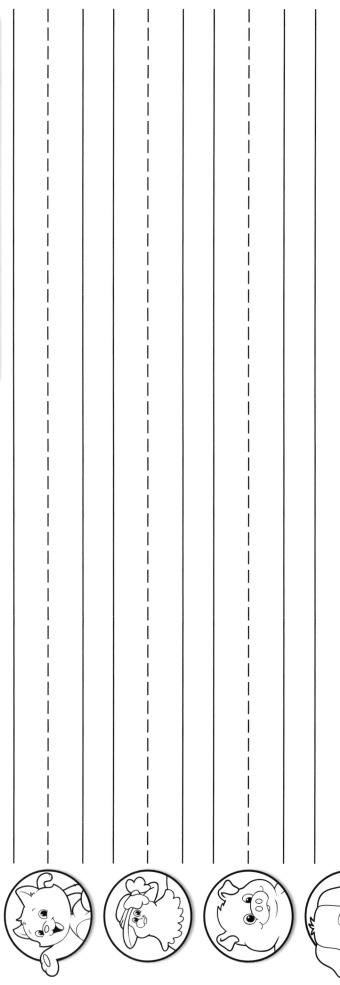

Bonus: Add two of these words—**big, fun, red, tan, wet**—to one of your sentences. Write the sentence.

Note to the teacher: Give each child a copy of the page. Identify the animals as a cat, a hen, a pig, and a dog.

Literature Units

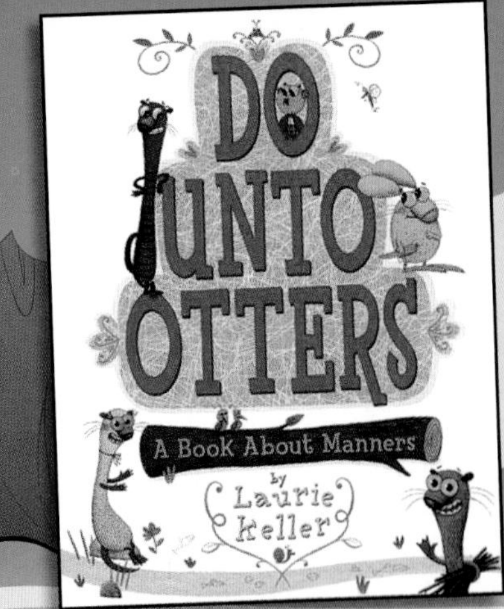

DO UNTO OTTERS: A BOOK ABOUT MANNERS

By Laurie Keller

When a family of otters moves next door to Mr. Rabbit, he is concerned that they won't get along. But once he learns a very special rule, he realizes that he should treat the otters the exact same way he would like to be treated.

ideas contributed by Karin Bulkow
Washington School for Comprehensive Literacy, Sheboygan, WI

Literacy

Have students recall story details to share why they, just like Mr. Rabbit, should "Do unto otters as you would have otters do unto you." Draw a supersize set of rabbit ears on a sheet of chart paper. Then have students name behaviors Mr. Rabbit expects of the otters and write each one on the ears. Finally, have each child sign the chart paper to show that this is how she would like to be treated as well. ***Recalling story details (RL.K.1)***

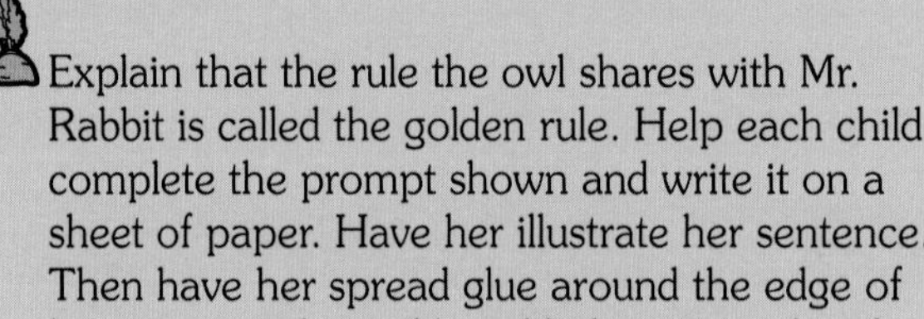

Explain that the rule the owl shares with Mr. Rabbit is called the golden rule. Help each child complete the prompt shown and write it on a sheet of paper. Have her illustrate her sentence. Then have her spread glue around the edge of her paper and sprinkle gold glitter over the glue! ***Making connections (W.K.8)***

I would show kindness by taking turns on the swings.

Social Studies

Take photographs of youngsters dramatizing ways to be kind and not so kind to others, such as sharing and not sharing crayons. Then place happy and sad face cutouts in your pocket chart and lead students to sort the photos accordingly. ***Understanding what it means to be a good citizen***

Science

Show students a picture of a real otter. Discuss true characteristics of otters such as living near rivers and eating fish. Then ask, "Do you think a real otter would wear clothes?" Guide students to understand that the book's illustrator put clothes on the otters because it makes the book more entertaining. Then have youngsters name more similarities and differences between real otters and the fictional ones in the story. ***Characteristics of real animals***

Story Discussion

- Think about a time that you had to apologize for something you did. Was it easy to apologize? Were you honest about what happened?
- How was Mr. Rabbit feeling about his neighbors at the beginning of the story? How do you think he felt at the end? Why?
- Why is it important to share? ***(SL.K.2)***

There Is a Bird on Your Head!

By Mo Willems

A relaxing day for Piggie and Elephant Gerald quickly changes when a bird lands on Gerald's head! His friend Piggie is more amused than bothered as she answers each of Gerald's many questions about one bird, then two birds, then a nest, and then a family of birds on his head. When Piggie finally suggests a friendly way to encourage the birds to move, Gerald is thrilled. But now Piggie has a family of birds on HER head!

ideas contributed by Stephanie Litwin, Mendham Township Elementary
Mendham, NJ

On an Elephant's Head

Retelling a story (RL.K.2)

Help youngsters recall major story events with this little ditty. Lead students in singing all five verses. For added fun, incorporate actions for youngsters to do while they sing. Then, after the last verse, have youngsters call out "Oh no!" Next, give each child a strip of paper with five boxes. Have him use the song verses to help him draw scenes in the boxes to retell the story.

(sung to the tune of "The Mulberry Bush")

This is the way [we fly like a bird],
[Fly like a bird, fly like a bird].
This is the way [we fly like a bird]
[To an elephant's head.]

Continue with the following verses: *we build a nest/on an elephant's head; we sit on a nest/on an elephant's head; the eggs will hatch/on an elephant's head; we fly away, onto Piggie's head!*

What Will Piggie Do Now?

Making predictions (RL.K.1)

When the birds move from Gerald's head to Piggie's head, students are sure to wonder what might happen next. Encourage youngsters to use the illustrations and the text to support what they think would happen if the story continued. Then give each child a copy of page 247. Instruct her to draw birds on the pig's head to match the end of the story. To the right of the pig, have her draw to show what she thinks will happen next. Then help her write a sentence that supports her prediction.

Be a Friend

Connecting characters to one's life experiences (RL.K.1)

This friendship-related shape book is sure to be popular with your youngsters! Invite pairs of students to act out different scenes from the story. Lead youngsters to draw conclusions about Piggie's and Gerald's friendship. After a dramatization of the last scene in the story, ask students to share times when they have helped a friend or asked a friend for help. Next, have each child draw on a rounded square cutout (booklet page) a personalized scene of a friend helping a friend. To make a shape book, staple the completed pages between matching gray covers. Then cut out paper ears and a trunk, glue them to the front cover as shown, and draw facial details.

Where Is Home, Little Pip?

By Karma Wilson and Jane Chapman

Little Pip the penguin wanders far from her home. Other arctic animals attempt to help her find her way back, but they only know their own homes. Finally, Little Pip's parents hear her singing, and she learns that home is where your loved ones are.

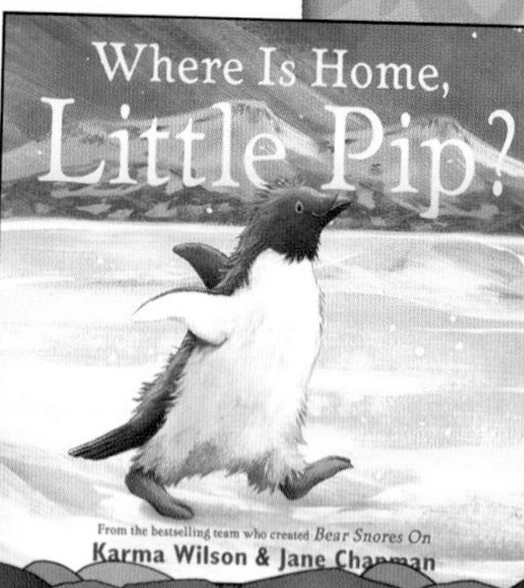

ideas contributed by Karin Bulkow
Washington School for Comprehensive Literacy, Sheboygan, WI

Literacy

Foster youngsters' success with learning new vocabulary with this simple visual aid. Draw a face and thought bubble on a large sheet of paper as shown and laminate it. After reading the story, use a dry-erase marker to write the word *wander* in the thought bubble. Explain that *wander* might be an unfamiliar word they need to think about. Next, use the word in a sentence, saying, "Don't wander far, Little Pip!" Then have students replace *wander* with words that mean nearly the same thing, such as *travel, trek*, or *hike.* Repeat the process with other words from the story, including *plodded* and *exhausted.* ***Building vocabulary (RL.K.4)***

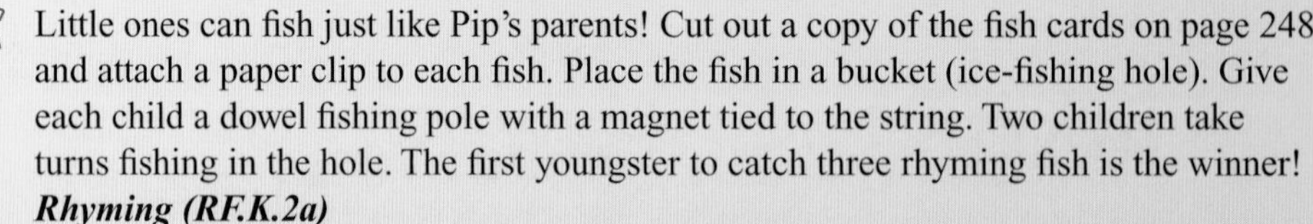

Little ones can fish just like Pip's parents! Cut out a copy of the fish cards on page 248 and attach a paper clip to each fish. Place the fish in a bucket (ice-fishing hole). Give each child a dowel fishing pole with a magnet tied to the string. Two children take turns fishing in the hole. The first youngster to catch three rhyming fish is the winner! ***Rhyming (RF.K.2a)***

Science

Have students recall the different animal homes mentioned in the story. Ask children why a penguin couldn't live successfully in the other animal homes. Then guide them to name necessary characteristics of a penguin's home for its survival. ***Animal homes and habitats***

Social Studies

Have students describe their homes. Invite volunteers to share why they would or would not be comfortable living in a home different from theirs. Then have each child draw a picture of his home and write a description. ***Text-to-self connections (L.K.1f)***

Story Discussion

Pip ran into many friends that tried to help her. What is something a friend has done to help you?

Have you ever wandered away from your family? How did it feel when you were alone? How did you find your family again?

If you got lost like Pip, how would you find help?

(SL.K.1a, b)

Lilly's Purple Plastic Purse

By Kevin Henkes

Lilly loves everything about her teacher, Mr. Slinger. But when he takes away her distracting new purple plastic purse, Lilly gets mad and writes him an unflattering letter. When she realizes her unkindness, she makes it up to Mr. Slinger and has a much better day!

ideas contributed by Janice Burch, Tri-Valley Elementary, Downs, IL

A Purse Full of Questions

Making text-to-self connections (RL.K.1), story discussion (RL.K.1)

Youngsters reflect on the story with questions pulled directly from Lilly's purse! Make a simple purple purse out of craft items. Then cut out a copy of the question cards on page 249 and place them in the purse. Have a child take a card from the purse. Then read the question aloud and encourage students to discuss the answer. Continue with each remaining question.

Sticks and Stones

Discussing feelings (SL.K.6)

Collect several sticks and stones and place them in your group-time area. Then gather youngsters around the sticks and stones. Discuss the meaning of the adage "Sticks and stones may break my bones, but words will never hurt me." Explain that words do hurt. Lilly used hurtful words and couldn't take them back, but she made the situation better. Have students share how they could make hurtful situations better. Then display the sticks and stones in the classroom as a reminder that words can be hurtful, and instead, youngsters should carefully choose words that are kind and helpful.

What Do You Think?

Writing to express an opinion (W.K.1)

Give each child a paper programmed with the title of the book. Instruct him to write and draw on his paper to show his opinion of the book. Next, have him glue his paper to a larger sheet of purple construction paper. Guide him to attach a paper handle to the project and add sequin or glitter details, as desired. Then display the resulting purses with the title "Our Thoughts on *Lilly's Purple Plastic Purse*."

Diary of a Worm
FROM THE AUTHOR OF CLICK, CLACK, MOO: COWS THAT TYPE

Written by Doreen Cronin
Illustrated by Harry Bliss

Worm shares important lessons and funny daily happenings in his diary, like how he tried to teach a spider how to dig, how it's nearly impossible for worms to dance, and how it is not easy being a worm. The hidden world of these earth-friendly creatures is revealed through the funny perspective of this endearing underground dweller.

My Critter Diary

Informative writing (W.K.2)

Students make their own unique diaries using a critter of their choice! To begin, discuss the definition of a diary, explaining that a diary is where personal thoughts are recorded. Then give each child a booklet with five pages of story paper. Have her choose a critter and make a diary entry on the first page, including at least one fact about the critter. Instruct students to add entries in a similar manner on four more days. If desired, have students decorate and attach a cover to the booklet.

Stephanie Litwin, Mendham, NJ

Anna
Dear Diary,
Today I landed on a flower. I got food from it. It tasted good. I like my pretty wings.

Read the Worm!

Differentiating between fact and fiction (RI.K.10)

Attaching paper worms to the correct plot of dirt is sure to be a hit with your students. Write factual and fictional details from the story on separate worm cutouts. Place the worms in a container. Label two pieces of brown paper (dirt) as shown. Next, invite a child to take a worm and help him read the text. Lead him to discuss whether the statement is fact or fiction. When classmates agree, have him glue the worm to the correct plot of dirt. Continue with each worm.

Stephanie Litwin

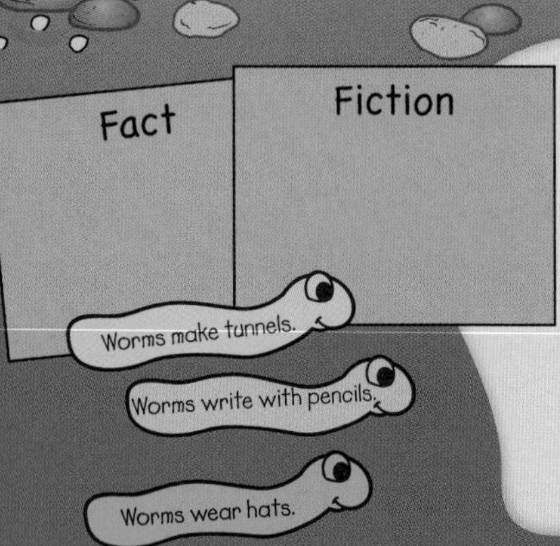

Worms make tunnels.
Worms write with pencils.
Worms wear hats.

What's Happening?

Understanding the relationship between text and illustrations (RL.K.7)

Have students sit in a circle and pass the book around as you lead them in singing the song shown. At the song's end, instruct the child with the book to open it, choose an illustration, and show it to his classmates. Encourage students to describe what is happening in the story based on the illustration. Continue as time permits.

(sung to the tune of "Clementine")

What is happening
In the story?
We can find out when we look
At the pictures on the pages
Of this pretty picture book!

Hey, Little Ant

Written by Phillip and Hannah Hoose
Illustrated by Debbie Tilley

What would your students do if they were the ants under a raised-up shoe? The author leaves students to ponder this question at the end of this thought-provoking tale.

Literacy

During a rereading of the story, read each of the two rhyming lines on each page, omitting the last word. Encourage youngsters to generate the unspoken rhyming word. ***Rhyming (RF.K.2a)***

Arrange students into small groups to discuss their responses to the question raised at the end of the book. Instruct youngsters to take turns, giving each child a chance to share her opinion. ***Speaking and listening (SL.K.1a, b)***

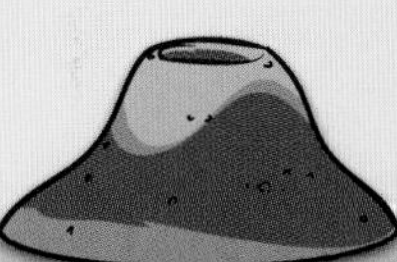

Writing and Science

Ask youngsters how their opinions about squishing ants did or did not change after reading the story. Then have each child write to tell why he would or would not step on the ant. If desired, encourage him to add illustrations to support his key points. ***Writing to share an opinion (W.K.1)***

Your students are sure to enjoy learning facts about these small insects! Set out books about ants for each of several small groups of students. Instruct each group to discuss and look through their books to answer a predetermined set of questions related to the information in *Hey, Little Ant*, such as the following: Are ants really crooks? Do ants really help each other? Is the ant really like the kid? Then gather youngsters to share how people and insects may and may not be alike. ***Facts about ants, participating in collaborative conversations (SL.K.1a, b)***

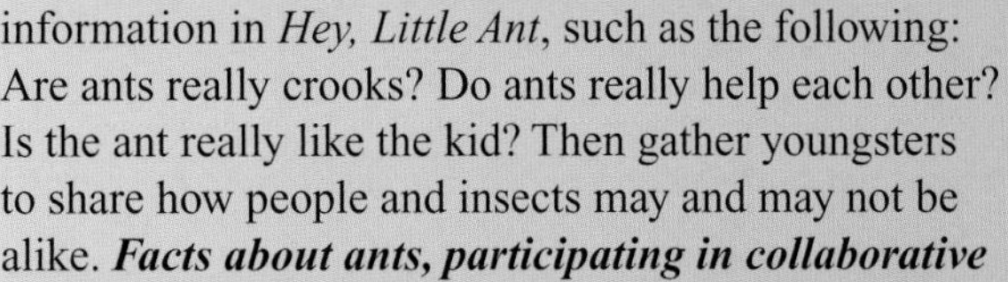
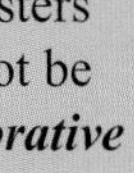

Stephanie Litwin, Mendham Township Elementary, Mendham, NJ

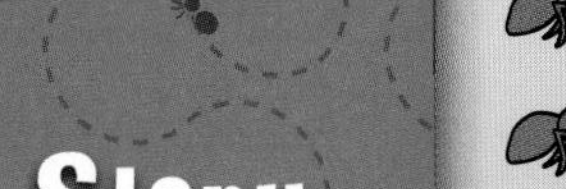

Story Discussion

- What other reasons might the boy have to squish the ant?
- What other reasons might the ant have to convince the boy not to squish it?
- How do you show respect toward animals?
- Was the boy being a bully toward the ant? Why or why not?

Stephanie Litwin

Six Seuss Classics

Entertain and inspire your young readers with the silly characters and tongue-twisting rhymes in these Dr. Seuss books. Then use the accompanying activities, and learning opportunities are sure to abound!

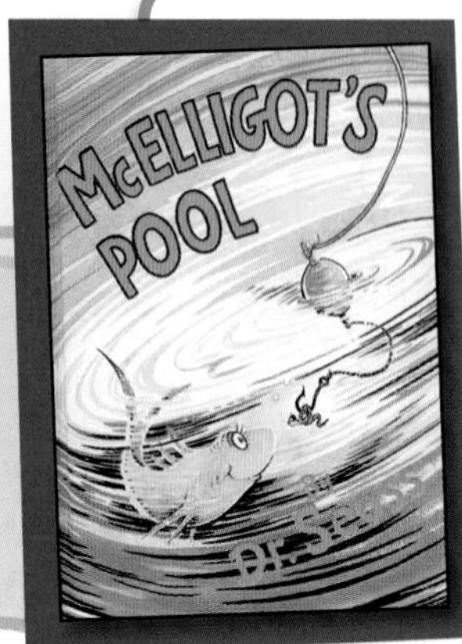

What a Catch!

Writing to share an idea (W.K.2)

Marco imagines there are many things he might catch if he sits patiently and fishes in *McElligot's Pool.* Encourage your youngsters to imagine what they might catch if they went fishing in "Mc[Your last name]'s pool"! Following some discussion, give each child a paper programmed with the sentence starter shown. Direct each child to complete the sentence and illustrate his catch on the top of the page. Display the pages with the title "Fishing in Mc[Your last name]'s Pool."

Stefan might catch an elephant fish.

Stephanie Litwin, Mendham Township Elementary, Mendham, NJ

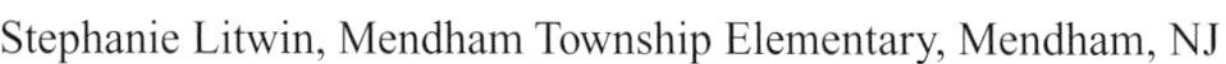

Faithful Like Horton?

Responding to literature (RL.K.10)

After reading *Horton Hatches the Egg* to your youngsters, remind them that Horton is faithful "one hundred 'per cent'." Ask students to share their ideas about what the word *faithful* means. Next, invite youngsters to tell about times they promised to help someone only to find that it was difficult to do. Lead students in discussing whether they, like Horton, were faithful to the end. Then have each student draw to show a time when Horton is faithful in the story and write to tell if he could be faithful just like Horton.

What Is Where?

Writing (L.K.1f)

Students create pages similar to those in the book *There's a Wocket in my Pocket!* with this silly activity. Invite a child to name an object and write its name on the board. Next, have a child name a silly word that rhymes with the object and write it on the board. After listing several different objects, direct each child to use a pair of rhyming words and write a sentence similar to the ones in the story. Then have her illustrate her sentence. If desired, bind the pages and title the book "There's a What Where?"

Monika
There's a spock behind the clock!

Stephanie Litwin

Make a Match!

Rhyming (RF.K.2a)

Invite a small group of students to go on an egg hunt after a read-aloud of *Green Eggs and Ham*. In advance, gather 15 plastic eggs and cut apart a copy of the cards from page 250. Place two cards in each egg so most of the pairs rhyme and secretly hide the eggs around the room. Then prepare a T chart as shown. To begin, encourage group members to go on an egg hunt to find all the eggs. Then invite a child to open an egg, name the pictures, and place the pair on the appropriate side of the chart. Have students take turns until all the eggs have been opened. **To extend the activity**, lead students in making rhyming pairs with nonrhyming cards until each card has a match!

Jennie Jensen
North Cedar Elementary
Lowden, IA

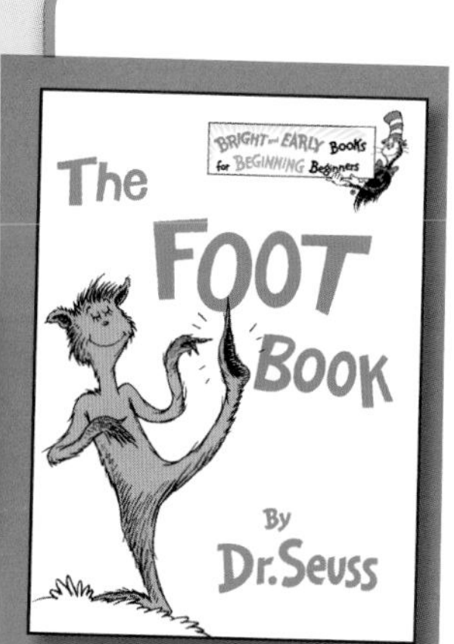

Two by Two

Counting by twos

After reading *The Foot Book*, your youngsters are sure to want to know how many feet they have altogether. So invite them to count and find out! Have students sit in a circle with their feet pointing toward the center. Guide youngsters to realize that they each have two feet. Then ask a volunteer to stand in the center of the circle. Have that student point to his feet and then a classmate's feet as he begins leading the group in counting the feet by twos. As a child's feet are pointed to, direct her to pull her feet in from the circle. Continue with a different student for more counting practice and to discover there will be the same number of feet each time.

Stephanie Litwin
Mendham Township Elementary
Mendham, NJ

Hat Snacks

Here's a prereading activity for *The Cat in the Hat* that's sure to hit the spot! Have each child spread frosting on a large marshmallow and wrap strips of red licorice laces around the marshmallow to make stripes. Then have each youngster set her prepared marshmallow atop a small white powdered donut. Have youngsters compare their hat snacks to the hat shown on the front cover of the book before settling in for a read-aloud of the story.

Kelly Buddenhagen
Breinigsville, PA

Not Just Fish Stories!

Some books are oldies but goodies! Use these classics to reel in "fin-tastic" teaching opportunities for essential skills.

ideas submitted by Stephanie Litwin, Mendham, NJ

LITERACY

Good Friends

After a read-aloud of *The Rainbow Fish* by Marcus Pfister, discuss with students why they think the Rainbow Fish did not want to share his glittery scales, why the fish changed his mind, and why the fish did indeed feel happy at the end of the story. Guide students to make text-to-self connections with how sharing and being kind to others affects their own friendships. Then lead youngsters in singing the song shown to foster fabulous friendships. ***Comprehension (RL.K.1)***

(sung to the tune of "If You're Happy and You Know It")

I can be a good friend, yes I can.	*Point to self.*
You can be a good friend, yes you can.	*Point to a classmate.*
We show kindness here and there.	*Shake hands with a classmate.*
We're respectful everywhere.	*Bow or curtsy.*
Oh, we can be good friends, yes we can!	*Put arms across shoulders of classmates.*

MATH

Ten Fish

The rhythmic text in *One Fish Two Fish Red Fish Blue Fish* by Dr. Seuss is the perfect introduction for this math activity! Write the poem shown on sentence strips, leaving blank spaces for the number words, and slide the strips into your pocket chart. Nearby, put sets of number word cards from *zero* to *ten*, with extra *five* cards for the doubles facts. Give each child two blue papers (water) and ten goldfish crackers or paper cutouts. Next, slide a word card atop the blank in the first sentence and read the first two lines of the poem. Encourage youngsters to arrange their fish to determine the correct word that completes the second sentence. Invite a child to use the correct words to complete the poem. Then have students record the number combination on paper and read the poem. Continue with different number combinations. ***Making ten (K.OA.A.4)***

One fish in a little pool.
Nine fish in a separate school.
One and nine fish do make ten.
Now let's start all over again!

SCIENCE & WRITING

Courageous Camouflage

In Leo Lionni's book *Swimmy*, the little black fish's idea for a creative disguise leads a large group of red fish into the open water. Find out what your students think about Swimmy's idea with this activity. Following a read-aloud of the story, discuss how some animals use camouflage for protection, such as a chameleon's ability to change colors to match its surroundings. Guide youngsters to discuss Swimmy's use of camouflage as a solution to the story problem. Then have each child draw and write to answer the questions "Do you think Swimmy's use of camouflage was a good idea? Why or why not?" ***Animal characteristics, writing to share an opinion (W.K.1)***

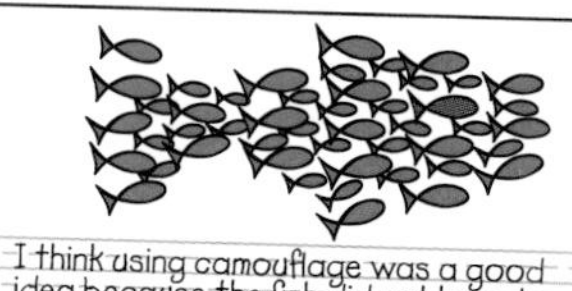

I think using camouflage was a good idea because the fish did not have to hide anymore.

Act it out!

Have the class mimic the movements of the fish in the story. Lead them to realize the importance of everyone moving at the same time and at the same speed.

Name ____________________

Making predictions
(RL.K.1)

What's Next?

____

____

Note to the teacher: Use with "What Will Piggie Do Now?" on page 239.

Fish Cards

Use with the second literacy activity on page 240.

Use with "A Purse Full of Questions" on page 241.

How would you feel if a teacher took something away that is special to you?

TEC42065

How do you think Lilly feels when she takes the note and bag of snacks out of her purse?

TEC42065

Have you ever done something mean that you felt bad about? What did you do to make up for it?

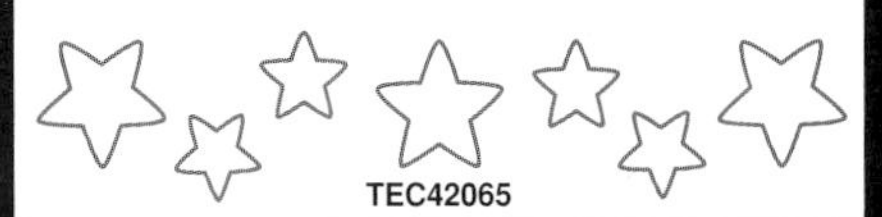

TEC42065

Is it easy to apologize for something you've done?

TEC42065

What are some things Lilly does that are wrong?

TEC42065

What are some things Lilly does that are right?

TEC42065

Talk about something that you would be excited to share.

TEC42065

Are Lilly's actions basically good or bad? Why?

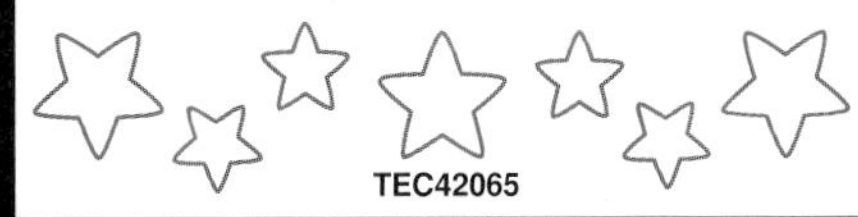

TEC42065

Lilly loves several things about school. What do you love about school?

TEC42065

Rhyming Picture Cards

Use with "Make a Match!" on page 245.

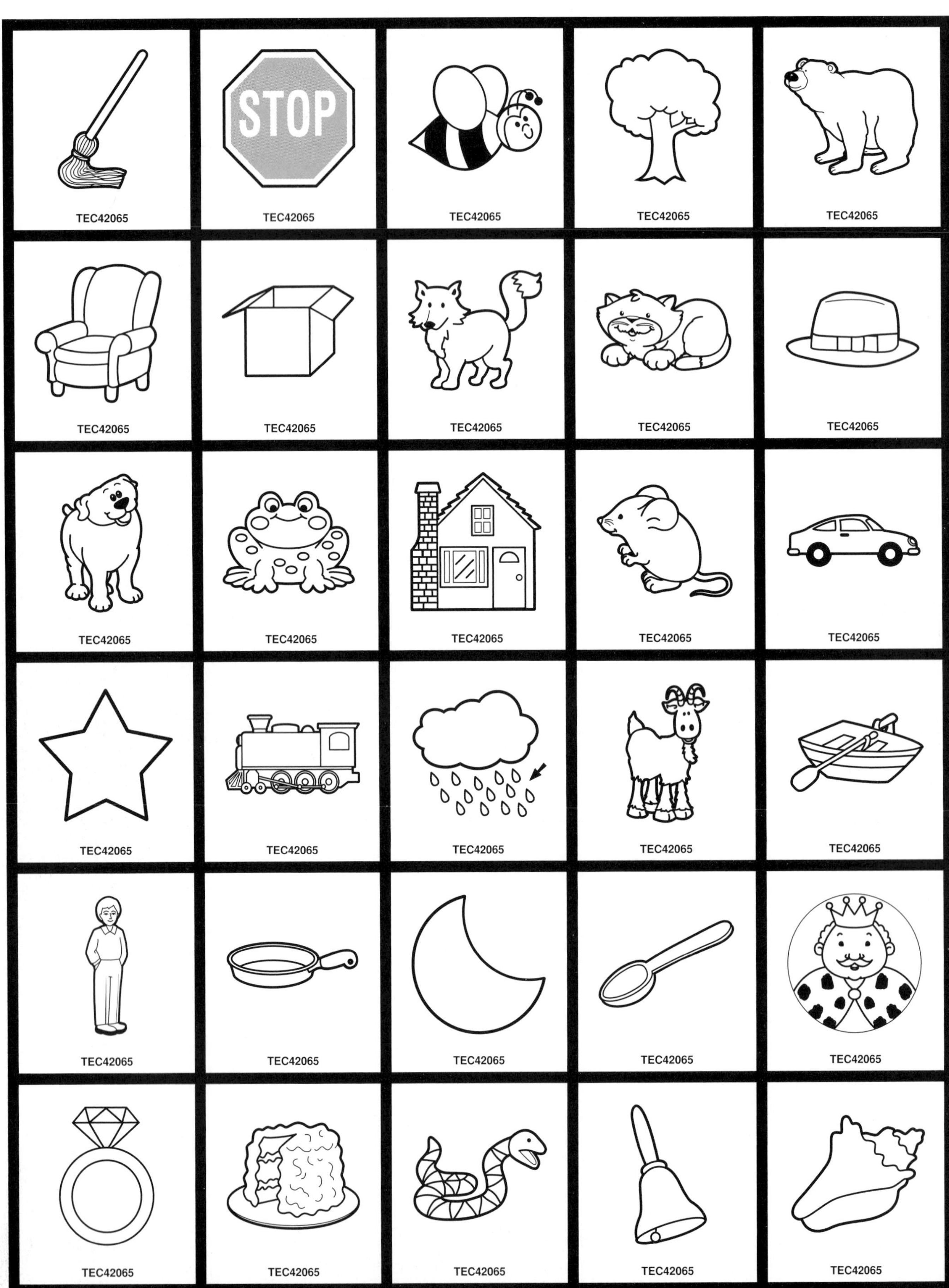

Math Units

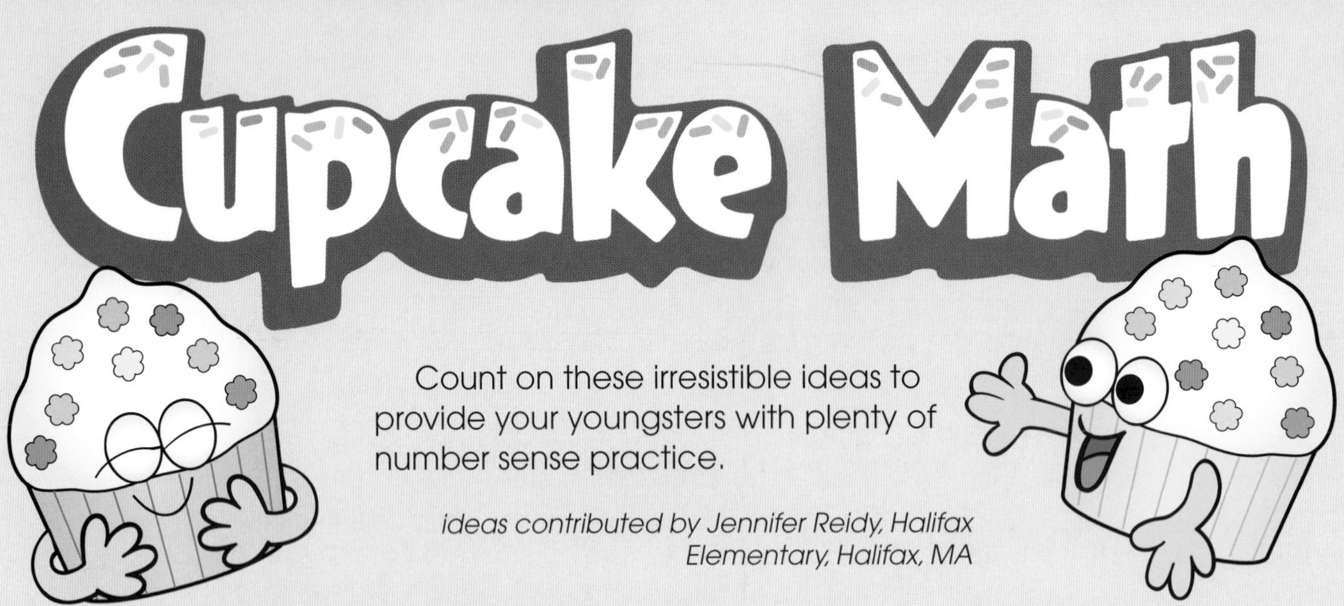

Cupcake Math

Count on these irresistible ideas to provide your youngsters with plenty of number sense practice.

ideas contributed by Jennifer Reidy, Halifax Elementary, Halifax, MA

A Cherry on Top

Number recognition, counting (K.CC.A.3)

Students collect colorful cupcakes while playing this small-group game. To prepare, write a different number from 2 to 12 on separate red sticky dots (cherries) and label a twelfth cherry with a star. Then attach each cherry to a separate supersize pom-pom (cupcake). Next, place a liner in each section of a cupcake tin and randomly place each cupcake in a liner. To play, a child rolls a pair of dice, counts the total number of dots, and removes the cupcake labeled with the matching number. If that cupcake is no longer in the tin, the child pretends to eat the cupcake with the star cherry and then returns it to the tin to complete her turn. Players continue taking turns until the star cupcake is the only one left in the tin.

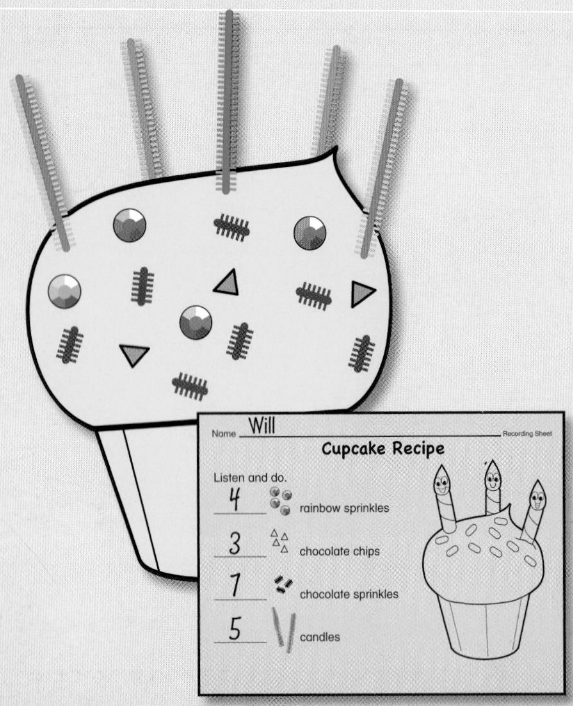

One of a Kind!

Counting, writing numbers (K.CC.A.3)

Invite your young bakers to put toppings of their choosing on these cupcakes! Place at a center small containers of each of the following: colorful sequins (rainbow sprinkles), 2" pieces of pipe cleaner (candles), small brown paper triangles (chocolate chips), and ¼" brown pipe cleaner pieces (chocolate sprinkles). For each child, set out a copy of the recording sheet from page 254 and a cupcake cutout (page 254). A child places a small number (fewer than ten) of each item on a cupcake. Next, he counts the total number of each topping and writes the numbers on his recording sheet. Then he glues the toppings to his cupcake.

How Many Sprinkles?

Matching numbers to sets, comparing sets (K.CC.A.3; K.CC.C.6)

These cupcakes can be used for several activities. Cut out a cupcake pattern from page 254 for each student. Next, write a different number on each liner, glue a matching number of colorful sequins (sprinkles) on each cupcake top, and then cut apart the liners and cupcake tops. To use the cupcakes, choose one or all of the options below.

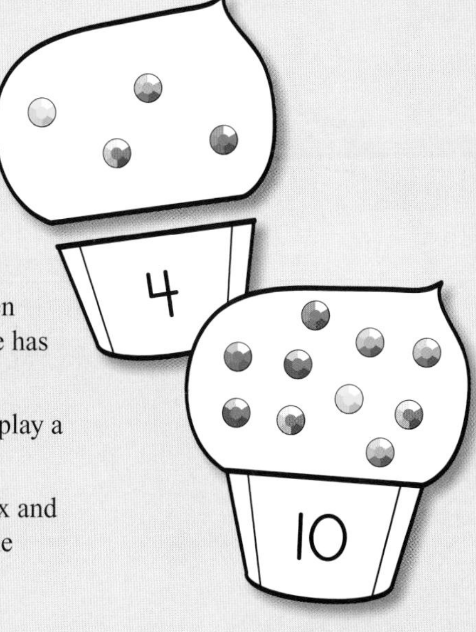

Whole group: Distribute the cupcake tops and have each youngster count his total number of sprinkles. Next, display two cupcake liners and have the students holding the cupcake tops with the corresponding number of sprinkles place them on the appropriate liners. Lead the class in counting the sprinkles on each cupcake top. Then have students compare the sets of sprinkles. Ask a volunteer to announce which cupcake has more sprinkles. Continue until each child has matched his cupcake top to a liner.

Small group: Students place the cupcake tops and liners facedown in an open area and play a game similar to Concentration.

Center: Store the cupcake parts in a clean, empty cake mix box. A child empties the box and matches each cupcake top to the corresponding liner. If desired, program the backs of the matching cupcake parts to make the activity self-checking.

Candle Comparison

Comparing sets (K.CC.C.6)

Who has more candles? Your youngsters will find out during this whole-group activity! Have each child decorate a cupcake cutout (patterns on page 254). Then give each child ten two-inch pipe cleaner pieces (candles) and a set of number cards labeled from 1 to 10. Next, pair students and lead them in saying the chant shown. Have each child in a twosome randomly pick a number card and place the corresponding number of candles on her cupcake. Direct the partners to compare their sets of candles and determine which cupcake has more candles and which has fewer or if the cupcakes have the same amount of candles. For different number comparisons, have students remove the candles from their cupcakes, set the two number cards aside, and chant the rhyme again. **For a more challenging version,** have each child in the duo record the number of each set of candles and circle the larger number.

Put candles on cupcakes!
Yes, you and me.
Which has more?
We'll check and see!

Unique Treats

Making sets with more and fewer (K.CC.C.6)

Students place fewer and more sprinkles on each of two tasty treats for this activity. To make a mat, glue two cupcake cutouts (patterns on page 254) to each side of a sheet of paper and label them as shown. Then give each child a copy of the prepared mat and 12 small pom-poms (sprinkles). Next, write a number less than 12 on the board and draw a corresponding number of dots. Guide youngsters to place an appropriate number of sprinkles on each of their two cupcakes. Continue with different numbers and sets. After sufficient practice, help each child write a number on her paper between the two cupcakes. Then have her glue sprinkles to each cupcake to match the labels.

Cupcake Patterns

Use with "One of a Kind!" on page 252 and "How Many Sprinkles?" "Candle Comparison," and "Unique Treats" on page 253.

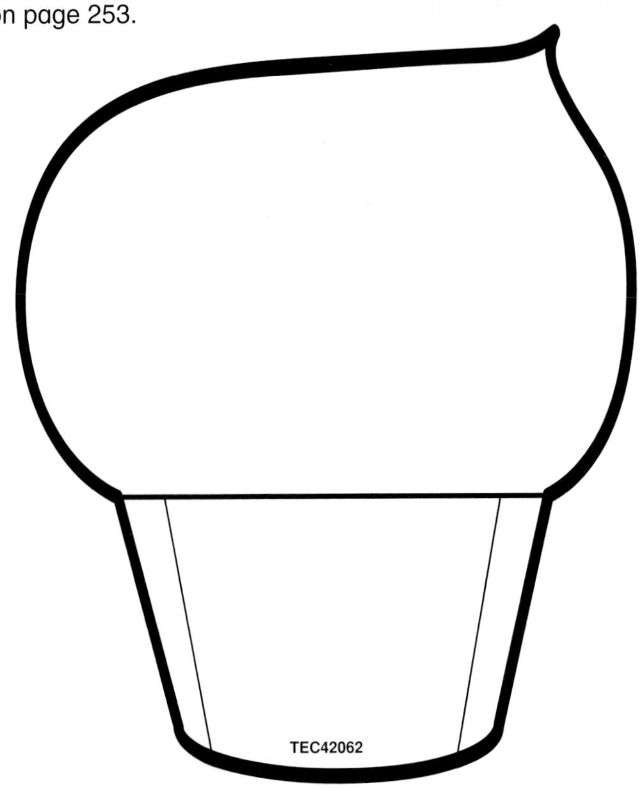

TEC42062

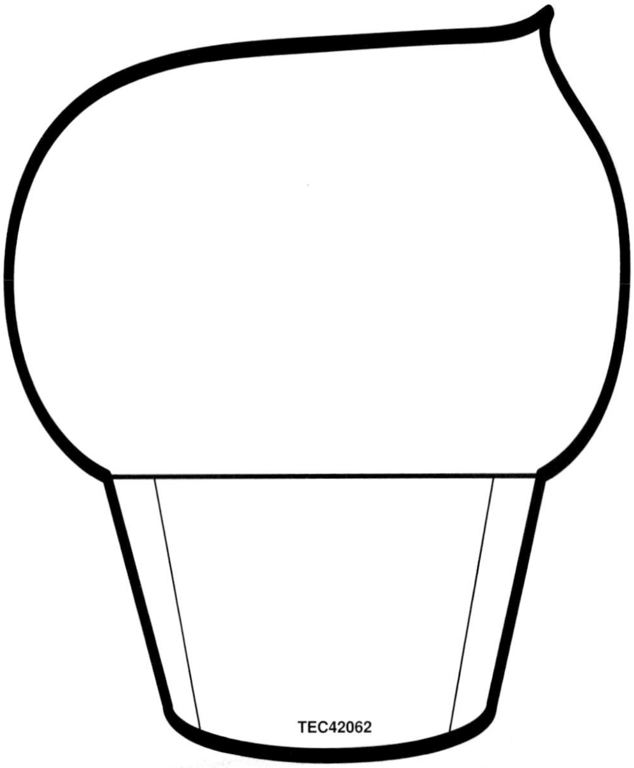

TEC42062

Name ______________________________ Recording Sheet (K.CC.A.3)

Cupcake Recipe

Listen and do.

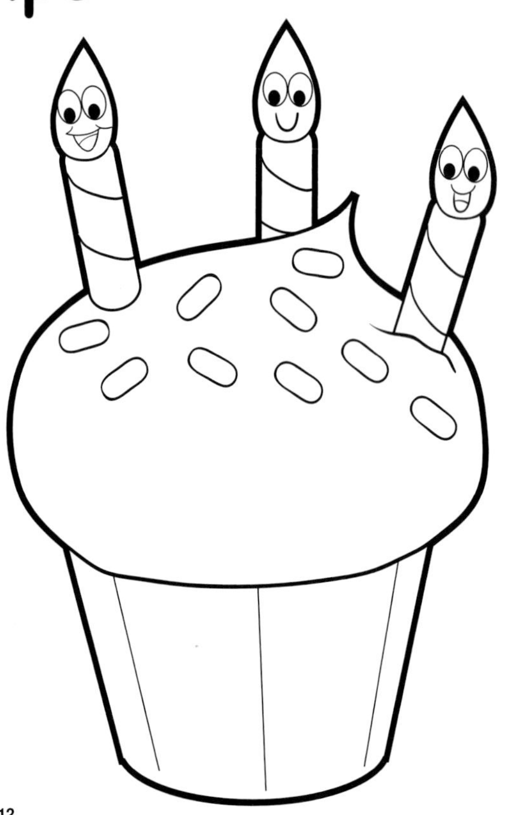

________ 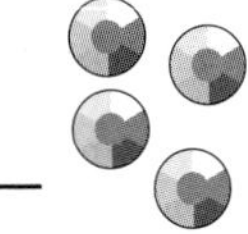 rainbow sprinkles

________ chocolate chips

________ chocolate sprinkles

________ candles

 Note to the teacher: Use with "One of a Kind!" on page 252.

Name ______________________ Comparing sets (K.CC.A.3; K.CC.C.6, 7)

Blow Them Out!

Count. Write.

Color the that has **more**.

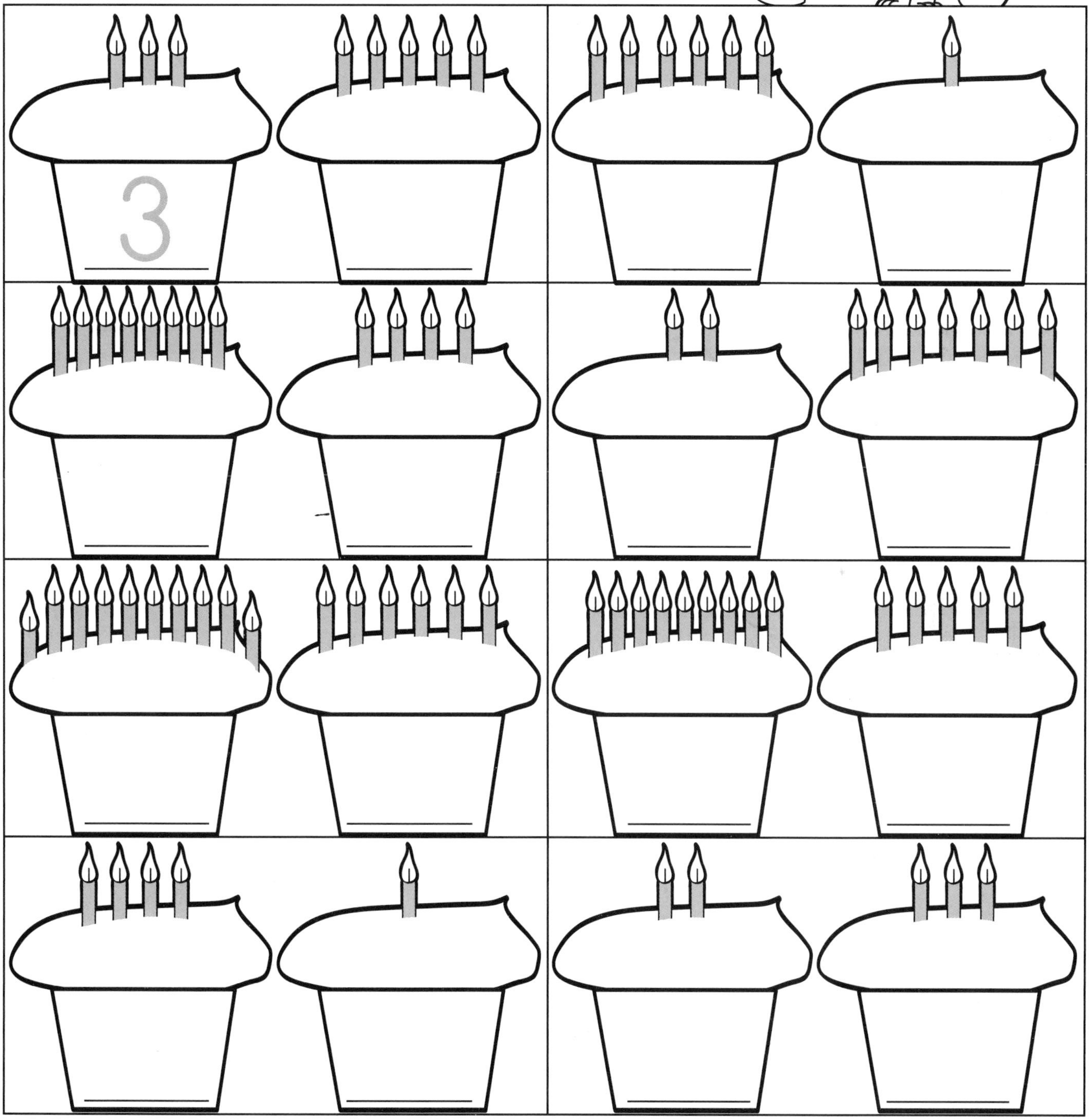

3

Bonus: Draw 2 . On one, draw **to equal your age**. On the other , draw **fewer** .

Shaping Up Geometry!

Give your students' math skills a workout with this collection of shapely ideas.

ideas contributed by Janice Burch, Tri-Valley Elementary, Downs, IL

Ready, Set, Roll?

Attributes of geometric figures (K.G.B.4)

Can spheres slide? Will a cylinder roll? Students will find out the answers to these questions and more during this whole-group activity. Have youngsters sit in pairs facing each other. Then provide each duo with a set of three-dimensional shapes. Name a shape and ask students, "Can it roll, or can it slide?" Encourage students to make predictions and then test each action by having partners roll and slide the shape to each other if possible. Encourage youngsters to record their findings and then continue with different shapes for more math practice!

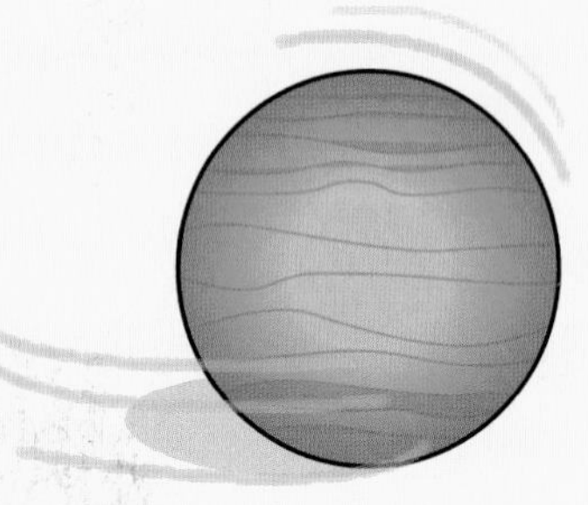

Searching for Shapes

Recognizing and drawing shapes in the environment (K.G.A.2)

Your youngsters will delight in hunting for familiar shapes with the help of these seasonal wands. Draw and label a different shape on each of several seasonal cutouts and glue each cutout to a craft stick. Place the resulting wands at a center along with a supply of drawing paper and crayons. A child folds her paper to make four boxes. Next, she chooses a wand and draws the featured shape in a box on her paper. Then she points the wand at different classroom objects in search of matching shapes. When she finds a match, she draws it in a box on her paper. She continues to search for shapes until she has one drawing in each box.

Super Sleuths!

Identifying shapes (K.G.A.2)

Students test their memory skills and name shapes at this partner center! Set out a supply of pattern blocks and a large paper cone. To begin, Partner 1 chooses five shapes and places them in front of her partner to study. Next, Partner 2 closes his eyes so Partner 1 can secretly cover one shape with the cone. When ready, Partner 1 asks, "What's undercover?" signaling her partner to open his eyes. Partner 2 names each visible shape; then he calls the name of the shape he thinks is hidden. If he is correct, Partner 1 says, "You are a super sleuth!" and lifts the cone. If he is not correct, Partner 1 gives clues about the hidden shape until her partner correctly names it. Then the players switch roles.

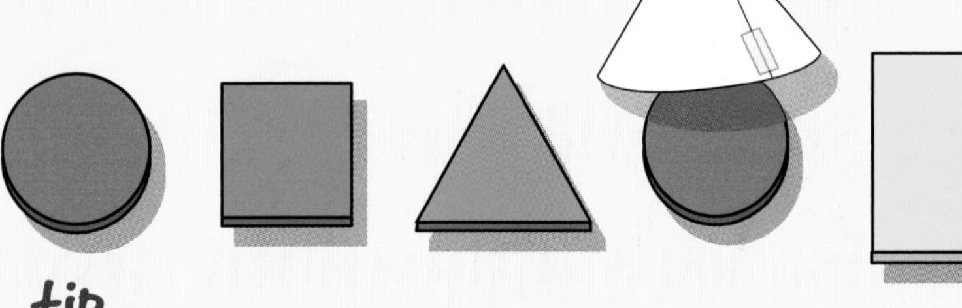

tip Cut a line to the center of a circle cutout and roll the paper to make a cone.

Feel for Facts

Attributes of geometric shapes (K.G.B.4)

This small-group activity encourages youngsters to use their sense of touch to identify shapes. Gather several shapes and a clean sock. To begin, secretly place a shape inside the sock and pass it to a student. As the child reaches his hand inside the sock to feel the shape, lead the group in the chant shown. Next, have the child name the number of flat surfaces and corners he feels. Then ask group members to name the shape before the child removes it from the sock. Review with students why their guesses were correct or incorrect. Continue with different shapes until each student has had a turn.

Count the corners and surfaces too;
What shape is in the sock for you?

What Am I?

Attributes of shapes in the environment (K.G.B.4)

Here's a great way for youngsters to connect shape names to the shapes they see in the environment. Place several three-dimensional objects, such as the ones on the chart, in a large paper bag. To begin, secretly choose an object hidden in the bag. Announce to students different clues that describe the selected object. For example, to describe a cube-shaped tissue box, say, "It has six flat sides. It can stack. It has eight corners. When someone sneezes, I might ask her to get something out of this object." After each clue, invite volunteers to guess the name of the shape and name the object. When a child solves the mystery, invite her to remove that object from the bag and show it to her classmates. Continue with each remaining object.

Shapes

Cube
- tissue box
- block

Cone
- ice cream cone
- party hat

Sphere
- ball
- orange

Cylinder
- soup can
- unsharpened pencil

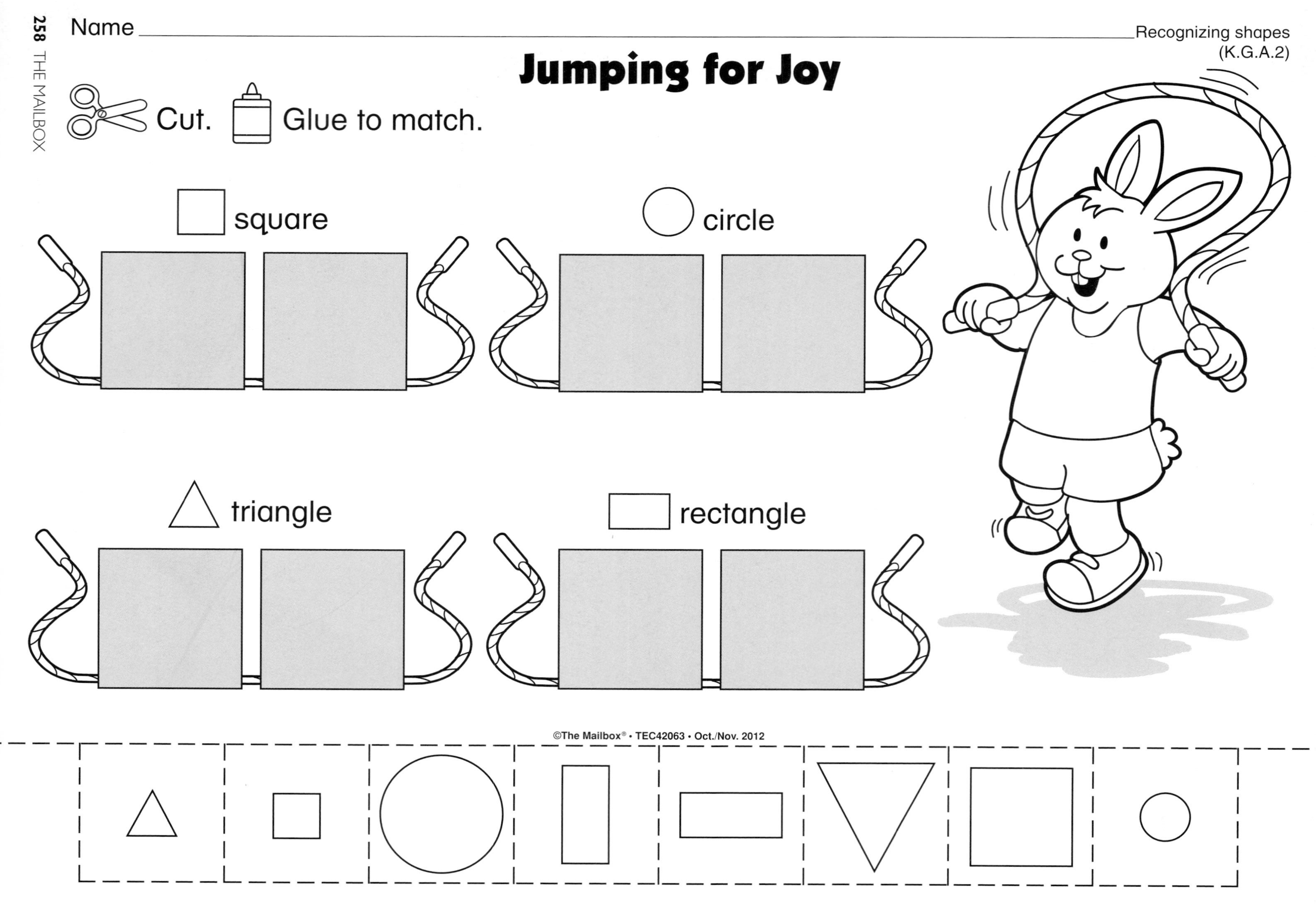
Name
Recognizing shapes
(K.G.A.2)
Jumping for Joy
Cut.
Glue to match.
square
circle
triangle
rectangle

Put It All Together!

Fabulous Addition Ideas

Count on your students' math skills improving when you use these kid-pleasing addition ideas.

Jump, Jump, Jump!

Beginning addition (K.OA.A.1)

This quick and easy idea pairs exercise with addition! Write an addition problem on the board. Have students jump the matching number of times for each addend. Then invite a child to solve the problem. If correct, have students applaud her by jumping that number of times. Continue with different addition problems. **For an added challenge**, write several addition problems with the same sum, one after the other. Lead youngsters to realize that for each problem, they jumped the same number of times. Then guide students to understand that different number combinations can have the same sum.

Stephanie Schmidt, Lester B. Pearson Public School, Waterloo, Ontario, Canada

Nine!
One, two, three,
four, five, six, seven,
eight, nine!

Draw and Solve

Modeling addition (K.OA.A.1)

Place at a center a supply of paper, crayons, and cards labeled with addition facts. A child divides a sheet of paper into four sections. He chooses a card and draws in a blank section of his paper pictures to match the equation. Then he writes the number sentence below his drawings. He continues with different addition facts to complete his paper. **For an alternative option**, encourage students to use a strategy of their choosing to solve the addition problem and draw or write to show the strategy he used.

Serve It Up!

Solving addition word problems (K.OA.A.2)

For this small-group activity, gather three bowls, write "+" and "=" on separate index cards, and place the bowls and cards in a row as shown. Also gather a supply of green and orange cubes (peas and carrots). Say a word problem and invite volunteers to put the corresponding number of peas and carrots in the appropriate addend bowls. Direct each child to write and solve the equation on a sheet of paper. Then have a child combine the contents of the bowls into the third bowl and have him count aloud to announce the correct sum. Continue with different problems.

Carrie ate four carrots. Then she ate six peas. How many vegetables did Carrie eat in all?

Leah Hurwitz
Yeshiva of Spring Valley
Monsey, NY

How Many More?

Ways to make ten (K.OA.A.4)

Have each youngster string ten jumbo beads onto a pipe cleaner and then fold over each end of the pipe cleaner. Guide students to slide all the beads to one side of the pipe cleaner. Then announce a number (ten or less) and have students slide the corresponding number of beads to the opposite end of the pipe cleaner. Ask students how many more beads are needed to make ten. Then have each child count the remaining beads on the pipe cleaner to find the answer. Finally, have each child record a matching number sentence on a sheet of paper. **For an added challenge**, guide students to write related math facts.

Melissa Moran, C. W. Harris School, Phoenix, AZ

Carson
6 + 4 = 10

Colorful Petals

Decomposing numbers (K.OA.A.3)

Label paper circles (flower centers) with different sums from 3 to 12. Place them at a center along with paper, crayons, and pom-poms of two colors. A student takes a paper circle. Then, to show one way to make the corresponding number, she places a combination of pom-poms (petals) around the flower center. She writes the featured number on a sheet of paper and then writes and draws her addition combination. She continues until she writes three or more combinations for the number. If time permits, she takes a different flower and repeats the activity.

adapted from an idea by Lauren Giles, Oakview Elementary, Simpsonville, SC

Abby 8
6 + 2 = 8

8

See page 261 for a **skill sheet** on making ten.

Name ______________________________ Addition (K.OA.A.4) Making ten

Stacking Snowballs

Count.

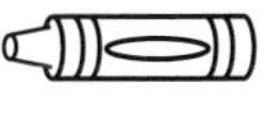
Draw ◯ to make 10.

Write.

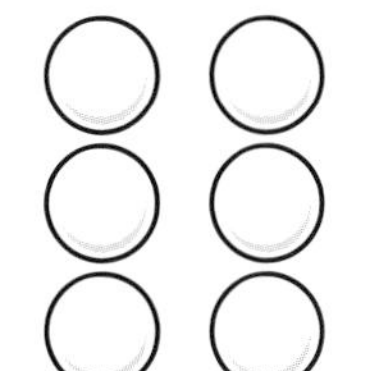
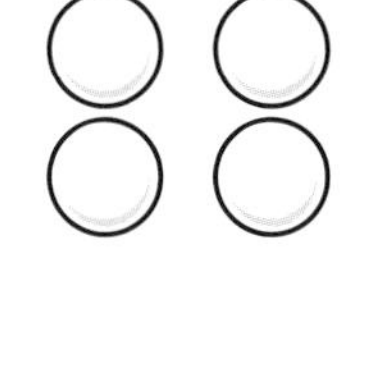

6 + ______ = 10

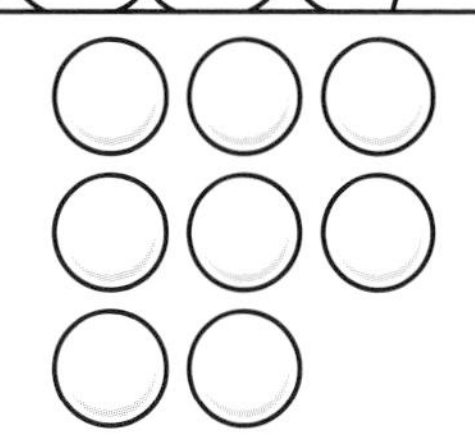

______ + ______ = 10

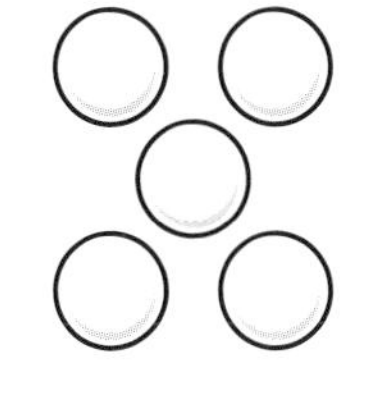

______ + ______ = 10

______ + ______ = 10

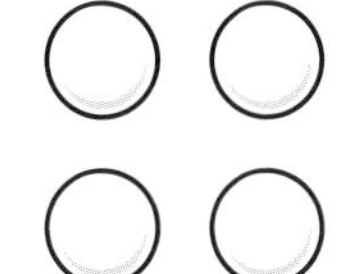

______ + ______ = 10

______ + ______ = 10

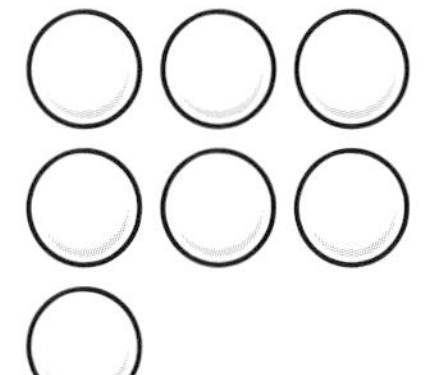

______ + ______ = 10

______ + ______ = 10

Bonus: Read and solve. Write a matching number sentence.
Max makes a snowball. How many more does he need to **make ten**?

Taking Math to Heart

Your students are sure to love this sweet assortment of math activities!

ideas contributed by Jennifer Reidy
Halifax Elementary
Halifax, MA

Heart to Heart

Patterning

These student-made heart strips make the perfect props for a hands-on center activity. To begin, provide each of several small groups a supply of paper strips and heart cutouts. Assign each group a different pattern, such as *AB*, *ABB*, or *ABC*. Challenge group members to use the hearts and show their pattern in different ways. Then have each child glue at least one heart pattern on a strip.

To set up a center activity, place the heart pattern strips, foam hearts, crayons, and paper at a center. A child chooses a strip and uses the foam hearts to extend the pattern. To document his work, he draws the extended pattern on his paper. He continues with different strips as time allows.

Candy Containers

Measurement

Candy boxes can be used to practice two different measurement skills! Gather several heart-shaped boxes in different sizes. Then choose one or both of the options below.

Exploring capacity (K.MD.A.2): For this small-group activity, gather a supply of brown Unifix cubes (chocolates). Lead students to compare the sizes of the boxes and predict which of the boxes will hold the greatest and least amount of chocolates. Next, have students place chocolates in the containers to discover how many chocolates each box holds. Guide students to order the boxes in ascending or descending order and then compare the results to their predictions.

Comparing weight (K.MD.A.2): Set out a balance scale. Next, invite a volunteer to choose two boxes and assign each box a different number: 1 or 2. Have each student hold up her finger or fingers to show which box she thinks is heavier. Then instruct the volunteer to place the boxes on the scale to compare their weights. After several volunteers have had a turn, guide youngsters to conclude that the larger box may not always be the heavier box.

Postage Due!

Counting pennies and nickels

Valentine cards add extra appeal to this center activity. Label a variety of cards with prices up to ten cents. For each card, use penny and nickel stampers to stamp a corresponding set of coins on an envelope. Label the inside flap of each envelope with the coin amount for self-checking. Place the cards and envelopes at a center. A child reads the postage-due price on a card. Then she counts coins to find a matching envelope, checks the inside flap for accuracy, and slips the card inside the envelope. She continues with each remaining valentine card.

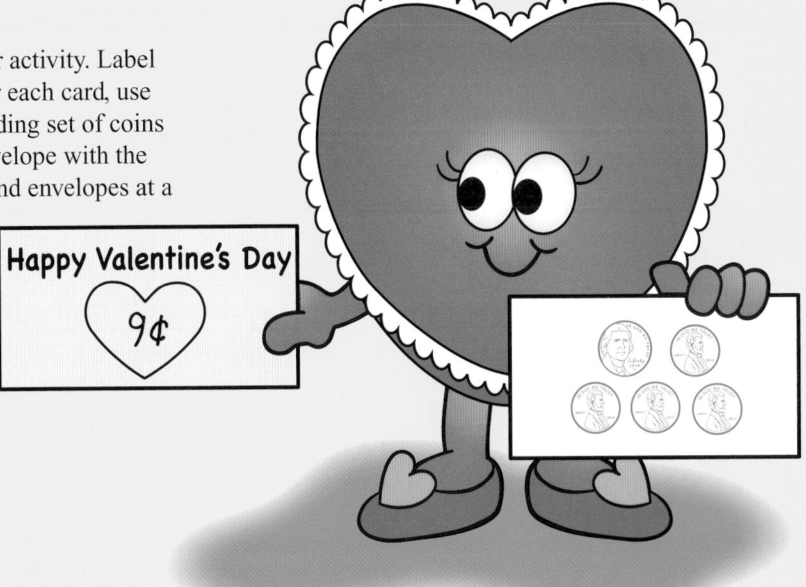

Sidney has five chocolates. Then she eats some and has three chocolates left. How many chocolates did she eat?

How Many Chocolates?

Subtraction (K.OA.A.2)

Try this tasty approach to introduce youngsters to subtraction. Draw on the board a large heart-shaped chocolate box. Provide each child with a heart-shaped mat and a supply of brown paper circles (chocolates). Next, announce a subtraction word problem. Encourage students to use their supplies to solve the problem. Then invite a volunteer to solve the problem on the board and have students check their work.

Get a **subtraction skill sheet** on page 265.

Cupid's Arrow

Odd and even numbers

Count on this cute heart character to help students identify odd and even numbers. At a center, set out a class supply of page 264, ten one-inch pipe cleaner pieces, blank paper, scissors, crayons, and glue. A child cuts apart her copy of page 264. Then she traces each box on her heart character card with a different-color crayon and glues it at the top of a blank paper. Next, she puts a number card on the arrow mat and places that number of pipe cleaner pieces on the mat, making pairs as is possible. She determines if the number is odd or even and then colors the heart to match that color on her heart character card. Finally, she glues the number card on her paper under the appropriate heading. She continues with the remaining number cards.

Arrow Mat, Heart Character Card, and Number Cards

Use with "Cupid's Arrow" on page 263.

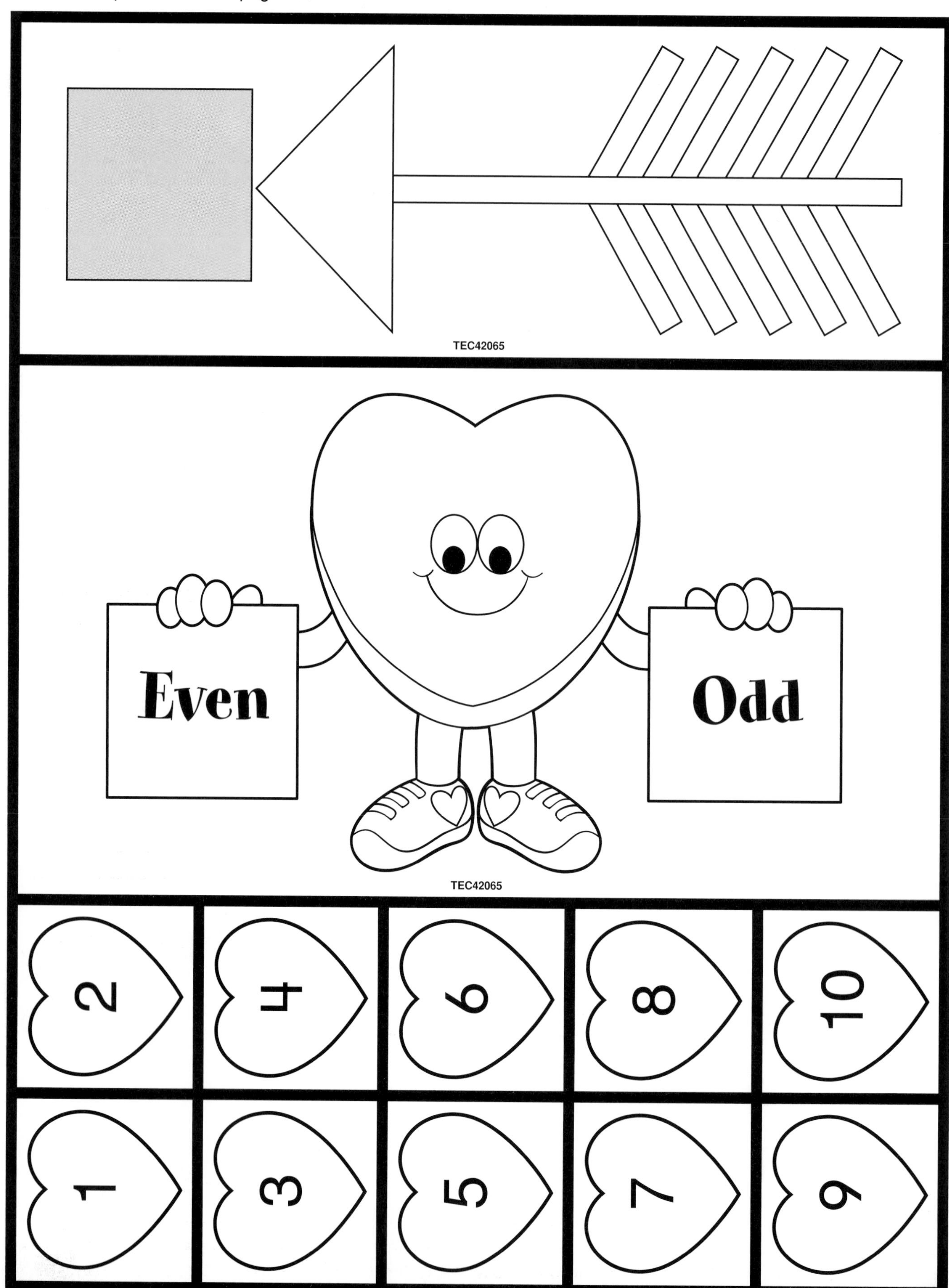

Name ______________________________ Subtraction (K.OA.A.1)

Tasty Treats

Subtract.
Cross out to help you.

7 – 4 = ____	5 – 3 = ____	
10 – 6 = ____	9 – 2 = ____	4 – 4 = ____
6 – 5 = ____	8 – 4 = ____	10 – 8 = ____

Bonus: Hal has 10 chocolates. He eats 5. How many are left? Write the subtraction sentence.

Addition and Subtraction Explorations

Your students will be eager to dive into this treasure trove of math ideas.

ideas contributed by Jennifer Reidy, Halifax Elementary, Halifax, MA

Take the Bait!

Representing addition and subtraction (K.OA.A.2)

Youngsters hunt for worms at this partner center! Label several plastic cups with addition and subtraction problems. Then hide two-inch pipe cleaner pieces (worms) in a tub of brown paper shreds (dirt). Put the cups and tub at a center. A child takes a cup and explains to her partner whether she will be adding or subtracting to solve the problem. Next, she digs for worms and explains her thinking as she works. For example, to solve 5 – 3, she may hunt for five worms, put them in her cup, and then throw back three worms, leaving two worms in her cup. Then her partner takes a turn. If desired, have youngsters write or draw to show their work.

Dolphin Diving

Acting out addition and subtraction (K.OA.A.2)

Students move a dolphin along a wavy number line to help them solve these math problems! Give each child a copy of page 268, a blue paper strip, and a length of yarn. Have each student color, cut out, and fold his dolphin card. Direct him to trim the top of the paper strip so that it looks like ocean waves and draw on it a number line from 0 to 10. Next, help him tape his dolphin card and wave strip to opposite ends of the yarn, taping the dolphin card closed at the same time. Then encourage him to pretend the dolphin is jumping over waves along the number line to help him solve the problems on his page.

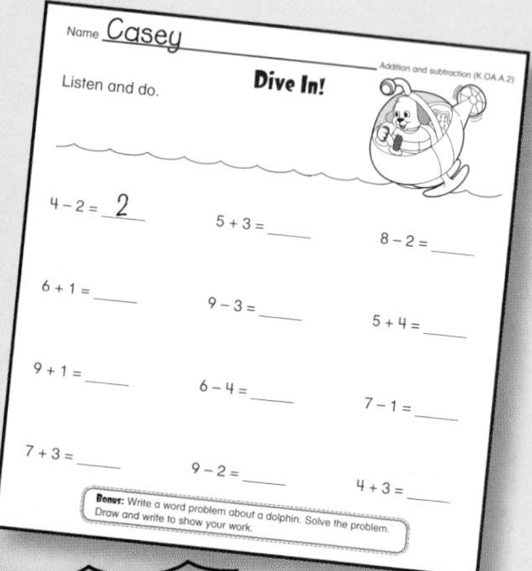

Name Casey

Addition and subtraction (K.OA.A.2)

Dive In!

Listen and do.

4 – 2 = 2	5 + 3 = ____	8 – 2 = ____
6 + 1 = ____	9 – 3 = ____	5 + 4 = ____
9 + 1 = ____	6 – 4 = ____	7 – 1 = ____
7 + 3 = ____	9 – 2 = ____	4 + 3 = ____

Bonus: Write a word problem about a dolphin. Solve the problem. Draw and write to show your work.

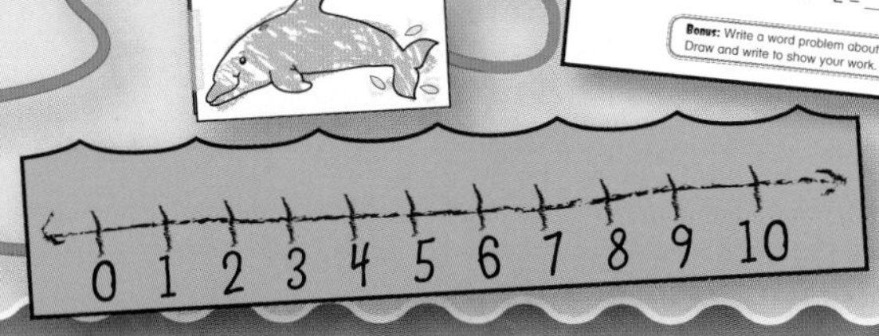

Frogs on a Log

Solving word problems (K.OA.A.2)

To prepare for this whole-group activity, attach a six-foot strip of masking tape to the floor. Have each child draw a log on paper and crumple green paper scraps to make little balls (frogs). Next, announce an addition or subtraction story about frogs and the log, such as "There are seven frogs sitting on a log. Two more frogs hop on the log. How many frogs are on the log?" Direct each child to use her props to act out and solve the word problem. Then ask student volunteers to act out the story, using the masking tape as a log. Guide youngsters to check their work before you announce the next word problem. **For an added challenge,** encourage students to record an equation for each word problem.

Swimmers High and Low

Decomposing numbers (K.OA.A.3)

How many fish swim at the top and at the bottom of the fish tank? Your youngsters will decide! To prepare, place at a center blue paper (fish tank), ten fish cards (cards on page 269), a set of cards numbered from 5 to 10, and blank paper. A child chooses a number card and places it on the tank. She takes a corresponding number of fish and places some at the top of the tank and the rest at the bottom. Then she writes a number sentence to match her work. Next, she rearranges the same number of fish and records that number sentence. She continues to make as many addition combinations as possible. If time permits, she repeats the activity with a different number card.

For added fun, set out fish-shaped crackers for youngsters to arrange in the tank!

Balancing Balls

Ways to make ten (K.OA.A.4)

How many different ways can these silly seals balance ten balls on their noses? Your students will find out with this hands-on activity. Give each child a copy of the seal card from page 269 and ten double-sided counters (balls). Announce a number between 0 and 10 and direct each child to arrange a corresponding number of same-color balls so it looks like the seal is balancing them on its nose. Next, ask, "How many more make ten?" and direct him to add the remaining balls (with the other color showing). Then have him write the corresponding addition equation. Continue in this manner, announcing different numbers each time.

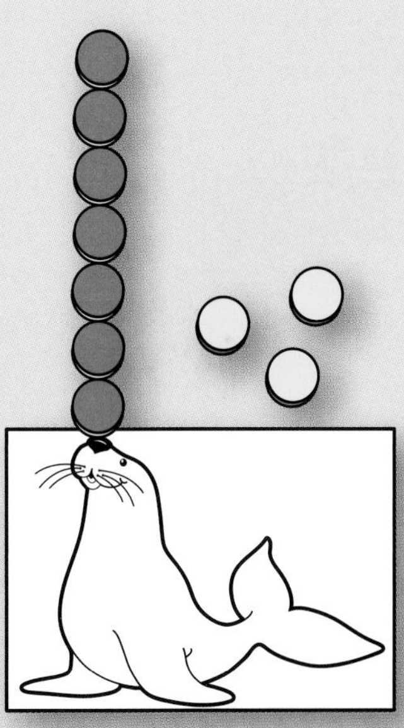

Name ______________________________ Addition and subtraction (K.OA.A.2)

Dive In!

Listen and do.

$4 - 2 =$ ______ $5 + 3 =$ ______ $8 - 2 =$ ______

$6 + 1 =$ ______ $9 - 3 =$ ______ $5 + 4 =$ ______

$9 + 1 =$ ______ $6 - 4 =$ ______ $7 - 1 =$ ______

$7 + 3 =$ ______ $9 - 2 =$ ______ $4 + 3 =$ ______

Bonus: Write a word problem about a dolphin. Solve the problem. Draw and write to show your work.

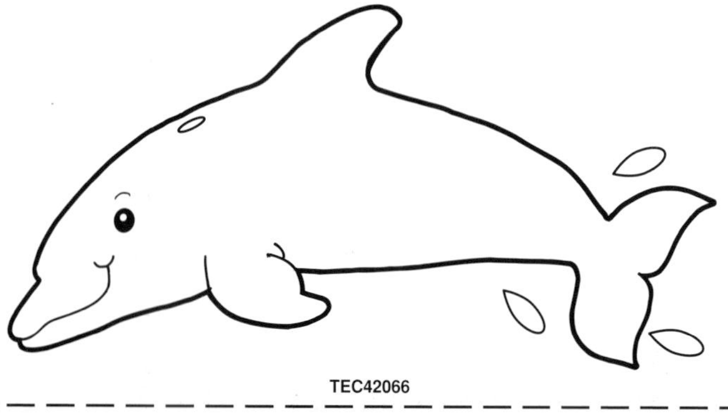

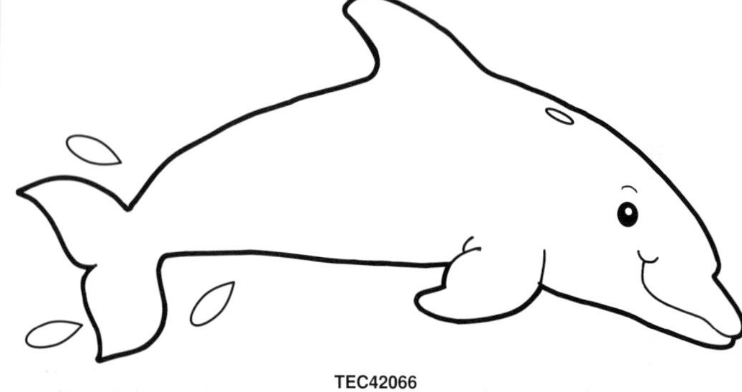

Note to the teacher: Use with "Dolphin Diving" on page 266.

Fish Cards

Use with "Swimmers High and Low" on page 267.

Seal Card

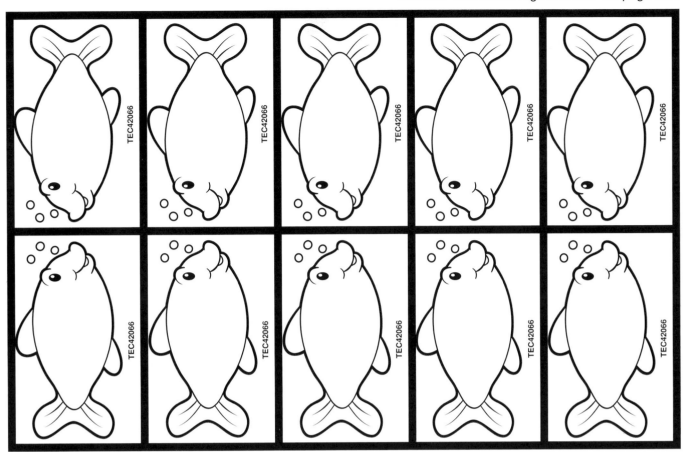

Use with "Balancing Balls" on page 267.

Mighty Math With CUBES: 7 Sensational Ideas

1 Make Mystery Bags

Label a set of nine bags from *A* to *I*. Then put a different set of from 11 to 19 Unifix cubes in each of the bags. Place the bags and paper at a center. A child lists the letters from *A* to *I* on her paper. Next, she takes a bag and removes the cubes. She counts the total number of cubes and predicts if she can make a group of ten. Then she connects cubes to show a group of ten and the remaining ones left. Beside that letter on her paper, she writes or draws to show her work. Then she takes the cubes apart and returns them to the bag. ***Composing and decomposing numbers from 11 to 19 (K.NBT.A.1)***

Jennifer Reidy, Halifax Elementary, Halifax, MA

Color	Tallies	Number
red	𝍸 𝍸 𝍸 I	16
blue	I	1
green		0

2 Use a Grab Bag

Draw a chart like the one shown. Have youngsters watch as you drop each of the following cubes into a bag: 17 red, two blue, and one green. Next, ask youngsters to predict which color will be chosen most often and give reasons for their predictions. Then invite each child to remove a cube, make a tally mark beside the matching color on the chart, and drop the cube back into the bag. After each child has had a turn, lead youngsters to count the tally marks and compare the results with their predictions. For added emphasis, repeat the activity to compare a second round of results. ***Representing data, probability***

Stephanie Litwin, Mendham, NJ

3 Count to 50!

To prepare this center activity, write each number counting by fives to 50 on separate pieces of tape. Attach each number to a Unifix cube. A student orders the cubes from least to greatest number. Then he starts with the number one and counts up to 50. As he names each number on a cube, he picks it up and snaps it together with the next cube so the cubes are in order. Then he uses the connected cubes to count to 50 by fives. ***Counting to 50, counting by fives***

Stephanie Litwin

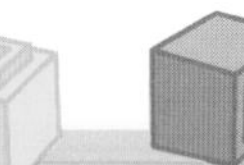

Solve Puppy Problems

The puppy has two bones. He already ate two bones. How many bones did the pup start with?

Have each child use a paper plate, paper scraps, and other desired materials to make a puppy prop. Then give him ten cubes (bones). Announce a theme-related word problem and have students use their props to solve the problem. Continue with several more problems. For added fun, give each child one last problem for him to draw spots on his pooch pal. For example, say, "Your dog has two black spots and three brown spots. How many spots does your dog have in all?" ***Solving word problems (K.OA.A.2)***

Jennifer Reidy
Halifax Elementary
Halifax, MA

Count and Click

Place a tub containing 100 Unifix cubes at a center. One at a time, a child places a cube on the table as he counts. After all 100 cubes are on the table, he links the cubes to make towers of ten. Then he counts the cubes by tens. ***Counting by ones and tens to 100 (K.CC.A.1)***

Compare Capacity

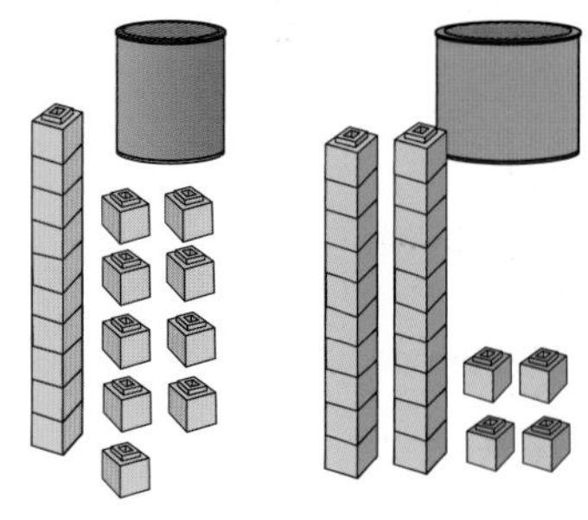

For this small-group activity, gather several containers of different shapes and sizes. Fill each container with a different color of Unifix cubes. Have each youngster choose a container and connect the cubes to make towers of ten. Next, he arranges the towers and leftover cubes to show how many cubes fit in his container. Then lead youngsters to compare the cube amounts to determine which container has the largest capacity and to compare the capacity of other containers. ***Comparing measurable attributes (K.MD.A.2)***

adapted from an idea by Stephanie Litwin, Mendham, NJ

Which is your favorite picnic food?
hamburger–

Show Answers

Pose a question and give youngsters two or more answer choices. Assign a color to each choice and set out a tub of corresponding-color Unifix cubes. Have each child respond by selecting the color cube to match her answer and then linking it with classmates' matching cubes to make a set. Then lead students in counting the number of cubes per answer and comparing the sets to determine the most and least popular choices. ***Data analysis***

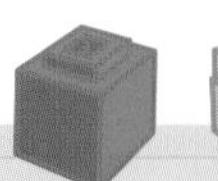
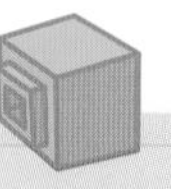
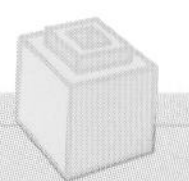

Hit a Home Run With Math!

Play ball! These baseball-themed activities are perfect for reinforcing a variety of math skills.

ideas contributed by Reubena Whitted, Roxboro, NC

Kindergarten MVPs!

Solving addition and subtraction word problems (K.OA.A.2)

Who are the most valuable players of this no-prep activity? Your students! For a time filler or transition activity, say a theme-related word problem or a problem that corresponds to an existing situation, such as "Ten baseball players are ready for lunch. *(Ten students are in line to go to lunch.)* There are eighteen players on the team. *(There are 18 students present.)* How many players are not yet ready for lunch?" Guide youngsters to then act out the word problem or use the existing model to solve the problem.

Four girls are at the top of the batting order. One more girl is in the lineup. How many girls are in the lineup altogether?

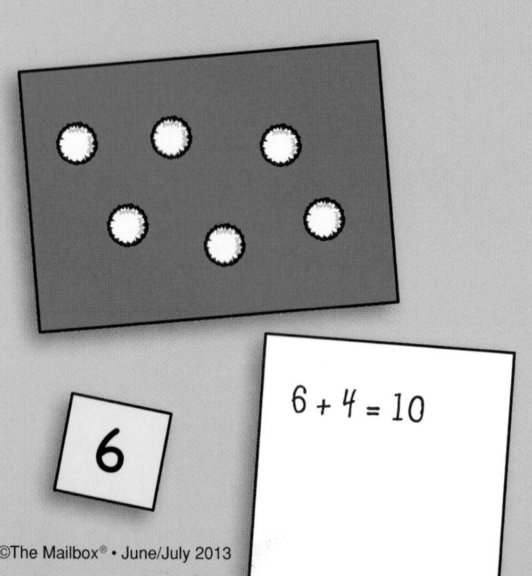

Swing Away!

Making ten (K.OA.A.4)

Your young baseball players aim for ten hits with this hands-on activity. Place at a center a green paper (batting-practice field), number cards from 1 to 9, ten white pom-poms (baseballs), and paper. A child takes a card and pretends to hit that many baseballs onto the field. Next, she uses the props to determine how many more hits she needs to make ten hits. Then she writes a corresponding equation on her paper. She continues with each remaining number card as time permits.

Round the Bases

Decomposing numbers (K.NBT.A.1)

This whole-group game is sure to be a hit with your students! Write "Strike!" and "Home run!" on separate cards. Put the word cards in a bag with a set of number cards from 11 to 19. Then place four papers on the floor so they resemble a baseball diamond and divide the group into two teams. To play, a player from Team 1 removes a card from the bag. For a number card, he draws on the board to illustrate the number. If a member of his team correctly names the number, he moves to first base; if the number is not named correctly, the team's turn is over. If he gets the "Home run!" card, he moves around the bases as in baseball and earns a run for his team. (Each player standing on a base will also earn a run for her team!) If he gets the "Strike!" card, his team's turn is over. After each turn, the card is returned to the bag. Alternate play continues until one team wins with a predetermined number of runs.

Batter Up!

Adding and subtracting within five (K.OA.A.5)

Players match bats to baseballs when they play this partner game. To prepare, write addition and subtraction problems within five on an even number of baseball bat cutouts. Write the answers to the problems on separate white paper circles (baseballs). Youngsters place the bats in facedown rows. Next, a player deals the baseballs. To begin, Player 1 takes a bat, solves the problem, and looks for the matching answer on her baseballs. If she makes a match, she puts the bat on the ball; if not, she returns the bat to its original position. Then Player 2 takes a turn. The first player to match all her bats and baseballs wins. **For more advanced students**, include addition and subtraction problems beyond five.

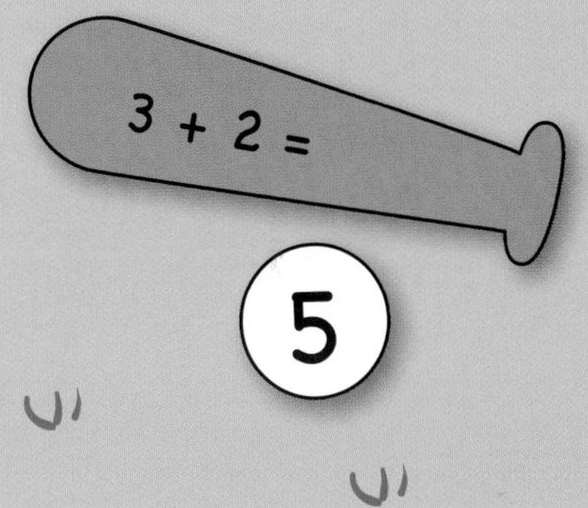

Bunches of Balls

Composing numbers (K.NBT.A.1)

How many baseballs? Students will take a look and tell during this center activity! Cut apart a copy of the baseball cards on page 274 and make a class supply of the recording sheet on the same page. Place the cards and recording sheets at a center. A child takes a card and writes on his recording sheet to compose the matching two-digit number. He continues with each remaining card.

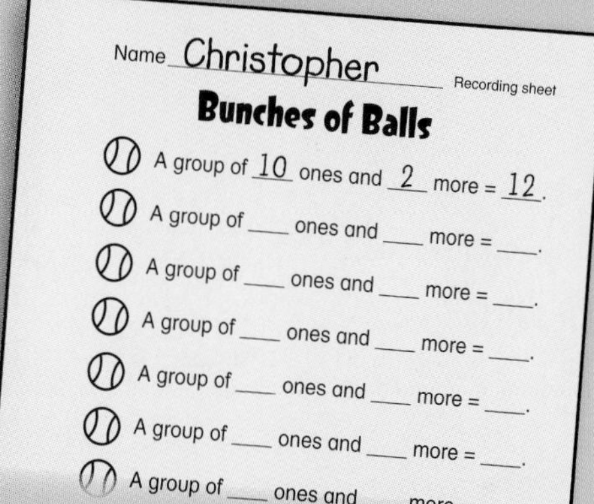

Name Christopher ____ Recording sheet

Bunches of Balls

A group of 10 ones and 2 more = 12.
A group of ____ ones and ____ more = ____.
A group of ____ ones and ____ more = ____.
A group of ____ ones and ____ more = ____.
A group of ____ ones and ____ more = ____.
A group of ____ ones and ____ more = ____.
A group of ____ ones and ____ more = ____.

Baseball Cards and Recording Sheet

Use with "Bunches of Balls" on page 273.

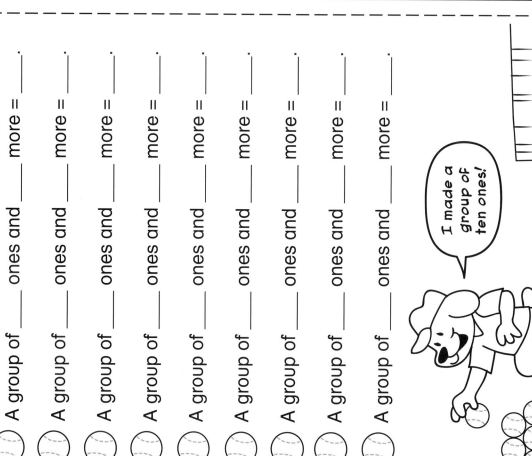

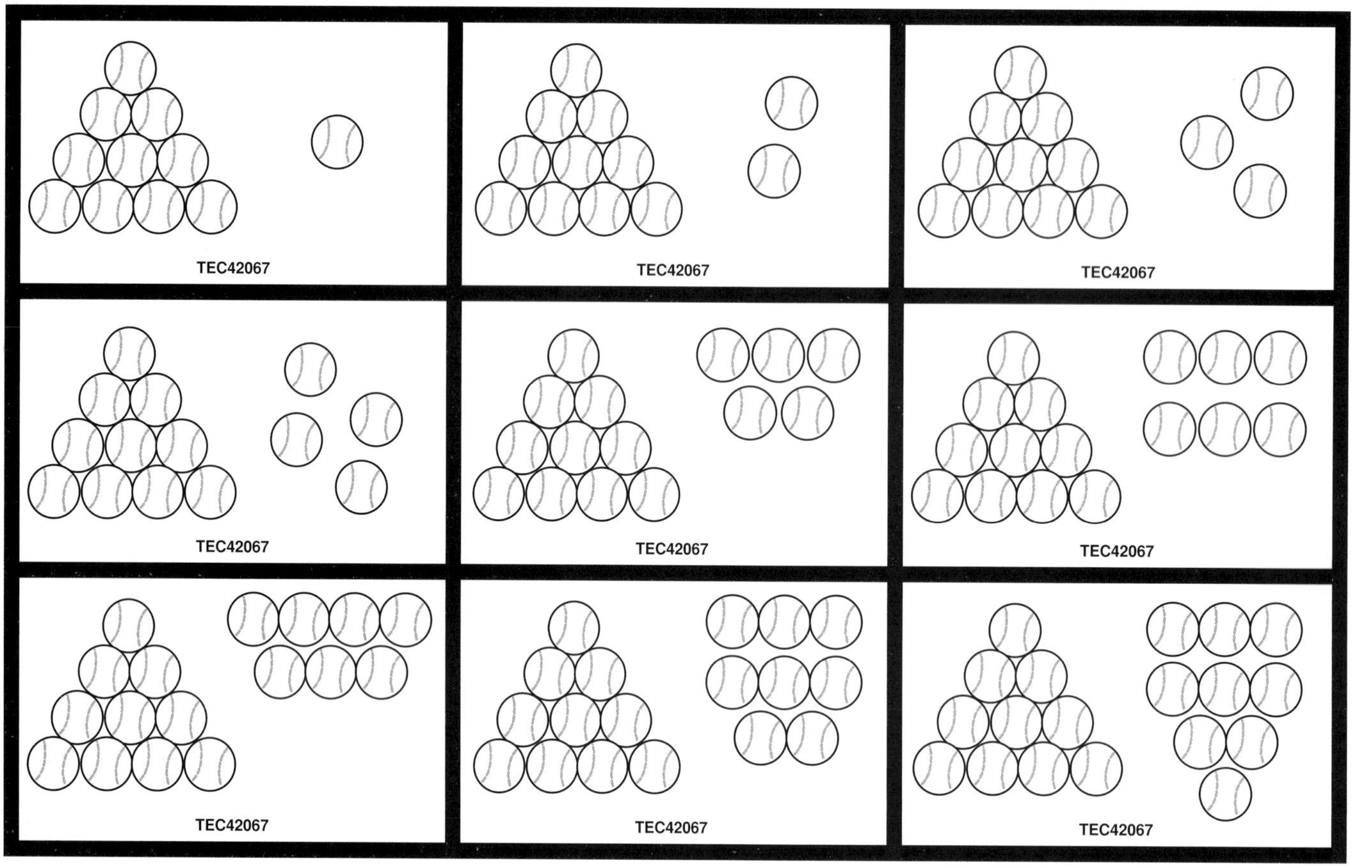
TEC42067
TEC42067
TEC42067
TEC42067
TEC42067
TEC42067
TEC42067
TEC42067
TEC42067

Name ____________ Recording sheet

Bunches of Balls

A group of ____ ones and ____ more = ____.

A group of ____ ones and ____ more = ____.

A group of ____ ones and ____ more = ____.

A group of ____ ones and ____ more = ____.

A group of ____ ones and ____ more = ____.

A group of ____ ones and ____ more = ____.

A group of ____ ones and ____ more = ____.

A group of ____ ones and ____ more = ____.

A group of ____ ones and ____ more = ____.

I made a group of ten ones!

Seasonal Units

Blastoff!

Rocketing Into a Great School Year

Choose one or all of these ideas for a blast of a beginning to kindergarten!

Look Around the Room

Kindergarten readiness

Here's a great way for youngsters to "tour" the classroom without ever leaving their seats! Display a different letter at each of several locations, such as the bookshelves, center areas, cubbies, "home" for the class mascot, and pencil sharpener. Then name each location, in turn, and encourage youngsters to name the featured letter in that area. The letter labeling is a great way for students to get to know the classroom and for you to pre-assess letter knowledge. *(RF.K.1d)*

Ana Catasus-Perez
Mother of Christ Catholic School
Miami, FL

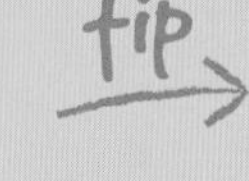
tip

For a high-frequency word review, replace the letters with word cards. *(RF.K.3c)*

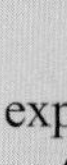

The Perfect Prop

Classroom rules

A Mr. Potato Head character makes the perfect prop for introducing expected behaviors to students. Assign each accessory a particular rule, such as the following: hat, put on your thinking cap; ears, be a good listener; and feet, no running or kicking. Then guide youngsters to make connections to the accessory and the school rule. To reinforce positive behavior throughout the year, point to the character's nose and say, "Mr. Potato Head 'knows' the rules. Do you?" Then lead youngsters to review the established rules.

Hands—I will keep my hands to myself.

Jodi Darter, Cabool Elementary, Cabool, MO

See the writing sheet on page 279.

Fantastic Frames

Kindergarten keepsake

A photograph of each child's first day in kindergarten is sure to be treasured forever! In advance, personalize a foam frame, similar to the one shown, for each student. On the back of the frame, reserve space to tape a photo and write your name and the date. On the first day of school, take a photo of each child. Invite her to decorate the front of her frame with craft materials and set it aside to dry. When the frames are dry, tape each student's photo to her frame and send it home with her as a special gift.

Christy Bentley-Dye, Eastminster School, Conyers, GA

Build a Book

Writing

How can a class mascot help youngsters become familiar with different school locations? Read this! First, pique students' interest by reading *If You Take a Mouse to School* by Laura Numeroff. Then lead students on a school tour, pretending the mascot is naming and telling about places visited, including the last stop, your room. Discuss with students each of the school's locations and its purpose. To continue, help each child complete a writing prompt similar to the one shown and write her dictation on a sheet of paper. Instruct her to draw an illustration to match her sentence. If desired, bind the completed pages to make a class book. **For a home-school connection**, assign each child a different day to take the mascot home and have her write and draw to complete the prompt "If you take mascot's name to student's name's home, he will _______." *(W.K.2)*

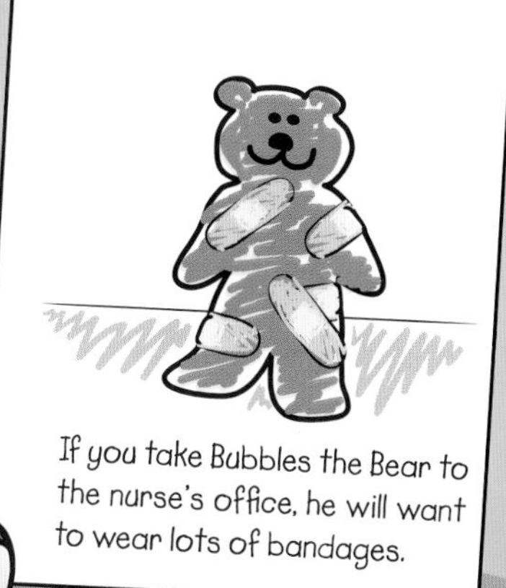

If you take Bubbles the Bear to the nurse's office, he will want to wear lots of bandages.

Lisa Clabaugh
Russell Elementary
Shelby, OH

A Banner Year

Cooperative learning

Each of your young learners helps decorate this wall display. Program the middle of a length of bulletin board paper (banner) with your class name and the school year. Next, draw lines to designate a section of the perimeter for each child. Put the banner and markers at a table. Invite each child to draw pictures and write his name in a section of the banner. Then display the completed banner as an early reminder that each member of the class is a welcome part of your kindergarten team.

Karen Guess
St. Richard's School
Indianapolis, IN

Nice to Meet You!

Getting acquainted

Here's a morning meet-and-greet activity that also helps youngsters learn each other's names. For each child, personalize a card with the child's name and photograph. Put the cards in a bag. Then invite a student to take a card, find the classmate featured on the card, and introduce him to the class. Lead the class to respond with a personalized greeting. Continue until each child has been introduced. *(SL.K.6)*

Debbie Patrick
State College, PA

Who, Me?

Getting acquainted

Students are sure to get to know who's who with this interactive circle-time activity. Lead youngsters in the chant shown, following the rhythmic beat of the familiar rhyme "Who Stole the Cookies From the Cookie Jar?" At the end of the rhyme, have the standing child sit. Then continue until each child has had a turn to wave and say, "Hello!" *(SL.K.6)*

All: Who is a kindergartner in our class?
Teacher: [Troy] is a kindergartner in our class.
Student named: Who me? *(Student stands.)*
All: Yes, you!
Student named: Hello, hello! *(Waves.)*
All: Hello to you! *(All students wave.)*

adapted from an idea by Lori Seay, Winfield, IL

Kindergarten Lotto

Getting acquainted

Students' photos are the center of attention on these gameboards. Make several copies of each student's photo. Then, for each child, prepare a lotto-style gameboard featuring nine different photos. Keep a matching set of photos to serve as callers cards.

To play, give each child a gameboard and nine game markers. Then show a student photo and lead the class in naming the student. Have players mark their boards, if possible, in accordance with the traditional game. Continue until a child has marked all the photos on her gameboard and says, "Friendly faces!" Then help her name each child on her board, have the corresponding children stand, and declare them all to be winners!

Lynn Downing, Pandora-Gilboa School, Pandora, OH

Name______________________________ Writing (W.K.2)

All About Me

Things I Like:

My Family

This Is Me!

What can students do with different sets of acorn cards? Check it out!
8

Awesome 8 Acorn Activities

Use copies of the acorn cards on page 282 for these math and literacy activities.

ideas contributed by Karin Bulkow
Washington School for Comprehensive Literacy
Sheboygan, WI

1 Play a Partner Game

Program pairs of acorn cards for a desired skill, such as matching letters, matching numbers to sets, or high-frequency words. Youngsters use the cards to play a game similar to Concentration. *(CCSS)*

2 Play a Small-Group Game

To prepare, make matching card pairs or sets (game cards) related to a math or literacy skill of your choice. (If desired, use the cards made for activity 1.) Have students use the cards to play a game similar to Go Fish. *(CCSS)*

3 Fine-Tune Listening Skills

Inspire students' desire to recognize words with this listen-and-do activity. Program a copy of the acorn cards page with different high-frequency words and give each child a copy of the page. Next, announce a direction such as "Use a brown crayon. Color the acorn that shows the word *me*." Have the child follow the direction. Continue with similar directions to have students identify each word. *(RF.K.3c)*

Find the acorn that shows the word *can*. Draw a green line under the word *can*.

Put Numbers in Order

Randomly display in a pocket chart acorn cards labeled with different numbers from 1 to 20. Invite youngsters to take turns switching two cards at a time until the numbers are in order. **For a center option**, have a youngster order the numbers on a line of tape to form a number line and then have him write the numbers on a sheet of paper.

Measure Objects With Acorn Rulers

Help each child glue acorn cards side by side on a paper strip to make a ruler. Direct each child to use his ruler to measure several objects and record the acorn measurements on a sheet of paper.

Review Print Concepts

Write the words for simple sentences on separate acorn cards. Store the cards for each sentence in a separate resealable plastic bag. Then lead students in reading the words from a bag and forming the sentence. Point out the uppercase letter at the beginning of the sentence and the punctuation at the end. To extend the activity, have each child write and illustrate one of the sentences. *(RF.K.1a, c)*

Play a Whole-Group Game

To play this version of Bingo, give each child a copy of page 282 to use as a gameboard and 12 game markers. Then have each child write a different number between 1 and 30 on each acorn. Randomly announce a number and direct her to cover the number on her board. When a child covers three numbers in a row, four numbers in a column, or the four corners, have her call out "Acorns!"

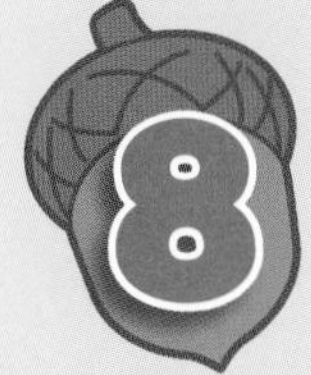

Practice Positional Words

Acorns are here, there, and everywhere for this whole-group activity. Give each child an acorn card. Then call out a direction that involves a positional word, such as "Put the acorn under your chair." Play several more rounds using a different positional word and location each time. *(K.G.A.1)*

Acorn Cards

Use with the ideas on pages 280 and 281.

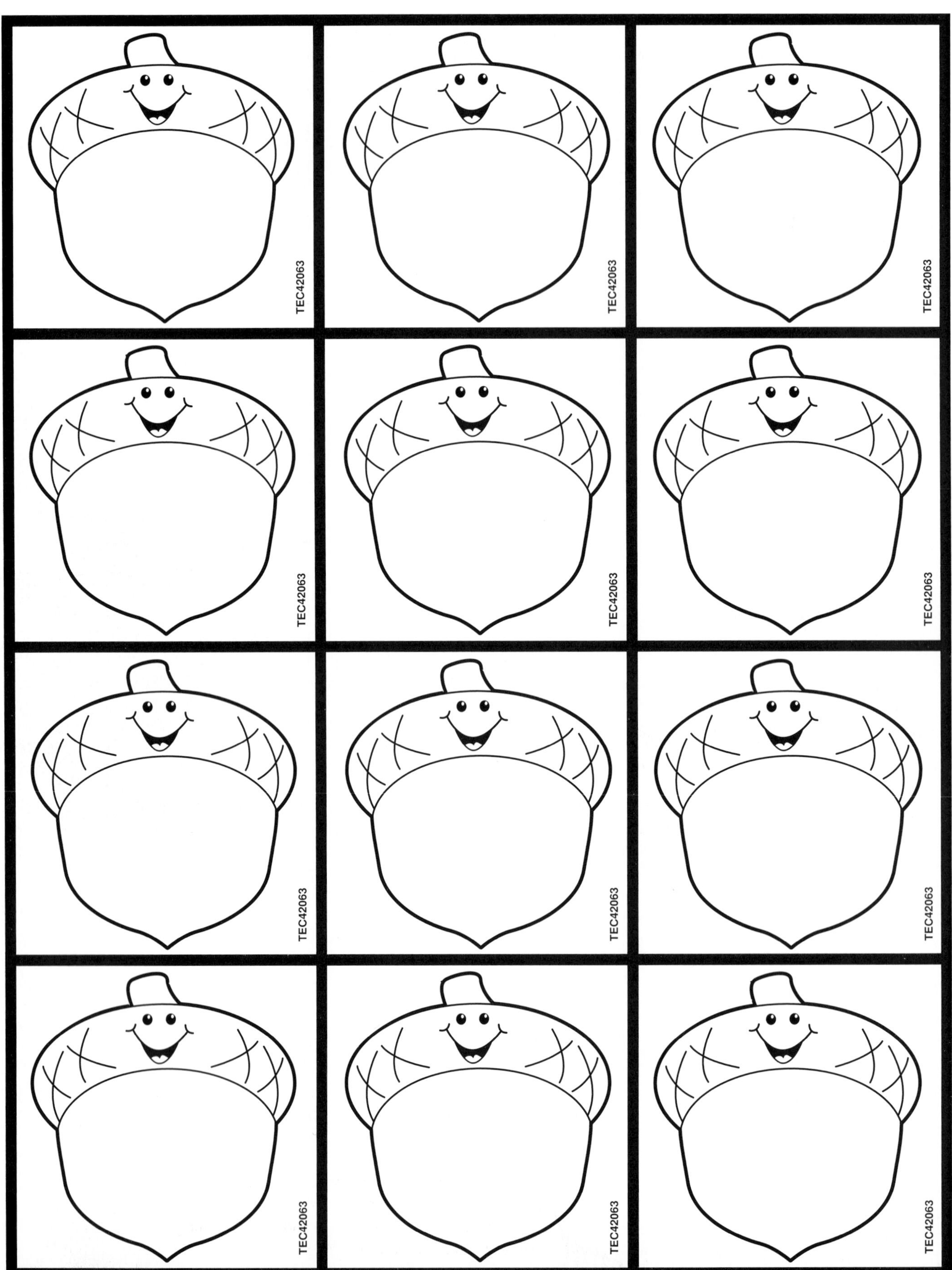

Seasonal Skill Practice

Penguins

Try these interactive penguin activities to foster students' success in literacy, math, and more!

ideas contributed by Laurie Gibbons, Huntsville, AL

SCIENCE AND LITERACY

Sea Swimmers!

Do some penguins live by the beach? Yes! Do all penguins live near water? Yes again! Write the poem shown on chart paper. Read the poem aloud to launch a discussion about penguins and their homes. Guide youngsters to answer the question in line six and explain their reasoning. **For a rhyming-word connection,** invite different students to circle each of the four rhyming word pairs in the poem. ***Animal habitats, reading response (RI.K.10)***

Some penguins live where the cold winds blow
Huddled close together in the ice and snow.
Other penguins live on rocky beaches
Far from where the cold wind reaches.
But ALL penguins live where they can swim in a sea.
Do you think it is their favorite place to be?
They swim. They dive. They fish and play
By saltwater seas, they live each day!

SCIENCE AND MATH

Penguin Preferences

Many people think all penguins live in very cold climates, but not Galapagos penguins—they prefer an environment at the equator! Draw pictures related to a cold climate to make a poster and then do the same for a warm climate. Lead students to discuss the icy habitat of most penguins and the warmer climate of Galapagos penguins. Next, say the chant shown and have students (penguins) waddle to their preferred climate. Then compare the total number of penguins in each habitat. For added fun, have each child wear a penguin headband similar to the one shown. ***Animal habitats, comparing numbers***

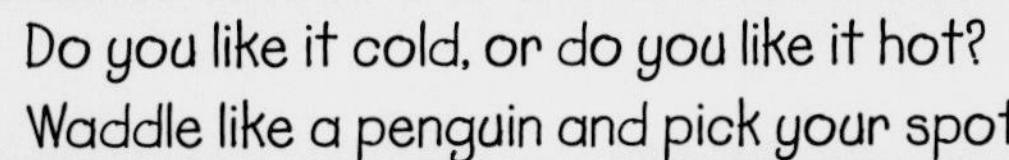

Do you like it cold, or do you like it hot?
Waddle like a penguin and pick your spot!

SPEAKING AND LISTENING

Waddle, Waddle

Have each child make a penguin headband similar to the one shown. Then encourage youngsters (penguins) to waddle around the room. On your signal, have your little penguins stop and stand in small groups of two or three. Encourage each penguin to take a turn answering a question such as "What do you like about being a penguin?" or "What do you think it would be like to slide on ice?" When each student in a group has had a turn, those penguins waddle quietly until all penguins are on the move and ready for the next question. ***Answering to express an opinion (SL.K.6)***

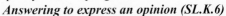

LITERACY
Alphabet on Ice

Have you ever noticed that packaging foam resembles ice floes? The foam is perfect for this center activity! Write lowercase letters on separate penguin cards (see page 285) and glue each one to a wooden ice cream spoon as shown. Push the penguins into a large piece of packing foam (ice floe) and write on the floe by each penguin the matching uppercase letter. Remove the penguins and place them and the ice floe at a center. A child puts each penguin on the floe by matching the letters. To record her work, she writes the letter pairs on a sheet of paper. ***Matching and writing uppercase and lowercase letters (RF.K.1d; L.K.1a)***

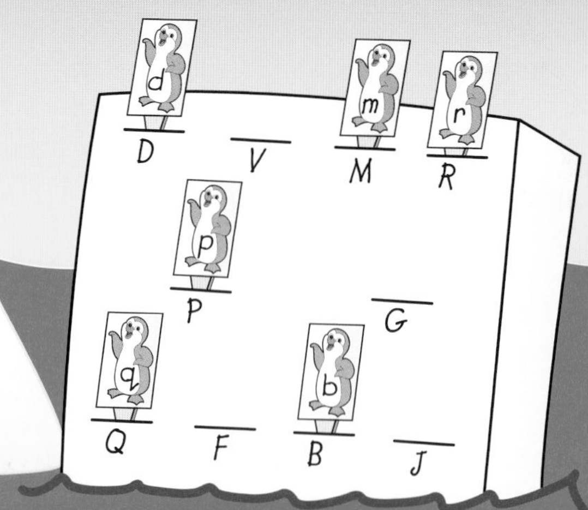

The penguin with green feet is third in line.

MATH
Penguins on Parade

First, second, third, fourth—these colorful-footed penguins provide partners plenty of ordinal number practice. Have each child set out the same ten colors of crayons. Then, on a copy of page 285, have her color each pair of penguin feet a different color and cut apart the cards. To use the cards, two students sit on opposite sides of a standing file folder or other partition. One child puts her penguins in a line. Then she gives directions, guiding her partner to put his penguins in the same order. When both sets of penguins are lined up, the partners check to see if the penguins are indeed in the same order. Then they switch roles and begin again. ***Ordinal numbers***

See the ordinal numbers **skill sheet** on page 287.

SCIENCE
Birds of a Feather Swim Together!

Students are sure to be curious about a penguin's ability to swim in icy waters without freezing. Share with students how a penguin has a soft layer of feathers close to its body for warmth and an outer layer of overlapping feathers coated with an oily substance that provides waterproofing. To demonstrate, smear petroleum jelly on the tummy and eyes of a large penguin cutout. Then paint over the entire penguin with black paint. When the paint dries, use a paper towel to show how the paint is easily wiped away from the coated parts of the penguin. Lead students to make connections with how the oily outer feathers are like the petroleum jelly and prevent the icy water from giving the penguin a chill! ***Characteristics of animals, animal adaptations***

Penguin Cards

Use with "Alphabet on Ice" and "Penguins on Parade" on page 284.

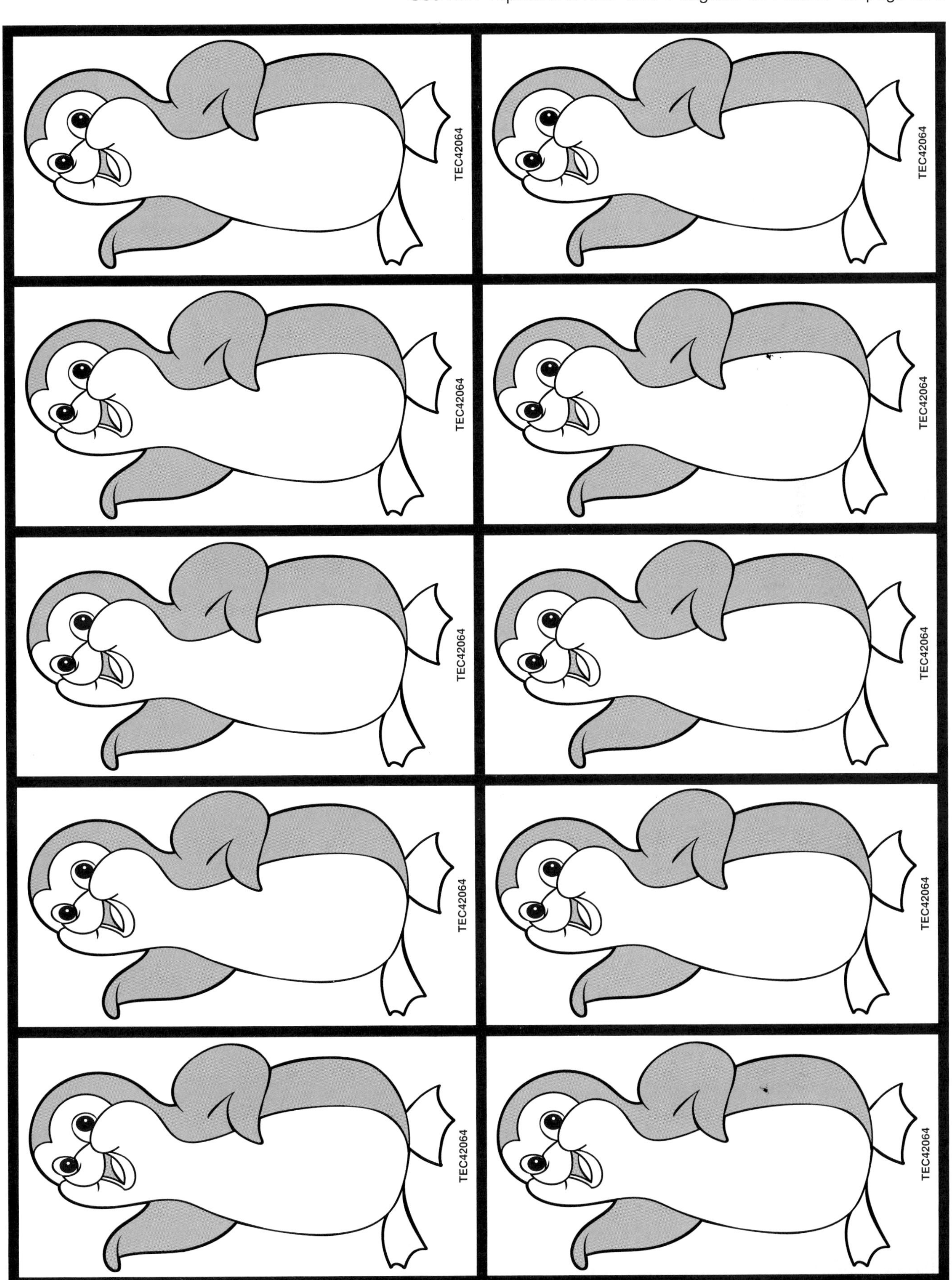

Name ____________________

High-frequency words
(RF.K.3c)

A Fresh Catch!

Color by the code.

Bonus: Read. Draw a picture to match. The *mom* and *dad* [penguin] love me!

Name ______________________

All in a Row

Read. Color to match.

The **7th** is pink.

The **4th** is blue.

The **10th** is brown.

The **1st** is red.

The **9th** is gray.

The **2nd** is orange.

The **5th** is green.

The **8th** is black.

The **3rd** is yellow.

The **6th** is purple.

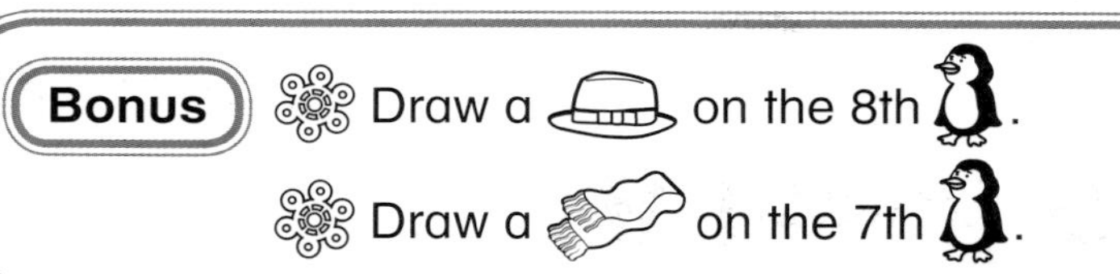

Bonus

Draw a hat on the 8th.

Draw a scarf on the 7th.

Draw a bow on the 10th.

Draw glasses on the 3rd.

What's the Buzz?

IT'S SPRING!

From a literary garden to counting by fives, these springtime activities are sure to keep your young learners buzzing with enthusiasm!

ideas contributed by Laurie K. Gibbons, Huntsville, AL

SCIENCE and LITERACY

A Garden of Promise

This display creates the perfect preview of students' springtime expectations. Encourage youngsters to share what they think the signs of spring are. Then help each child write on two leaf cutouts a different word or phrase related to the season. Next, have her draw a picture related to her chosen words on a blossom cutout. To assemble her flower, give her a green rectangle (stem) and instruct her to glue her flower parts together. Display the completed flowers with the title "Spring brings…" For added fun, when a student's expectation is observed, ask her to draw a simple ladybug on that leaf of her craft. ***Characteristics of spring, seasonal words and phrases (L.K.6)***

SCIENCE and WRITING

Show What You Know!

egg
tadpole
frog
adult frog

How Does It Grow?

Students illustrate the growth of different living things with this booklet activity. Give each child a blank booklet with a desired number of pages. To begin, ask students how plants and animals grow and change over time. For each named topic, draw and label a simple chart to record students' responses. Next, instruct each youngster to choose a chart and label the front cover of a booklet. Then encourage her to use the chart to help her draw chronological pictures of change on the pages. On the remaining pages, have her write about her topic. ***Living things grow and change, writing informative text (W.K.2)***

Cool Flipbook! To demonstrate knowledge of two topics in one booklet, try this alternative!

LITERACY

Two in One!

This interactive activity is sure to expand students' vocabularies. Write compound words on separate cards to have one word for every two students. Puzzle-cut the cards, separating the two individual words, and read each word aloud as you hand each child a puzzle card. Next, have students match their cards to form compound words. Instruct each child to write the compound word on a bow cutout and draw a picture to match. Then collect, shuffle, and redistribute the cards for more matching. When a child has three completed bows, provide craft materials for her to create a kite on which to attach her bows. ***Compound words***

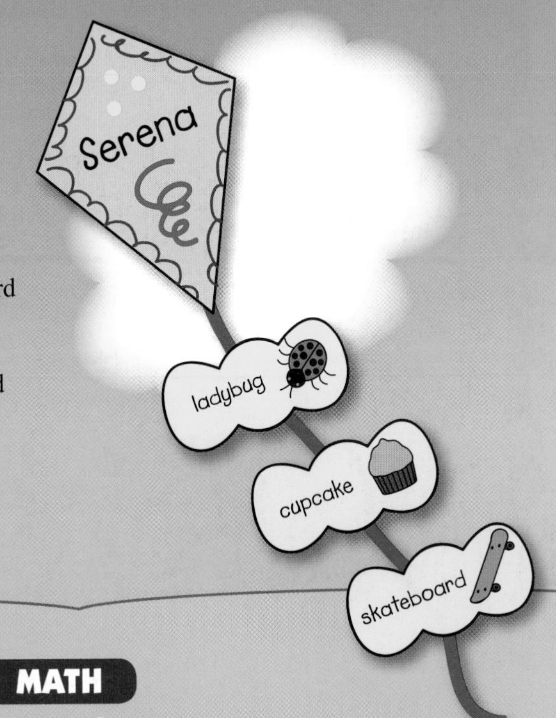

MATH

Busy Little Honeybees

The bees in this counting book are made by your students! Have each child use a yellow ink pad and a black marker to make five fingerprint bees on a hive-shaped page (use the booklet cover on page 290 for a template). Next, invite each child, in turn, to hand you her bee page as you lead youngsters in counting by fives. Then have youngsters count aloud by fives as you record each number to label the pages. Staple the completed pages together, in order, behind a copy of the booklet cover on page 290. Then read the poem aloud and have students count the bees by fives one more time as you flip the pages. Set out the math booklet for independent practice when time permits. ***Counting by fives***

To reserve space for the numbers, draw a pencil line on the booklet pages and have youngsters make their bees above the line.

Read the Critters

A whiteboard and markers are all you need for this buggy activity. Draw two caterpillar heads and speech bubbles as shown. To the left of the heads, list singular and plural words. To begin, read a word and invite a child to tell if it means one or more than one. Guide him to write the word next to the corresponding caterpillar head and draw a circle around the word (body part). Next, erase that word from the list and continue with different words until the two caterpillars are complete. Then have each child choose one word from each caterpillar; instruct him to write and illustrate a sentence for each word. ***Plurals with* s *(L.K.1)***

Booklet Cover

Use with "Busy Little Honeybees" on page 289.

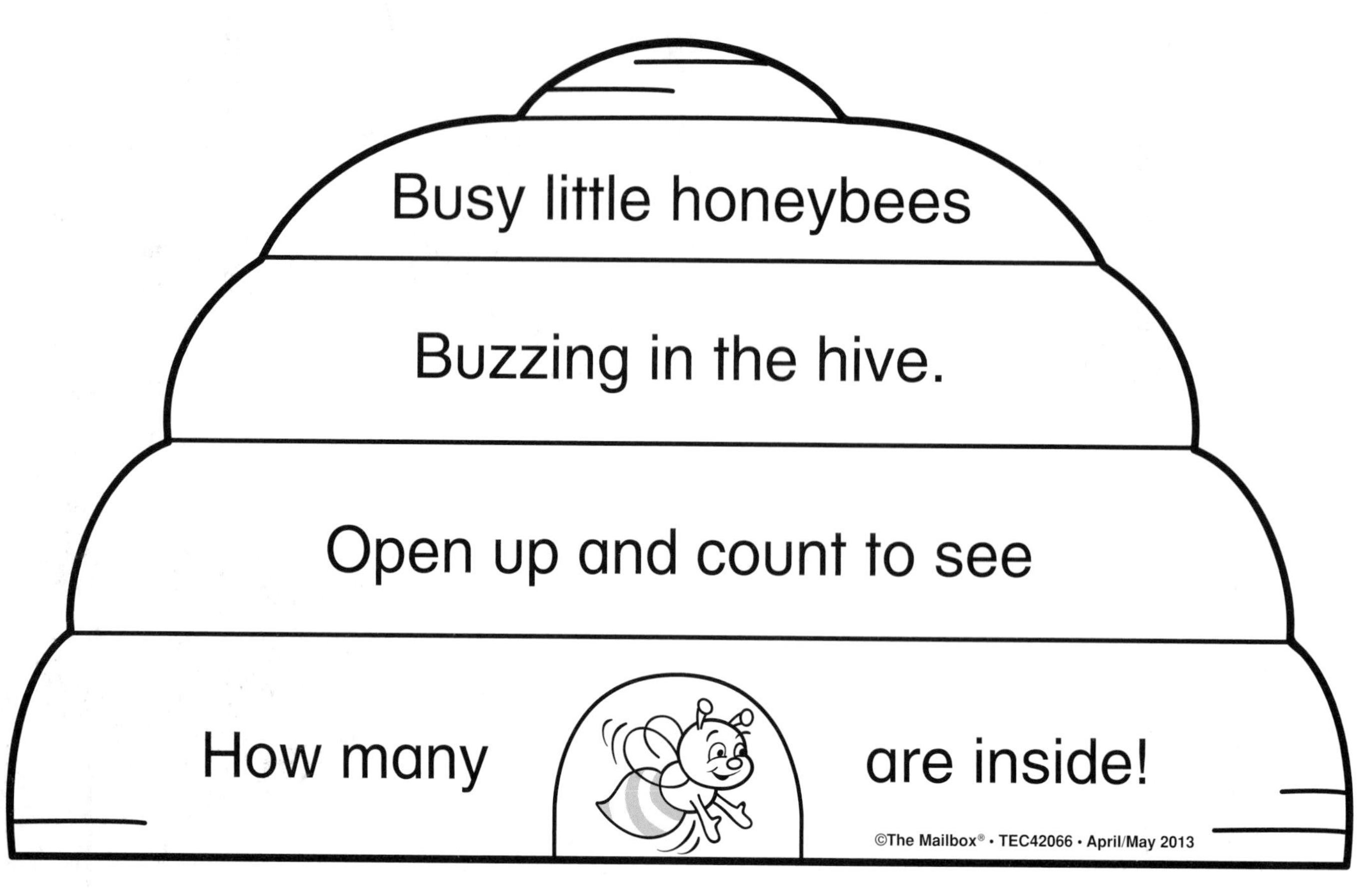

Busy little honeybees
Buzzing in the hive.
Open up and count to see
How many
are inside!
©The Mailbox® • TEC42066 • April/May 2013

Name ____________________

Counting by fives

Fives in the Hive

Count by **5s**.

Write.

5, ___, ___, 20, ___

30, ___, 40, ___, ___

Bonus: Color each number as you count by **10s** to 50.

Name ______________________

Spring Is in the Air!

Write to label the pictures. Use the word bank.
Add **s** to show **more than one**.

Word Bank

ant	bee	kite	tree
log	egg	nest	bird

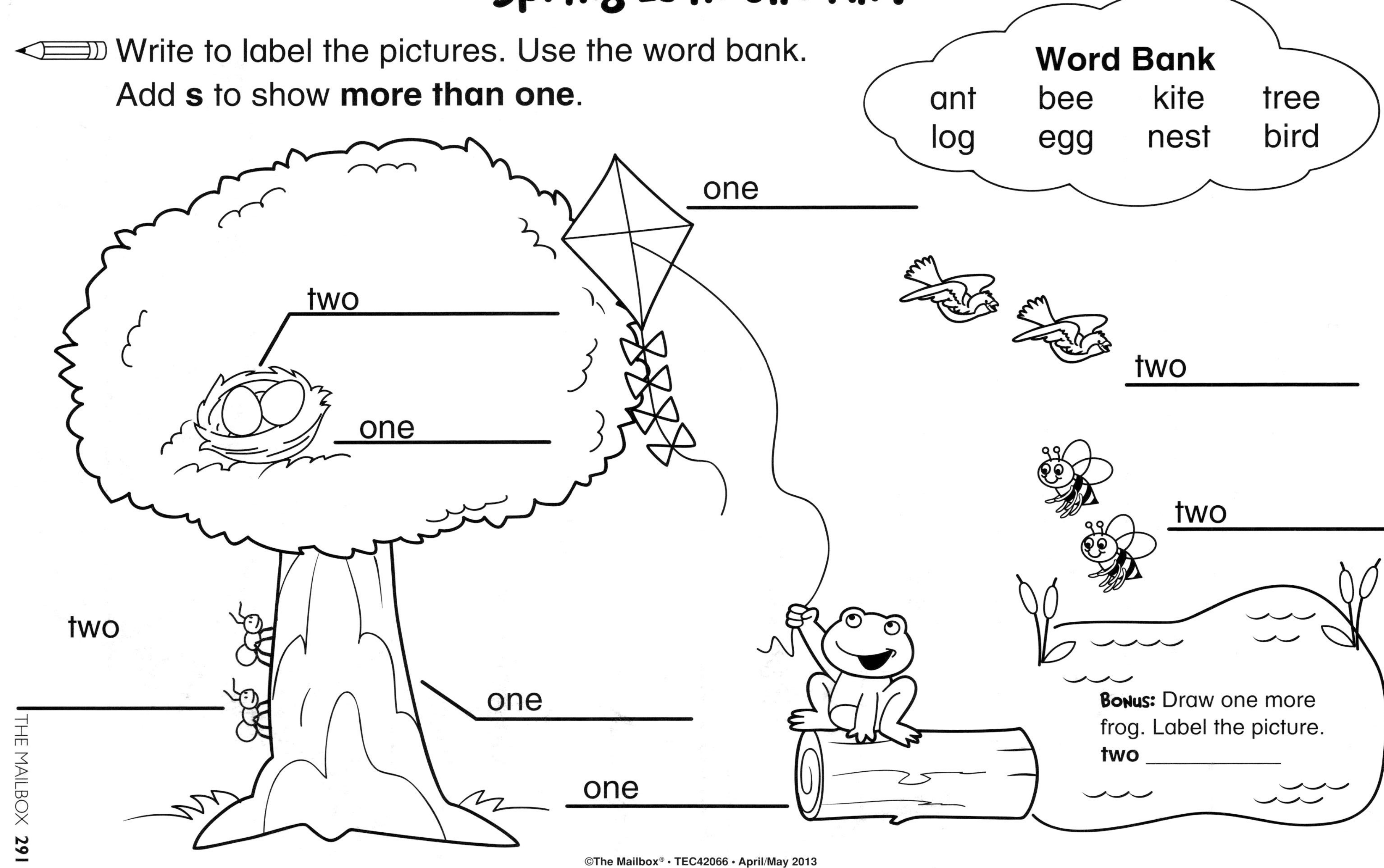

Bonus: Draw one more frog. Label the picture.
two ______

Butterflies

SCIENCE

Flutter, Flutter, Fly

Do your youngsters like surprises? If so, they are sure to enjoy this ***butterfly life-cycle*** activity!

1. Glue onto a leafy display a white pom-pom for each student.
2. Have students use craft sticks, pom-poms, and adhesive wiggle eyes to make caterpillars. Attach a personalized label to the back of each child's caterpillar craft.
3. Gently replace the eggs on the display with students' caterpillars. For several days, trim the leaves to mimic caterpillars eating the leaves.
4. When students are out of the room, cover each caterpillar with a tissue so it resembles a chrysalis.
5. Have each child predict what her caterpillar might look like when it emerges from its chrysalis. Then have her color and cut out a copy of the wings pattern on page 294 so the wings resemble her butterfly prediction. Attach a personalized label to the back of each child's wings.
6. When students are out of the room, break open the tissues to remove each child's caterpillar and glue it to her decorative wings. Display the butterflies around the room for a wonderful surprise upon students' return.

ideas contributed by Diane Flohr Henderson, Kentwood, MI

PHONICS

What a View!

Encourage youngsters to fly their butterflies around the room while looking for words and objects associated with a designated letter and sound. Then have each child write and draw to show the findings on its flight. ***Letter-sound associations (RF.K.3)***

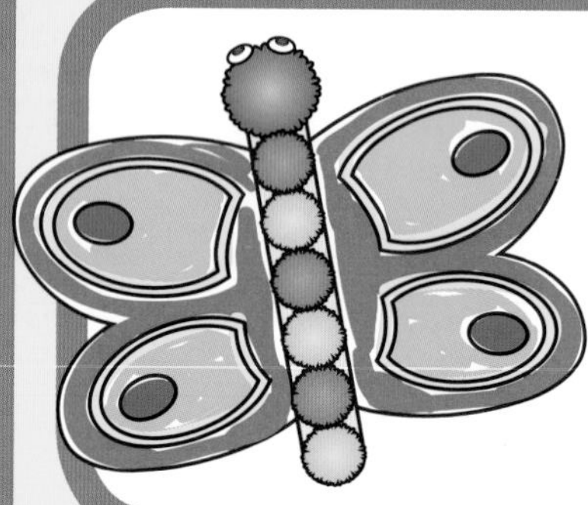

MATH

Beautiful Butterfly

Have each child show an *AB* pattern to form a butterfly's body. ***Patterning***

SONG

Sing a Song!

Have each child keep her butterfly hidden while singing the first verse, pretending to look around for her caterpillar. For the second verse, have her lift her butterfly into the air and then fly it around the room.

(sung to the tune of "Oh Where, Oh Where Has My Little Dog Gone?")

Oh where, oh where has my caterpillar gone?
Oh where, oh where can it be?
It has munched and crunched on a bunch of leaves.
Oh where, oh where can it be?

Oh there, oh there, look up into the air.
Oh there, oh there, do you see?
It's my caterpillar; it has changed a lot.
It can flutter and fly; it is free!

Plants

SCIENCE AND MATH

Green Hair and Hairspray!

Students are sure to be eager to use hairspray (water) on their green-headed (grass) animations with this **plant growth** and **measurement** activity!

1. Have each child plant grass seeds in a plastic cup and water them well. Instruct him to draw a face on the cup to personalize it.
2. Provide a spray bottle (hairspray) for youngsters to water their grass heads as needed. If desired, encourage them to use the phrase "H_2O to make the grass grow!"
3. Instruct students to record observations during the next couple weeks.
4. Have each child measure the length of his grass. Then encourage him to give the grass head a haircut. Challenge him to record how long it takes for the grass to grow to its original length.

ideas contributed by Tina Gagliana, Churchville Elementary Churchville, PA

SONG

Sing a Song!

The echo song "The Green Grass Grows All Around" is perfect for singing in springtime! If desired, establish motions that correspond with the verses for students to act out as they sing. **For a literacy connection**, write the song on chart paper with a related illustration for students to point to as they sing the words.

Name

A Grassy Green Head!

Writing (W.K.1–3)

Write.

See page 294!

WRITE

A Grassy Green Head!

Label a copy of the writing skill sheet on page 294 with a prompt (see the suggestions below); then make a class supply. Put the pages at a center and have youngsters sit with their grass heads for inspiration and respond to the prompt! ***Responding to a prompt (W.K.1–3)***

- My Grass Head Needs a Haircut
- I liked it when…
- Do Not Use Too Much Hairspray!

Wings Pattern

Use with "Flutter, Flutter, Fly" on page 292.

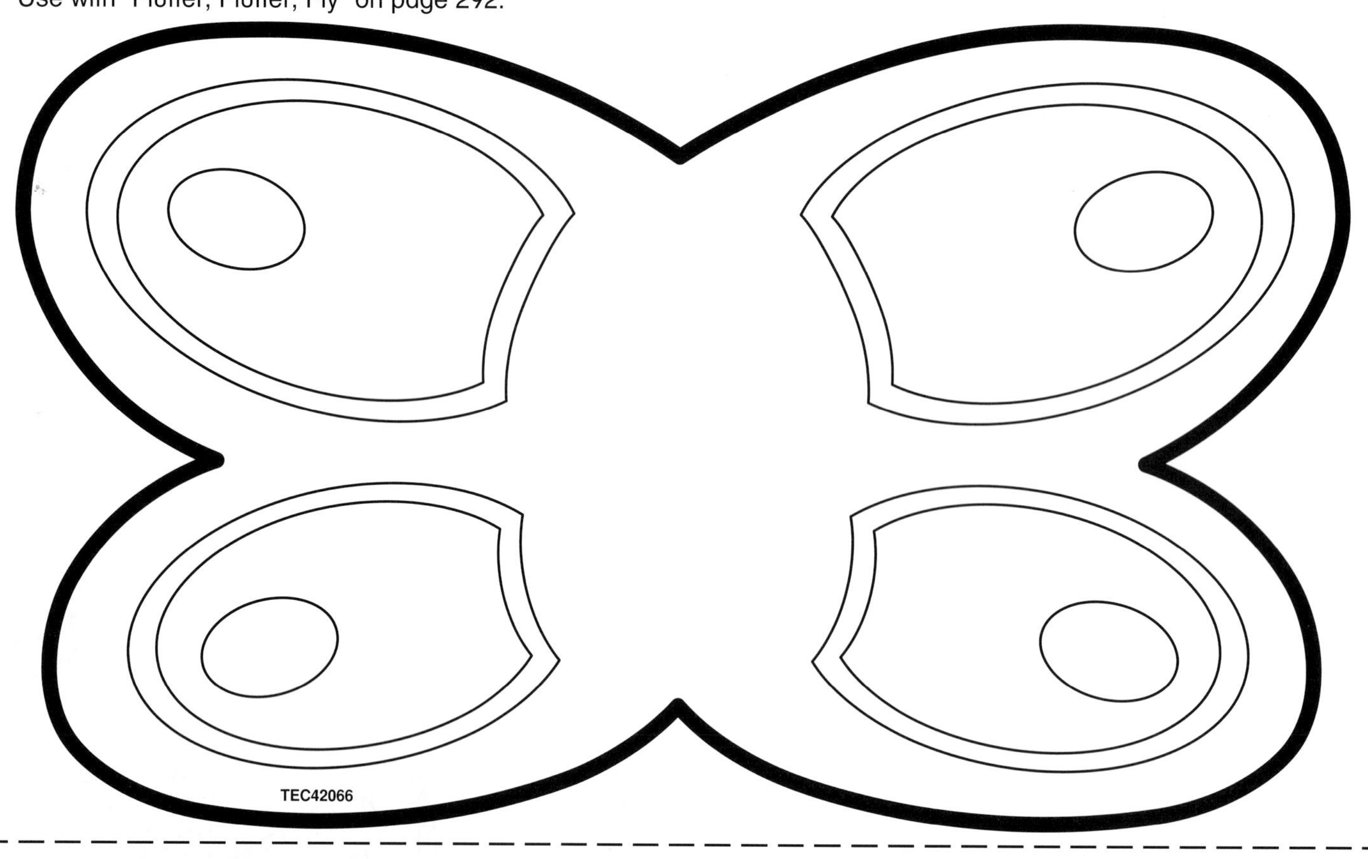

Name ______________________________ Writing (W.K.1–3)

A Grassy Green Head!

Write. ______________________________

____

____

____

____

 Note to the teacher: Use with "A Grassy Green Head!" on page 293.

A Splashing Good Time at the Pond!

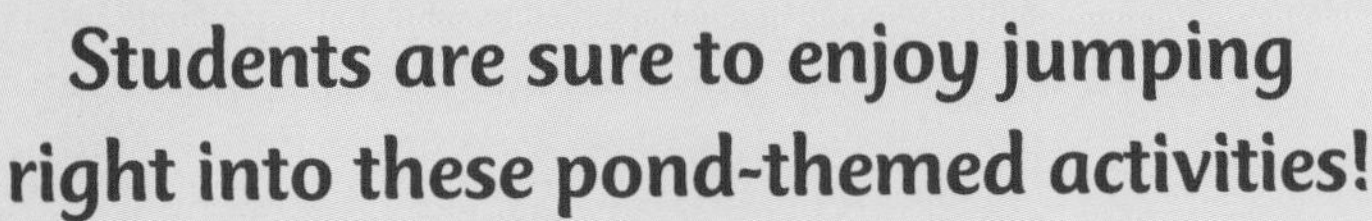

Students are sure to enjoy jumping right into these pond-themed activities!

ideas contributed by Laurie K. Gibbons, Huntsville, AL

SCIENCE & LITERACY

A Hoppin' Habitat

What Lives in a Pond?

These student-made shape booklets include a 3-D element for a pretend field trip to the pond! For each child, staple a 6" x 9" piece of blue construction paper atop several same-size white pages. Trim the corners of each resulting booklet so it resembles a pond and staple it to a 6" x 9" piece of brown paper (land). After sharing a favorite story about pond life, a child writes "What Lives in a Pond?" on the cover and, on each booklet page, she writes and illustrates a different sentence to tell about things that live at the pond. To make the stand-up grass, she folds in half each of two green rectangles, glues half of each rectangle to the back of her booklet, and fringe-cuts the halves that are pointing up to create blades of grass. Then she embellishes the scene with other pond details as desired. ***Life at the pond, informative writing (W.K.2)***

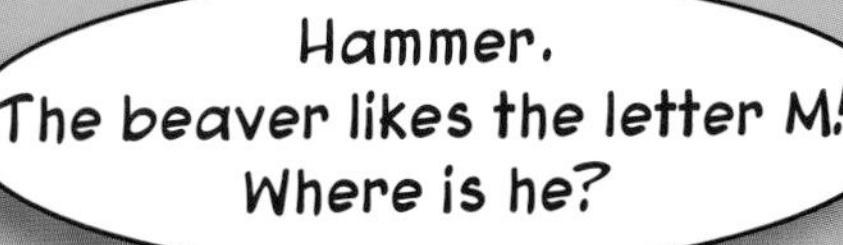
Hammer.
The beaver likes the letter M!
Where is he?

beginning
middle
end

LITERACY

Busy Beavers

Students use their phonics skills to find the beaver during this small-group activity. Cut away the bottoms of three paper bags (beaver-made dams) and label each dam as shown. To begin, secretly drop a brown pom-pom (beaver) into a dam. Next, name a word and a letter clue associated with the beaver's location. Then challenge youngsters to use their letter knowledge to find the beaver. When a child thinks he has solved the mystery, have him raise the matching dam to see if he is correct. Continue until the beaver is revealed before beginning the next round. ***Matching letters and sounds (RF.K.3)***

MATH

Life on a Log

Critters' pond play is the inspiration for these hopping word problems. Staple paper strips between log-shaped paper covers to make a booklet for each child. Have each child write her name and draw simple log details on her front cover. For the first word problem, tell youngsters how many frogs are playing at the pond, such as five. Instruct her to draw five frogs on her first booklet page. Then tell students more frogs join them (for addition) or some frogs hop away (for subtraction) and have youngsters write or draw to solve the problem. Continue with similar teacher-directed word problems for each remaining booklet page. **For independent practice**, provide cards with easy-to-read word problems for students to solve and show their work. ***Word problems to ten (K.OA.A.2)***

SCIENCE & MATH

From Egg to Frog!

Students find out how many spins it will take for a frog to grow up with this partner game. Use a brad to attach a paper clip to a copy of the spinner pattern on page 297. Have each player write his name on a copy of the game card from page 297. To play, a child spins the spinner. If the paper clip rests on the first stage of the frog's life cycle, the eggs, he colors the first box on his game card; if it does not, he makes a tally mark where indicated and his turn is over. Play continues until each child has colored the stages of the frog's life cycle in order. Then players count their tally marks and record that number. The player with the fewest tally marks wins. ***Life cycle of a frog, counting tally marks***

MATH

Critter Classification

Compare turtles and frogs with this variation of a Venn diagram. On separate cards, write characteristics of each critter and a few characteristics that the critters have in common. Next, draw and label a log, turtle, and frog on the board as shown. To begin, help a child read a card and lead youngsters to determine on what section of the log the card belongs; attach the card to the board. Continue with each remaining card. Then discuss the results of the diagram. **For an added challenge**, encourage youngsters to name different characteristics to add to the board, including facts that pertain to neither animal, such as "have fur," to display around the log. ***Classification (K.MD.B.3)***

Use with "From Egg to Frog!" on page 296.

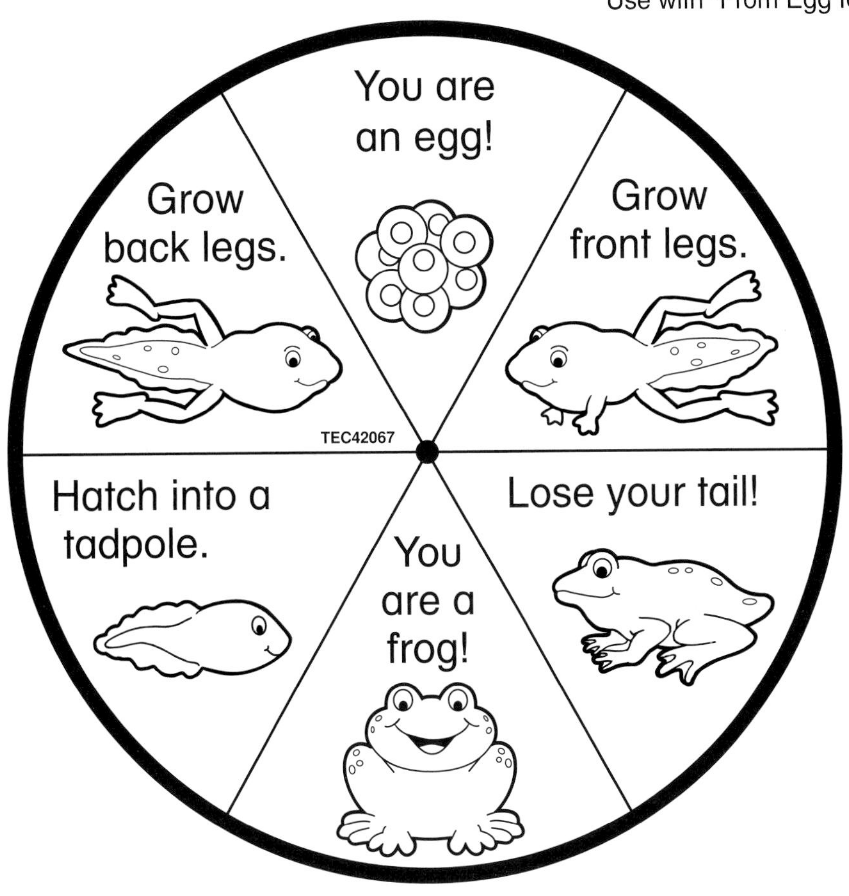
You are an egg!
Grow front legs.
Lose your tail!
You are a frog!
Hatch into a tadpole.
Grow back legs.
TEC42067

Name ____ Game card

From Egg to Frog!

1
2
3
4
5
6 Frog!

Tally Marks

Total: ______

Name ________________________________ Conventions (L.K.2)

Fix It!

Don't forget the punctuation!

Circle two mistakes in each sentence.

Write each sentence correctly.

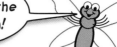

Bonus: Read sentence 5. Draw a picture to match.

1 You and i can go to the pond

____

2 i see bugs on the log

____

3 Do you see what i see

____

4 are there five frogs

____

5 i see three frogs in the pond

____

Teacher Resource

Decorating Your Classroom on a Shoestring Budget

10 Inexpensive Tips

1 Reuse Fabulous Fabrics

Use fabric for bulletin board backgrounds year after year. Seasonal fabrics can often be purchased for a fraction of the cost at end-of-season sales. What's even better is that the fabric does not fade the way paper does!

Nancy Berger, Montessori School 27, Yonkers, NY

tip To make fabrics flame retardant, mix 13 ounces of borax with one gallon of hot water. Pour the mixture into a spray bottle and shake it well. Then spray classroom fabrics and allow them to dry.

2 Trim Gift Wrap

Keep the leftover wrap from the end of a roll! This seasonal or holiday paper makes bright and colorful liners for small baskets, pencil trays, and center tubs. To make the liners last longer, simply laminate them!

Nancy Berger

3 Use Carpet Squares

Make welcoming doormats! Ask a home improvement store to donate carpet squares. Then use fabric paint to decorate different mats to match desired themes, holidays, and seasons. Interchange the mats by your classroom door throughout the year to welcome visitors.

Debbie Musser, Washington Lee Elementary, Bristol, VA

4 Decorate With Photos

Student photos are appealing and guaranteed to be a hit with classroom visitors! Use paper frames to enhance the photos and then display them on walls, bulletin boards, file cabinets, and desks!

Tammy Lutz, George E. Greene Elementary, Bad Axe, MI

5 Cut Cool Curtains

New or gently used bedsheets are perfect for making curtains to cover storage areas!

Nancy Berger

Create a Display

Rather than purchase a number-recognition bulletin board set, make your own! Write different numbers from 1 to 30 on separate fishbowl cutouts. Then attach a matching number of foam fish or fish stickers on each bowl. For a reading connection, label each bowl with the matching number word.

Add Burlap to Displays

Save burlap scraps to dress up cutouts on your displays. For example, add burlap to an apple basket cutout, create seed pods in the center of a sunflower, or add texture to ice cream cone cutouts. This sturdy cloth adds a unique touch to various objects and holds up well even after many little hands have tested its durability.

Janice Shuman, Saint Brigid School, South Boston, MA

Visit a Bookstore

Ask your local bookstore to donate old freestanding book characters, cardboard book displays, and children's posters. These free finds are perfect for decorating your reading areas, enhancing classroom displays, and showcasing class-made books.

Colleen Dabney, Williamsburg, VA

Use Plastic Pails

Purchase colorful plastic pails during end-of-summer deals. These containers are perfect for storing center materials and manipulatives, and they brighten up the room. As an added bonus, if a shovel is attached to the pail, label it with the pail's contents.

Waynetta Jordan, Follet Independent School District, Follet, TX

Adorn Your Desk Lamp

Here's a fast and frugal way to add a little pizzazz to a lamp. Simply feature a favorite storybook character or classroom theme art on the lamp shade. For added fun, hang sequin strips, stringed beads, or fabric fringes along the base of the shade.

Karen Cook, McDonough Primary, McDonough, GA

8 Easy Ideas for No-Prep Skill Practice

Tuck these supersimple activities into your lesson plans or use them as time fillers when you have a few minutes to spare!

1 Practice Counting (K.CC.A.1)

Have students stand in a circle. Show the group a number. Choose a child to begin counting from one and direct students to count on around the circle. When a child names the featured number, she sits down and the next child who is standing begins counting from one again. Continue in this manner until one child remains standing. ***Susan Bunyan, Linn Elementary, Dodge City, KS***

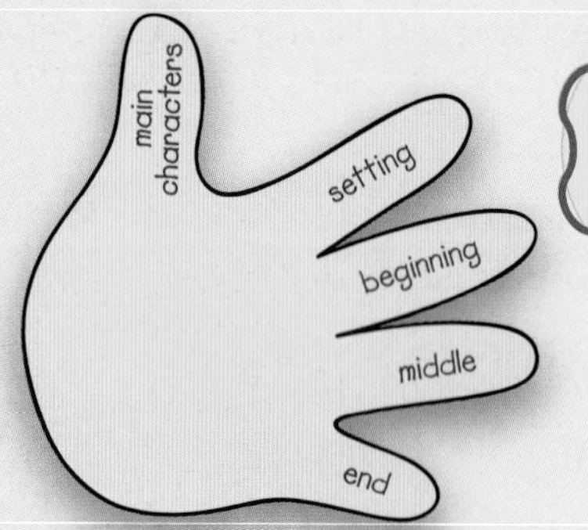

2 Give Story Details (RL.K.3)

Try this "hand-y" helper! Use your hand to make connections to story details. After reading a story, invite a child to "give you a high-five" by sharing the corresponding information featured on the hand (as is possible). When the child is finished, give him a real high-five to reward his effort. ***Jan Trautman, Raleigh, NC***

3 Copy and Extend Patterns

Start a simple pattern by producing actions such as snapping and clapping. Invite students to copy and continue the pattern. **For added fun,** invite a volunteer to introduce a pattern that involves tapping different body parts, such as "knees, elbows, and toes." Guide her classmates to copy and continue the pattern. ***Lisa Igou, Silbernagel Elementary, Dickinson, TX***

4 Identify Numbers

Display a hundred chart. Then lead students in one of the rhymes shown, inserting an appropriate number or equation where indicated. Have a volunteer point to the corresponding number on the chart. ***Myra Ingram, Yorktown Elementary, Yorktown, VA***

Numbers, numbers, 1, 2, 3,
Can you find number [15] for me?

Numbers, numbers, 1, 2, 3,
Can you find the sum of [6 + 3] for me?

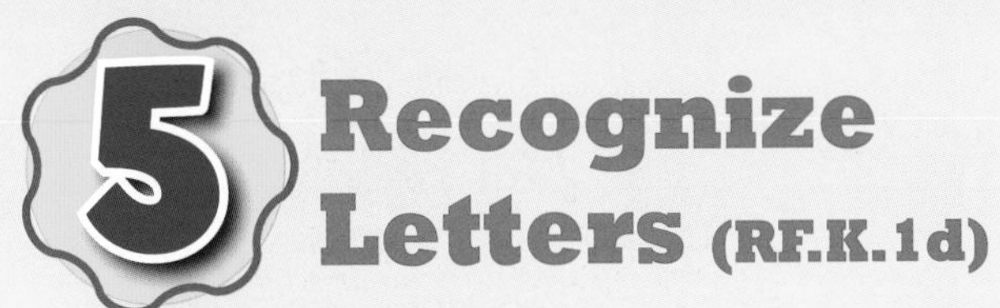

5 Recognize Letters (RF.K.1d)

There's an *e* in the exit sign!

This game is perfect to play while waiting in the hallway, or it can be played in the classroom anytime! Find a familiar letter and describe its location to students. Invite a child to guess the letter and name its location. Then have that child find a different letter to begin a new round. ***Rebecca Henry, Windsor Elementary, Windsor, ME***

6 Practice Literacy Skills (CCSS)

Squirt a generous amount of nonmentholated shaving cream onto each child's desk and have students smooth the shaving cream into a thin layer. Then choose a skill to practice, such as letters, sight words, CVC words, or word family words. Announce a letter or a word and have each youngster use a finger to write it in the shaving cream. After scanning for accuracy, have students smooth the shaving cream to "erase" the word. Continue as time permits. ***Sara Fox, Franklin Moore Elementary, Arcanum, OH***

7 Review Number Order

Display a hundred chart. Secretly cover a number with a small sticky note (trimmed to fit if necessary). Next, show the chart and have students write the missing number. Then remove the sticky note so students can check their answers. **For a no-prep partner activity**, put the hundred chart and a small sticky note at a center. ***Suzanne Moore, Tucson, AZ***

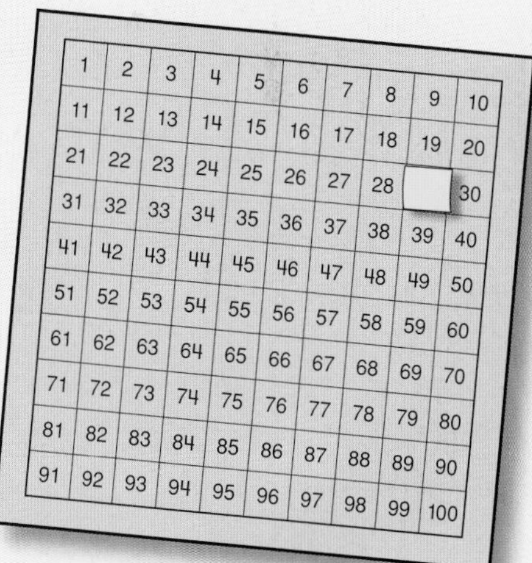

8 Identify Letters in One's Name (RF.K.1d)

Line students up on one side of a large playing area and stand opposite them. Announce a letter and ask each student who has this letter in her first name to run over and join you. Play continues until only a few children are left in the original location. Invite these youngsters to skip with big fanfare to join their classmates and you! ***Meagan Naumann, St. Paul's Lutheran School, East Troy, WI***

Growing Bookworms!

Terrific Tips That Encourage Reading

1 Create a Reading Zone

Give students a fun place to read that goes with your classroom theme, such as a kiddie pool called the "Ribbit Reading Pond" for a frog theme. Then invite youngsters to read in the zone! ***Rebecca Henry, Windsor Elementary, Windsor, ME***

2 Boost Buddy Reading

For each of several themes, put related books and a sign-up sheet in a basket. Have youngsters sign their names on the sheets for the themes that interest them. Then, when a child wants to read with a buddy, she has a list of interested friends to choose from! ***Barbara Mason, Deposit Elementary, Deposit, NY***

3 Foster Book Recommendations

When a student really likes a book, have him write his name and draw a happy face on a small sticky note. Then have him place the note on the inside of the front cover. Youngsters' opinions are sure to encourage others to read more books. ***Barbara Mason***

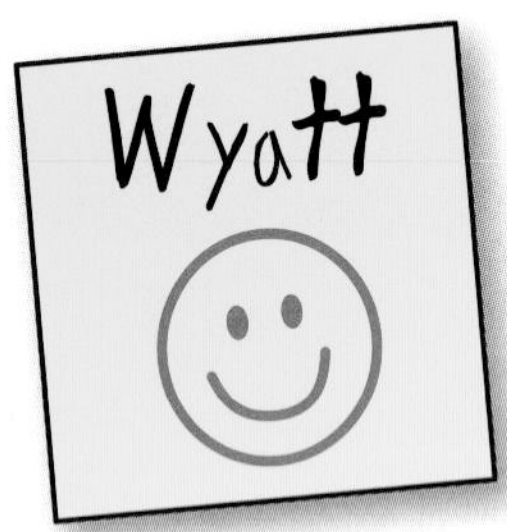

4 Attract Rockin' Readers

Invite a child who has mastered reading a storybook to sit in a rocking chair and read the book to the class. Then reward his success with a "Rockin' Reader" certificate. Students are sure to eagerly prepare to read in the rocker. ***Nichole Hutchins, Spencer County Elementary, Taylorsville, KY***

5 Enhance Book Displays

Adorn book areas with personalized leaves in the fall, holiday decor in the winter, flowers in the spring, and fabulous fish cutouts for summer. To increase display space, secure eaves and baseboards to a length of picket fence, paint the resulting display, and decorate it for each season. ***Cami Ashley, Countryside Charter School, Benton Harbor, MI***

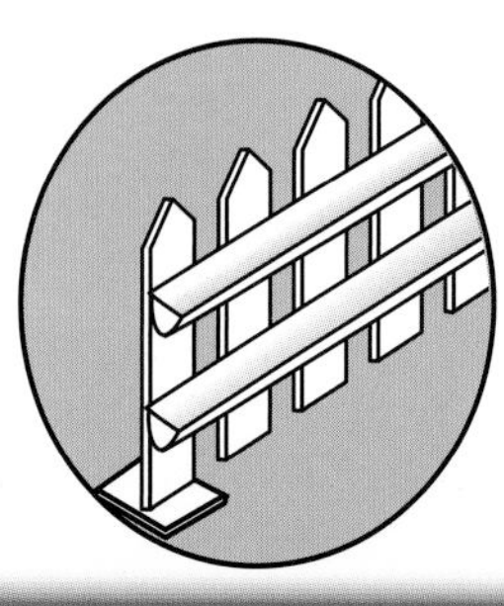

6 Build Students' Confidence

Encourage youngsters to read to an audience of stuffed critters! The plush book buddies are very patient and never complain! ***Janice Burch, Tri-Valley Elementary, Downs, IL***

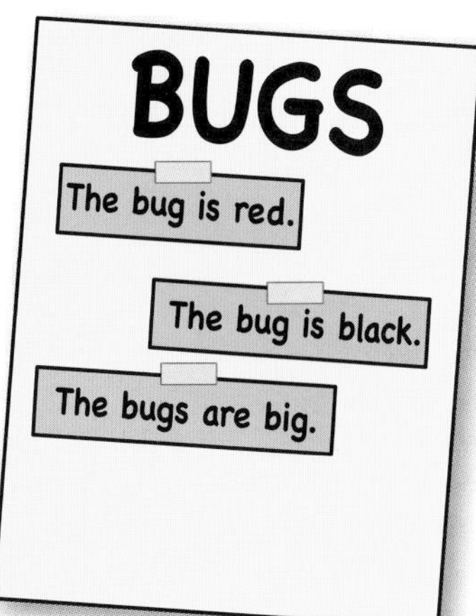

7 Promote Reading for Meaning

Write simple sentences, most of which relate to a specific topic, and give one to each child. Name the topic and have each child read her sentence aloud, in turn, and tape it to a chart paper if it is on topic. If it is not on topic, she hands her paper to you. *(RI.K.10)*

8 Increase Book Selections

Set apart a little library of books all students can read. Guide youngsters to recognize the increasing number of books they can read independently throughout the year. ***Stephanie Litwin, Mendham Township Elementary, Mendham, NJ***

9 Get Gutters!

Rain gutters are great for displaying books! The gutters can be attached to just about any surface, the books don't fall out, and little hands can get the books without knocking them off shelves. ***Janis Mederich, Long Beach Elementary, Montgomery, IL***

10 Use Technology

Set up a sound center with CD players, tape players, or computers. Place each book and its audio version in separate resealable plastic bags. For added interest, provide audio versions of yourself reading different books. Youngsters will surely look forward to following along and joining the readers, or singers, of the tales. ***Janice Burch***

11 Write Mystery Messages

Prior to students' arrival at school, write a message from a "mystery guest." Encourage youngsters to read the message upon their arrival and determine who the visitor might have been. Continue with different messages from time to time to inspire interest in reading. *(RI.K.1)*

12 Congratulate Reading Success!

Write the titles from a leveled reader collection on a card for each child. When he successfully reads a book, put a sticker by that title. When each title has a sticker, write his name on a bookworm cutout and display it in the room. Regularly praise the growing collection of beautiful bookworms.

Eyes on Me!

What are some ways to get students to listen quickly? Try these easy-to-implement tips!

Chime Time

Designate a particular sound, such as a wind chime or soft bell, to call students to order. Then simply sound the chime or ring the bell, and students will know right away that it's time to listen.

Hands Up!

Clap a short rhythm and have students repeat it. Then have youngsters hold up their hands to verify all toys and materials have been set aside. Continue with directions in a soft voice to maintain students' attention.

Suzanne Ward
Caledonia Centennial Public School
Caledonia, Ontario, Canada

One, Two, Three

The twist to this familiar poem silences students' voices quickly. After saying the poem, encourage students to look at you and pretend to zip their lips.

Rebecca Needham, Luce Road Early Childhood Learning Center, Alma, MI

1, 2, 3,
All eyes on me!
3, 2, 1,
All voices done!

Tuned In!

Students are sure to tune in to instructions with this musical idea. Sing the first line of a song youngsters are likely to know, signaling to them to stop what they are doing. Prompt students to sing the next line and then wait quietly for your instructions. To heighten students' interest and keep them on their toes, sing several different tunes throughout the year.

Nicole Kucharski, Monsignor Gadoury, Woonsocket, RI

Old MacDonald had a Farm.

Sing and Listen

Begin group activities by leading students in singing this little ditty. Challenge youngsters to be in their places and ready to listen by the time you're finished singing the song.

Jodi Darter, Cabool Elementary, Cabool, MO

(sung to the tune of "I'm a Little Teapot")

I'm a good listener,
Watch and see!
I can sit very quietly.
My body's still—no wiggles in sight!
My mouth is closed up tight, tight, tight!

Thank You, Volunteers!

A Classy Photo

Each time a volunteer looks at this cute keepsake, she is sure to have fond memories of her time with your students. Print a copy of a class photograph for each volunteer. Use a craft foam border as a frame and write "Thank You!" across the top. Next, have each child use a marker to write his name on the frame. Embellish the frame with glitter glue or stickers as desired. Then tape the photo to the back of the frame and glue on a construction paper backing. To make a hanger, thread and twist the ends of a pipe cleaner through two hole-punched holes.

Reubena Whitted, Roxboro, NC

tip This idea is easy to adapt for volunteers that work with a small group of students!

Personalized Performance

Singing is a heartwarming way to make a volunteer feel special. Invite a volunteer to sit in a special seat and lead youngsters in singing a song, such as "You Are My Sunshine." For added fun, have students perform actions for desired words or lines of the song.

Barbara Mason, Deposit Elementary
Deposit, NY

Berry Thankful

Check out this adorable thank-you note! For each volunteer, color and cut out a sturdy copy of the bear pattern on page 309. Set out the bears, berry-colored ink pads, and a black marker. Have each child choose an ink color and make a fingerprint (berry) in the bear's basket. To make a strawberry, guide him to make two fingerprints as shown. Then write the child's name beside his prints. After each child has made a berry, add appropriate berry details to each print. If desired, write a personal note on the back of the bear and present the sentiment with a treat, such as chocolate-dipped strawberries or a berry pie.

Laurie K. Gibbons
Huntsville, AL

Quick and Simple

Here are a few more ways to send a fast thank-you to a volunteer.

- Attach a tag that says "You Are So Sweet" to a chocolate bar.
- Attach a tag that says "Thanks a Million" to a bag of coin candies.
- Attach a tag that says "You Take the Cake!" to a decorated cupcake.
- Place a sign in the soil of a plant that says "Thanks for Helping Us Grow!"
- Create a class-made book for a volunteer; insert a dedication page at the front of the book.

Karin Bulkow, Washington School for Comprehensive Literacy, Sheboygan, MI

Clever Countdowns

Encourage students to track the number of days until the last day of school with these multiskill ideas!

From A to Z

Make the final days of school special with this alphabetic countdown! To determine a starting date, count back 26 school days from the last day of school. To begin the countdown, tape an arrow cutout to the letter *A* on an alphabet display and have students do a letter-related celebration activity. (See the list of ideas.) Next, pointing to one letter at a time, lead students in counting how many school days are left until the last day of school. Continue each day, moving the arrow to point to the next letter in sequence.

Ashley Dockett, Montpelier Elementary, Laurel, MD

Alphabet Countdown Ideas

Autograph: Make a class autograph book.
Buddy: Read a favorite book with a buddy!
Castle: Create a castle with paper shapes.
Dance: Share some favorite dance moves.
Exercise: Join in a classwide exercise routine.
Fantasy: Draw to create and then write about a friendly space creature.
Game: Play a game.
Hula hoop: Practice hooping skills.
Icy treat: Enjoy an icy treat.
Jump: Jump 100 times while counting to one hundred.
Keepsakes: Make something to help you remember the school year.
Listen: Listen to some fun music.
Memories: Write about three kindergarten memories.
Nice: Write a nice note to a school staff member.
Outside: Have storytime outdoors.
Pick your seat: Sit wherever you would like.
Question: Ask your teacher questions.
Recess: Enjoy extra recess time.
Sing: Sing a favorite song from the year.
Teacher: Write a note to your teacher.
Use manipulatives: Use math manipulatives in desired ways.
Vote: Vote on a favorite class activity.
Write: Enjoy some free writing time.
***X* marks the spot:** Make an *X* on paper. On the back, draw a desired treasure.
Yearbook: Make a page to put in a class yearbook.
Zip it up: Celebrate the last day of school!

Student of the Day

This idea spotlights a different student on each day leading up to the last day of school. Gather a set of student name cards. To determine the starting date, count back from the last day of school one day for each member of your class. On the appropriate countdown date, remove a card at random and give clues about that child. Encourage youngsters to use the clues to correctly name the student of the day. Invite that child to sit in a special seat, be your helper all day, or wear a paper crown. The next day, invite the previous day's featured student to choose a card and give the clues for classmates to determine the new student of the day.

Hanging On Until Summer

Students are ready to swing into summer after moving this monkey day after day! Write each number from 1 to 10 on separate leaf cutouts. When there are ten school days left until summer, create this display by stapling the leaves in descending order along a yarn vine and posting a monkey cutout (pattern on page 310) to the left of the leaves with the title shown. The next day, remove the "10" leaf and pretend the monkey swings into its place, showing there are nine days left until summer. Continue until it is time to celebrate the last day of school with students.

Alyson Severino, Ocean Day School, Lakewood, NJ

Bear Pattern

Use with "Berry Thankful" on page 307.

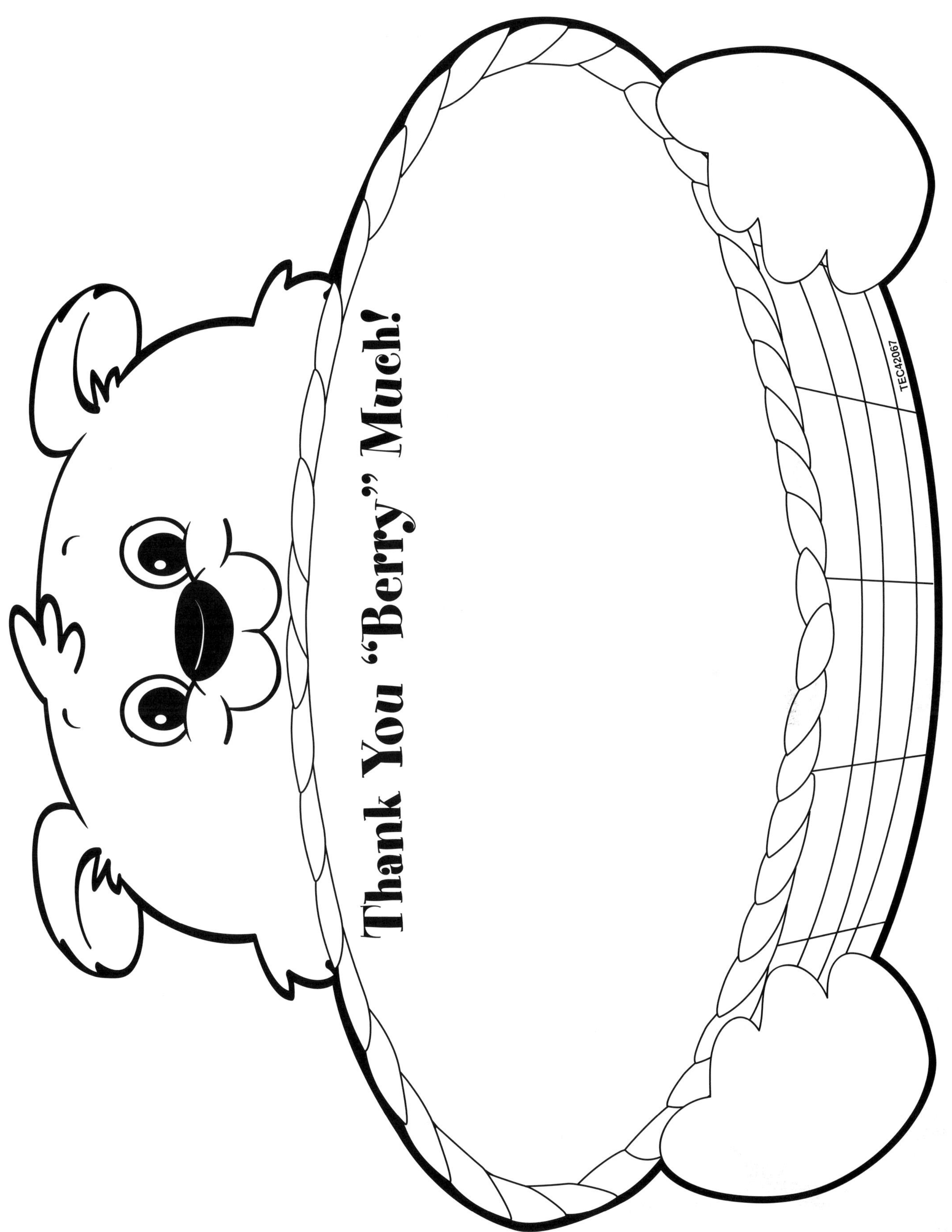
Thank You "Berry" Much!
TEC42067

Monkey Pattern

Use with "Hanging On Until Summer" on page 308.

INDEX